Common Sense in the

Household

A Manual of Practical Housewifery

Marion Harland

Alpha Editions

ISBN : 9789353295349

Design and Setting By
Alpha Editions
email - alphaedis@gmail.com

Contents

INTRODUCTORY OF REVISED EDITION

It is not yet quite ten years since the publication of "COMMON SENSE IN THE HOUSEHOLD. GENERAL RECEIPTS." In offering the work to the publishers, under whose able management it has prospered so wonderfully, I said: "I have written this because I felt that such a Manual of Practical Housewifery is needed." That I judged aright, taking my own experience as a housekeeper as the criterion of the wants and perplexities of others, is abundantly proved by the circumstance which calls for this new and revised edition of the book. Through much and constant use—nearly 100,000 copies having been printed from them—the stereotype plates have become so worn that the impressions are faint and sometimes illegible. I gladly avail myself of the opportunity thus offered to re-read and so far to alter the original volume as may, in the light of later improvements in the culinary art and in my understanding of it, make the collection of family receipts more intelligible and available. Nor have I been able to resist the temptation to interpolate a few excellent receipts that have come into my hands at a later period than that of the publication of the last, and in my estimation, perhaps the most valuable of the "Common Sense Series," viz.: "THE DINNER YEAR-BOOK."

I am grateful, also, to the courtesy of my publishers for the privilege of thanking those to whom this book was, and is dedicated, "My fellow-housekeepers—North, East, South and West"—for their substantial endorsement of the work I have done in their behalf. A collection of the private letters I have received from those who have used the "General Receipts" would make a volume very nearly as large as this. If I have, as the writers of these testimonials assure me—"done them good,"—they have done me more in letting me know that I have not spent my strength for naught. I acknowledge with pleasure sundry pertinent suggestions and inquiries which have led me, in this revision, to examine warily the phraseology of some receipts and to modify these, I believe, for the better. But, by far, the best "good" done me through this work has been the conscious sisterhood into which I have come with the great body of American housewives. This is a benefit not to be rated by dollars and cents, or measured by time. I hope my fellow-workers will find their old kitchen-companion, in fresh dress, yet more serviceable than before, and that their daughters may, at the close of a second decade, demand new stereotype plates for still another, and, like this, a progressive edition.

MARION HARLAND.

October 1, 1880.

FAMILIAR TALK WITH MY
FELLOW-HOUSEKEEPER AND READER

A TALK as woman to woman, in which each shall say, "I" and "you," and "my dear," and "you know," as freely as she pleases. It would not be a womanly chat if we omitted these forms of expression. An informal preface to what I mean shall be an informal book—bristling with "I's" all the way through. If said bristles offend the critic's touch, let him remember that this work is not prepared for the library, but for readers who trouble themselves little about editorial "we's" and the circumlocutions of literary modesty.

I wish it were in my power to bring you, the prospective owner of this volume, in person, as I do in spirit, to my side on this winter evening, when the bairnies are "folded like the flocks;" the orders for breakfast committed to the keeping of Bridget, or Gretchen, or Chloe, or the plans for the morrow definitely laid in the brain of that ever-busy, but most independent of women, the housekeeper who "does her own work." I should perhaps summon to our cozy conference a very weary companion—weary of foot, of hand—and I should not deserve to be your confidant, did I not know how often heart-weary with discouragement; with much producing of ways and means; with a certain despondent looking forward to the monotonous grinding of the household machine; to the certainty, proved by past experience, that toilsome as has been this day, the morrow will prove yet more abundant in labors, in trials of strength and nerves and temper. You would tell me what a dreary problem this of "woman's work that is never done" is to your fainting soul. How, try as you may and as you do to be systematic and diligent, something is always "turning up" in the treadmill to keep you on the strain. How you often say to yourself, in bitterness of spirit, that it is a mistake of Christian civilization to educate girls into a love of science and literature, and then condemn them to the routine of a domestic drudge. You do not see, you say, that years of scholastic training will make you a better cook, a better wife or mother. You have seen the time—nay, many times since assuming your present position—when you would have exchanged your knowledge of ancient and modern languages, belles-lettres, music, and natural science, for the skill of a competent kitchen-maid. The "learning how" is such hard work! Labor, too, uncheered by encouraging words from mature housewives, unsoftened by sympathy even from your husband, or your father or brother, or whoever may be the "one" to whom you "make home lovely." It may be that, in utter discouragement, you have made up your mind that you have "no talent for these things."

I have before me now the picture of a wife, the mother of four children, who, many years ago, sickened me for all time with that phrase. In a slatternly morning-gown at four in the afternoon, leaning back in the laziest and most ragged of rocking-chairs, dust on the carpet, on the open piano, the mantel, the mirrors, even on her own hair, she rubbed the soft palm of one hand with the grimy fingers of the other, and with a sickly-sweet smile whined out—

"Now, I am one of the kind who have no talent for such things! The kitchen and housework and sewing are absolutely hateful to me—utterly uncongenial to my turn of mind. The height of my earthly ambition is to have nothing to do but to paint on velvet all day!"

I felt then, in the height of my indignant disgust, that there was propriety as well as wit in the "Spectator's" suggestion that every young woman should, before fixing the wedding-day, be compelled by law to exhibit to inspectors a prescribed number of useful articles as her outfit—napery, bed-linen, clothing, etc., made by her own hands, and that it would be wise legislation which should add to these proofs of her fitness for her new sphere a practical knowledge of housework and cookery.

If you have not what our Yankee grandmothers termed a "faculty" for housewifery—yet are obliged, as is the case with an immense majority of American women, to conduct the affairs of a household, bills of fare included—there is the more reason for earnest application to your profession. If the natural taste be dull, lay to it more strength of will—resolution born of a just sense of the importance of the knowledge and dexterity you would acquire.

Do not scoff at the word "profession." Call not that common and unclean which Providence has designated as your life-work. I speak not now of the labors of the culinary department alone; but, without naming the other duties which you and you only can perform, I do insist that upon method, skill, economy in the kitchen, depends so much of the well-being of the rest of the household, that it may safely be styled the root—the foundation of housewifery. I own it would be pleasanter in most cases, especially to those who have cultivated a taste for intellectual pursuits, to live above the heat and odor of this department. It must be very fine to have an efficient aide-de-camp in the person of a French cook, or a competent sub-manager, or an accomplished head-waiter who receives your orders for the day in your boudoir or library, and executes the same with zeal and discretion that leave you no room for anxiety or regret. Such mistresses do not need cookery-books. The few—and it must be borne in mind that in this country these are *very* few—born in an estate like this would not comprehend what I am now writing; would not enter into the depths of that compassionate yearning which moves me as I think of what I have known for myself in the earlier years of my wedded life, what I have heard and seen in other households of honest intentions brought to contempt; of ill-directed toil; of mortification, and the heavy, wearing sense of inferiority that puts the novice at such a woful disadvantage in a community of notable managers.

There is no use in enlarging upon this point. You and I might compare experiences by the hour without exhausting our store.

"And then"—you sigh, with a sense of resentment upon you, however amiable your disposition, for the provocation is dire— "cookery-books and young housekeepers' assistants, and all that sort of thing, are such humbugs!—Dark lanterns at best—too often Will-o'-the-wisps."

My dear, would you mind handing me the book which lies nearest you on the table there? "Dickens?" Of course. You will usually find something of his in every room in this house—almost as surely as you will a Bible. It rests and refreshes one to pick him up at odd times, and dip in anywhere. Hear the bride, Mrs. John Rokesmith, upon our common grievance.

"She was under the constant necessity of referring for advice and support to a sage volume, entitled 'The Complete British Family Housewife,' which she would sit consulting, with her elbows upon the table, and her temples in her hands, like some perplexed enchantress poring over the Black Art. This, principally because the Complete British Housewife, however sound a Briton at heart, was by no means an expert Briton at expressing herself with clearness in the British tongue, and sometimes might have issued her directions to equal purpose in the Kamtchatkan language."

Don't interrupt me, my long-suffering sister! There is more of the same sort to come.

"There was likewise a coolness on the part of 'The Complete British Housewife' which Mrs. John Rokesmith found highly exasperating. She would say, 'Take a salamander,' as if a general should command a private to catch a Tartar. Or, she would casually issue the order, 'Throw in a handful' of something entirely unattainable. In these, the housewife's most glaring moments of unreason, Bella would shut her up and knock her on the table, apostrophizing her with the compliment—'O you ARE a stupid old donkey! Where am I to get it, do you think?'"

When I took possession of my first real home, the prettily furnished cottage to which I came as a bride, more full of hope and courage than if I had been wiser, five good friends presented me with as many cookery-books, each complete, and all by different compilers. One day's investigation of my *ménage* convinced me that my lately-hired servants knew no more about cookery than I did, or affected stupidity to develop my capabilities or ignorance. Too proud to let them suspect the truth, or to have it bruited abroad as a topic for pitying or contemptuous gossip, I shut myself up with *my* "Complete Housewives," and inclined seriously to the study of the same, comparing one with the other, and seeking to shape a theory which should grow into practice in accordance with the best authority. I don't like to remember that time! The question of disagreeing doctors, and the predicament of falling between two stools, are trivial perplexities when compared with my strife and failure.

Said the would-be studious countryman to whom a mischievous acquaintance lent "Webster's Unabridged Dictionary" as an entertaining volume,—"I wrastled, and I wrastled, *and* I wrastled with it, but I couldn't get up much of an int'rest."

My wrestling begat naught save pitiable confusion, hopeless distress, and a three-days' sick headache, during which season I am not sure that I did not darkly contemplate suicide as the only sure escape from the meshes that girt me. At the height—or depth—of my despondency a friend, one with a great heart and steady brain, came to my rescue. Her cheerful laugh over my dilemma rings down to me now, through all these years, refreshingly as it then saluted my ears.

"Bless your innocent little heart!" she cried, in her fresh, gay voice, "Ninety-nine out of a hundred cookbooks are written by people who never kept house, and the hundredth by a good cook who yet doesn't know how to express herself to the enlightenment of others. Compile a receipt book for yourself. Make haste slowly. Learn one thing at a time, and when you have mastered it, 'make a note on it,' as Captain Cuttle says—never losing sight of the principle that you *must do it in order to learn how.*"

Then she opened to me her own neatly-written "Manual"—the work of years, recommending, as I seized it that I should commence my novitiate with simple dishes.

This was the beginning of the hoard of practical receipts I now offer for your inspection. For twenty years, I have steadily pursued this work, gleaning here and sifting there, and levying such remorseless contributions upon my friends, that I fear the sight of my paper and pencil has long since become a bugbear. For the kindness and courtesy which have been my invariable portion in this quest, I hereby return hearty thanks. For the encouraging words and good wishes that have ever answered the hint of my intention to collect what had proved so valuable to me into a printed volume, I declare myself to be yet more a debtor. I do not claim for my compend the proud pre-eminence of the "Complete American Housewife." It is no boastful system of "Cookery Taught in Twelve Lessons." And I should write myself down a knave or a fool, were I to assert that a raw cook or ignorant mistress can, by half-a-day's study of my collection, equal Soyer or Blot, or even approximate the art of a half-taught scullion.

We may as well start from the right point, if we hope to continue friends. You must learn the rudiments of the art for yourself. Practice, and practice alone, will teach you certain essentials. The management of the ovens, the requisite thickness of boiling custards, the right shade of brown upon bread and roasted meats—these and dozens of other details are hints which cannot be imparted by written or oral instructions. But, once learned, they are never forgotten, and henceforward your fate is in your own hands. You are mistress of yourself, though servants leave. Have faith in your own abilities. You will be a better cook for the mental training you have received at school and from books. Brains tell everywhere, to say nothing of intelligent observation, just judgment, a faithful memory, and orderly habits. Consider that you have a profession, as I said just now, and resolve to understand it in all its branches. My book is designed to help you. I believe it will, if for no other reason, because it has been a faithful guide to myself—a reference beyond value in seasons of doubt and need. I have brought every receipt to the test of common sense and experience. Those which I have not tried myself were obtained from trustworthy housewives—the best I know. I have enjoyed the task heartily, and from first to last the persuasion has never left me that I was engaged in a good cause. Throughout I have had you, my dear sister, present before me, with the little plait between your brows, the wistful look about eye and mouth that reveal to me, as words could not, your desire to "do your best."

"In a humble home, and in a humble way," I hear you add, perhaps. You "are not ambitious;" you "only want to help John, and to make him and the children comfortable and happy."

Heaven reward your honest, loyal endeavors! Would you mind if I were to whisper a word in your ear I don't care to have progressive people hear?—although progress is a grand thing when it takes the right direction. My dear, John and the children, and the humble home, make your sphere for the present, you say. Be sure you fill it—*full!* before you seek one wider and higher. There is no better receipt between these covers than that. Leave the rest to God. Everybody knows those four lines of George Herbert's, which ought to be framed and hung up in the work-room of every house:—

> "A servant, with this clause,
> Makes drudgery divine;
> Who sweeps a room as for Thy laws
> Makes that and th' action fine."

I wonder if the sainted poet knows—in that land where drudgery is one of the rough places forever overpast, and work is unmingled blessing—to how many sad and striving hearts those words have brought peace?

And by way of helping John, not only by saving money and preparing palatable and wholesome dishes for his table, but by sparing the wife he loves many needless steps and much hurtful care, will you heed a homely hint or two relative to the practice of your art? Study method, and economy of time and strength, no less than of materials. I take it for granted that you are too intelligent to share in the vulgar prejudice against labor-saving machines. A raisin-seeder costs a trifle in comparison with the time and patience required to stone the fruit in the old way. A *good* egg-beater—the Dover, for instance—is a treasure. So with farina-kettles, syllabub churns, apple-corers, potato-peelers and slicers, clothes wringers and sprinklers, and the like. Most of these are made of tin—are therefore cheap and easily kept clean. Let each article have its own place in the closet and kitchen, to which restore it so soon as you have done using it. Before undertaking the preparation of any dish, read over the receipt carefully, unless you are thoroughly familiar with the manufacture of it. Many excellent housewives have a fashion of saying loftily, when asked how such things are made— "I carry all my receipts in my head. I never wrote out one in my life."

And you, if timid and self-distrustful, are smitten with shame, keep your receipt-book out of sight, and cram your memory with ingredients and measures, times and weights, for fear Mrs. Notable should suspect you of rawness and inefficiency. Whereas the truth is, that if you have a mind worthy of the name, its powers are too valuable to be laden with such details. Master the general principles, as I said just now, and for particulars look to your marching-orders. Having refreshed your memory by this reference, pick out from your household stores, and set in convenient order, within reach of your hand, everything you will need in making ready the particular compound under consideration. Then, take your stand in the midst—or sit, if you can. It is common sense—oftentimes a pious duty, to take judicious care of your physical health. I lay it down as a safe and imperative rule for kitchen use—*Never stand when you can do your work as well while sitting.* If I could have John's ear for a minute, I would tell him that which would lead him to watch you and exercise wholesome authority in this regard.

Next, prepare each ingredient for mixing, that the bread, cake, pudding, soup, or ragoût may not be delayed when half finished because the flour is not sifted, or the "shortening" warmed, the sugar and butter are not creamed, the meat not cut up, or the herbs not minced. Don't begin until you are ready; then go steadily forward, "without haste, without rest," and think of what you are doing.

"Dickens again?"

Why not, since there is no more genial and pertinent philosopher of common life and every-day subjects? To quote, then—

"It was a maxim of Captain Swosser's," said Mrs. Badger, "speaking in his figurative, naval manner, that when you make pitch hot, you cannot make it too hot, and that if you have only to swab a plank, you should swab it as if Davy Jones were after you. It appears to me that this maxim is applicable to the medical as well as the nautical profession."

"To all professions!" observed Mr. Badger. "It was admirably said by Captain Swosser; beautifully said!"

But it will sometimes happen that when you have heated your pitch, or swabbed your deck, or made your pudding according to the lights set before you, the result is a failure. This is especially apt to occur in a maiden effort. You have wasted materials and time, and suffered, moreover, acute demoralization—are enwrapped in a wet blanket of discouragement, instead of the seemly robe of complacency. Yet no part of the culinary education is more useful, if turned to proper account, than this very discipline of failure. It is a stepping-stone to excellence—sharp, it is true, but often sure. You have learned how *not* to do it right, which is the next thing to success. It is pretty certain that you will avoid, in your second essay, the rock upon which you have split this time. And, after all, there are few failures which are utter and irremediable. Scorched soups and custards, sour bread, biscuit yellow with soda, and cake heavy as lead, come under the head of "hopeless." They are absolutely unfit to be set before civilized beings and educated stomachs. Should such mishaps occur, lock the memory of the attempt in your own bosom, and do not vex or amuse John and your guests with the narration, still less with visible proof of the calamity. Many a partial failure would pass unobserved but for the clouded brow and earnest apologies of the hostess. Do not apologize except at the last gasp! If there is but one chance in ten that a single person present may not discover the deficiency which has changed all food on the table to dust and gravel-stones to you, trust to the one chance, and carry off the matter bravely. You will be astonished to find, if you keep your wits about you how often even your husband will remain in blissful ignorance that aught has gone wrong, if you do not tell him. You know so well what should have been the product of your labor that you exaggerate the justice of others' perceptions. Console yourself, furthermore, with the reflection that yours is not the first failure upon record, nor the million-and-first, and that there will be as many to-morrows as there have been yesterdays.

Don't add to a trifling *contretemps* the real discomfort of a discontented or fretful wife. Say blithely, if John note your misfortune—"I hope to do better another time," and do not be satisfied until you have redeemed your pledge. Experience and your quick wit will soon teach you how to avert impending evils of this nature, how to snatch your preparations from imminent destruction, and, by ingenious correctives or concealments, to make them presentable. These you will soon learn for yourself if you keep before you the truism I have already written, to wit, that few failures are beyond repair.

Never try experiments for the benefit of invited guests nor, when John is at home, risk the success of your meal upon a new dish. Have something which you know he can eat, and introduce experiments as by-play. But do not be too shy of innovations in the shape of untried dishes. Variety is not only pleasant, but healthful. The least pampered palate will weary of stereotyped bills of fare. It is an idea which should have been exploded long ago, that plain roast, boiled, and fried, on Monday, Tuesday, Wednesday, and Thursday, cod-fish on Friday, with pork-and-beans every Saturday, are means of grace, because economical. And with this should have vanished the prejudice against warmed-over meals—or *réchauffés*, as our French friends term them. I have tried, in the following pages, to set forth the attractions of these, and their claims to your attention as being savory, economical, nourishing, and often elegant. In preparing these acceptably, everything depends upon your own taste and skill. Season with judgment, cook just enough and not a minute too long, and dish nicely. The recommendation of the eye to the palate is a point no cook can afford to disregard. If you can offer an unexpected visitor nothing better than bread-and-butter and cold ham, he will enjoy the luncheon twice as much if the bread be sliced thinly and evenly, spread smoothly, each slice folded in the middle upon the buttered surface, and piled symmetrically; if the ham be also cut thin, scarcely thicker than a wafer, and garnished with parsley, cresses, or curled lettuce. Set on mustard and pickles; let the table-cloth and napkin be white and glossy; the glass clear, and plate shining clean; and add to these accessories to comfort a bright welcome, and, my word for it, you need fear no dissatisfaction on his part, however epicurean may be his tastes. Should your cupboard be bare of aught more substantial than crackers and cheese, do not yield to dismay; split the crackers (if splittable), toast the inside lightly, and butter while hot. Grate your cheese into a powdery mound, garnishing the edges of the plate. If you have no beverage except water to set before him, let this be cool, and pour it out for him yourself, into an irreproachable glass. A dirty table-cloth, a smeared goblet, or a sticky plate, will spoil the most luxurious feast. A table well set is half-spread.

I have not said one-tenth of that which is pressing upon my heart and mind, yet I fear you may think me trite and tedious. One suggestion more, and we will proceed to the details of business.

I believe that, so far as care can avail in securing such a result, my receipts are accurate. But in the matter of seasoning and other minor details, consult your judgment and John's taste. Take this liberty with whatever receipt you think you can improve. If I chance to find in your work-basket, or upon the kitchen dresser, a well-thumbed copy of my beloved "Common Sense," with copious annotations in the margin, I shall, so far from feeling wounded, be flattered in having so diligent a student, and, with your permission, shall engraft the most happy suggestions upon the next edition.

For the speedy issue of which, the petitioner doth humbly pray.

MARION HARLAND.

NOTE

In looking over this book the reader will notice certain receipts marked thus— ✠. I do not claim for these greater merit than should of right be accorded to many others. I merely wish to call the attention of the novice to them as certainly safe, and for the most part simple. Every one thus marked has been tried by myself; most of them are in frequent, some in daily use, in my own family.

My reason for thus singling out comparatively a small number of receipts from the rest, is the recollection of my own perplexities—the loss of time and patience to which I have been subjected in the examination of a new cookery-book, with an eye to immediate use of the directions laid down for various dishes. I have often and vainly wished for a finger-board to guide me in my search for those which were easy and sure, and which would result satisfactorily. This sort of directory I have endeavored to supply, taking care, however, to inform the reader in advance that, so far as I know, there is not an unsafe receipt in the whole work.

Of course it was not necessary or expedient to append the above sign to plain "roast and boiled," which are in common use everywhere.

SOUPS

THE base of your soup should always be uncooked meat. To this may be added, if you like, cracked bones of cooked game, or of underdone beef or mutton; but for flavor and nourishment, depend upon the juices of the meat which was put in raw. Cut this into small pieces, and beat the bone until it is fractured at every inch of its length. Put them on in cold water, without salt, and heat very slowly. *Do not boil fast at any stage of the operation.* Keep the pot covered, and do not add the salt until the meat is thoroughly done, as it has a tendency to harden the fibres, and restrain the flow of the juices. Strain—always through a cullender, after which clear soups should be filtered through a hair-sieve or coarse bobbinet lace. The bag should not be squeezed.

It is slovenly to leave rags of meat, husks of vegetables and bits of bone in the tureen. Do not uncover until you are ready to ladle out the soup. Do this neatly and quickly, having your soup-plates heated beforehand.

Most soups are better the second day than the first, unless they are warmed over too quickly or left too long upon the fire after they are hot. In the one case they are apt to scorch; in the other they become insipid.

VEGETABLE SOUPS.

GREEN PEA. (No. 1.) ✠

- 4 lbs. beef—cut into small pieces.
- ½ peck of green peas.
- 1 gallon water.
- ½ cup of rice-flour, salt, pepper and chopped parsley.

Boil the empty pods of the peas in the water one hour before putting in the beef. Strain them out, add the beef, and boil slowly for an hour and a half longer. Half an hour before serving, add the shelled peas; and twenty minutes later, the rice-flour, with salt, pepper and parsley. After adding the rice-flour, stir frequently, to prevent scorching. Strain into a hot tureen.

GREEN PEA (No. 2.)

- 2 qts. of strong veal or beef broth.
- ½ teaspoonful sugar.
- 1 tablespoonful butter.
- 1 qt. shelled peas.

Bring the broth to a boil; put in the peas, and boil for twenty minutes. Add the sugar, and a sprig of green mint. Boil a quarter of an hour more, and stir in the butter, with pepper and salt, if the broth be not sufficiently salted already. Strain before serving, and send to table with small squares of toasted bread floating upon the top.

SPLIT PEA (*dried*). ✠

- 1 gallon water.
- 1 qt. split peas, which have been soaked over night.
- 1 lb. salt pork, cut into bits an inch square.
- 1 lb. beef, cut into bits an inch square.
- Celery and sweet herbs.
- Fried bread.

Put over the fire, and boil slowly for two hours, or until the quantity of liquor does not exceed two quarts. Pour into a cullender, and press the peas through it with a wooden or silver spoon. Return the soup to the pot, adding a small head of celery, chopped up, a little parsley, or, if preferred, summer savory or sweet marjoram. Have ready three or four slices of bread (stale) which have been fried in butter until they are brown; cut into slices and scatter them upon the surface of the soup after it is poured into the tureen.

PEA AND TOMATO. ✠

This is made according to either of the foregoing receipts, in summer with green—in winter with dried and split peas. Just before straining the soup, add a quart of tomatoes, which have already been stewed soft; let the whole come to a good boil, and strain as above directed. If the stewed tomato be watery, strain off the superfluous liquid before pouring into the pea soup, or it will be too thin.

BEAN (*dried.*) ✠

The beans used for this purpose may be the ordinary kidney, the rice or field bean, or, best of all, the French mock-turtle soup bean. Soak a quart of these over night in soft lukewarm water; put them over the fire next morning, with one gallon of cold water and about two pounds of salt pork. Boil slowly for three hours, keeping the pot well covered; shred into it a head of celery, add pepper— cayenne, if preferred—simmer half an hour longer, strain through a cullender, and serve, with slices of lemon passed to each guest.

Mock-turtle beans, treated in this way, yield a very fair substitute for the fine calf's-head soup known by the same name.

BEAN AND CORN. ✠

This is a winter soup, and is made of white beans prepared according to the foregoing receipt, but with the addition of a quart of dried or canned corn. If the former is used—and the Shaker sweet corn is nearly, salted corn quite as good for the purpose as the more expensive canned green corn—soak it overnight in warm water—changing this early in the morning, and pouring on more warm water, barely enough to cover the corn, and keeping it in a close vessel until ready to put on the beans. Let all boil together, with pork as in the bean soup proper. Strain out as usual, rubbing hard through the cullender. Some persons have a habit of neglecting the use of the cullender in making bean soup, and serving it like stewed beans which have been imperfectly drained. The practice is both slovenly and unwholesome, since the husks of the cereal are thus imposed upon the digestive organs of the eater, with no additional nutriment. To the beans and corn may be added a pint of stewed tomato, if desired.

ASPARAGUS (*White soup.*)

- 3 lbs. veal. The knuckle is best.

- 3 bunches asparagus, as well bleached as you can procure.

- 1 gallon water.

- 1 cup milk.

- 1 tablespoonful rice flour.

- Pepper and salt.

Cut off the hard green stem, and put half of the tender heads of the asparagus into the water with the meat. Boil in closely covered pot for three hours, until the meat is in rags and the asparagus dissolved. Strain the liquor and return to the pot, with the remaining half of the asparagus heads. Let this boil for twenty minutes more, and add, before taking up, a cup of sweet milk (cream is better) in which has been stirred a tablespoonful of rice-flour, arrow-root, or corn-starch. When it has fairly boiled up, serve without further straining, with small squares of toast in the tureen. Season with salt and pepper.

ASPARAGUS (*Green soup.*)

- 3 lbs. veal—cut into small pieces.

- ½ lb. salt pork.

- 3 bunches asparagus.

- 1 gallon water.

Cut the entire stalk of the asparagus into pieces an inch long, and when the meat has boiled one hour, add half of the vegetable to the liquor in the pot. Boil two hours longer and strain, pressing the asparagus pulp very hard to extract all the green coloring. Add the other half of the asparagus—(the heads only, which should be kept in cold water until you are ready for them), and boil twenty minutes more. Then proceed as with the asparagus white soup, omitting the milk, thickening, and salt. The pork will supply the latter seasoning.

TOMATO (Winter soup.) ✠

- 3 lbs. beef.
- 1 qt. canned tomatoes.
- 1 gallon water.
- A little onion.
- Pepper and salt.

Let the meat and water boil for two hours, until the liquid is reduced to little more than two quarts. Then stir in the tomatoes, and stew all slowly for three-quarters of an hour longer. Season to taste, strain, and serve.

TOMATO (*Summer soup*). ✠

- 2½ lbs. veal, or lamb.
- 1 gallon water.
- 2 qts. fresh tomatoes, peeled and cut up fine.
- 1 tablespoonful butter.
- 1 teaspoonful white sugar.
- Pepper and salt. Chopped parsley.

Boil the meat to shreds and the water down to two quarts. Strain the liquor, put in the tomatoes, stirring them very hard that they may dissolve thoroughly; boil half an hour. Season with parsley or any other green herb you may prefer, pepper, and salt. Strain again, and stir in a tablespoonful of butter, with a teaspoonful of white sugar, before pouring into the tureen.

This soup is more palatable still if made with the broth in which chickens were boiled for yesterday's dinner.

TURNIP.

- Knuckle of veal, well cracked.
- 5 qts. water.

Cover closely and stew gently for four hours, the day before the soup is wanted. On the morrow, skim off the fat and warm the stock gradually to a boil. Have ready an onion and six large winter or a dozen small summer turnips, sweet marjoram or thyme minced very finely. Put these into the soup and let them simmer together for an hour. Strain: return to the fire and add a cup of milk—in which has been stirred a tablespoonful of rice-flour or other thickening—and a tablespoonful of butter. Season with salt and pepper, let it boil up once, stirring all the time, as is necessary in all soups where milk is added at last, and remove instantly, or it will scorch.

POTATO.

- A dozen large mealy potatoes.
- 2 onions.
- 1 lb. salt pork.
- 3 qts. water.
- 1 tablespoonful butter.
- 1 cup milk or cream.
- 1 well-beaten egg.
- Chopped onion.

Boil the pork in the clear water for an hour and a half, then take it out. Have ready the potatoes, which, after being peeled and sliced, should lie in cold water for half an hour. Throw them into the pot, with the chopped onion. Cover and boil three-quarters of an hour, stirring often. Beat in butter, milk and egg. Add the latter ingredients carefully, a little at a time; stir while it heats to a final boil, and then serve.

This is a cheap wholesome dish, and more palatable than one would suppose from reading the receipt.

GRAHAM SOUP. ✠

- 3 onions.
- 3 carrots.

- 4 turnips.
- 1 small cabbage.
- 1 bunch celery.
- 1 pt. stewed tomatoes.

Chop all the vegetables, except the tomatoes and cabbage, very finely, and set them over the fire with rather over three quarts of water. They should simmer gently for half an hour, at the end of which time the cabbage must be added, having previously been parboiled and chopped up. In fifteen minutes more put in the tomatoes and a bunch of sweet herbs, and give all a lively boil of twenty minutes. Rub through a cullender, return the soup to the fire, stir in a good tablespoonful of butter, pepper, and salt, half a cup of cream if you have it, thickened with corn-starch; let it boil up, and it is ready for the table.

OCHRA, OR GUMBO.

Ochra, or *okra*, is a vegetable little known except in the far South, where it is cultivated in large quantities and is very popular. A favorite soup is prepared from it in the following manner:—

- 2 qts. of ochras, sliced thin.
- 1 qt. of tomatoes, also sliced.
- 4 tablespoonfuls of butter.
- 2 lbs. of beef, cut into small pieces.
- ½ lb. corned ham or pork, also cut up.

Put the meat and ochras together in a pot with a quart of cold water—just enough to cover them—and let them stew for an hour. Then add the tomatoes and two quarts of *boiling* water—more, if the liquid in the pot has boiled away so as to expose the meat and vegetables. Boil three-quarters of an hour longer, skimming often with a *silver* spoon. When the contents of the vessel are boiled to pieces, put in the butter, with cayenne pepper and salt, if the ham has not seasoned it sufficiently. Strain and send up with squares of light, crisp toast floating upon it.

CORN. ✠

- 1 large fowl, cut into eight pieces.

- 1 doz. ears green corn—cut from the cobs.

Boil the chicken with the cobs in a gallon of water until the fowl is tender—if tough, the boiling must be slow and long. Then, put the corn into the pot, and stew an hour longer—still gently. Remove the chicken with a cupful of the liquid, if you wish to make other use of the meat. Set this aside, take out the cobs, season the corn-soup with pepper, salt, and parsley; thicken with rice or wheat flour, boil up once, and serve without straining, if the corn be young and tender.

A tolerable fricassee may be made of the chicken, unless it has boiled to rags, by beating up an egg and a tablespoonful of butter, adding this to the cupful of reserved liquor from which the corn must be strained. Boil this for a moment, thicken with flour, throw in a little chopped parsley, pepper, and salt; pour, while scalding, over the chicken, which you have arranged in a dish; garnish with circular slices of hard-boiled eggs and curled parsley.

MEAT SOUPS.

BEEF SOUP (*à la Julienne*). ✠

- 6 lbs. of lean beef. The shin is a good piece for this purpose. Have the bones well cracked, carefully extracting the marrow, every bit of which should be put into the soup.

- 6 qts. of water.

The stock must be prepared the day before the soup is needed. Put the beef, bones and all, with the water in a close vessel, and set it where it will heat gradually. Let it boil very slowly for six hours at least, only uncovering the pot once in a great while to see if there is danger of the water sinking too rapidly. Should this be the case, replenish with boiling water, taking care not to put in too much. During the seventh hour, take off the soup and set it away in a cool place, until next morning. About an hour before dinner, take out the meat, which you can use for mince-meat, if you wish; remove the cake of fat from the surface of the stock, set the soup over the fire, and throw in a little salt to bring up the scum. When this has been skimmed carefully off, put in your vegetables. These should be:—

- 2 carrots.

- 3 turnips.

- Half a head of white cabbage.

- 1 pt. green corn—or dried Shaker corn, soaked over night.

- 1 head celery.

- 1 qt. tomatoes.

These should be prepared for the soup by slicing them very small, and stewing them in barely enough water to cover them, until they break to pieces. Cook the cabbage by itself in two waters—throwing the first away. The only exception to the general dissolution, is in the case of a single carrot, which should likewise be cooked alone and whole, until thoroughly done, and set aside to cool, when the rest of the vegetables, with the water in which they were boiled, are added to the soup. Return the pot to the fire with the vegetables and stock, and boil slowly for half an hour from the time ebullition actually begins. Strain without pressing, only shaking and lightly stirring the contents of the cullender. The vegetables having been added with all their juices already cooked, much boiling and squeezing are not needed, and only make the soup cloudy. Cut the reserved carrot into dice and drop into the clear liquor after it is in the tureen,—also, if you like, a handful of vermicelli, or macaroni which has been boiled tender in clear water.

The seasoning of this excellent soup is a matter of taste. Some use only salt and white pepper. Others like with this a few blades of mace, and boil in the stock a handful of sweet herbs. And others fancy that, in addition to these, a glass of brown sherry imparts a flavor that renders it peculiarly acceptable to most palates. Send to table very hot, and have the soup-plates likewise heated.

VEAL SOUP WITH MACARONI. ✠

- 3 lbs. of veal knuckle or scrag, with the bones broken and meat cut up.
- 3 qts. water.
- ¼ lb. Italian macaroni.

Boil the meat alone in the water for nearly three hours until it is reduced to shreds; and the macaroni until tender, in enough water to cover it, in a vessel by itself. The pieces should not be more than an inch in length. Add a little butter to the macaroni when nearly done. Strain the meat out of the soup, season to your taste, put in the macaroni, and the water in which it was boiled; let it boil up, and serve.

You can make macaroni soup of this by boiling a pound, instead of a quarter of a pound, in the second vessel, and adding the above quantity of veal broth. In this case, send on with it a plate of grated cheese, that those who cannot relish macaroni without this accompaniment may put it into their soup. Take care that the macaroni is of uniform length, not too long, and that it does not break while stewing. Add butter in proportion to the increased quantity of macaroni.

BEEF SOUP (*brown*).

- 3 lbs. beef cut into strips.
- 3 onions.
- 3 qts. water.

Put beef and water into the saucepan and boil for one hour. Meanwhile, slice the onions and fry them in butter to a light brown. Drop into the pot with a teaspoonful of cloves, half as much pepper, same quantity of mace as pepper, a pinch of allspice, and a teaspoonful of essence of celery, if you cannot get a head of fresh celery; also half a teaspoonful of powdered savory or sweet marjoram, and a teaspoonful of Worcestershire sauce. Stew all for two hours more, or until the beef has boiled to pieces. Strain the soup and return to the fire. Salt to taste, and just before taking it off, pour in a glass of brown sherry or Madeira wine.

MUTTON OR LAMB BROTH. ✠

- 4 lbs. mutton or lamb—*lean*—cut into small pieces.
- 1 gallon water.
- ½ teacupful rice.

Boil the unsalted meat for two hours, slowly, in a covered vessel. Soak the rice in enough warm water to cover it, and at the end of this time add it, water and all, to the boiling soup. Cook an hour longer, stirring watchfully from time to time, lest the rice should settle and adhere to the bottom of the pot. Beat an egg to a froth and stir into a cup of cold milk, into which has been rubbed smoothly a tablespoonful rice or wheat flour. Mix with this, a little at a time, some of the scalding liquor, until the egg is so far cooked that there is no danger of curdling in the soup. Pour into the pot, when you have taken out the meat, season with parsley, thyme, pepper, and salt. Boil up fairly, and serve. If allowed to stand on the fire, it is apt to burn.

This soup may be made from the liquor in which a leg of mutton has been boiled, provided too much salt was not put in with it. It is especially good when the stock is chicken broth. For the sick it is palatable and nutritious with the rice left in. When strained it makes a nice white table soup, and is usually relished by all.

VERMICELLI SOUP. ✠

- 4 lbs. lamb, from which every particle of fat has been removed.
- 1 lb. veal.
- A slice of corned ham.
- 5 qts. water.

Cut up the meat, cover it with a quart of water, and set it back on the range to heat very gradually, keeping it covered closely. At the end of an hour, add four quarts of boiling water, and cook until the meat is in shreds. Season with salt, sweet herbs, a chopped shallot, two teaspoonfuls Worcestershire sauce, and when these have boiled in the soup for ten minutes, strain and return to the fire. Have ready about a third of a pound of vermicelli (or macaroni), which has been boiled tender in clear water. Add this; boil up once, and pour out.

MOCK-TURTLE OR CALF'S HEAD SOUP. ✠

- 1 large calf's head, well cleaned and washed.
- 4 pig's feet, well cleaned and washed.

This soup should always be prepared the day before it is to be served up. Lay the head and feet in the bottom of a large pot, and cover with a gallon of water. Let it boil three hours, or until the flesh will slip easily from the bones. Take out the head, leaving in the feet, and allow these to boil steadily while you cut the meat from the head. Select with care enough of the fatty portions which lie on the top of the head and the cheeks to fill a teacup, and set them aside to cool. Remove the brains to a saucer and also set aside. Chop the rest of the meat with the tongue very fine, season with salt, pepper, powdered marjoram and thyme, a teaspoonful of cloves, the same of mace, half as much allspice, and a grated nutmeg, and return to the pot. When the flesh falls from the bones of the pig's feet, take out the latter, leaving in the gelatinous meat. Let all boil together slowly, without removing the cover, for two hours more; take the soup from the fire and set it away until the next day. An hour before dinner, set on the stock to warm. When it boils strain carefully, and drop in the meat you have reserved, which, when cold, should be cut into small squares. Have these all ready as well as the force-meat balls. To prepare these, rub the yolks of five hard-boiled eggs to a paste in a Wedgewood mortar, or in a bowl, with the back of a silver tablespoon, adding gradually the brains to moisten them, also a little butter and salt. Mix with these two eggs beaten very light, flour your hands, and make this paste into balls about the size of a pigeon's egg. Throw them into the soup five minutes before you take it from the fire; stir in three large tablespoonfuls of browned flour rubbed smooth in three great spoonfuls of melted butter, let it boil up well, and finish the seasoning by the addition of a glass and a half of *good* wine—Sherry or Madeira—and the juice of a lemon. It should not boil more than half an hour on the second day. Serve with sliced lemon. Some lay the slices upon the top of the soup, but the better plan is to pass to the guests a small dish containing these.

If the directions be closely followed, the result is sure to be satisfactory, and the task is really much less troublesome than it appears to be.

GIBLET SOUP.

- Feet, neck, pinions, and giblets of three chickens, or of two ducks or two geese.
- 1½ lb. veal.
- ½ lb. ham.
- 3 qts. water.

Crack the bones into small pieces, and cut the meat into strips. Put all together with the giblets over the fire, with a bunch of sweet herbs and a pinch of allspice. Stew slowly for two hours. Take out the giblets and set them aside in a pan where they will keep warm. Take up a teacupful of the hot soup and stir into this a large tablespoonful of flour which has been wet with cold water and rubbed to a smooth paste; then, two tablespoonfuls of butter. Return to the pot and boil for fifteen minutes; season at the last with a glass of brown sherry and a tablespoonful of tomato or walnut catsup. A little Worcestershire sauce is an improvement. Finally, chop and add the giblets, and boil up once.

BROWN GRAVY SOUP.

- 3 lbs. beef.
- 1 carrot.
- 1 turnip.
- 1 head of celery.
- 6 onions, if small button onions—one, if large.
- 3½ qts. water.

Have ready some nice dripping in a frying-pan. Slice the onions and fry them brown. Take them out and set them by in a covered pan to keep warm. Cut the beef into bits an inch long and half an inch thick, and fry them brown also, turning frequently lest they should burn. Chop the vegetables and put them with the meat and onions into a covered pot. Pour on the water and let all stew together for two hours. Then throw in salt and pepper and boil one hour longer, skimming very carefully. Strain; put back over the fire; boil up once more to make the liquid perfectly clear, skim, and add a handful of vermicelli that has been boiled separately and drained dry. The safest plan is to put in the vermicelli after the soup is poured into the tureen. Do not stir before it goes to table. The contents of the tureen should be clear as amber. Some add half a glass of *pale* Sherry. This is a fine show soup, and very popular.

VEAL AND SAGO SOUP.

- 2½ lbs. veal chopped fine.
- ¼ lb. pearl sago.
- 1 pt. milk.
- 4 eggs.
- 3 qts. water.

Put on the veal and water, and boil slowly until the liquid is reduced to about one-half the original quantity. Strain out the shreds of meat, and put the soup again over the fire. Meanwhile the sago should be washed in several waters, and soaked half an hour in warm water enough to cover it. Stir it into the strained broth and boil—stirring very often to prevent lumping or scorching—half an hour more. Heat the milk almost to boiling; beat the yolks of the eggs very light; mix with the milk gradually, as in making boiled custard, and pour—stirring all the while—into the soup. Season with pepper and salt; boil up once to cook the eggs, and serve. Should the liquid be too thick after putting in the eggs, replenish with boiling water. It should be about the consistency of hot custard.

This soup is very good, if chicken broth be substituted for the veal. It is very strengthening to invalids, and especially beneficial to those suffering from colds and pulmonary affections.

CHICKEN SOUP. ✠

- 2 young fowls, or one full-grown.
- ½ lb. corned ham.
- 1 gallon of water.

Cut the fowls into pieces as for fricassee. Put these with the ham into the pot with a quart of water, or enough to cover them fairly. Stew for an hour, if the fowls are tender; if tough, until you can cut easily into the breast. Take out the breasts, leaving the rest of the meat in the pot, and add the remainder of the water—boiling hot. Keep the soup stewing slowly while you chop up the white meat you have selected. Rub the yolks of four hard-boiled eggs smooth in a mortar or bowl, moistening to a paste with a few spoonfuls of the soup. Mix with these a handful of fine bread-crumbs and the chopped meat, and make it into small balls. When the soup has boiled in all, two hours and a half, if the chicken be reduced to shreds, strain out the meat and bones. Season with salt and white pepper, with a bunch of chopped parsley. Drop in the prepared force-meat, and after boiling ten minutes to incorporate the ingredients well, add, a little at a time, a pint of rich milk thickened with flour. Boil up once and serve.

A chicken at least a year old would make better soup than a younger fowl.

VENISON SOUP. ✠

- 3 lbs. of venison. What are considered the inferior pieces will do.
- 1 lb. corned ham or salt pork.
- 1 onion.
- 1 head of celery.

Cut up the meat; chop the vegetables, and put on with just enough water to cover them, keeping on the lid of the pot all the while, and stew slowly for one hour. Then add two quarts of boiling water, with a few blades of mace and a dozen whole peppers. Or, should you prefer, a little cayenne. Boil two hours longer, salt, and strain. Return the liquor to the pot; stir in a tablespoonful of butter, thicken with a tablespoonful of browned flour wet into a smooth thin paste with cold water; add a tablespoonful of walnut or mushroom catsup, a teaspoonful of Worcestershire or other pungent sauce, and a generous glass of Madeira or brown Sherry.

HARE OR RABBIT SOUP.

Dissect the rabbit, crack the bones, and prepare precisely as you would the venison soup, only putting in three small onions instead of one, and a bunch of sweet herbs. Hares which are too tough to be cooked in any other way, make excellent game soup. Also, the large gray squirrel of the Middle and Southern States.

OX-TAIL SOUP.

- 1 ox-tail.
- 2 lbs. lean beef.
- 4 carrots.
- 3 onions.
- Thyme.

Cut the tail into several pieces and fry brown in butter. Slice the onions and two carrots, and when you remove the ox-tail from the frying-pan, put in these and brown them also. When done, tie them in a bag with a bunch of thyme and drop into the soup-pot. Lay the pieces of ox-tail in the same; then the meat cut into small slices. Grate over them the two whole carrots, and add four quarts of cold water, with pepper and salt. Boil from four to six hours, in proportion to the size of the tail. Strain fifteen minutes before serving it, and thicken with two tablespoonfuls of browned flour. Boil ten minutes longer.

FISH SOUPS.

OYSTER SOUP (No. 1). ✠

- 2 qts. of oysters.
- 1 qt. of milk.
- 2 tablespoonfuls butter.
- 1 teacupful water.

Strain the liquor from the oysters, add to it the water, and set it over the fire to heat slowly in a covered vessel. When it is near boiling, season with pepper and salt; add the oysters, and let them stew until they "ruffle" on the edge. This will be in about five minutes. Then put in the butter with the milk which has been heated in a separate vessel, and stir well for two minutes.

Serve with sliced lemon and oyster or cream crackers. Some use mace and nutmeg in seasoning. The crowning excellence in oyster soup is to have it cooked just enough. Too much stewing ruins the bivalves, while an underdone oyster is a flabby abomination. The plumpness of the main body and ruffled edge are good indices of their right condition.

OYSTER SOUP (No. 2).

- 2 qts. of oysters.
- 2 eggs.
- 1 qt. of milk.
- 1 teacupful of water.

Strain the liquor from the oysters into a saucepan, pour in with it the water. Season with cayenne pepper and a little salt, a teaspoonful of mingled nutmeg, mace, and cloves. When the liquor is almost boiling, add half the oysters chopped finely and boil five minutes quite briskly. Strain the soup and return to saucepan. Have ready some force-meat balls, not larger than marbles, made of the yolks of the eggs boiled hard and rubbed to a smooth paste with a little butter, then mix with six raw oysters chopped very finely, a little salt, and a raw egg well beaten, to bind the ingredients together. Flour your hands well and roll the force-meat into pellets, laying them upon a cold plate, so as not to touch one another until needed. Then put the reserved whole oysters into the hot soup, and when it begins to boil again, drop in the force-meat marbles. Boil until the oysters "ruffle," by which time the balls will also be done. Add the hot milk.

Serve with sliced lemon and crackers. A liberal tablespoonful of butter stirred in gently at the last is an improvement.

CLAM SOUP.

- 50 clams.
- 1 qt. milk.
- 1 pint water.
- 2 tablespoonfuls butter.

Drain off the liquor from the clams and put it over the fire with a dozen whole peppers, a few bits of cayenne pods, half a dozen blades of mace, and salt to taste. Let it boil for ten minutes, then put in the clams and boil half an hour quite fast, keeping the pot closely covered. If you dislike to see the whole spices in the tureen, strain them out before the clams are added. At the end of the half hour add the milk, which has been heated to scalding, not boiling, in another vessel. Boil up again, taking care the soup does not burn, and put in the butter. Then serve without delay. If you desire a thicker soup stir a heaping tablespoonful of rice-flour into a little cold milk, and put in with the quart of hot.

CAT-FISH SOUP. ✠

Those who have only seen the bloated, unsightly "hornpouts" that play the scavengers about city wharves, are excusable for entertaining a prejudice against them as an article of food. But the small cat-fish of our inland lakes and streams are altogether respectable, except in their unfortunate name.

- 6 cat-fish, in average weight half a pound apiece.
- ½ lb. salt pork.
- 1 pint milk.

- 2 eggs.
- 1 head of celery, or a small bag of celery seed.

Skin and clean the fish and cut them up. Chop the pork into small pieces. Put these together into the pot, with two quarts of water, chopped sweet herbs, and the celery seasoning. Boil for an hour, or until fish and pork are in rags, and strain, if you desire a regular soup for a first course. Return to the saucepan and add the milk, which should be already hot. Next the eggs, beaten to a froth, and a lump of butter the size of a walnut. Boil up once, and serve with dice of toasted bread on the top. Pass sliced lemon, or walnut or butternut pickles with it.

EEL SOUP.

Eel soup is made in precisely the same manner as cat-fish, only boiled longer. A chopped onion is no detriment to the flavor of either, and will remove the muddy taste which these fish sometimes acquire from turbid streams.

LOBSTER SOUP.

- 2 qts. veal or chicken broth, well strained.
- 1 large lobster.
- 2 eggs—boiled hard.

Boil the lobster and extract the meat, setting aside the coral in a cool place. Cut or chop up the meat found in the claws. Rub the yolks of the eggs to a paste with a teaspoonful of butter. Pound and rub the claw-meat in the same manner, and mix with the yolks. Beat up a raw egg, and stir into the paste; season with pepper, salt, and, if you like, mace; make into force-meat balls, and set away with the coral to cool and harden. By this time the stock should be well heated, when, put in the rest of the lobster-meat cut into square bits. Boil fifteen minutes, which time employ in pounding the coral in a Wedgewood mortar, or earthenware bowl, rubbing it into a fine, even paste, with the addition of a few spoonfuls of the broth, gradually worked in until it is about the consistency of boiled starch. Stir *very* carefully into the hot soup, which should, in the process, blush into a roseate hue. Lastly, drop in the force-meat balls, after which do not stir, lest they should break. Simmer a few minutes to cook the raw egg; but, if allowed to boil, the soup will darken.

Crab soup may be made in the same way, excepting the coralline process, crabs being destitute of that dainty.

GREEN TURTLE SOUP.

- A glass of Madeira.

- 2 onions.

- Bunch of sweet herbs.

- Juice of one lemon.

- 5 qts of water.

Chop up the coarser parts of the turtle-meat, with the entrails and bones. Add to them four quarts of water, and stew four hours with the herbs, onions, pepper, and salt. Stew very slowly, but do not let it cease to boil during this time. At the end of four hours strain the soup, and add the finer parts of the turtle and the green fat, which has been simmered for one hour in two quarts of water. Thicken with browned flour; return to the soup-pot, and simmer gently an hour longer. If there are eggs in the turtle, boil them in a separate vessel for four hours, and throw into the soup before taking it up. If not, put in force-meat balls; then the juice of the lemon and the wine; beat up once and pour out. Some cooks add the finer meat before straining, boiling all together five hours; then strain, thicken, and put in the green fat, cut into lumps an inch long. This makes a handsomer soup than if the meat is left in.

For the mock eggs, take the yolks of three hard-boiled eggs, and one raw egg well beaten. Rub the boiled eggs into a paste with a teaspoonful of butter, bind with the raw egg, roll into pellets the size and shape of turtle-eggs, and lay in boiling water for two minutes before dropping into the soup.

Force-meat balls for the above.

Six tablespoonfuls turtle-meat chopped very fine. Rub to a paste with the yolks of two hard-boiled eggs; tablespoonful of butter, and, if convenient, a little oyster-liquor. Season with cayenne, mace, and half a teaspoonful of white sugar. Bind with a well-beaten egg; shape into balls; dip in egg, then powdered cracker, fry in butter, and drop into the soup when it is served.

Green turtle for soups is now within the reach of every private family, being well preserved in air-tight cans.

FISH.

BOILED CODFISH. (*Fresh.*) ✠

Lay the fish in cold water, slightly salted, for half an hour before it is time to cook it. When it has been wiped free of the salt and water, wrap it in a clean linen cloth kept for such purposes. The cloth should be dredged with flour, to prevent sticking. Sew up the edges in such a manner as to envelop the fish entirely, yet have but one thickness of the cloth over any part. The wrapping should be fitted neatly to the shape of the piece to be cooked. Put into the fish-kettle, pour on plenty of hot water, and boil briskly— fifteen minutes for each pound.

Have ready a sauce prepared thus:—

To one gill boiling water add as much milk, and when it is scalding-hot, stir in—leaving the sauce-pan on the fire—two tablespoonfuls of butter, rolled thickly in flour; as this thickens, two beaten eggs. Season with salt and chopped parsley, and when, after one good boil, you withdraw it from the fire, add a dozen capers, or pickled nasturtium seeds, or, if you prefer, a spoonful of vinegar in which celery-seeds have been steeped. Put the fish into a hot dish, and pour the sauce over it. Some serve in a butter-boat; but I fancy that the boiling sauce applied to the steaming fish imparts a richness it cannot gain later. Garnish with sprigs of parsley and circles of hard-boiled eggs, laid around the edge of the dish.

ROCK-FISH.

Rock-fish and river-bass are very nice, cooked as above, but do not need to be boiled so long as codfish.

BOILED CODFISH. (*Salt.*)

Put the fish to soak over night in lukewarm water—as early as eight o'clock in the evening. Change this for more warm water at bed-time and cover closely. Change again in the morning and wash off the salt. Two hours before dinner plunge into *very* cold water. This makes it firm. Finally, set over the fire with enough lukewarm water to cover it, and boil for half an hour. Drain well; lay it on a hot dish, and pour over it egg-sauce prepared as in the foregoing receipt, only substituting the yolks of two hard-boiled eggs, rubbed to a paste with butter, for the beaten raw egg.

This is a useful receipt for country housekeepers who can seldom procure fresh cod. Salt mackerel, prepared in the same way, will repay the care and time required, so superior is it to the Friday's dish of salt fish, as usually served.

Should the cold fish left over be used for fish-balls—as it should be—it will be found that the sauce which has soaked into it while hot has greatly improved it.

CODFISH BALLS. ✠

Prepare the fish precisely as for boiling whole. Cut in pieces when it has been duly washed and soaked, and boil twenty minutes. Turn off the water, and cover with fresh from the boiling tea-kettle. Boil twenty minutes more, drain the fish very dry, and spread upon a dish to cool. When perfectly cold, pick to pieces with a fork, removing every vestige of skin and bone, and shredding very fine. When this is done, add an equal bulk of mashed potato; work into a stiff batter by adding a lump of butter and sweet milk, and if you want to have them very nice, a beaten egg. Flour your hands and make the mixture into balls or cakes. Drop them into boiling lard or good dripping, and fry to a light brown. Plainer fish-cakes may be made of the cod and potatoes alone, moulded round like biscuit. In any shape the dish is popular.

SALT CODFISH STEWED WITH EGGS.

Prepare the fish as for balls. Heat almost to boiling a pint of rich, sweet milk, and stir into it, gradually and carefully, three eggs, well beaten, a tablespoonful of butter, a little chopped parsley and butter, with pepper, lastly the fish. Boil up once and turn into a deep covered dish, or chafing dish lined with buttered toast. Eat hot for breakfast or supper.

CODFISH AND POTATO STEW. ✠

Soak, boil, and pick the fish, if salt, as for fish-balls. If fresh, boil and pick into bits. Add an equal quantity of mashed potatoes, a large tablespoonful of butter and milk, enough to make it very soft. Put into a skillet, and add a little boiling water to keep it from burning. Turn and toss constantly until it is smoking hot but not dry; add pepper and parsley, and dish.

BOILED MACKEREL. (*Fresh.*) ✠

Clean the mackerel and wipe carefully with a dry, clean cloth; wash them lightly with another cloth dipped in vinegar; wrap each in a coarse linen cloth (floured) basted closely to the shape of the fish. Put them into a pot with enough salted water to cover them, and boil them gently for three quarters of an hour. Drain them well. Take a teacupful of the water in which they were boiled, and put into a saucepan with a tablespoonful of walnut catsup, some anchovy paste or sauce, and the juice of half a lemon. Let this boil up well and add a lump of butter the size of an egg, with a tablespoonful browned flour wet in cold water. Boil up again and serve in the sauce-boat. This makes a brown sauce. You can substitute egg-sauce if you like. Garnish with parsley and nasturtium blossoms.

BROILED MACKEREL. (*Fresh.*)

Clean the mackerel, wash, and wipe dry. Split it open, so that when laid flat the backbone will be in the middle. Sprinkle lightly with salt, and lay on a buttered gridiron over a clear fire, with the inside downward, until it begins to brown; then turn the other. When quite done, lay on a hot dish and butter it plentifully. Turn another hot dish over the lower one, and let it stand two or three minutes before sending to table.

BROILED MACKEREL. (*Salt.*)

Soak over night in lukewarm water. Change this early in the morning for very cold, and let the fish lie in this until time to cook. Then proceed as with the fresh mackerel.

BOILED HALIBUT. ✠

Lay in cold salt and water for an hour. Wipe dry and score the skin in squares. Put into the kettle with cold salted water enough to cover it. It is so firm in texture that you can boil without a cloth if you choose. Let it heat gradually, and boil from half to three-quarters of an hour, in proportion to the size of the piece. Four or five pounds will be enough for most private families. Drain and accompany by egg-sauce—either poured over the fish, or in a sauce-boat.

Save the cold remnants of the fish and what sauce is left until next morning. Pick out as you would cod, mix with an equal quantity of mashed potato, moisten with the sauce, or with milk and butter if you have no sauce, put it into a skillet, and stir until it is very hot. Do not burn. Season with pepper and salt.

BAKED HALIBUT. ✠

Take a piece of halibut weighing five or six pounds, and lay in salt and water for two hours. Wipe dry and score the outer skin. Set in the baking-pan in a tolerably hot oven, and bake an hour, basting often with butter and water heated together in a saucepan or tin cup. When a fork will penetrate it easily it is done. It should be of a fine brown. Take the gravy in the dripping-pan—add a little boiling water should there not be enough—stir in a tablespoonful of walnut catsup, a teaspoonful of Worcestershire sauce, the juice of a lemon, and thicken with browned flour, previously wet with cold water. Boil up once and put into sauce-boat.

There is no finer preparation of halibut than this, which is, however, comparatively little known. Those who have eaten it usually prefer it to boiled and broiled. You can use what is left for the same purpose as the fragments of boiled halibut.

HALIBUT STEAK. ✠

Wash and wipe the steaks dry. Beat up two or three eggs, and roll out some Boston or other brittle crackers upon the kneading-board until they are fine as dust. Dip each steak into the beaten egg, then into the bread crumbs (when you have salted the fish), and fry in hot fat, lard, or nice dripping.

Or, you can broil the steak upon a buttered gridiron, over a clear fire, first seasoning with salt and pepper. When done, lay in a hot dish, butter well, and cover closely.

DEVILLED HALIBUT.

Mince a pound of cold boiled or baked halibut, or the fragments of halibut steak, and make for it the following dressing: The yolks of three hard-boiled eggs rubbed smooth with the back of a silver spoon, or in a Wedgewood mortar, and when there remain no lumps in it, work into a soft paste with a tablespoonful salad oil. Next beat in two teaspoonfuls white sugar, a teaspoonful made mustard, a pinch of cayenne, teaspoonful salt, one of Worcestershire sauce, a little anchovy paste if you have it, and finally, a little at a time to prevent lumping, a *small* teacupful of vinegar in which celery-seed have been steeped. It is easy to keep a bottle of this on hand for salads and sauces. Stir all thoroughly into the minced fish, garnish with a chain of the whites of the eggs cut into rings, with a small round slice of pickled beet laid within each link, and you have a *piquant* and pretty salad for the supper-table.

BOILED SALMON. (*Fresh.*) ✠

Wrap the fish, when you have washed and wiped it, in a clean linen cloth—not too thick—baste it up securely, and put into the fish-kettle. Cover with cold water in which has been melted a handful of salt. Boil slowly, allowing about a quarter of an hour to each pound. When the time is up, rip open a corner of the cloth and test the salmon with a fork. If it penetrate easily, it is done. If not, hastily pin up the cloth and cook a little longer. Skim off the scum as it rises to the top. Have ready in another saucepan a pint of cream—or half milk and half cream will do—which has been heated in a vessel set in boiling water; stir into this a large spoonful of butter, rolled in flour, a little salt and chopped parsley, and a half-gill of the water in which the fish is boiled. Let it boil up once, stirring all the while. When the fish is done, take it instantly from the kettle, lay it an instant upon a folded cloth to absorb the drippings; transfer with great care, for fear of breaking, to a hot dish, and pour the boiled cream over it, reserving enough to fill a small sauce-boat. Garnish with curled parsley and circular slices of hard-boiled yolks—leaving out the whites of the eggs.

After serving boiled salmon with cream-sauce, you will never be quite content with any other. If you cannot get cream, boil a pint of milk and thicken with arrow-root. It is not so nice, but many will not detect the difference—*real* cream being a rare commodity in town.

You may pickle what is left, if it is in one piece. Or devil it, as I have directed you to treat cold halibut. *Or* mince, mixed with mashed potato, milk, and butter, and stir into a sort of stew. Or, once again, mix with mashed potato, milk, butter, and a raw egg well-beaten; make into cakes or balls, and fry in hot lard or dripping. At any rate, let none of it be lost, it being at once one of our most expensive and most delicious fish.

BAKED SALMON. ✠

Wash and wipe dry, and rub with pepper and salt. Some add a soupçon of cayenne and powdered mace. Lay the fish upon a grating set over your baking-pan, and roast or bake, basting it freely with butter, and, toward the last, with its own drippings only. Should it brown too fast, cover the top with a sheet of white paper until the whole is cooked. When it is done, transfer to a hot dish and cover closely, and add to the gravy a little hot water thickened with arrow-root, rice, or wheat flour,—wet, of course, first with cold water,—a great spoonful of strained tomato sauce, and the juice of a lemon. Boil up and serve in a sauce boat, or you can serve with cream sauce, made as for boiled salmon. Garnish handsomely with alternate sprigs of parsley and the bleached tops of celery, with ruby bits of firm currant jelly here and there. This is a fine dish for a dinner-party. A glass of Sherry improves the first-named sauce.

SALMON STEAKS. ✠

Dry well with a cloth, dredge with flour, and lay them upon a well-buttered gridiron, over clear hot coals. Turn with a broad-bladed knife slipped beneath, and a flat wire egg-beater above, lest the steak should break. When done to a light brown, lay in a hot dish, butter each steak, seasoning with salt and pepper, cover closely, and serve.

PICKLED SALMON. (*Fresh.*) ✠

Having cleaned your fish, cut into pieces of a convenient size to go into the fish-kettle, and boil in salted water as for the table. Drain it very dry, wipe it with a clean cloth, and set it aside in a cool place until next morning.

Make pickle enough to cover it in the following proportions: 2 quarts vinegar, a dozen blades of mace, dozen white peppers, dozen cloves, two teaspoonfuls made mustard, three tablespoonfuls white sugar, and a pint of the water in which the fish was boiled. Let them boil up once hard, that you may skim the pickle. Should the spices come away with the scum in large quantities, pick them out and return to the kettle. Set the liquor away in an earthenware jar, closely covered, to keep in the flavor. Next morning hang it over a brisk fire in a bell-metal kettle (covered), and heat to boiling. Meanwhile, prepare the salmon by cutting into pieces an inch and a half long and half an inch wide. Cut cleanly and regularly with a sharp knife. When they are all ready, and the liquor is on the boil, drop them carefully into the kettle. Let the pickle boil up once to make sure the salmon is heated through. Have ready some air-tight glass jars, such as you use for canning fruit and tomatoes. Take the salmon from the kettle, while it is still on the stove or range, with a wire-egg-beater, taking care you do not break the pieces. Drop them rapidly into the jar, packing closely as you go on; fill with the boiling pickle until it overflows, screw on the top, and set away in a dark, cool place. Proceed in the same way with each can until all are full. Salmon thus put up will keep good for *years*, as I can testify from experience, and will well repay the trouble of preparation. You can vary the seasoning to your taste, adding a shallot or two minced very fine, some celery and small pods of cayenne pepper, which always *look* well in vinegar.

Be sure that the contents of the kettle are boiling when transferred to the cans, that they are not allowed time to cool in the transit, that the elastic on the can is properly adjusted, and the top screwed down tightly, and success is certain. I would call the attention of those who are fond of the potted spiced salmon, sold at a high price in grocery stores, to this receipt for making the same luxury at home. It costs less by one-half, is as good, and is always on hand.

PICKLED SALMON. (*Salt.*)

Wash the salmon in two or three waters, rubbing it lightly with a coarse cloth to remove the salt-crystals. Then soak over night in tepid water. Exchange this in the morning for ice-cold, and let the fish lie in the latter for three hours. Take it out, wipe dry, and cut in strips as directed in the foregoing receipt. Drop these, when all are ready, in a saucepan of boiling water, placed alongside of a kettle of pickle prepared as for fresh salmon. Beside these have your air-tight jars, covers laid in readiness, and when the salmon has boiled five minutes—fairly boiled, not simmered—fish out the pieces with your wire spoon, pack rapidly into your can; fill up with the boiling pickle from the other kettle, and seal instantly. In two days the pickled salmon will be fit for use, and is scarcely distinguishable from that made of fresh fish. It has the advantage of being always procurable, and of comparative cheapness, and in the country is a valuable stand-by in case of unexpected supper company.

SMOKED SALMON. (*Broiled.*)

Take a piece of raw smoked salmon the size of your hand, or larger in proportion to the number who are to sit down to supper. Wash it in two waters, rubbing off the salt. Lay in a skillet with enough warm—not hot—water to cover it; let it simmer fifteen minutes, and boil five. Remove it, wipe dry, and lay on a buttered gridiron to broil. When it is nicely browned on both sides, transfer to a hot dish; butter liberally, and pepper to taste. Garnish with hillocks of grated horse-radish interspersed with sprays of fresh or pickled fennel-seed, or with parsley.

Raw smoked salmon is in common use upon the supper-table, cut into smooth strips as long as the middle finger, and rather wider; arranged neatly upon a garnished dish, and eaten with pepper-sauce or some other pungent condiment.

BOILED SHAD. (*Fresh.*) ✠

Clean, wash, and wipe the fish. A roe shad is best for this purpose. Cleanse the roes thoroughly, and having sprinkled both shad and eggs with salt, wrap in separate cloths and put into a fish-kettle, side by side. Cover with salted water, and boil from half an hour to three-quarters, in proportion to the size. Experience is the best rule as to the time. When you have once cooked fish to a turn, note the weight and time, and you will be at no loss thereafter. A good rule is to make a pencilled memorandum in the margin of the receipt-book opposite certain receipts.

Serve the shad upon a hot dish, with a boat of drawn butter mingled with chopped eggs and parsley, or egg-sauce. Lay the roes about the body of the fish. Garnish with capers and slices of hard boiled eggs.

BOILED SHAD. (*Salt.*)

Soak the fish six or seven hours in warm water, changing it several times; wipe off all the salt and immerse in ice-cold water. When it has lain in this an hour, put into a fish-kettle with enough fresh water to cover it, and boil from fifteen to twenty minutes, in proportion to the size. Serve in a hot dish, with a large lump of butter spread over the fish.

BROILED SHAD. (*Fresh.*) ✠

Wash, wipe, and split the fish. Sprinkle with salt and pepper, and lay it upon a buttered gridiron, inside downward. When the lower side is browned, turn the fish. One of medium size will be done in about twenty minutes. Serve upon a hot dish, and lay a good piece of butter upon the fish.

BROILED SHAD. (*Salt.*)

Soak over night in lukewarm water. Take out in the morning and transfer to ice-cold for half an hour. Wipe very dry, and broil as you do fresh shad.

FRIED SHAD.

This is a popular dish upon Southern tables, and is good anywhere. Clean, wash, and wipe a fine roe-shad; split and cut each side into four pieces, leaving out the head, and removing fins and tail. Sprinkle with salt and pepper, and dredge with flour. Have ready a frying pan of boiling hot lard or drippings; put in the fish and fry, turning at the end of five minutes to cook the other side. Fry the roe in the same way; lay the fish in the middle of the dish, and the roe outside of it; garnish with water-cresses and sprigs of pickled cauliflower, and eat with catsup.

BAKED SHAD. ✠

Clean, wash, and wipe the fish, which should be a large one. Make a stuffing of grated bread-crumbs, butter, salt, pepper, and sweet herbs. Stuff the shad and sew it up. Lay it in the baking-pan, with a cupful of water to keep it from burning, and bake an hour, basting with butter and water, until it is tender throughout and well browned. Take it up, put in a hot dish and cover tightly, while you boil up the gravy with a great spoonful of catsup, a tablespoonful of browned flour which has been wet with cold water, the juice of a lemon, and, if you want to have it very fine, a glass of Sherry or Madeira. Garnish with sliced lemon and water-cresses. You may pour the gravy around the fish, or serve in a sauce-boat. Of course you take out the thread with which it has been sewed up before serving the fish.

BOILED SEA-BASS.

Clean and put the fish into the fish-kettle, with salted water enough to cover it when you have enveloped it in the fish-cloth. A medium-sized fish will be done in a little over half an hour. But do not boil too fast. When done, drain and serve in a hot dish. Lay sliced boiled eggs upon and about it, and serve with egg-sauce, mingled with capers and nasturtium seed.

FRIED SEA-BASS.

Use smaller fish for this purpose than for boiling. Clean, wipe dry, inside and out, dredge with flour and season with salt. Fry in hot butter or dripping. A mixture, half butter, half lard, is good for frying fish. The bass should be done to a delicate brown—not to a crisp. The fashion affected by some cooks of drying fried fish to a crust is simply abominable.

Fried bass are a most acceptable breakfast dish.

STURGEON STEAK.

Skin the steaks carefully and lay in salted water (cold) for an hour, to remove the oily taste, so offensive to most palates. Then wipe each steak dry, salt, and broil over hot coals on a buttered gridiron. Serve in a hot dish when you have buttered and peppered them, and send up garnished with parsley and accompanied by a small glass dish containing sliced lemon.

Or,

You can pour over them a sauce prepared in this way:—

Put a tablespoonful of butter into a frying-pan, and stir until it is brown—*not* burned. Add a half-teacupful of boiling water in which has been stirred a tablespoonful of browned flour previously wet with cold water. Add salt, a teaspoonful Worcestershire sauce or anchovy, the juice of a lemon, and let it boil up well. Pour over the steaks when you have arranged them in the dish.

BAKED STURGEON.

A piece of sturgeon weighing five or six pounds is enough for a handsome dish. Skin it and let it stand in salt and water for half an hour. Parboil it to remove the oil. Make a dressing of bread-crumbs, minute bits of fat salt pork, sweet herbs, and butter. Gash the upper part of the fish quite deeply, and rub this force-meat well in; put in a baking-pan with a little water to keep it from burning, and bake for an hour.

Serve with a sauce of drawn butter, in which has been stirred a spoonful of caper sauce and another of catsup.

This is a Virginia receipt, and an admirable one.

MAYONNAISE. (*Fish.*)

Take a pound or so of cold boiled fish (halibut, rock, or cod), cut—not chop—into pieces an inch in length. Mix in a bowl a dressing as follows: the yolks of four boiled eggs rubbed to a smooth paste with salad oil; add to these salt, pepper, mustard, two teaspoonfuls white sugar, and, lastly, six tablespoonfuls of vinegar. Beat the mixture until light, and just before pouring it over the fish, stir in lightly the frothed white of a raw egg. Serve the fish in a glass dish, with half the dressing stirred in with it. Spread the remainder over the top, and lay blanched lettuce-leaves around the edges, to be eaten with it.

BAKED SALMON-TROUT. ✠

Those who have eaten this prince of game fish in the Adirondacks, within an hour after he has left the lake, will agree with me that he never has such justice done him at any other time as when baked with cream.

Handle the beauty with gentle respect while cleaning, washing, and wiping him, and lay him at full length, still respectfully, in a baking-pan, with just enough water to keep him from scorching. If large, score the back-bone with a sharp knife, taking care not to mar the comeliness of his red-spotted sides. Bake slowly, basting often with butter and water. By the time he is done—and he should be so well-looked after that his royal robe hardly shows a seam or rent, and the red spots are still distinctly visible—have ready in a saucepan a cup of cream—diluted with a *few* spoonfuls of hot water, lest it should clot in heating—in which have been stirred cautiously two tablespoonfuls of melted butter and a little chopped parsley. Heat this in a vessel set within another of boiling water, add the gravy from the dripping-pan, boil up once to thicken, and when the trout is laid—always respectfully—in a hot dish, pour the sauce around him as he lies in state. He will take kindly to the creamy bath, and your guests will take kindly to him. Garnish with a wreath of crimson nasturtium blooms and dainty sprigs of parsley, arranged by your own hands on the edge of the dish, and let no sharply-spiced sauces come near him. They would but mar his native richness—the flavor he brought with him from the lake and wild-wood. Salt him lightly, should he need it, eat and be happy.

If the above savor of bathos rather than "common sense," my excuse is, I have lately eaten baked salmon-trout with cream-gravy.

BOILED SALMON-TROUT. ✠

Clean, wash, and dry the trout; envelop in a thin cloth fitted neatly to the shape of the fish, lay within a fish-kettle, cover with salted water (cold), and boil gently half an hour or longer, according to the size. When done, unwrap and lay in a hot dish. Pour around it cream-sauce made as for baked salmon-trout—only, of course, with the omission of the fish-gravy—and serve.

FRIED TROUT.

Brook trout are generally cooked in this way, and form a rarely delightful breakfast or supper dish.

Clean, wash, and dry the fish, roll lightly in flour, and fry in butter or clarified dripping, or butter and lard. Let the fat be hot, fry quickly to a delicate brown, and take up the instant they are done. Lay for an instant upon a hot folded napkin, to absorb whatever grease may cling to their speckled sides; then range side by side in a heated dish, garnish, and send to the table. Use no seasoning except salt, and that only when the fish are fried in lard or unsalted dripping.

FRIED PICKEREL. ✠

The pickerel ranks next to trout among game-fish, and should be fried in the same manner. Especially—and I urge this with groaning of spirit, in remembrance of the many times in which I have had my sense of fitness, not to say my appetite, outraged by seeing the gallant fish brought to table dried to a crisp throughout, all his juices wasted and sweetness utterly departed—especially, do not fry him slowly and too long; and when he is done, take him out of the grease!

CREAM PICKEREL. ✠

Reserve your largest pickerel—those over three pounds in weight—for baking, and proceed with them as with baked salmon-trout—cream-gravy and all. If you cannot afford cream, substitute rich milk, and thicken with rice or wheat flour. The fish are better cooked in this way than any other.

FRIED PERCH, AND OTHER PAN-FISH.

Clean, wash, and dry the fish. Lay them in a large flat dish, salt, and dredge with flour. Have ready a frying-pan of hot dripping, lard, or butter; put in as many fish as the pan will hold without crowding, and fry to a light brown. Send up hot in a chafing-dish.

The many varieties of pan-fish—porgies, flounders, river bass, weak-fish, white-fish, etc., may be cooked in like manner. In serving, lay the head of each fish to *the tail of the one* next him.

STEWED CAT-FISH. ✠

Skin, clean, and cut off the horribly homely heads. Sprinkle with salt, to remove any muddy taste they may have contracted from the flats or holes in which they have fed, and let them lie in a cool place for an hour or so. Then put them into a saucepan, cover with cold water, and stew very gently for from half to three-quarters of an hour, according to their size. Add a chopped shallot or button-onion, a bunch of chopped parsley, a little pepper, a large tablespoonful of butter, a tablespoonful of flour mixed to a paste with cold water; boil up once, take out the fish carefully, and lay in a deep dish. Boil up the gravy once more, and pour over the fish. Send to table in a covered dish.

FRIED CAT-FISH. ✠

Skin, clean, and remove the heads. Sprinkle with salt, and lay aside for an hour or more. Have ready two or three eggs beaten to a froth, and, in a flat dish, a quantity of powdered cracker. Dip the fish first in the egg, then in the cracker, and fry quickly in hot lard or dripping. Take up as quick as done.

CAT-FISH CHOWDER.

Skin, clean, and cut off the heads. Cut the fish into pieces two inches long, and put into a pot with some fat pork cut into shreds—a pound to a dozen medium-sized fish, two chopped onions, or half a dozen shallots, a bunch of sweet herbs, and pepper. The pork will salt it sufficiently. Stew slowly for three-quarters of an hour. Then stir in a cup of milk, thickened with a tablespoonful of flour; take up a cupful of the hot liquor, and stir, a little at a time, into two well-beaten eggs. Return this to the pot, throw in half a dozen Boston or butter crackers, split in half; let all boil up once, and turn into a tureen. Pass sliced lemon or cucumber pickles, also sliced, with it. Take out the backbones of the fish before serving.

STEWED EELS. ✠

Inquire, before buying, where they were caught, and give so decided a preference to country eels as to refuse those fattened upon the offal of city wharves. Nor are the largest eels the best for eating. One weighing a pound is better for your purpose than a bulky fellow that weighs three.

Skin and clean, carefully extracting all the fat from the inside. Cut into lengths of an inch and a half; put into a saucepan, with enough cold water to cover them; throw in a little salt and chopped parsley, and stew slowly, closely covered, for at least an hour. Add, at the last, a great spoonful of butter, and a little flour wet with cold water, also pepper. Serve in a deep dish. The appearance and odor of this stew are so pleasing as often to overcome the prejudices of those who "Wouldn't touch an eel for the world! They look like snakes!" And those who have tasted them rarely enter a second demurrer.

FRIED EELS.

Prepare as for stewing; roll in flour, and fry, in hot lard or dripping, to a light brown.

CHOWDER (*No. 1.*) ✠

Take a pound of salt pork, cut into strips, and soak in hot water five minutes. Cover the bottom of a pot with a layer of this. Cut four pounds of cod or sea-bass into pieces two inches square, and lay enough of these on the pork to cover it. Follow with a layer of chopped onions, a little parsley, summer savory, and pepper, either black or cayenne. Then a layer of split Boston, or butter, or whole cream crackers, which have been soaked in warm water until moist through, but not ready to break. Above this lay a stratum of pork, and repeat the order given above—onions, seasoning, (not too much,) crackers, and pork, until your materials are exhausted. Let the topmost layer be buttered crackers, well soaked. Put in enough cold water to cover all barely. Cover the pot, stew gently for an hour, watching that the water does not sink too low. Should it leave the upper layer exposed, replenish constantly from the tea-kettle. When the chowder is thoroughly done, take out with a perforated skimmer and put into a tureen. Thicken the gravy with a tablespoonful of flour and about the same quantity of butter. Boil up and pour over the chowder. Send sliced lemon, pickles, and stewed tomatoes to the table with it, that the guests may add, if they like.

CHOWDER (*No. 2.*)

Slice six large onions, and fry them in the gravy of fried salt pork. Cut five pounds of bass or cod into strips three inches long and one thick, and line the bottom of a pot with them. Scatter a few slices of onion upon them, a little salt, half a dozen whole black peppers, a clove or two, a pinch of thyme and one of parsley, a tablespoonful tomato or mushroom catsup, and six oysters; then comes a layer of oyster crackers, well-soaked in milk and buttered thickly. Another layer of fish, onions, seasoning, and crackers, and so on until all are used up. Cover with water, boil slowly for an hour and pour out. Serve with capers and sliced lemon. A cup of oyster liquor added to the chowder while boiling improves it.

SHELL-FISH.

TO BOIL A LOBSTER.

Choose a lively one—not too large, lest he should be tough. Put a handful of salt into a pot of boiling water, and having tied the claws together, if your fish merchant has not already skewered them, plunge him into the prepared bath. He will be restive under this vigorous hydropathic treatment; but allay your tortured sympathies by the reflection that he is a cold-blooded animal, destitute of imagination, and that pain, according to some philosophers, exists only in the imagination. However this may be, his suffering will be short-lived. Boil from half an hour to an hour, as his size demands. When done, draw out the scarlet innocent, and lay him, face downward, in a sieve to dry. When cold, split open the body and tail, and crack the claws to extract the meat, throwing away the "lady fingers" and the head. Lobsters are seldom served without dressing, upon private tables, as few persons care to take the trouble of preparing their own salad after taking their seats at the board.

DEVILLED LOBSTER.

Extract the meat from a boiled lobster, as for salad, and mince it finely; reserve the coral. Season highly with mustard, cayenne, salt, and some pungent sauce. Toss and stir until it is well mixed, and put into a porcelain saucepan (covered), with just enough hot water to keep it from burning. Rub the coral smooth, moistening with vinegar until it is thin enough to pour easily, then stir into the contents of the saucepan. It is necessary to prepare the dressing, let me say, before the lobster-meat is set on the fire. It ought to boil up but once before the coral and vinegar are put in. Next stir in a heaping tablespoonful of butter, and when it boils again, take the pan from the fire. Too much cooking toughens the meat. This is a famous supper dish for sleighing parties.

LOBSTER CROQUETTES. ✠

To the meat of a well-boiled lobster, chopped fine, add pepper, salt, and powdered mace. Mix with this one-quarter as much bread-crumbs, well rubbed, as you have meat; make into ovates, or pointed balls, with two tablespoonfuls of melted butter. Roll these in beaten egg, then in pulverized cracker, and fry in butter or very nice sweet lard. Serve dry and hot, and garnish with crisped parsley. This is a delicious supper dish or *entrée* at dinner.

DEVILLED CRAB. ✠

This is prepared according to the receipt for devilled lobster—substituting for the coral in the vinegar some pulverized cracker, moistened first with a tablespoonful of rich cream. You can serve up in the back-shell of the crab if you like. Send in with cream crackers, and stick a sprig of parsley in the top of each heap, ranging the shells upon a large flat dish.

CRAB SALAD.

Mince the meat and dress as in lobster salad. Send in the back-shell of the crab.

SOFT CRABS. ✠

Many will not eat hard-shell crabs, considering them indigestible, and not sufficiently palatable to compensate for the risk they run in eating them. And it must be owned that they are, at their best, but an indifferent substitute for the more aristocratic lobster. But in the morning of life, for him so often renewed, his crabship is a different creature, and greatly affected by epicures.

Do not keep the crabs over night, as the shells harden in twenty-four hours. Pull off the spongy substance from the sides and the sand bags. These are the only portions that are uneatable. Wash well, and wipe dry. Have ready a pan of seething hot lard or butter, and fry them to a fine brown. Put a little salt into the lard. The butter will need none. Send up hot, garnished with parsley.

WATER-TURTLES, OR TERRAPINS.

Land-terrapins, it is hardly necessary to say, are uneatable, but the large turtle that frequents our mill-ponds and rivers can be converted into a relishable article of food.

Plunge the turtle into a pot of boiling water, and let him lie there five minutes. You can then skin the underpart easily, and pull off the horny parts of the feet. Lay him for ten minutes in *cold* salt and water; then put into more hot water—salted, but not too much. Boil until tender. The time will depend upon the size and age. Take him out, drain, and wipe dry; loosen the shell carefully, not to break the flesh; cut open also with care, lest you touch the gall-bag with the knife. Remove this with the entrails and sand-bag. Cut up all the rest of the animal into small bits, season with pepper, salt, a chopped onion, sweet herbs, and a teaspoonful of some spiced sauce, or a tablespoonful of catsup—walnut or mushroom. Save the juice that runs from the meat, and put all together into a saucepan with a closely fitting top. Stew gently fifteen minutes, stirring occasionally, and add a great spoonful of butter, a tablespoonful of browned flour wet in cold water, a glass of brown Sherry, and lastly, the beaten yolk of an egg, mixed with a little of the hot liquor, that it may not curdle. Boil up once, and turn into a covered dish. Send around green pickles and delicate slices of dry toast with it.

STEWED OYSTERS.

Drain the liquor from two quarts of firm, plump oysters; mix with it a small teacupful of hot water, add a little salt and pepper, and set over the fire in a saucepan. Let it boil up once, put in the oysters, let them boil for five minutes or less—not more. When they "ruffle," add two tablespoonfuls of butter. The instant it is melted and well stirred in, put in a large cupful of boiling milk and take the saucepan from the fire. Serve with oyster or cream crackers, as soon as possible. Oysters become tough and tasteless when cooked too much, or left to stand too long after they are withdrawn from the fire.

FRIED OYSTERS. ✠

Use for frying the largest and best oysters you can find. Take them carefully from the liquor; lay them in rows upon a clean cloth, and press another lightly upon them to absorb the moisture. Have ready some crackers crushed fine. In the frying-pan heat enough nice butter to cover the oysters entirely. Dip each oyster into the cracker, rolling it over that it may become completely incrusted. Drop them carefully into the frying-pan, and fry quickly to a light brown. If the butter is hot enough they will soon be ready to take out. Test it by putting in one oyster before you risk the rest. Do not let them lie in the pan an instant after they are done. Serve dry, and let the dish be warm. A chafing-dish is best.

OYSTER FRITTERS. ✠

Drain the liquor from the oysters, and to a cupful of this add the same quantity of milk, three eggs, a little salt, and flour enough for a thin batter. Chop the oysters and stir into the batter. Have ready in the frying-pan a few spoonfuls of lard, or half lard, half butter; heat very hot, and drop the oyster-batter in by the tablespoonful. Try a spoonful first, to satisfy yourself that the lard is hot enough, and that the fritter is of the right size and consistency. Take rapidly from the pan as soon as they are done to a pleasing yellow brown, and send to table very hot.

Some fry the oyster whole, enveloped in batter, one in each fritter. In this case, the batter should be thicker than if the chopped oysters were to be added.

SCALLOPED OYSTERS. ✠

Crush and roll several handfuls of Boston or other friable crackers. Put a layer in the bottom of a buttered pudding-dish. Wet this with a mixture of the oyster liquor and milk, slightly warmed. Next, have a layer of oysters. Sprinkle with salt and pepper, and lay small bits of butter upon them. Then another layer of moistened crumbs, and so on until the dish is full. Let the top layer be of crumbs, thicker than the rest, and beat an egg into the milk you pour over them. Stick bits of butter thickly over it, cover the dish, set it in the oven, bake half an hour; if the dish be large, remove the cover, and brown by setting it upon the upper grating of oven, or by holding a hot shovel over it.

BROILED OYSTERS. ✠

Choose large, fat oysters; wipe them very dry; sprinkle salt and cayenne pepper upon them, and broil upon one of the small gridirons sold for that purpose. You can dredge the oyster with cracker-dust or flour if you wish to have it brown, and some fancy the juices are better kept in in this way. Others dislike the crust thus formed. Butter the gridiron well, and let your fire be hot and clear. If the oyster drip, withdraw the gridiron for an instant until the smoke clears away. Broil quickly and dish hot, putting a tiny piece of butter, not larger than a pea, upon each oyster.

CREAM OYSTERS ON THE HALF-SHELL.

Pour into your inner saucepan a cup of hot water, another of milk, and one of cream, with a little salt. Set into a kettle of hot water until it boils, when stir in two tablespoonfuls of butter and a little salt, with white pepper. Take from the fire and add two heaping tablespoonfuls of arrow-root, rice-flour, or corn-starch, wet with cold milk. By this time your shells should be washed and buttered, and a fine oyster laid within each. Of course, it is *selon les régles* to use oyster-shells for this purpose; but you will find clam-shells more roomy and manageable, because more regular in shape. Range these closely in a large baking-pan, propping them with clean pebbles or fragments of shell, if they do not seem inclined to retain their contents. Stir the cream *very* hard and fill up each shell with a spoon, taking care not to spill any in the pan. Bake five or six minutes in a hot oven after the shells become warm. Serve on the shell. Some substitute oyster-liquor for the water in the mixture, and use all milk instead of cream.

OYSTER OMELET. ✠

- 12 oysters, if large; double the number of small ones.

- 6 eggs.

- 1 cup milk.

- 1 tablespoonful butter.

- Chopped parsley, salt, and pepper.

Chop the oysters very fine. Beat the yolks and whites of the eggs separately as for nice cake—the white until it stands in a heap. Put three tablespoonfuls of butter in a frying-pan, and heat while you are mixing the omelet. Stir the milk into a deep dish with the yolk, and season. Next put in the chopped oysters, beating vigorously as you add them gradually. When they are thoroughly incorporated, pour in the spoonful of melted butter; finally, whip in the whites lightly and with as few strokes as possible. If the butter is hot, and it ought to be, that the omelet may not stand uncooked, put the mixture into the pan. *Do not stir it*, but when it begins to stiffen—"to set," in culinary phrase, slip a broad-bladed, round-pointed dinner-knife around the sides, and cautiously under the omelet, that the butter may reach every part. As soon as the centre is fairly "set," turn out into a hot dish. Lay the latter bottom upward over the frying-pan, which must be turned upside-down dexterously. This brings the browned side of the omelet uppermost. This omelet is delicious and easily made.

OYSTER PIE. ✠

Make a rich puff-paste; roll out twice as thick as for a fruit-pie for the top crust—about the ordinary thickness for the lower. Line a pudding-dish with the thinner, and fill with crusts of dry bread or light crackers. Some use a folded towel to fill the interior of the pie, but the above expedient is preferable. Butter the edges of the dish, that you may be able to lift the upper crust without breaking. Cover the mock-pie with the thick crust, ornamented heavily at the edge, that it may lie the more quietly, and bake. Cook the oysters as for a stew, only beating into them at the last two eggs, and thickening with a spoonful of fine cracker-crumbs or rice-flour. They should stew but five minutes, and time them so that the paste will be baked just in season to receive them. Lift the top crust, pour in the smoking hot oysters, and send up hot.

I know that many consider it unnecessary to prepare the oysters and crust separately; but my experience and observation go to prove that, if this precaution be omitted, the oysters are apt to be wofully overdone. The reader can try both methods and take her choice.

PICKLED OYSTERS. ✠

- 100 large oysters.
- 1 pt. white wine vinegar.
- 1 doz. blades of mace.
- 2 doz. whole cloves.
- 2 doz. whole black peppers.
- 1 large red pepper broken into bits.

Put oysters, liquor and all, into a porcelain or bell-metal kettle. Salt to taste. Heat slowly until the oysters are very hot, but not to boiling. Take them out with a perforated skimmer, and set aside to cool. To the liquor which remains in the kettle add the vinegar and spices. Boil up fairly, and when the oysters are almost cold, pour over them scalding hot. Cover the jar in which they are, and put away in a cool place. Next day put the pickled oysters into glass cans with tight tops. Keep in the dark, and where they are not liable to become heated.

I have kept oysters thus prepared for three weeks in the winter. If you open a can, use the contents up as soon as practicable. The air, like the light, will turn them dark.

It is little trouble for every housekeeper to put up the pickled oysters needed in her family; and besides the satisfaction she will feel in the consciousness that the materials used are harmless, and the oysters sound, she will save at least one-third of the price of those she would buy ready pickled. The colorless vinegar used by "professionals" for such purposes is usually sulphuric or pyroligneous acid. If you doubt this, pour a little of the liquor from the pickled oysters put up by your obliging oyster-dealer into a bell-metal kettle. I tried it once, and the result was a liquid that matched the clear green of Niagara in hue.

ROAST OYSTERS.

There is no pleasanter frolic for an Autumn evening, in the regions where oysters are plentiful, than an impromptu "roast" in the kitchen. There the oysters are hastily thrown into the fire by the peck. You may consider that your fastidious taste is marvellously respected if they are washed first. A bushel basket is set to receive the empty shells, and the click of the oyster-knives forms a constant accompaniment to the music of laughing voices. Nor are roast oysters amiss upon your own quiet supper-table, when the "good man" comes in on a wet night, tired and hungry, and wants "something heartening." Wash and wipe the shell-oysters, and lay them in the oven, if it is quick; upon the top of the stove, if it is not. When they open, they are done. Pile in a large dish and send to table. Remove the upper shell by a dexterous wrench of the knife, season the oyster on the lower, with pepper-sauce and butter, or pepper, salt, and vinegar in lieu of the sauce, and you have the very aroma of this pearl of bivalves, pure and undefiled.

Or, you may open while raw, leaving the oysters upon the lower shells; lay in a large baking-pan, and roast in their own liquor, adding pepper, salt, and butter before serving.

RAW OYSTERS.

It is fashionable to serve these as one of the preliminaries to a dinner-party; sometimes in small plates, sometimes on the half-shell. They are seasoned by each guest according to his own taste.

STEAMED OYSTERS.

If you have no steamer, improvise one by the help of a cullender and a pot-lid fitting closely into it, at a little distance from the top. Wash some shell oysters and lay them in such a position in the bottom of the cullender that the liquor will not escape from them when the shell opens, that is, with the upper shell down. Cover with a cloth thrown over the top of the cullender, and press the lid hard down upon this to exclude the air. Set over a pot of boiling water so deep that the cullender, which should fit into the mouth, does not touch the water. Boil hard for twenty minutes, then make a hasty examination of the oysters. If they are open, you are safe in removing the cover. Serve on the half-shell, or upon a hot chafing dish. Sprinkle a little salt over them and a few bits of butter; but be quick in whatever you do, for the glory of the steamed oyster is to be eaten hot.

OYSTER PÂTÉS. ✠

- 1 qt. oysters.
- 2 tablespoonfuls of butter.
- Pepper, and a pinch of salt.

Set the oysters, with enough liquor to cover them, in a saucepan upon the range or stove; let them come to a boil; skim well, and stir in the butter and seasoning. Two or three spoonsful of cream will improve them. Have ready small tins lined with puff paste. Put three or four oysters in each, according to the size of the *pâté*; cover with paste and bake in a quick oven twenty minutes. For open *pâtés*, cut the paste into round cakes: those intended for the bottom crust less than an eighth of an inch thick; for the upper, a little thicker. With a smaller cutter, remove a round of paste from the middle of the latter, leaving a neat ring. Lay this carefully upon the bottom crust; place a second ring upon this, that the cavity may be deep enough to hold the oysters; lay the pieces you have extracted also in the pan with the rest, and bake to a fine brown in a *quick* oven. When done, wash over with beaten egg, around top and all, and set in the oven three minutes to glaze. Fill the cavity with a mixture prepared as below, fit on the top lightly, and serve.

Mixture.

Boil half the liquor from a quart of oysters. Put in all the oysters, leaving out the uncooked liquor; heat to boiling, and stir in—

- ½ cup of hot milk.

- 1 tablespoonful butter.

- 2 tablespoonfuls corn starch, wet with a little milk.

- A little salt.

Boil four minutes, stirring all the time until it thickens, and fill the cavity in the paste shells. These *pâtés* are very nice.

SCALLOPS.

The heart is the only part used. If you buy them in the shell, boil and take out the hearts. Those sold in our markets are generally ready for frying or stewing.

Dip them in beaten egg, then in cracker-crumbs and fry in hot lard.

Or,

You may stew like oysters. The fried scallops are generally preferred.

SCALLOPED CLAMS.

Chop the clams fine, and season with pepper and salt. Cayenne pepper is thought to give a finer flavor than black or white; but to some palates it is insufferable. Mix in another dish some powdered cracker, moistened first with warm milk, then with the clam liquor, a beaten egg or two, and some melted butter. Stir in with this the chopped clams. Wash as many clam-shells as the mixture will fill;

wipe and butter them; fill, heaping up and smoothing over with a silver knife or teaspoon. Range in rows in your baking-pan, and cook until nicely browned. Or, if you do not care to be troubled with the shells, bake in patty-pans, sending to table hot in the tins, as you would in the scallop-shells.

CLAM FRITTERS. ✠

- 12 clams, minced fine.

- 1 pint of milk.

- 3 eggs.

Add the liquor from the clams to the milk; beat up the eggs and put to this, with salt and pepper, and flour enough for thin batter; lastly, the chopped clams. Fry in hot lard, trying a little first to see that fat and batter are right. A tablespoonful will make a fritter of moderate size. Or, you can dip the whole clams in batter and cook in like manner. Fry quickly, or they are apt to be too greasy.

CLAM CHOWDER. ✠

Fry five or six slices of fat pork crisp, and chop to pieces. Sprinkle some of these in the bottom of a pot; lay upon them a stratum of clams; sprinkle with cayenne or black pepper and salt, and scatter bits of butter profusely over all; next, have a layer of chopped onions, then one of small crackers, split and moistened with warm milk. On these pour a little of the fat left in the pan after the pork is fried, and then comes a new round of pork, clams, onion, etc. Proceed in this order until the pot is nearly full, when cover with water, and stew slowly—the pot closely covered—for three-quarters of an hour. Drain off all the liquor that will flow freely, and, when you have turned the chowder into the tureen, return the gravy to the pot. Thicken with flour, or, better still, pounded crackers; add a glass of wine, some catsup, and spiced sauce; boil up, and pour over the contents of the tureen. Send around walnut or butternut pickles with it.

POULTRY.

Poultry should never be eaten in less than six or eight hours after it is killed; but it should be picked and drawn as soon as possible. There is no direr disgrace to our Northern markets than the practice of sending whole dead fowls to market. I have bought such from responsible poultry dealers, and found them uneatable, from having remained undrawn until the flavor of the craw and intestines had impregnated the whole body. Those who are conversant with the habit of careful country housewives, of keeping up a fowl without food for a day and night before killing and dressing for their own eating, cannot but regard with disgust the surcharged crops and puffy sides of those sold *by weight* in the shambles. If you want to know what you really pay for poultry bought in these circumstances, weigh the offal extracted from the fowl by your cook, and deduct from the market weight. "But don't you know it actually poisons a fowl to lie so long undressed?" once exclaimed a Southern lady to me. "In *our* markets they are offered for sale ready picked and drawn, with the giblets—also cleaned— tucked under their wings."

I know nothing about the poisonous nature of the entrails and crops. I do assert that the custom is unclean and unjust. And this I do without the remotest hope of arousing my fellow-housekeepers to remonstrance against established usage. Only it relieves my mind somewhat to grumble at what I cannot help. The best remedy I can propose for the grievance is to buy live fowls, and, before sending them home, ask your butcher to decapitate them; the probabilities being greatly in favor of the supposition that your cook is too "tinder-hearted" to attempt the job.

One word as to the manner of roasting meats and fowls. In this day of ranges and cooking-stoves, I think I am speaking within bounds when I assume that not one housekeeper in fifty uses a spit, or even a tin kitchen, for such purposes. It is in vain that the writers of receipt-books inform us with refreshing *naïveté* that all our meats are baked, not roasted, and expatiate upon the superior flavor of those prepared upon the English spits and in old fashioned kitchens, where enormous wood-fires blazed from morning until night. I shall not soon forget my perplexity when, an inexperienced housekeeper and a firm believer in all "that was writ" by older and wiser people, I stood before my neat Mott's

"Defiance," a fine sirloin of beef ready to be cooked on the table behind me, and read from my Instruction-book that my "fire should extend at least eight inches beyond the roaster on either side!" I am not denying the virtues of spits and tin kitchens—only regretting that they are not within the reach of every one. In view of this fact, let me remark, for the benefit of the unfortunate many, that, in the opinion of excellent judges, the practice of roasting meat in close ovens has advantages. Of these I need mention but two, to wit, the preservation of the flavor of the article roasted, and the prevention of its escape to the upper regions of the dwelling.

ROAST TURKEY.

After drawing the turkey, rinse out with several waters, and in next to the last mix a teaspoonful of soda. The inside of a fowl, especially if purchased in the market, is sometimes very sour, and imparts an unpleasant taste to the stuffing, if not to the inner part of the legs and side-bones. The soda will act as a corrective, and is moreover very cleansing. Fill the body with this water, shake well, empty it out, and rinse with fair water. Then prepare a dressing of bread-crumbs, mixed with butter, pepper, salt, thyme or sweet marjoram. You may, if you like, add the beaten yolks of two eggs. A little chopped sausage is esteemed an improvement when well incorporated with the other ingredients. Or, mince a dozen oysters and stir into the dressing. The effect upon the turkey-meat, particularly that of the breast, is very pleasant.

Stuff the craw with this, and tie a string tightly about the neck, to prevent the escape of the stuffing. Then fill the body of the turkey, and sew it up with strong thread. This and the neck-string are to be removed when the fowl is dished. In roasting, if your fire is brisk, allow about ten minutes to a pound; but it will depend very much upon the turkey's age whether this rule holds good. Dredge it with flour before roasting, and baste often; at first with butter and water, afterward with the gravy in the dripping-pan. If you lay the turkey in the pan, put in with it a teacup of hot water. Many roast always upon a grating placed on the top of the pan. In that case the boiling water steams the underpart of the fowl, and prevents the skin from drying too fast, or cracking. Roast to a fine brown, and if it threaten to darken too rapidly, lay a sheet of white paper over it until the lower part is also done.

Stew the chopped giblets in just enough water to cover them, and when the turkey is lifted from the pan, add these, with the water in which they were boiled, to the drippings; thicken with a spoonful of browned flour, wet with cold water to prevent lumping, boil up once, and pour into the gravy-boat. If the turkey is fat, skim the drippings well before putting in the giblets.

Serve with cranberry sauce. Some lay fried oysters in the dish around the turkey.

BOILED TURKEY.

Chop about two dozen oysters, and mix with them a dressing compounded as for roast turkey, only with more butter. Stuff the turkey as for roasting, craw and body, and baste about it a thin cloth, fitted closely to every part. The inside of the cloth should be dredged with flour to prevent the fowl from sticking to it. Allow fifteen minutes to a pound, and boil slowly.

Serve with oyster-sauce, made by adding to a cupful of the liquor in which the turkey was boiled, eight oysters chopped fine. Season with minced parsley, stir in a spoonful of rice or wheat flour, wet with cold milk, a tablespoonful of butter. Add a cupful of hot milk. Boil up once and pour into an oyster-tureen. Send around celery with it.

TURKEY SCALLOP. ✠

Cut the meat from the bones of a cold boiled or roasted turkey left from yesterday's dinner. Remove the bits of skin and gristle, and chop up the rest very fine. Put in the bottom of a buttered dish a layer of cracker or bread-crumbs; moisten slightly with milk, that they may not absorb all the gravy to be poured in afterward; then spread a layer of the minced turkey, with bits of the stuffing, pepper, salt, and small pieces of butter. Another layer of cracker, wet with milk, and so on until the dish is nearly full. Before putting on the topmost layer, pour in the gravy left from the turkey, diluted—should there not be enough—with hot water, and seasoned with Worcestershire sauce, or catsup, and butter. Have ready a crust of cracker-crumbs soaked in warm milk, seasoned with salt, and beaten up light with two eggs. It should be just thick enough to spread smoothly over the top of the scallop. Stick bits of butter plentifully upon it, and bake. Turn a deep plate over the dish until the contents begin to bubble at the sides, showing that the whole is thoroughly cooked; then remove the cover, and brown. A large pudding-dish full of the mixture will be cooked in three-quarters of an hour.

This, like many other economical dishes, will prove so savory as to claim a frequent appearance upon any table.

Cold chicken may be prepared in the same way

Or,

The minced turkey, dressing, and cracker-crumbs may be wet with gravy, two eggs beaten into it, and the force-meat thus made rolled into oblong shapes, dipped in egg and pounded cracker, and fried like croquettes, for a side dish, to "make out" a dinner of ham or cold meat.

RAGOÛT OF TURKEY.

This is also a cheap, yet nice dish. Cut the cold turkey from the bones and into bits an inch long with knife and fork, tearing as little as possible. Put into a skillet or saucepan the gravy left from the roast, with hot water to dilute it should the quantity be small. Add a lump of butter the size of an egg, a teaspoonful of pungent sauce, a large pinch of nutmeg, with a little salt. Let it boil, and put in the meat. Stew very slowly for ten minutes—not more—and stir in a tablespoonful of cranberry or currant jelly, another of browned flour which has been wet with cold water; lastly, a glass of brown Sherry or Madeira. Boil up once, and serve in a covered dish for breakfast. Leave out the stuffing entirely; it is no improvement to the flavor, and disfigures the appearance of the ragoût.

ROAST CHICKENS.

Having picked and drawn them, wash out well in two or three waters, adding a little soda to the last but one should any doubtful odor linger about the cavity. Prepare a stuffing of bread-crumbs, butter, pepper, salt, &c. Fill the bodies and crops of the chickens, which should be young and plump; sew them up, and roast an hour or more, in proportion to their size. Baste two or three times with butter and water, afterward with their own gravy. If laid flat within the dripping pan, put in at the first a little hot water to prevent burning.

Stew the giblets and necks in enough water to cover them, and, when you have removed the fowls to a hot dish, pour this into the drippings; boil up once; add the giblets, chopped fine; thicken with browned flour; boil again, and send to table in a gravy-boat.

Serve with crab-apple jelly or tomato sauce.

BOILED CHICKENS.

Clean, wash, and stuff as for roasting. Baste a floured cloth around each, and put into a pot with enough boiling water to cover them well. The hot water cooks the skin at once, and prevents the escape of the juices. The broth will not be so rich as if the fowls are put on in cold water, but this is a proof that the meat will be more nutritious and better flavored. Stew very slowly, for the first half hour especially. Boil an hour or more, guiding yourself by size and toughness.

Serve with egg or bread sauce. (See *Sauces*.)

FRICASSEED CHICKEN. (*White.*) ✠

Clean, wash, and cut up the fowls, which need not be so tender as for roasting. Lay them in salt and water for half an hour. Put them in a pot with enough cold water to cover them, and half a pound of salt pork cut into thin strips. Cover closely, and let them heat very slowly; then stew for over an hour, if the fowls are tender. I have used chickens for this purpose that required four hours stewing, but they were tender and good when done. Only put them on in season, and cook very slowly. If they boil fast, they toughen and shrink into uneatableness. When tender, add a chopped onion or two, parsley, and pepper. Cover closely again, and, when it has heated to boiling, stir in a teacupful of milk, to which have been added two beaten eggs and two tablespoonfuls of flour. Boil up fairly; add a great spoonful of butter. Arrange the chicken neatly in a deep chafing-dish, pour the gravy over it, and serve.

In this, as in all cases where beaten egg is added to hot liquor, it is best to dip out a few spoonfuls of the latter, and drop a little at a time into the egg, beating all the while, that it may heat evenly and gradually before it is put into the scalding contents of the saucepan or pot. Eggs managed in this way will not curdle, as they are apt to do if thrown suddenly into hot liquid.

FRICASSEED CHICKEN. (*Brown*.) ✠

Clean, wash, and cut up a pair of young chickens. Lay in clear water for half an hour. If they are old, you cannot brown them well. Put them in a saucepan, with enough cold water to cover them well, and set over the fire to heat slowly. Meanwhile, cut half a pound of salt pork into strips, and fry crisp. Take them out, chop fine, and put into the pot with the chicken. Fry in the fat left in the frying-pan one large onion, or two or three small ones, cut into slices. Let them brown well, and add them also to the chicken, with a quarter teaspoonful of allspice and cloves. Stew all together slowly for an hour or more, until the meat is very tender; you can test this with a fork. Take out the pieces of fowl and put in a hot dish, covering closely until the gravy is ready. Add to this a great spoonful of walnut or other dark catsup, and nearly three tablespoonfuls of browned flour, a little chopped parsley, and a glass of brown Sherry. Boil up once; strain through a cullender, to remove the bits of pork and onion; return to the pot, with the chicken; let it come to a final boil, and serve, pouring the gravy over the pieces of fowl.

BROILED CHICKEN.

It is possible to render a tough fowl eatable by boiling or stewing it with care. *Never* broil such! And even when assured that your "broiler" is young, it is wise to make this doubly sure by laying it upon sticks extending from side to side of a dripping-pan full of boiling water. Set this in the oven, invert a tin pan over the chicken, and let it steam for half an hour. This process relaxes the muscles, and renders supple the joints, besides preserving the juices that would be lost in parboiling. The chicken should be split down the back, and wiped perfectly dry before it is steamed. Transfer from the vapor-bath to a buttered gridiron, inside downward. Cover with a tin pan or common plate, and broil until tender and brown, turning several times; from half to three-quarters of an hour will be sufficient. Put into a hot chafing-dish, and butter very well. Send to table smoking hot.

FRIED CHICKEN (*No. 1*).

Clean, wash, and cut to pieces a couple of Spring chickens. Have ready in a frying-pan enough boiling lard or dripping to cover them well. Dip each piece in beaten egg when you have salted it, then in cracker-crumbs, and fry until brown. If the chicken is large, steam it before frying, as directed in the foregoing receipt. When you have taken out the meat, throw into the hot fat a dozen sprigs of parsley, and let them remain a minute—just long enough to crisp, but not to dry them. Garnish the chicken by strewing these over it.

FRIED CHICKEN (*No. 2*).

Cut up half a pound of fat salt pork in a frying-pan, and fry until the grease is extracted, but not until it browns. Wash and cut up a young chicken (broiling size), soak in salt and water for half an hour; wipe dry, season with pepper, and dredge with flour; then fry in the hot fat until each piece is a rich brown on both sides. Take up, drain, and set aside in a hot covered dish. Pour into the gravy left in the frying-pan a cup of milk—half cream is better; thicken with a spoonful of flour and a tablespoonful of butter; add some chopped parsley, boil up, and pour over the hot chicken. This is a standard dish in the Old Dominion, and tastes nowhere else as it does when eaten on Virginia soil. The cream gravy is often omitted, and the chicken served up dry, with bunches of fried parsley dropped upon it.

CHICKEN POT-PIE.

Line the bottom and sides of a pot with a good rich paste, reserving enough for a top crust and for the square bits to be scattered through the pie. Butter the pot very lavishly, or your pastry will stick to it and burn. Cut up a fine large fowl, and half a pound of corned ham or salt pork. Put in a layer of the latter, pepper it, and cover with pieces of the chicken, and this with the paste dumplings or squares. If you use potatoes, parboil them before putting them into the pie, as the first water in which they are boiled is rank and unwholesome. The potatoes should be sliced and laid next the pastry squares; then another layer of pork, and so on until your chicken is used up. Cover with pastry rolled out quite thick, and slit this in the middle. Heat very slowly, and boil two hours. Turn into a large dish, the lower crust on top, and the gravy about it.

This is the old-fashioned pot-pie, dear to the memory of men who were school-boys thirty and forty years ago. If you are not experienced in such manufactures, you had better omit the lower crust; and, having browned the upper, by putting a hot pot-lid or stove-cover on top of the pot for some minutes, remove dexterously without breaking. Pour out the chicken into a dish, and set the crust above it.

Veal, beef-steak, lamb (not mutton), hares, &c., may be substituted for the chicken. The pork will salt it sufficiently.

BAKED CHICKEN PIE ✠

Is made as above, but baked in a buttered pudding-dish, and, in place of the potatoes, three hard-boiled eggs are chopped up and strewed among the pieces of chicken. If the chickens are tough, or even doubtful, parboil them before making the pie, adding the water in which they were boiled, instead of cold water, for gravy. If they are lean, put in a few bits of butter. Ornament with leaves cut out with a cake-cutter, and a star in the centre. Bake an hour— more, if the pie is large.

CHICKEN PUDDING. ✠

Cut up as for fricassee, and parboil, seasoning well with pepper, salt, and a lump of butter the size of an egg, to each chicken. The fowls should be young and tender, and divided at every joint. Stew slowly for half an hour, take them out, and lay on a flat dish to cool. Set aside the water in which they were stewed for your gravy.

Make a batter of one quart of milk, three cups of flour, three tablespoonfuls melted butter, half a teaspoonful soda, and one spoonful of cream tartar, with four eggs well beaten, and a little salt. Put a layer of chicken in the bottom of the dish, and pour about half a cupful of batter over it—enough to conceal the meat; then, another layer of chicken, and more batter, until the dish is full. The batter must form the crust. Bake one hour, in a moderate oven, if the dish is large.

Beat up an egg, and stir into the gravy which was set aside; thicken with two teaspoonfuls of rice or wheat flour, add a little chopped parsley; boil up, and send it to table in a gravy-boat.

CHICKEN AND HAM. ✠

Draw, wash, and stuff a pair of young fowls. Cut enough large, thick slices of cold boiled ham to envelop these entirely, wrapping them up carefully, and winding a string about all, to prevent the ham from falling off. Put into your dripping-pan, with a little water to prevent scorching; dashing it over the meat lest it should dry and shrink. Invert a tin pan over all, and bake slowly for one hour and a quarter, if the fowls are small and tender—longer, if tough. Lift the cover from time to time to baste with the drippings—the more frequently as time wears on. Test the tenderness of the fowls, by sticking a fork through the ham into the breast. When done, undo the strings, lay the fowls in a hot dish, and the slices of ham about them. Stir into the dripping a little chopped parsley, a tablespoonful of browned flour wet in cold water; pepper, and let it boil up once. Pour some of it over the chickens—not enough to float the ham in the dish; serve the rest in a gravy-boat.

ROAST DUCKS.

Clean, wash, and wipe the ducks very carefully. To the usual dressing add a little sage (powdered or green), and a minced shallot. Stuff, and sew up as usual, reserving the giblets for the gravy. If they are tender, they will not require more than an hour to roast. Baste well. Skim the gravy before putting in the giblets and thickening. The giblets should be stewed in a very little water, then chopped fine, and added to the gravy in the dripping-pan, with a chopped shallot and a spoonful of browned flour.

Accompany with currant or grape jelly.

TO USE UP COLD DUCK. ✠

I may say, as preface, that cold duck is in itself an excellent supper dish, or side dish, at a family dinner, and is often preferred to hot. If the duck has been cut into at all, divide neatly into joints, and slice the breast, laying slices of dressing about it. Garnish with lettuce or parsley, and eat with jelly.

But if a warm dish is desired, cut the meat from the bones and lay in a saucepan, with a little minced cold ham; pour on just enough water to cover it, and stir in a tablespoonful of butter. Cover, and heat gradually, until it is *near* boiling. Then add the gravy, diluted with a little hot water; a great spoonful of catsup, one of Worcestershire sauce, and one of currant or cranberry jelly, with a glass of wine and a tablespoonful of browned flour.

Or,

You may put the gravy, with a little hot water and a lump of butter, in a frying-pan, and when it is hot lay in the pieces of duck, and warm up quickly, stirring in at the last a teaspoonful of Worcestershire sauce and a tablespoonful of jelly.

Serve in a hot chafing-dish.

(For wild ducks, see GAME.)

STEWED DUCK.

This is a good way to treat an old tough fowl.

Clean and divide, as you would a chicken for fricassee. Put in a saucepan, with several (minced) slices of cold ham or salt pork which is not too fat, and stew slowly for at least an hour—keeping the lid on all the while. Then stir in a chopped onion, a half-spoonful of powdered sage, or of the green leaves cut fine, half as much parsley, a tablespoonful catsup, and black pepper. Stew another half-hour, or until the duck is tender, and add a teaspoonful brown sugar, and a tablespoonful of browned flour, previously wet with cold water. Boil up once, and serve in a deep covered dish, with green peas as an accompaniment.

GUINEA FOWLS.

Many are not aware what an excellent article of food these speckled Arabs of the poultry-yard are. They are kept chiefly for the beauty of their plumage, and their delicious eggs, which are far richer than those of chickens.

Unless young they are apt to be tough, and the dark color of the meat is objected to by those who are not fond of, or used to eating game. Cooked according to the foregoing receipt they are very savory, no matter how old they may be. Put them on early, and stew *slowly*, and good management will bring the desired end to pass. There is nothing in the shape of game or poultry that is not amenable to this process, providing the salt be omitted until the meat is tender.

But a pair of young Guinea fowls, stuffed and roasted, basting them with butter until they are half done, deserve an honorable place upon our bill of fare. Season the gravy with a chopped shallot, parsley, or summer savory, not omitting the minced giblets, and thicken with browned flour. Send around currant, or other tart jelly, with the fowl. A little ham, minced fine, improves the dressing.

ROAST GOOSE.

Clean and wash the goose—not forgetting to put a spoonful of soda in next to the last water, rinse out well, and wipe the inside quite dry. Add to the usual stuffing of bread-crumbs, pepper, salt, etc., a tablespoonful melted butter, an onion chopped fine, a tablespoonful chopped sage, the yolks of two eggs, and some minute bits of fat pork. Stuff body and craw, and sew up. It will take fully two hours to roast, if the fire is strong. Cover the breast, until it is half done, with white paper, or a paste of flour and water, removing this when you are ready to brown.

Make a gravy as for roast duck, adding a glass of Sherry or Madeira, or (if you can get it) old Port.

Send to table with cranberry or apple sauce.

GOOSE PIE.

An old goose is as nearly good for nothing as it is possible for anything which was once valuable, and is not now absolutely spoiled, to be. The best use to put it to is to make it into a pie, in the following manner. Put on the ancient early in the morning, in cold water enough to cover it, unsalted, having cut it to pieces at every joint. Warm it up gradually, and let it stew—not boil hard—for four or five hours. Should the water need replenishing, let it be done from the boiling kettle. Parboil a beef's tongue (corned), cut into slices nearly half an inch thick; also slice six hard-boiled eggs. Line a deep pudding-dish with a good paste; lay in the pieces of goose, the giblets chopped, the sliced tongue and egg, in consecutive layers; season with pepper, salt, and bits of butter, and proceed in this order until the dish is full. If the goose be large, cut the meat from the bones after stewing, and leave out the latter entirely. Intersperse with strips of paste, and fill up with the gravy in which the goose was stewed, thickened with flour. Cover with a thick paste, and when it is done, brush over the top with beaten white of egg.

In cold weather this pie will keep a week, and is very good.

ROAST PIGEONS.

Clean, wash, and stuff as you would chickens. Lay them in rows, if roasted in the oven, with a little water in the pan to prevent scorching. Unless they are very fat, baste with butter until they are half done, afterwards with their own gravy. Thicken the gravy that drips from them, and boil up once; then pour into a gravy-boat. The pigeons should lie close together in the dish.

STEWED PIGEONS.

Pick, draw, clean and stuff as above directed. Put the pigeons in a deep pot with enough cold water to cover them, and stew gently for an hour, or until, testing them with a fork, you find them tender. Then season with pepper, salt, a few blades of mace, a little sweet marjoram, and a good piece of butter. Stew, or rather simmer, for five minutes longer—then stir in a tablespoonful of browned flour. Let it boil up once; remove the pigeons, draw out the strings with which they were sewed up, and serve, pouring the hot gravy over them. A little salt pork or ham, cut into strips, is an improvement. This should be put in when the pigeons have stewed half an hour.

BROILED PIGEONS OR SQUABS.

Young pigeons or "squabs" are rightly esteemed a great delicacy. They are cleaned, washed, and dried carefully with a clean cloth; then split down the back, and broiled like chickens. Season with pepper and salt, and butter liberally in dishing them. They are in great request in a convalescent's room, being peculiarly savory and nourishing.

They may, for a change, be roasted whole, according to the receipt for roast pigeons.

PIGEON PIE.

Is best made of wild pigeons. (SEE GAME.)

MEATS.

ROAST BEEF.

The best pieces for roasting are the sirloin and rib pieces. The latter are oftenest used by small families. Make your butcher remove most of the bone, and skewer the meat into the shape of a round. If you roast in an oven, it is a good plan to dash a small cup of *boiling* water over the meat in first putting it down, letting it trickle into the pan. This, for a season, checks the escape of the juices, and allows the meat to get warmed through before the top dries by said escape. If there is much fat upon the upper surface, cover with a paste of flour and water until it is nearly done. Baste frequently, at first with salt and water, afterward with the drippings. Allow about a quarter of an hour to a pound, if you like your meat rare; more, if you prefer to have it well done. Some, when the meat is almost done, dredge with flour and baste with butter—only once.

Remove the beef, when quite ready, to a heated dish; skim the drippings; add a teacupful of boiling water, boil up once, and send to table in a gravy-boat. Many reject made gravy altogether, and only serve the red liquor that runs from the meat into the dish as it is cut. This is the practice with some—indeed most of our best housekeepers. If you have made gravy in a sauce-boat, give your guest his choice between that and the juice in the dish.

Serve with mustard, or scraped horse-radish and vinegar.

ROAST BEEF WITH YORKSHIRE PUDDING. ✠

Set a piece of beef to roast upon a grating, or several sticks laid across a dripping-pan. Three-quarters of an hour before it is done, mix the pudding and pour into the pan. Continue to roast the beef, the dripping meanwhile falling upon the latter below. When both are done, cut the pudding into squares, and lay around the meat when dished. If there is much fat in the dripping-pan before the pudding is ready to be put in, drain it off, leaving just enough to prevent the batter from sticking to the bottom.

Receipt for Pudding.

- 1 pint of milk.
- 4 eggs, whites and yolks beaten separately.
- 2 cups of prepared flour.
- 1 teaspoonful salt.

Be careful, in mixing, not to get the batter too stiff.

This pudding, which the cook who introduced it into my family persisted in calling "*Auction* pudding," is very palatable and popular, and not so rich as would be thought from the manner of baking. It should be a yellow-brown when done.

BEEF-STEAK.

It is not customary to fry beef-steaks for people who know what really good cookery is. To speak more plainly, a steak, *killed* by heat and swimming in grease, is a culinary solecism, both vulgar and indigestible.

Cut the steak thick, at least three-quarters of an inch in thickness, and if you cannot get tender meat for this purpose, it is best to substitute some other dish for it. But since tender meat is not always to be had, if the piece you have purchased is doubtful, lay it on a clean cloth, take a blunt heavy carving-knife, if you have not a steak mallet, and hack *closely* from one end to the other; then turn and repeat the process upon the other side. The knife should be so dull you cannot cut with it, and the strokes not the sixtieth part of an inch apart. Wipe all over on both sides with *lemon-juice*, cover, and leave it in a cool place for one hour. Lay on a buttered gridiron over a clear fire, turning very often as it begins to drip. Do not season until it is done, which will be in about twelve minutes, if the fire is good and the cook attentive. Rub your hot chafing dish with a split raw onion, lay in the steak, salt and pepper on both sides, and put a liberal lump of butter upon the upper. Then put on a hot cover, and let it stand five minutes to draw the juices to the surface before it is eaten. If you have neither chafing-dish nor cover, lay the steak between two hot platters for the same time, sending to table without uncovering. A gridiron fitting *under* the grate is better than any other. If a gridiron is not at hand, rub a little butter upon the bottom of a hot, clean frying-pan, put in the meat, set over a bright fire, and turn frequently. This will not be equal to steak cooked upon a gridiron, but it is infinitely preferable to the same fried.

I shall never forget the wondering distrust with which my first cook, a sable "professional," watched me when I undertook to show her how to prepare a steak for the third breakfast over which I presided as mistress of ceremonies. And when, at the end of twelve minutes, I removed the meat, "rare and hot," to the heated dish in readiness, her sniff of lofty contempt was as eloquent as indescribable.

"Call dat *cooked!* Folks 'bout here would 'a had dat steak on by day-break!"

A remark that has been recalled to my mind hundreds of times since at the tables of so-called capital housewives.

The best—nay, the only pieces for steak are those known as porter-house and sirloin. The former is the more highly esteemed by gourmands; but a really tender sirloin is more serviceable where there are several persons in the family, the porter-house having a narrow strip of extremely nice meat lying next the bone, while the rest is often inferior to any part of the sirloin. If the meat be tender omit the hacking process and lemon-juice.

BEEF-STEAK AND ONIONS.

Prepare the steak as above directed. While it is broiling put three or four chopped onions in a frying-pan with a little beef-dripping or butter. Stir and shake them briskly until they are done, and begin to brown. Dish your steak and lay the onions thickly on top. Cover and let all stand five or six minutes, that the hot onions may impart the required flavor to the hot meat. In helping your guests, inquire if they will take onions with the slices of steak put upon their plates. I need hardly remind the sensible cook how necessary it is to withdraw the gridiron from the fire for an instant, should the fat drip upon the coals below, and smoke or blaze. Yet those who have eaten steaks flavored with creosote may thank me for the suggestion.

BEEF À-LA-MODE. ✠

Take a round of beef; remove the bone from the middle, and trim away the tougher bits about the edges, with such gristle, &c., as you can reach. Set these aside for soup-stock.

Bind the beef into a symmetrical shape by passing a strip of stout muslin, as wide as the round is high, about it, and stitching the ends together at one side. Have ready at least a pound of fat salt pork, cut into strips as thick as your middle finger, and long enough to reach from top to bottom of the trussed round. Put a half pint of vinegar over the fire in a tin or porcelain saucepan;

season with three or four minced shallots or button onions, two teaspoonfuls made mustard, a teaspoonful nutmeg, one of cloves, half as much allspice, half-spoonful black pepper, with a bunch of sweet herbs minced fine, and a tablespoonful brown sugar. Let all simmer for five minutes, then boil up once, and pour, while scalding hot, upon the strips of pork, which should be laid in a deep dish. Let all stand together until cold. Remove the pork to a plate, and mix with the liquor left in the dish enough bread-crumbs to make a tolerably stiff force-meat. If the vinegar is very strong, dilute with a little water before moistening the crumbs. With a long, thin-bladed knife, make perpendicular incisions in the meat, not more than half an inch apart, even nearer is better; thrust into these the strips of fat pork, so far down that the upper ends are just level with the surface, and work into the cavities with them a little of the force-meat. Proceed thus until the meat is fairly riddled and plugged with the pork. Fill the hole from which the bone was taken with the dressing and bits of pork; rub the upper side of the beef well with the spiced force-meat. Put into a baking-pan; half-fill this with boiling water; turn a large pan over it to keep in the steam, and roast slowly for five or six hours, allowing half an hour to each pound of meat. If the beef be tough, you had better stew the round by putting it in a pot with half enough cold water to cover it. Cover tightly and stew very slowly for six hours; then set in the oven with the gravy about it, and brown half an hour, basting frequently.

If you roast the round, do not remove the cover, except to baste (and this should be done often), until fifteen minutes before you draw it from the oven. Set away with the muslin band still about it, and pour the gravy over the meat.

When cold, lift from the gravy,—which, by the way, will be excellent seasoning for your soup-stock,—cut the stitches in the muslin girdle, remove carefully and send the meat to table, cold, garnished with parsley and nasturtium blossoms. Carve horizontally, in slices thin as a shaving. Do not offer the outside to any one; but the second cut will be handsomely marbled with the white pork, which appearance should continue all the way down.

I cannot too highly commend this as a side-dish at dinner, and a supper and breakfast stand-by. In winter it will keep a week and more, and as long in summer, if kept in the refrigerator—except when it is on the table.

BREAKFAST STEW OF BEEF. ✠

Cut up two pounds of beef—not too lean—into pieces an inch long; put them into a saucepan with just enough water to cover them, and stew gently for two hours. Set away until next morning, when season with pepper, salt, sweet marjoram or summer savory, chopped onion, and parsley. Stew half an hour longer, and add a teaspoonful of sauce or catsup, and a tablespoonful of browned flour wet up with cold water; finally, if you wish to have it very good, half a glass of wine. Boil up once, and pour into a covered deep dish.

This is an economical dish, for it can be made of the commoner parts of the beef, and exceedingly nice for winter breakfasts. Eaten with corn-bread and stewed potatoes, it will soon win its way to a place in the "stock company" of every judicious housewife.

ANOTHER BREAKFAST DISH.

Cut thin slices of cold roast beef, and lay them in a tin saucepan set in a pot of boiling water. Cover them with a gravy made of three tablespoonfuls of melted butter, one of walnut catsup, a teaspoonful of vinegar, a little salt and pepper, a spoonful of currant jelly, a teaspoonful made mustard, and some warm water. Cover tightly, and steam for half an hour, keeping the water in the outer vessel on a hard boil.

If the meat is underdone, this is particularly nice.

BEEF HASH.

To two parts cold roast or boiled corned beef, chopped fine, put one of mashed potatoes, a little pepper, salt, milk, and melted butter. Turn all into a frying-pan, and stir until it is heated through and smoking hot, but not until it browns. Put into a deep dish, and if stiff enough, smooth as you would mashed potato, into a hillock.

Or, you can cease stirring for a few minutes, and let a brown crust form on the under side; then turn out whole into a flat dish, the brown side uppermost.

Or, mould the mixture into flat cakes; dip these in beaten egg flour, and fry in hot drippings.

The remains of beef *à-la-mode* are very good prepared in any of these ways. A little catsup and mustard are an improvement to plain cold beef, thus hashed.

BEEF-STEAK PIE.

Cut the steak into pieces an inch long, and stew with the bone (cracked) in just enough water to cover the meat until it is half-done. At the same time parboil a dozen potatoes in another pot. If you wish a bottom crust—a doubtful question—line a pudding-dish with a good paste, made according to the receipt given below. Put in a layer of the beef, with salt and pepper, and a very little chopped onion; then one of sliced potatoes, with a little butter scattered upon them, and so on, until the dish is full. Pour over all the gravy in which the meat is stewed, having first thrown away the bone and thickened with browned flour. Cover with a crust thicker than the lower, leaving a slit in the middle.

CRUST FOR MEAT-PIES. ✠

- 1 quart of flour.

- 3 tablespoonfuls of lard.

- 2½ cups milk.

- 1 teaspoonful of soda wet with hot water, and stirred into the milk.

- 2 teaspoonfuls of cream-tartar sifted into the dry flour.

- 1 teaspoonful of salt.

Work up very lightly and quickly, and do not get too stiff.

If you can get prepared flour, omit the soda and cream-tartar.

BEEF PIE, WITH POTATO CRUST. ✠

Mince some rare roast beef or cold corned beef, if it is not too salt; season with pepper and salt, and spread a layer in the bottom of a pudding-dish. Over this put one of mashed potato, and stick bits of butter thickly all over it; then another of meat, and so on until you are ready for the crust.

To a large cupful of mashed potato add two tablespoonfuls of melted butter, a well-beaten egg, two cups of milk, and beat all together until very light. Then work in enough flour to enable you to roll out in a sheet—not too stiff—and, when you have added to the meat and potato in the dish a gravy made of warm water, butter, milk, and catsup, with what cold gravy or dripping remains from "roast," cover the pie with a thick, tender crust, cutting a slit in the middle.

You can use the potato crust, which is very wholesome and good, for any kind of meat-pie. It looks well brushed over with beaten white of egg before it goes to table.

BEEF'S HEART—STEWED.

Wash the heart well, and cut into squares half an inch long. Stew them for ten minutes in enough water to cover them. Salt the water slightly to draw out the blood, and throw it away as it rises in scum to the top. Take out the meat, strain the liquor, and return the chopped heart to it, with a sliced onion, a great spoonful of catsup, some parsley, a head of celery chopped fine, and cayenne pepper, with a large lump of butter. Stew until the meat is very tender, when add a tablespoonful of browned flour to thicken. Boil up once, and serve.

TO CORN BEEF.

Rub each piece of beef well with salt mixed with one-tenth part of saltpetre, until the salt lies dry upon the surface. Put aside in a cold place for twenty-four hours, and repeat the process, rubbing in the mixture very thoroughly. Put away again until the next day, by which time the pickle should be ready.

- 5 gallons of water.
- 1 gallon of salt.
- 4 ounces saltpetre.
- 1½ lb. brown sugar.

Boil this brine ten minutes; let it get perfectly cold; then pour over the beef, having wiped the latter entirely dry.

Examine the pickle from time to time to see if it keeps well; if not, take out the meat without delay, wipe it, and rub in dry salt, covering it well until you can prepare new and stronger brine.

BOILED CORNED BEEF.

If your piece is a round, skewer it well into shape, and tie it up with stout tape or twine when you have washed it in three or four waters and removed all the salt from the outside. Put into a pot, and cover with cold water. Allow, in boiling, about twenty minutes to a pound. Turn the meat three times while cooking.

When done, drain very dry, and serve with drawn butter in a sauce-boat. Send around mashed turnips with the meat. They should be boiled in a separate pot, however, or they will impart a disagreeable taste to the beef.

The brisket is a good piece for a family dinner.

BEEF TONGUE.

Soak over night in cold water when you have washed it well. Next morning put into a pot with plenty of cold water, and boil slowly until it is tender throughout. This you can determine by testing it with a fork. Leave in the liquor until quite cold.

Pare off the thick skin, cut in round slices, and dish for tea, garnishing with fresh parsley.

Tongue sandwiches are generally held in higher esteem than those made of ham.

DRIED BEEF.

The most common way of serving dried or smoked beef is to shave it into thin slices or chips, raw; but a more savory relish may be made of it with little trouble.

Put the slices of uncooked beef into a frying-pan with just enough boiling water to cover them; set them over the fire for ten minutes, drain off all the water, and with a knife and fork cut the meat into small bits. Return to the pan, which should be hot, with a tablespoonful of butter and a little pepper. Have ready some well-beaten eggs, allowing four to a half-pound of beef; stir them into the pan with the minced meat, and toss and stir the mixture for about two minutes. Send to table in a covered dish.

MUTTON AND LAMB.

ROAST MUTTON.

The parts which are usually roasted are:—

- The shoulder,
- The saddle, or chine, and
- The loin and haunch (a leg and part of the loin).

The leg is best boiled, unless the mutton is young and very tender. To roast—wash the meat well, and dry with a clean cloth. Let your fire be clear and strong; put the meat on with a little water in the dripping-pan. If you think well of the plan (and I do), let there be a cupful of boiling water dashed over the meat when it is first put down to roast, and left to trickle into the pan. I have elsewhere explained the advantages of the method. Allow, in roasting, about twelve minutes per pound, if the fire is good. Baste often—at first with salt and water, afterward with the gravy. If it is in danger of browning too fast, cover with a large sheet of white paper. Roast lamb in the same manner, but not so long. Skim the gravy well, and thicken very slightly with browned flour. Serve with currant jelly.

ROAST MUTTON *à la Venison.*

A Christmas saddle of mutton is very fine prepared as follows: Wash it well, inside and out, with vinegar. Do not wipe it, but hang it up to dry in a cool cellar. When the vinegar has dried off, throw a clean cloth over it, to keep out the dust. On the next day but one, take down the meat and sponge it over again with vinegar, then put it back in its place in the cellar. Repeat this process three times a week for a fortnight, keeping the meat hung in a cold place, and covered, except while you are washing it. When you are ready to cook it, wipe it off with a dry cloth, but do not wash it. Roast—basting for the first hour with butter and water; afterward with the gravy, and keeping the meat covered with a large tin pan for two hours. A large saddle of mutton will require four hours to roast. When it is done, remove to a dish, and cover to keep it hot. Skim the gravy, and add half a teacupful of walnut, mushroom or tomato catsup, a glass of Madeira wine, and a tablespoonful of browned flour. Boil up once, and send to table in a sauce-boat. Always send around currant or some other tart jelly with roast mutton. If properly cooked, a saddle of mutton, prepared in accordance with these directions, will strongly resemble venison in taste. An old Virginia gentleman whom I used to know, always hung up the finest saddle his plantation could furnish *six weeks* before Christmas, and had it sponged off with vinegar every other day, until the morning of the important 25th; and the excellence of his mutton was the talk of the neighborhood. It can certainly be kept a fortnight anywhere at that season.

BOILED MUTTON.

Wash a leg of mutton clean, and wipe dry. Do not leave the knuckle and shank so long as to be unshapely. Put into a pot with hot water (salted) enough to cover it, and boil until you ascertain, by probing with a fork, that it is tender in the thickest part. Skim off all the scum as it rises. Allow *about* twelve minutes to each pound. Take from the fire, drain perfectly dry, and serve with melted butter, with capers, or nasturtium seed; or, if you have neither of these, some cucumber or gherkin-pickle stirred into it. If you wish to use the broth for soup, put in very little salt while boiling; if not, salt well, and boil the meat in a cloth.

MUTTON STEW. ✠

Cut up from three to four pounds of mutton,—the inferior portions will do as well as any other,—crack the bones, and remove all the fat. Put on the meat—the pieces not more than an inch and a half in length—in a pot with enough cold water to cover well, and set it where it will heat gradually. Add nothing else until it has stewed an hour, closely covered; then throw in half a pound of salt pork cut into strips, a little chopped onion, and some pepper; cover and stew an hour longer, or until the meat is very tender. Make out a little paste, as for the crust of a meat-pie; cut into squares, and drop in the stew. Boil ten minutes, and season further by the addition of a little parsley and thyme. Thicken with two spoonfuls of flour stirred into a cup of cold milk. Boil up once, and serve in a tureen or deep covered dish.

If green corn is in season, this stew is greatly improved by adding, an hour before it is taken from the fire, the grains of half a dozen ears, cut from the cob.

Try it for a cheap family dinner, and you will repeat the experiment often. Lamb is even better for your purpose than mutton.

MUTTON CHOPS.

If your butcher has not done it,—and the chances are that he has not, unless you stood by to see it attended to,—trim off the superfluous fat and skin, so as to give the chops a certain litheness and elegance of shape. Dip each in beaten egg, roll in pounded cracker, and fry in hot lard or dripping. If the fat is unsalted, sprinkle the chops with salt before rolling in the egg. Serve up dry and hot.

Or,

You may omit the egg and cracker, and broil on a gridiron over a bright fire. Put a little salt and pepper upon each chop, and butter them before they go to table. Cook lamb chops in the same way.

MUTTON CUTLETS. (*Baked*).

Cut them from the neck, and trim neatly. Lay aside the bits of bone and meat you cut off, to make gravy. Pour a little melted butter over the cutlets, and let them lie in it for fifteen minutes, keeping them just warm enough to prevent the butter from hardening; then dip each in beaten egg, roll in cracker-crumbs, and lay them in your dripping-pan with a *very* little water at the bottom. Bake quickly, and baste often with butter and water. Put on the bones, etc., in enough cold water to cover them; stew, and season with sweet herbs, pepper, and salt, with a spoonful of tomato catsup. Strain when all the substance is extracted from the meat and bones; thicken with browned flour, and pour over the cutlets when they are served.

MUTTON HAM.

For a leg of mutton weighing 12 lbs., take—

- 1 ounce of black pepper, or ½ ounce of cayenne,

- ¼ lb. brown sugar,

- 1 ounce saltpetre,

- 1¼ lb. salt.

The day after the sheep is killed, mix the sugar, pepper, and saltpetre, and rub well into the meat for nearly fifteen minutes, until the outer part of it is thoroughly impregnated with the seasoning. Put the ham into a large earthenware vessel, and cover it with the salt. Let it remain thus for three weeks, turning it every day and basting it with the brine; adding to this, after the first week, a teacupful of vinegar. When the ham is removed from the pickle, wash with cold water, then with vinegar, and hang it up in a cool cellar for a week, at least, before it is used.

Soak an hour in fair water before boiling.

Or if you choose to smoke it for several days after it is corned, it can be chipped and eaten raw, like jerked venison or dried beef.

Most of the receipts above given will apply as well to lamb as to mutton. There are several exceptions, however, which you will do well to note. Lamb should never be boiled except in stews. It is tasteless and sodden cooked in this manner, on account of its immaturity. But, on the other hand, a lamb-pie, prepared like one of beef or venison, is excellent, while mutton-pies have usually a strong, tallowy taste, that spoils them for delicate palates.

Roast lamb should be eaten with mint sauce (if you fancy it), currant jelly, and asparagus or green peas. Lettuce-salad is likewise a desirable accompaniment.

MUTTON OR LAMB RÉCHAUFFÉ. ✠

Cut some slices of cold underdone mutton or lamb; put them in a frying-pan with enough gravy or broth to cover them. Or, if you have neither of them, make a gravy of butter, warm water, and catsup. Heat to boiling, and stir in pepper and a great spoonful of currant jelly. Send to table in a chafing-dish, with the gravy poured about the meat.

Or,

You can put a lump of the butter in the bottom of the pan, and when it boils, lay in the slices of meat, turning them before they have time to crisp. As soon as they are thoroughly heated take them out, lay upon a hot dish, sprinkle with pepper and salt, and serve with a small spoonful of jelly laid upon each.

VEAL.

Despite the prejudice, secret or expressed, which prevails in many minds against veal,—one which the wise and witty "Country Parson" has as surely fostered among reading people, as did Charles Lamb the partiality for roast pig,—the excellent and attractive dishes that own this as their base are almost beyond number. For soups it is invaluable, and in *entrees* and *réchauffés* it plays a distinguished part. From his head to his feet, the animal that furnishes us with this important element of success in what should be the prime object of cookery, to wit, to please while we nourish, has proved himself so useful as an ally that it behooves us to lift the stigma from the name of "calf," provided he be not *too* infantine. In that case he degenerates into an insipid mass of pulpy muscle and gelatine, and deserves the bitterest sneers that have been flung at his kind.

ROAST VEAL.

LOIN.

Veal requires a longer time to roast than mutton or lamb. It is fair to allow *at least* a quarter of an hour to each pound. Heat gradually, baste frequently—at first with salt and water, afterward with gravy. When the meat is nearly done, dredge lightly with flour, and baste once with melted butter. Skim the gravy; thicken with a tablespoonful of flour, boil up, and put into the gravy-boat.

Should the meat brown too fast, cover with white paper. The juices, which make up the characteristic flavor of meat, are oftener dried out of veal than any other flesh that comes to our tables.

BREAST.

Make incisions between the ribs and the meat, and fill with a force-meat made of fine bread-crumbs, bits of pork, or ham chopped "exceeding small," salt, pepper, thyme, sweet marjoram, and beaten egg. Save a little to thicken the gravy. Roast slowly, basting often, and the verdict of the eaters will differ from theirs who pronounce this the coarsest part of the veal. Dredge, at the last, with flour, and baste well once with butter, as with the loin.

FILLET.

Make ready a dressing of bread-crumbs, chopped thyme and parsley; a little nutmeg, pepper and salt, rubbed together with some melted butter or beef suet; moisten with milk or hot water, and bind with a beaten egg.

Take out the bone from the meat, and pin securely into a round with skewers; then pass a stout twine several times about the fillet, or a band of muslin. Fill the cavity from which the bone was taken with this stuffing, and thrust between the folds of the meat, besides making incisions with a thin, sharp knife to receive it. Once in a while slip in a strip of fat pork or ham. Baste at first with salt and water, afterward with gravy. At the last, dredge with flour and baste with butter.

SHOULDER.

Stuff as above, making horizontal incisions near the bone to receive the dressing, and roast in like manner.

Veal Cutlets.

Dip in beaten egg when you have sprinkled a little pepper and salt over them; then roll in cracker-crumbs, and fry in hot dripping or lard. If you use butter or dripping, add a little boiling water to the gravy when the meat is dished; thicken with browned flour, boil up once, sending to table in a boat.

Or,

You can rub the cutlets well with melted butter, pepper, and broil on a gridiron like beef-steak, buttering *very* well after dishing.

Veal Chops

Are more juicy and less apt to be tough and solid than cutlets. Trim the bone as with mutton chops, and fry, dipping in beaten egg and cracker-crumbs. Add a little parsley and a minced shallot to the gravy.

Veal Steak.

This should be thinner than beef-steak, and be done throughout. Few persons are fond of rare veal. Broil upon a well-greased gridiron over a clear fire, and turn frequently while the steaks are cooking. Put into a saucepan four or five young onions minced fine, a great teaspoonful of tomato catsup, or twice the quantity of stewed tomato, a lump of butter the size of an egg, and a little thyme or parsley, with a small teacupful of hot water. Let them stew together while the steaks are broiling, thickening, before you turn the gravy out, with a spoonful of browned flour. Add, if you please, a half-glass of wine. Boil up once hard, and when the steaks are dished, with a small bit of butter upon each, pour the mixture over and around them.

Spinach is as natural an accompaniment to veal as are green peas to lamb.

VEAL PIES.

Let your veal be juicy and not too fat. Take out all the bone, and put with the fat and refuse bits, such as skin or gristle, in a saucepan, with a large teacupful of cold water to make gravy. Instead of chopping the veal, cut in thin, even slices. Line a pudding-dish with a good paste and put a layer of veal in the bottom; then one of hard-boiled eggs sliced, each piece buttered and peppered before it is laid upon the veal; cover these with sliced ham or thin strips of salt pork. Squeeze a few drops of lemon-juice upon the ham. Then another layer of veal, and so on until you are ready for the gravy. This should have been stewing for half an hour or so, with the addition of pepper and a bunch of aromatic herbs. Strain through a thin cloth and pour over the pie. Cover with crust and bake two hours.

Or,

Butter a large bowl very thickly, and line with sliced hard-boiled eggs. Then put in, in perpendicular layers, a lining of veal cut in thin slices, and seasoned with pepper. Next, one of sliced ham, each slice peppered and sprinkled with lemon-juice, more veal and more ham, until the dish is packed to the brim. Cover with a thick paste made of flour and hot water, just stiff enough to handle with ease. Press this closely to the outside of the bowl, which should not be at all greasy. Let it overlap the rim about half an inch. Some cooks substitute a cloth well floured, but it does not keep in the essence of the meats as well as the paste. Set the bowl in a pot of hot water, not so deep that it will bubble over the top. It is better that it should not touch the paste rim. Boil steadily—not hard—for at least three hours. Remove the paste the next day, when bowl and contents are perfectly cold, and turn out the pie into a large plate or flat dish. Cut in circular slices—thin as a wafer—beginning at the top, keeping your carver horizontal, and you have a delicious relish for the supper-table, or side-dish for dinner. Set in a cool place, and in winter it will keep several days.

This is the "weal and hammer pie" endorsed by Mr. Wegg as a good thing "for mellering the organ," and is a great favorite in England. It is a good plan to butter the eggs as well as the dish, as much of the success of the pie depends upon the manner in which it is turned out. Also, upon the close packing of the sliced meat. The salt ham prevents the need of other salt.

STEWED FILLET OF VEAL.

Stuff, and bind with twine as for roasting. Then cover the top and sides with sliced ham which has been already boiled, securing with skewers, or twine crossing the meat in all directions. Lay in a pot, put in two large cups of boiling water, cover immediately and closely, and stew gently—never letting it cease to boil, yet never boiling hard, for four or five hours. A large fillet will require nearly five hours. Remove the cover as seldom as possible, and only to ascertain whether the water has boiled away. If it is too low, replenish from the boiling kettle. Take off the strings when the meat is done; arrange the ham about the fillet in the dish, and serve a bit with each slice of veal. Strain the gravy, thicken with flour, boil up once, and send in a boat.

Serve with stewed tomatoes and spinach.

STEWED KNUCKLE OF VEAL.

Put the meat into a pot with two quarts of boiling water, half a pound of salt pork or ham cut into strips, a carrot, two onions, a bunch of parsley and one of summer savory—all cut fine—two dozen whole pepper-corns, and stew, closely covered, for three hours. When done, take the meat from the pot and lay in the dish. Strain the gravy, thicken with rice-flour, boil up once, and pour over the meat.

VEAL SCALLOP. ✠

Chop some cold roast or stewed veal very fine, put a layer in the bottom of a buttered pudding dish, and season with pepper and salt. Next have a layer of finely powdered crackers. Strew some bits of butter upon it and wet with a little milk; then more veal seasoned as before, and another round of cracker-crumbs, with butter and milk. When the dish is full, wet well with gravy or broth, diluted with warm water. Spread over all a thick layer of cracker seasoned with salt, wet into a paste with milk and bound with a beaten egg or two, if the dish be large. Stick butter-bits thickly over it; invert a tin pan so as to cover all and keep in the steam, and bake—if small, half an hour; three-quarters will suffice for a large dish. Remove the cover ten minutes before it is served, and brown.

This simple and economical dish should be an acquaintance with all who are fond of veal in any shape. Children generally like it exceedingly, and I have heard more than one gentleman of excellent judgment in culinary affairs declare that the best thing he knew about roast veal was that it was the harbinger of scallop on the second day.

Try it, and do not get it too dry.

VEAL PÂTÉS.

Mince the veal as above, and roll three or four crackers to powder. Also, chop up some cold ham and mix with the veal in the proportion of one-third ham and two-thirds veal. Then add the cracker, and wet well with gravy and a little milk. If you have no gravy, stir into a cup of hot milk two tablespoonfuls of butter and a beaten egg. Season well to your taste, and bake in pâté pans lined with puff-paste. If eaten hot, send to table in the tins. If cold, slip the pâtés out and pile upon a plate, with sprigs of parsley between. A little oyster liquor is a marked improvement to the gravy.

STEWED CALF'S-HEAD.

Wash the head in several waters, and taking out the brains, set them by in a cool place. Tie the head in a floured cloth and boil it two hours in hot water slightly salted. Wash the brains carefully, picking out all the bits of skin and membrane, cleansing them over and over until they are perfectly white. Then stew in just enough water to cover them. Take them out, mash smooth with the back of a wooden spoon, and add gradually, that it may not lump, a small teacupful of the water in which the head is boiled. Season with chopped parsley, a pinch of sage, pepper, salt, and powdered cloves, with a great spoonful of butter. Set it over the fire to simmer in a saucepan until you are ready. When the head is tender, take it up and drain very dry. Score the top, and rub it well over with melted butter; dredge with flour and set in the oven to brown. Or, you can use beaten egg and cracker-crumbs in place of the butter and flour.

When you serve the head, pour the gravy over it.

Never skin a calf's-head. Scald as you would that of a pig. A little lye in the water will remove the hair—as will also pounded rosin, applied before it is put into the water.

CALF'S-HEAD (*Scalloped.*) ✠

Clean the head, remove the brains, and set in a cool place. Boil the head until the meat slips easily from the bones. Take it out and chop fine, season with herbs, pepper, and salt; then put in layers into a buttered pudding-dish with bits of butter between each layer. Moisten well with the liquor in which the head was boiled. Wash the brains very thoroughly, removing all the membrane. Beat them into a smooth paste, season with pepper and salt, and stir in with them two eggs beaten very light. Spread this evenly over the scallop, dredge the top with a little flour, and bake to a delicate brown. Half an hour will be long enough.

SWEET-BREADS (*Fried.*) ✠

Wash very carefully, and dry with a linen cloth. Lard with narrow strips of fat salt pork, set closely together. Use for this purpose a larding-needle. Lay the sweet-breads in a clean, hot frying-pan, which has been well buttered or greased, and cook to a fine brown, turning frequently until the pork is crisp.

SWEET BREADS (*Broiled.*) ✠

Parboil, rub them well with butter, and broil on a clean gridiron. Turn frequently, and now and then roll over in a plate containing some hot melted butter. This will prevent them from getting too dry and hard.

SWEET-BREADS (*Stewed.*) ✠

When you have washed them, and removed all bits of skin and fatty matter, cover with cold water, and heat to a boil. Pour off the hot water, and cover with cold until the sweet-breads are firm. If you desire to have them very rich, lard as for frying before you put in the second water. They are more delicate, however, if the pork be left out. Stew in a very little water the second time. When they are tender, add for each sweet-bread a heaping teaspoonful of butter, and a little chopped parsley, with pepper, and salt, and a little cream. Let them simmer in this gravy for five minutes, then take them up. Send to table in a covered dish, with the gravy poured over them.

If you lard the sweet-breads, substitute for the cream in the gravy a glass of good wine. In this case, take the sweet-breads out before it is put into the gravy. Boil up once and pour over them.

SWEET-BREADS (*Roasted.*)

Parboil and throw into cold water, where let them stand for fifteen minutes. Then change to more cold water for five minutes longer. Wipe perfectly dry. Lay them in your dripping-pan, and roast, basting with butter and water until they begin to brown. Then withdraw them for an instant, roll in beaten egg, then in cracker-crumbs, and return to the fire for ten minutes longer, basting meanwhile twice with melted butter. Lay in a chafing-dish while you add to the dripping half a cup hot water, some chopped parsley, a teaspoonful browned flour, and the juice of half a lemon. Pour over the sweet-breads before sending to table.

JELLIED VEAL.

Wash a knuckle of veal, and cut it into three pieces. Boil it slowly until the meat will slip easily from the bones; take out of the liquor; remove all the bones, and chop the meat fine. Season with salt, pepper, two shallots chopped as fine as possible, mace and thyme, or, if you like, sage. Put back into the liquor, and boil until it is almost dry and can be stirred with difficulty. Turn into a mould until next day. Set on the table cold, garnish with parsley, and cut in slices. The juice of a lemon, stirred in just before it is taken from the fire, is an improvement.

CALF'S-HEAD IN A MOULD.

Boil a calf's-head until tender, the day before you wish to use it. When perfectly cold, chop—not too small—and season to taste with pepper, salt, mace, and the juice of a lemon. Prepare half as much cold ham, fat and lean—also minced—as you have of the chopped calf's-head. Butter a mould well, and lay in the bottom a layer of the calf's-head, then one of ham, and so on until the shape is full, pressing each layer hard, when you have moistened it with veal gravy or the liquor in which the head was boiled. Pour more gravy over the top, and when it has soaked in well, cover with a paste made of flour and water. Bake one hour. Remove the paste when it is quite cold, and turn out carefully. Cut perpendicularly.

This is quite as good a relish when made of cold roast or stewed veal and ham. It will keep several days in cool weather.

VEAL OLIVES WITH OYSTERS.

Cut large, smooth slices from a fillet of veal, or veal chops will do quite as well. Trim them into a uniform shape and size, and spread each neatly with forced-meat made of bread-crumbs and a little chopped pork, seasoned with pepper and salt. Over this spread some chopped oysters, about three to a good-sized slice of veal. Roll them up carefully and closely, and pin each with two small tin or wooden skewers. Lay them in a dripping-pan; dash a teacupful of boiling water over them, and roast, basting at least twice with melted butter. When they are brown, remove to a chafing-dish, and cover, while you add a little oyster-liquor to the gravy left in the dripping-pan. Let this simmer for three or four minutes; thicken with a teaspoonful of browned flour, and boil up at once. Withdraw the skewers cautiously, so as not to break the olives; pour the gravy over and around them, and serve. If you have no skewers, bind the olives with pack-thread, cutting it, of course, before sending to table.

Serve with cranberry jelly.

MINCED VEAL.

Take the remains of a cold roast of veal fillet, shoulder, or breast, and cut all the meat from the bones. Put the latter, with the outside slices and the gristly pieces, into a saucepan, with a cup of cold water, some sweet herbs, pepper, and salt. If you have a bit of bacon convenient, or a ham-bone, add this and omit the salt. Stew all together for an hour, then strain, thicken with flour, return to the fire, and boil five minutes longer, stirring in a tablespoonful of butter.

Meanwhile, mince the cold veal, and when the gravy is ready put this in a little at a time. Let it *almost* boil, when add two tablespoonfuls of cream, or three of milk, stirring all the while. Lastly, squeeze in the juice of a lemon, and a moment later half a glass of Sherry or Madeira wine.

The mince-meat should be dry enough to heap into a shape in a flat dish or chafing-dish. Lay triangles of buttered toast about the base of the mound, and on the top a poached egg.

The remains of cold roast beef treated in this manner, substituting for the toast balls of mashed potato, will make a neat and palatable dish.

Send around spinach or stewed tomatoes with minced veal; scraped horseradish steeped in vinegar with the beef.

VEAL CUTLETS À LA MAINTENON.

The cutlets should be nearly three-quarters of an inch thick, and trim in shape. Dip each in beaten egg, then into pounded cracker which has been seasoned with powdered sweet herbs, pepper, and salt. Wrap each cutlet in a half-sheet of note or letter paper, well buttered; lay them upon a buttered gridiron and broil over a clear fire, turning often and dexterously. You can secure the papers by fringing the ends, and twisting these after the cutlets are put in. This is neater than to pin them together. In trying this dish for the first time, have ready a sufficient number of duplicate papers in a clean, hot dish. If your envelopes are much soiled or darkened while the cutlets are broiling, transfer quickly when done to the clean warm ones, twist the ends, and serve. Cutlets prepared in this manner are sent to table in their cloaks, ranged symmetrically upon a hot chafing-dish.

The expedient of the clean papers is a "trick of the trade," amateur housewives will observe with satisfaction. Epicures profess to enjoy veal cooked in covers far more than when the flavor and juices escape in broiling without them. Empty every drop of gravy from the soiled papers into the clean over the cutlets.

CROQUETTES OF CALF'S BRAINS.

Wash the brains very thoroughly until they are free from membranous matter and perfectly white. Beat them smooth; season with a pinch of powdered sage, pepper, and salt. Add two tablespoonfuls fine bread-crumbs moistened with milk, and a beaten egg. Roll into balls with floured hands, dip in beaten egg, then cracker-crumbs, and fry in butter or veal-drippings.

These make a pleasant accompaniment to boiled spinach. Heap the vegetable in the centre of the dish, arrange the balls about it, and give one to each person who wishes spinach.

CALF'S LIVER (*Roasted.*)

Soak the liver in salt and water an hour to draw out the blood. Wipe perfectly dry, and stuff with a force-meat made of bread-crumbs, two slices of fat salt pork, chopped small, a shallot, pepper, salt, and nutmeg; sweet marjoram and thyme, and if you choose, a little sage. Moisten this with butter melted in a very little hot water, and two raw eggs, well beaten. In order to get this into the liver, make an incision with a narrow sharp knife, and without enlarging the aperture where the blade entered, move the point dexterously to and fro, to enlarge the cavity inside. Stuff this full of the force-meat, sew or skewer up the outer orifice; lard with strips of salt pork, and roast for an hour, basting twice with butter and water, afterward with the gravy in the dripping-pan. Pour the gravy over the liver when done.

Roasted liver is very good cold, cut into slices like tongue.

CALF'S LIVER (*Fried*).

Slice the liver smoothly, and lay in salt and water to draw out the blood. Lard each slice, when you have wiped it dry, with slices of fat salt pork, drawn through at regular distances, and projecting slightly on each side. Lay in a clean frying-pan and fry brown. When done, take out the slices, arrange them neatly on a hot dish, and set aside to keep warm. Add to the gravy in the frying-pan a chopped onion, a half-cup of hot water, pepper, the juice of a lemon, and thicken with brown flour. Boil up well, run through a cullender to remove the onion and the bits of crisped pork that may have been broken off in cooking, pour over the liver, and serve hot.

Pigs' livers can be cooked in the same way.

CALF'S LIVER (*Stewed*).

Slice the liver and lay in salt and water an hour. Then cut into dice and put over the fire, with enough cold water to cover it well. Cover and stew steadily for an hour, when add salt, pepper, a little mace, sweet marjoram, parsley, and a teaspoonful Worcestershire sauce. Stew again steadily, not fast, for half an hour longer, when put in a tablespoonful of butter, two of browned flour—wet with cold water, a teaspoonful of lemon-juice and one of currant jelly. Boil five minutes longer, and dish. A little wine is an improvement.

Or,

Put in with the liver-dice some of salt pork—say a handful—and when you season, a chopped onion, and omit the jelly at the last, substituting some tomato catsup.

IMITATION PÂTÉS DE FOIE GRAS. ✠

Boil a calf's liver until very tender in water that has been slightly salted, and in another vessel a nice calf's tongue. It is best to do this the day before you make your *pâté*, as they should be not only cold, but firm when used. Cut the liver into bits, and rub these gradually to a smooth paste in a Wedgewood mortar, moistening, as you go on, with melted butter. Work into this paste, which should be quite soft, a quarter-teaspoonful of cayenne pepper, or twice the quantity of white or black, half a grated nutmeg, a little cloves, a teaspoonful of Worcestershire sauce, salt to taste, a full teaspoonful of made mustard, and a tablespoonful of boiling water, in which a minced onion has been steeped until the flavor is extracted. Work all together thoroughly, and pack in jelly-jars with air-tight covers, or, if you have them, in *pâté*-jars. They give a foreign air to the compound, and aid imagination in deceiving the palate. Butter the inside of the jars well, and pack the *pâté* very hard, inserting here and there square and triangular bits of the tongue, which should be pared and cut up for this purpose. These simulate the truffles imbedded in the genuine *pâtés* from Strasbourg. When the jar is packed, and smooth as marble on the surface, cover with melted butter. Let this harden, put on the lid, and set away in a cool place. In winter it will keep for weeks, and is very nice for luncheon or tea. Make into sandwiches, or set on in the jars, if they are neat and ornamental.

The resemblance in taste to the real *pâté de foie gras* is remarkable, and the domestic article is popular with the lovers of that delicacy. Pigs' livers make a very fair *pâté*. If you can procure the livers of several fowls and treat as above, substituting bits of the inside of the gizzard for truffles, you will find the result even more satisfactory.

VEAL MARBLE.

Boil a beef-tongue the day before it is to be used, and a like number of pounds of lean veal. Grind first one, then the other, in a sausage-cutter, keeping them in separate vessels until you are ready to pack. If you have no machine for this purpose, chop *very* fine. Season the tongue with pepper, powdered sweet herbs, a teaspoonful of made mustard, a little nutmeg, and cloves—just a pinch of each; the veal in like manner, with the addition of salt. Pack in alternate spoonfuls, as irregularly as possible, in cups, bowls, or jars, which have been well buttered. Press very hard as you go on, smooth the top, and cover with melted butter. When this cools, close the cans, and keep in a cool, dry place. Turn out whole, or cut in slices for tea. It is a pretty and savory relish, garnished with parsley or the blanched tops of celery.

You can use ground ham instead of tongue. It is hardly so good, but is more economical.

PORK.

At the South, where, in spite of the warm climate, the consumption of pork is double that of the North, the full-grown hog is seldom represented by any of his parts at the table, fresh or pickled, unless it be during killing-time, when fresh spare-ribs, chine, and steak, with other succulent bits, are welcome upon the choicest bills of fare. The rest of the animal—ham, shoulders, and middlings—is consigned to the packing barrel, and ultimately to the smoke-house. But, in cool weather, "shoat"—*i. e.*, pig under six months of age—is abundantly displayed in market, and highly esteemed by all classes. The meat is fine and sweet, and, unless too fat, nearly as delicate as that of chicken—a very different-looking and tasting dish from the gross oleaginous joints and "chunks" offered for sale in many other regions as "nice young pork." Those of my readers who can command "shoat" are to be heartily congratulated. Those whose butchers dispense only portions of the mature porker will do well, in my opinion, if they rarely admit him to their families before he has been salted, and been thereby purged of many unwholesome properties. Few stomachs, save those of out-door laborers, can digest the fresh meat of a two or three, or even one year old hog. This is the truthful, but, to unaccustomed ears, offensive name for him at the South and West, where his qualities and habits are best known.

The parts of a properly dissected hog are the hams, shoulders, griskin or chine, the loin, middlings, spare-ribs, head, feet, liver, and haslet. The choice portions are hams, shoulders, and, for roasting, the loin. All hogs should be kept up and well fed for three weeks, at least, before they are killed; their styes be frequently cleaned, and furnished with abundance of water, renewed every day. Sir Grunter would be a more cleanly creature if he were allowed more extensive water privileges. If it were possible—and in the country this may sometimes be done—to build his pen on the bank of a running stream, he would speedily redeem his character from the stain cast upon it by the popular verdict, and the superior quality of the meat repay the thoughtful kindness of his owner. It is a disgrace to humanity, hardly second to the barbarities of swill-milk manufactories, this compulsory filth of any domestic animal. Those who, like myself, have been loathing witnesses of the pig-pens upon the premises of well-to-do farmers—the receptacles of the vilest slops and offal, never cleaned except during the yearly removal of manure from barnyard to field—cannot marvel at the growing prejudice against pork in all its varieties that pervades our best classes. We feed the hog with the offscourings (this is literal) of house, garden, and table; bed him in mire, and swell him with acetous fermentation, not to say active decomposition, and then abuse him for being what we have made him. I am persuaded—and wiser people than I declare—that hog-scrofula and cholera, and the rest of the train of fleshly ills that are the terror of pork-raisers, have, one and all, their root in this unseemly inhumanity. Eschew fresh pork we may, but we cannot dispense with hams, shoulders, and, most valuable of all to the cook, lard and pickled pork. Real sausage, porcine and home-made, is still sweet and pleasant to the unpampered palate; and of roast pig, the gentlest and most genial of English essayists did not disdain to become the eulogist. In memory of his usefulness, in belief of the healthfulness which should be his birthright, and the safeguard of his consumers, let us treat Bristle well—I do not say philosophically, but sensibly and kindly.

A pig should not be allowed to eat anything for twenty-four hours before he is killed. After he is butchered, great care should be exercised to keep the pork from tainting; it spoils more readily, when fresh, than any other meat. Cook all kinds of pork thoroughly. When underdone it is not only unpalatable, but exceedingly unwholesome.

ROAST LEG OF PORK.

One weighing about seven pounds is enough, even for a large family. If the pig be young, the leg will be even smaller. Score the skin in squares, or parallel lines running from side to side, for the convenience of the carver. Put it down to roast with a *very* little water in the pan below. Heat gradually until the fat begins to ooze from the meat, when quicken the fire to a red, steady glow. Baste only with its own gravy, and do this often, that the skin may not be hard or tough. When done take it up, skim the gravy thoroughly, put in half a cup of boiling water, thicken with brown flour, add pepper, salt, and the juice of a lemon, and serve in a boat.

Or,

If the joint be that of a full-grown hog, rub into the top, after scoring it deeply, a force-meat of bread-crumbs seasoned with sage and chopped onion, wet with the juice of a lemon or a very little vinegar; pepper and salt to taste. Rub this in hard until the cracks are filled. With a sharp knife make incisions close to the knuckle-bone, and stuff with the force-meat, tying a string tightly about it afterward, to prevent the escape of the seasoning. Rub over once with butter, when the meat is warm throughout; then baste with the fat. Skim all the fat from the drippings that can be removed before making the gravy.

Send around tomato or apple sauce, and pickles, with roast pork.

LOIN OF PORK.

Cook as you would a leg, allowing twenty minutes to a pound in roasting. This is a good rule for fresh pork, the flesh being coarser and of closer grain than are more delicate meats.

A shoulder is roasted in the same way.

ROAST SPARE-RIB.

When first put down to the fire, cover with a greased paper until it is half-done. Remove it then, and dredge with flour. A few minutes later, baste once with butter, and afterward, every little while, with its own gravy. This is necessary, the spare-rib being a very dry piece. Just before you take it up, strew over the surface thickly with fine bread-crumbs seasoned with powdered sage, pepper, and salt, and a small onion minced into almost invisible bits. Let it cook five minutes and baste once more with butter. Skim the gravy, add a half cupful of hot water, thicken with brown flour, squeeze in the juice of a lemon, strain, and pour over the meat in the dish.

Send tomato catsup around with it, or if you prefer, put a liberal spoonful in the gravy, after it is strained.

ROAST CHINE.

A chine is treated precisely as is the spare-rib, except that the strip of skin running along the back is scored closely. If you wish, you can omit the bread-crumb crust, the onion and sage. In carving, cut thin horizontal slices from the ribs. Chine is best cold. The meat next the ribs is delicious when scraped off and made into sandwiches, or laid upon buttered toast.

Or,

You can wash the chine over with beaten egg, dredge with cracker-crumbs, seasoned with salt and pepper, and roast, basting with butter and water once when the meat is heated through, afterward with its own gravy. This is a palatable supper-dish when cold. Garnish with cucumber pickles cut in round slices.

ROAST PIG.

A month-old pig, if it be well-grown and plump, is best for this purpose. It is hardly possible that any lady-housekeeper will ever be called upon to do the butcher's work upon the bodies of full-grown hogs, or even "shoat"—a task that requires the use of hatchet or cleaver. It is well that she should know how to clean and dress the baby pig, which is not larger than a Thanksgiving turkey.

As soon as it is really cold, make ready a large boiler of scalding water. Lay the pig in cold water for fifteen minutes; then, holding it by the hind-leg, plunge it into the boiling water, and shake it about violently until you can pull the hair off by the handful. Take it out, wipe it dry, and with a crash cloth or whisk broom rub the hair off, brushing from the tail to the head, until the skin is perfectly clean. Cut it open, take out the entrails, and wash very thoroughly with cold water, then with soda and water, to remove any unpleasant odor; next with salt and water. Rinse with fair water and wipe inside. Then wrap in a wet cloth, and keep this saturated with cold water until you are ready to stuff it. If these directions be followed implicitly, the pig will be fair and white, as if intrusted to a professional butcher.

For stuffing, take a cupful of bread-crumbs, half a chopped onion, two teaspoonfuls powdered sage, three tablespoonfuls melted butter, a saltspoonful of pepper, half a grated nutmeg, half a teaspoonful of salt, two well-beaten eggs. Mix all these ingredients, except the egg, together, incorporating them well; beat in the eggs, and stuff the pig into his natural size and shape. Sew him up, and bend his fore-feet backward, his hind-feet forward, under and close to the body, and skewering them into the proper position. Dry it well, and dredge with flour. Put it to roast with a little hot water, slightly salted, in the dripping-pan. Baste with butter and water three times, as the pig gradually warms, afterward with the dripping. When it begins to smoke or steam, rub it over every five minutes or so, with a cloth dipped in melted butter. Do not omit this precaution if you would have the skin tender and soft after it begins to brown. A month-old pig will require about an hour and three-quarters or two hours—sometimes longer—to roast, if the fire be brisk and steady.

Should you or your guests dislike onion, prepare your stuffing without it. The following is a good receipt for rich and savory force-meat for a pig:—

One cup of bread-crumbs, an ounce of suet, a bunch of parsley minced fine, teaspoonful of powdered sage, pepper, salt, and nutmeg, a little thyme, half a glass Madeira or Sherry, juice of a lemon, two tablespoonfuls melted butter, a cup of oyster-liquor, and two well-beaten eggs. For a Christmas pig, it is worth one's while to take the trouble to prepare this stuffing.

If your pig is large, you can cut off his head and split him down the back before sending to table. Do this with a sharp knife, and lay the backs together. But it is a pity! I have before me now the vision of a pig I once saw served whole on the table of a friend, that forbids me ever to mutilate him before the guests have a chance to feast their eyes upon the goodly picture. He was done to a turn—a rich, even brown, without a seam or crack from head to tail, and he knelt in a bed of deep-green parsley, alternately with bunches of whitish-green celery tops (the inner and tender leaves); a garland of the same was about his neck, and in his mouth was a tuft of white cauliflower, surrounded by a setting of curled parsley. Very simple, you see; but I never beheld a more ornamental roast.

Skim your gravy well; add a little hot water, thicken with brown flour, boil up once, strain, and, when you have added half a glass of wine and half the juice of a lemon, serve in a tureen.

In carving the pig, cut off the head first; then split down the back, take off hams and shoulders, and separate the ribs. Serve some of the dressing to each person.

I have been thus minute in describing the preparation of this holiday dish, because it is erroneously considered a difficult task. Any cook with a moderate degree of judgment and experience can undertake it with a reasonable expectation of success.

PORK STEAKS.

Those from the loin are best, but they can be cut from the neck. Remove the skin and trim neatly. Broil over a clear fire, without seasoning, adding pepper, salt, a pinch of sage, another of minced onion, and a lump of butter after they are put into the hot dish. Then cover closely and set in the oven for five minutes, until the aroma of the condiments flavors the meat. Try this method. You can cook spare-rib in the same manner.

PORK CHOPS.

Remove the skin, trim them, and dip first in beaten egg, then in cracker-crumbs seasoned with salt, pepper, minced onion, and a little sage. Fry in hot lard or drippings twenty or thirty minutes, turning often. The gravy of this dish is usually too rich or fat to accompany the meat.

Pork cutlets are cooked in like manner. Send apple-sauce to the table with them, and season with tomato catsup.

STEWED PORK.

Take some lean slices from the leg, or bits left from trimming the various pieces into shape. Cut into dice an inch square, put into a pot with enough cold water to cover them, and stew gently for three-quarters of an hour, closely covered. Meanwhile parboil half a dozen Irish potatoes, cut in thick slices, in another vessel. When the pork has stewed the allotted time, drain off the water from these and add to the meat. Season with pepper, salt, a minced shallot, a spoonful of pungent catsup, and a bunch of aromatic herbs. Cover again, and stew twenty minutes longer, or until the meat is tender throughout.

If your meat be not too fat, this stew will be very good, especially on a cold day.

You can stew cutlets in the same way.

PIG'S HEAD (*Roasted*).

Take the head of a half-grown pig; clean and split it, taking out the brains and setting these aside in a cool place. Parboil the head in salted water, drain off this, wipe the head dry, and wash all over with beaten egg; dredge thickly with bread-crumbs, seasoned with pepper, sage, and onion, and roast, basting twice with butter and water; then with the liquor in which the head was boiled; at last with the gravy that runs from the meat. Wash the brains in several waters until they are white; beat to a smooth paste, add one-quarter part fine bread-crumbs, pepper, and salt; make into balls, binding with a beaten egg; roll in flour and fry in hot fat to a light brown. Arrange about the head when it is dished. Skim the gravy left in the dripping-pan, thicken with brown flour, add the juice of a lemon, and boil up once. Pour it over the head.

PIG'S HEAD WITH LIVER AND HEART (*Stewed*).

Clean and split the head, taking out the brains and setting aside. Put the head in a pot with water enough to cover it and parboil it. Have ready another pot with the liver and heart, cut into inch-long pieces, stewed in just enough water to keep them from scorching. When the head is half-done, add the entire contents of the second vessel to the first, and season with salt, pepper, a little onion, parsley, and sage. Cover and stew until the head is very tender, when take it out and lay it in the middle of a flat dish. With a perforated skimmer remove the liver and heart and spread about the head, surrounding, but not covering it. Strain the gravy and return to the pot, thicken with brown flour, squeeze in the juice of a lemon, and drop in carefully force-meat balls of the brains, prepared according to the foregoing receipt and fried a light brown. Boil once and pour about the head, arranging the balls upon it, to cover the split between the two sides of the head.

You may improve this dish, which is very savory, by boiling a couple of pigs' feet with the head until the meat will slip from the bones. Take them from the liquor, cut off and chop the meat, and put into the large pot when you add the liver, etc.

SOUSE OF PIGS' EARS AND FEET.

Clean the ears and feet well; cover them with cold water slightly salted, and boil until tender. Pack in stone jars while hot, and cover while you make ready the pickle. To half a gallon of good cider vinegar allow half a cup of white sugar, three dozen whole black peppers, a dozen blades of mace, and a dozen cloves. Boil this one minute, taking care that it really boils, and pour while hot over the still warm feet and ears. It will be ready to use in two days, and will keep in a cool, dry place two months.

If you wish it for breakfast, make a batter of one egg, one cup of milk, salt to taste, and a teaspoonful of butter, with enough flour for a thin muffin-batter; dip each piece in this, and fry in hot lard or dripping. Or dip each in beaten egg, then in pounded cracker, before frying.

Souse is also good eaten cold, especially the feet.

HEAD CHEESE. (OR SOUSE.)

This is made of the head, ears and tongue. Boil them in salted water until very tender. Strip the meat from the bones and chop fine. Season with salt, pepper, sage, sweet marjoram, a little powdered cloves, and half a cup of strong vinegar. Mix all together thoroughly, taste to see that it is flavored sufficiently, remembering that the spice tends to keep it, and pack hard in moulds or bowls, interspersing the layers with bits of the tongue cut in oblongs, squares and triangles not less than an inch in length. Press down and keep the meat in shape by putting a plate on the top of each mould (first wetting the plate) and a weight upon this. In two days the cheese will be ready for use. Turn out from the shapes as you wish to use it; or, should you desire to keep it several weeks, take the cheese from the moulds and immerse in cold vinegar in stone jars. This will preserve it admirably, and you have only to pare away the outside, should it be too acid for your taste.

This is generally eaten cold for tea, with vinegar and mustard; but it is very nice cut in slices, seasoned slightly with mustard, and warmed in a frying-pan with enough butter to prevent burning. Or, you may dip in beaten egg, then cracker-crumbs, and fry for breakfast.

If the tongue is arranged judiciously the slices will be prettily marbled.

PORK POT-PIE.

You can make this of lean pork cut from any part of the pig, but the chine is best. Crack the bones well, and cut up the chine into *riblettes* two inches long. Line your pot, which should be round at the bottom and well greased, with a good light paste; put in the meat, then a layer of parboiled potatoes, split in half, seasoning with pepper and salt as you go on. When the pot is nearly full, pour in a quart of cold water and put on the upper crust, cutting a small round hole out of the middle, through which you can add hot water should the gravy boil away too fast. Slips of paste may also be strewed among the meat and potatoes. Put on the pot-lid, and boil from one hour and a half to two hours. When done, remove the upper crust carefully, turn out the meat and gravy into a bowl, that you may get at the lower. Lay this upon a hot dish, put the meat, etc., in order upon it, pour the gravy over it, and cover with the top crust. This can be browned with a red-hot shovel, or oven-lid.

CHESHIRE PORK-PIE.

Cut two or three pounds of lean fresh pork into strips as long and as wide as your middle finger. Line a buttered dish with puff-paste; put in a layer of pork seasoned with pepper, salt, and nutmeg or mace; next a layer of juicy apples, sliced and covered with about an ounce of white sugar; then more pork, and so on until you are ready for the paste cover, when pour in half a pint of sweet cider or wine, and stick bits of butter all over the top. Cover with a thick lid of puff-paste, cut a slit in the top, brush over with beaten egg, and bake an hour and a half.

This is an English dish, and is famous in the region from which it takes its name. It is much liked by those who have tried it, and is considered by some to be equal to our mince-pie.

Yorkshire pork-pie is made in the same way, with the omission of the apples, sugar, and nutmeg, and the addition of sage to the seasoning.

SAUSAGE (*No. 1*).

- 6 lbs. lean fresh pork.
- 3 lbs. fat fresh pork.
- 12 teaspoonfuls powdered sage.
- 6 teaspoonfuls black pepper.
- 6 teaspoonfuls salt.
- 2 teaspoonfuls powdered mace.
- 2 teaspoonfuls powdered cloves.
- 1 grated nutmeg.

Grind the meat, fat and lean, in a sausage-mill, or chop it very fine. The mill is better, and the grinding does not occupy one-tenth of the time that chopping does, to say nothing of the labor. One can be bought for three or four dollars, and will well repay the purchaser. Mix the seasoning in with your hands, taste to be sure all is right, and pack down in stone jars, pouring melted lard on top. Another good way of preserving them is, to make long, narrow bags of stout muslin, large enough to contain, each, enough sausage for a family dish. Fill these with the meat, dip in melted lard, and hang from the beams of the cellar.

If you wish to pack in the intestines of the hog, they should be carefully prepared as follows: Empty them, cut them in lengths, and lay for two days in salt and water. Turn them inside out, and lay in soak one day longer. Scrape them, rinse well in soda and water, wipe, and blow into one end, having tied up the other with a bit of twine. If they are whole and clear, stuff with the meat; tie up and hang in the store-room or cellar.

These are fried in the cases, in a clean, dry frying-pan, until brown. If you have the sausage-meat in bulk, make into small, round flat cakes, and fry in the same way. Some dip in egg and pounded cracker—others roll in flour before cooking. Their own fat will cook them. Send to table dry and hot, but do not let them fry hard. When one side is done, turn the other. The fire should be very brisk. Ten minutes, or twelve at the outside, is long enough to cook them.

SAUSAGE (*No. 2.*)

- 4 lbs. pork, lean.
- 1½ lbs. pork, fat.
- 10 teaspoonfuls sage.
- 5 teaspoonfuls pepper.
- 5 teaspoonfuls salt.

Grind and season as directed in No. 1.

This will not keep so long as that made according to the former receipt, but is very good for immediate family use.

SAUSAGE (*No. 3.*)

- 2 lbs. lean pork.
- 2 lbs. lean veal.
- 2 lbs. beef suet.
- Peel of half a lemon.

- 1 grated nutmeg.

- 1 teaspoonful black pepper.

- 1 teaspoonful cayenne.

- 5 teaspoonfuls salt.

- 3 teaspoonfuls sweet marjoram and thyme, mixed.

- 2 teaspoonfuls of sage.

- Juice of a lemon.

Stuff in cases. This is very fine.

BOLOGNA SAUSAGE (*Uncooked.*)

- 6 lbs. lean pork.

- 3 lbs. lean beef.

- 2 lbs. beef suet.

- 4 ounces salt.

- 6 tablespoonfuls black pepper.

- 3 tablespoonfuls cayenne.

- 2 teaspoonfuls powdered cloves.

- 1 teaspoonful allspice.

- One minced onion, very finely chopped.

Chop or grind the meat, and mix the seasoning well through it. Pack it in beef-skins (or entrails) prepared as you do those of pork. In the city, you can have these cleaned by your butcher, or get them ready for use from a pork merchant. Tie both ends tightly, and lay them in brine strong enough to bear up an egg. Let them be in this for a week; change the brine, and let them remain in this a week longer. Turn them over every day of the fortnight. Then take them out, wipe them, and send them to be smoked, if you have no smoke-house of your own. When well smoked, rub them over with sweet oil or fresh butter, and hang them in a cool, dark place.

Bologna sausage is sometimes eaten raw, but the dread of the fatal *trichinæ* should put at end to this practice, did not common sense teach us that it must be unwholesome, no less than disgusting. Cut in round, thick slices, and toast on a gridiron, or fry in their own fat. If you mean to keep it some time, rub over the skins with pepper to keep away insects.

BOLOGNA SAUSAGE (*Cooked.*)

- 2 lbs. lean beef.
- 2 lbs. lean veal.
- 2 lbs. lean pork
- 2 lbs. *fat* salt pork—not smoked.
- 1 lb. beef suet
- 10 teaspoonfuls powdered sage.
- 1 oz. marjoram, parsley, savory, and thyme, mixed.
- 2 teaspoonfuls cayenne pepper, and the same of black.
- 1 grated nutmeg.
- 1 teaspoonful cloves.
- 1 minced onion.
- Salt to taste.

Chop or grind the meat and suet; season, and stuff into beef-skins; tie these up; prick each in several places to allow the escape of the steam; put into hot—not boiling water, and heat gradually to the boiling-point. Cook slowly for one hour; take out the skins and lay them to dry in the sun, upon clean, sweet straw or hay. Rub the outside of the skins with oil or melted butter, and hang in a cool, dry cellar. If you mean to keep it more than a week, rub pepper or powdered ginger upon the outside. You can wash it off before sending to table. This is eaten without further cooking. Cut in round slices, and lay sliced lemon around the edge of the dish, as many like to squeeze a few drops upon the sausage before eating.

LARD.

Every housekeeper knows how unfit for really nice cooking is the pressed lard sold in stores as the "best and cheapest." It is close and tough, melts slowly, and is sometimes diversified by fibrous lumps. And even when lard has been "tried out" by the usual process, it is often mixed with so much water as to remind us unpleasantly that it is bought by weight.

The best way of preparing the "leaf lard," as it is called, is to skin it carefully, wash, and let it drain; then put it, cut into bits, into a large, clean tin kettle or bucket, and set this in a pot of boiling water. Stir from time to time until it is melted; throw in a very little salt, to make the sediment settle; and when it is hot—(it should not boil fast at any time, but simmer gently until clear)—strain through a close cloth into jars. Do not squeeze the cloth so long as the clear fat will run through, and when you do, press the refuse into a different vessel, to be used for commoner purposes than the other.

Most of the lard in general use is, however, made from the fatty portions of pork lying next the skin of the hog, and are left for this purpose by the butcher. Scrape from the rind, and cut all into dice. Fill a large pot, putting in a teacupful of water to prevent scorching, and melt very slowly, stirring every few minutes. Simmer until there remains nothing of the meat but fibrous bits. Remove these carefully with a perforated skimmer; throw in a little salt, to settle the fat, and when it is clear strain through a fine cullender, a sieve, or a coarse cloth. Dip the latter in boiling water, should it become clogged by the cooling lard. Observe the directions about squeezing the strainer. If your family is small, bear in mind that the lard keeps longer in small than large vessels. Set away the jars, closely covered, in a cool, dry cellar or store-room.

In trying out lard, the chief danger is of burning. Simmer gently over a steady fire, and give it your whole attention until it is done. A moment's neglect will ruin all. Stir very often—almost constantly at the last—and from the bottom, until the salt is thrown in to settle it, when withdraw to a less hot part of the fire. Bladders tied over lard jars are the best protection; next to these, paper, and outside of this, cloths dipped in melted grease.

BRAWN (No. 1.)

- Pig's head weighing 6 lbs.

- 1 lb. lean beef.

- 1 teaspoonful salt.

- ½ teaspoonful pepper (black or white).

- ½ teaspoonful cayenne pepper.

- ½ teaspoonful mace.

- A pinch of cloves.

- A small onion minced very fine.

Clean and wash the head, and stew with the beef in enough cold water to cover. When the bones will slip out easily, remove them, after draining off the liquor. Chop the meat finely while it is hot, season, and pour all into a mould, wet inside with cold water. If you can have a tin mould made in the shape of a boar's head, your brawn will look well at a Christmas feast.

BRAWN (No. 2.)

- Pig's head, feet, and ears.

- ½ teaspoonful of black pepper, and same of cayenne.

- 4 teaspoonfuls powdered sage.

- 1 teaspoonful mace.

- An onion minced.

- Salt and saltpetre.

Soak the head twelve hours, and lay in a strong brine, with a tablespoonful of saltpetre. Let it lie three days in this; rinse; then boil it until you can draw out the bones. Do this very carefully from the back and under-side of the head, breaking the outline of the top as little as possible. Chop the meat of the feet and ears, which should have been boiled with the head, season to taste with the spices I have indicated (tastes vary in these matters), beat in the brains, or two tablespoonfuls of melted butter. Fill up the hollows left by the removal of the bones with this mixture. Tie in a flannel cloth, sewing this tightly into the shape of the head; boil an hour and a quarter, and set aside to drain and cool. Do not remove the cloth until next day. This will be found very nice.

SAVELOYS.

- 8 lbs. pork.
- 4 teaspoonfuls black pepper.
- 1 teaspoonful cayenne.
- 1 teaspoonful cloves or mace.
- 8 teaspoonfuls sage, sweet marjoram, and thyme, mixed.
- 1 teacupful bread-crumbs.

Lay the meat, which should be young pork, in a brine of salt and water, with a tablespoonful of saltpetre, and leave it for three days. Dry and mince it, season, and add the grated bread. Stuff in skins, and bake, closely covered, in an oven for half an hour. Or, what is better, steam over boiling water one hour.

Eat either hot or cold.

TO PICKLE PORK. (NO. 1.)

Hams, shoulders, chines, and "middlings," are the parts of the hog which are usually pickled. This should be done as soon as may be after the meat is fairly cold—especially in moderate weather. When you can pack down pork, within twenty-four hours after butchering, it is best to do so, unless the cold be severe enough to preserve it longer.

- 4½ lbs. salt.
- 1 lb. brown sugar.
- 1 oz. saltpetre in 3 gallons of water.

Put into a large saucepan and boil for half an hour, skimming off the scum. When cold, pour over the meat, and let it lie for a few days.

This is intended to corn a small quantity of meat for family use.

(NO. 2.)

- 80 lbs. of meat.

- 2 quarts and 1 pint of fine salt.

- 4 lbs. sugar, or 1 quart best molasses.

- 3 oz. saltpetre.

Pulverize and mix the seasoning, with the exception of the two quarts of salt, using the one pint only. Rub the meat *well* all over, and lay upon boards on the cellar-floor for twenty-four hours. Then, put a few clean stones in the bottom of a barrel; lay sticks across these, that the meat may not soak in the liquor that drains from it. Pack the meat in layers, strewing between these the remaining two quarts of salt. Let it lie in the cask for fifteen or sixteen days, every day during this time tipping the cask to drain off the liquor, or drawing it through a bung-hole near the bottom. Pour this back in cupfuls over the meat.

If you do not mean to smoke the meat, take it out at the end of the fortnight, rub each piece well over with dry salt, and return to the barrel. If the liquor does not cover it, make fresh brine in the proportion of two pounds of salt, a quarter of an ounce of saltpetre, and a quart of water, and pour in when you have boiled it half an hour and let it cool. Lay a round piece of board upon the upper layer and keep this down with stones. Examine from time to time, to be sure the meat is keeping well. Should it seem likely to taint, throw away the pickle, rub each piece over with dry salt, and pack anew. Pork pickled in this way will keep two years.

TO CURE HAMS.

Having pickled your hams with the rest of your pork as just directed, take them, after the lapse of sixteen days, from the packing barrel, with the shoulders and jowls. At the South they empty the cask, and consign the "whole hog" to the smoke-house. Wash off the pickle, and, while wet, dip in bran. Some use saw-dust, but it is not so good. Others use neither, only wipe the meat dry and smoke. The object in dipping in bran or saw-dust is to form a crust which prevents the evaporation of the juices. Be sure that it is well covered with the bran, then hang in the smoke, the hock end downward. Keep up a good smoke, by having the fire partially smothered with hickory chips and saw dust, for four weeks, taking care the house does not become hot. Take down the meat, brush off the bran, examine closely, and if you suspect insects, lay it in the hot sun for a day or two.

The various ways of keeping hams—each strongly recommended by those who have practised it—are too numerous to mention here. Some pack in wood ashes; others, in dry oats; others, in bran. But the best authorities discard packing altogether. I will name one or two methods which I know have been successful. "I hang mine on hooks from wires, at the top of my granary, which is tight and dark," says an excellent judge and manufacturer of hams. "They are good and sweet when a year old." Another admirable housekeeper covers with brown paper, then with coarse muslin stitched tightly and fitting closely, then whitewashes. But for the paper, the lime would be apt to eat away the grease. Still another covers with muslin, and coats with a mixture of bees-wax and rosin. There is no doubt that the covers are an excellent precaution—provided always, that the insects have not already deposited their eggs in the meat. The bran coating tends to prevent this.

I have eaten ham twenty years old in Virginia, which had been kept sweet in *slaked* ashes. Unslaked will act like lime upon the fat.

BOILED HAM.

Soak in water over night. Next morning wash hard with a coarse cloth or stiff brush, and put on to boil with plenty of cold water. Allow a quarter of an hour to each pound in cooking, and do not boil too fast. Do not remove the skin until cold; it will come off easily and cleanly then, and the juices are better preserved than when it is stripped hot. Send to table with dots of pepper or dry mustard on the top, a tuft of fringed paper twisted about the shank, and garnish with parsley.

Cut very thin in carving.

GLAZED HAM. ✠

Brush the ham—a cold boiled one, from which the skin has been taken—well, all over with beaten egg. To a cup of powdered cracker allow enough rich milk or cream to make into a thick paste, salt, and work in a teaspoonful of melted butter. Spread this evenly a quarter of an inch thick over the ham, and set to brown in a moderate oven.

STEAMED HAM.

This is by far the best way of cooking a ham. Lay in cold water for twelve hours; wash very thoroughly, rubbing with a stiff brush, to dislodge the salt and smoke on the outside. Put into a steamer, cover closely, and set it over a pot of boiling water. Allow at least twenty minutes to a pound. Keep the water at a hard boil.

If you serve ham hot, skin, and immediately strew thickly with cracker or bread-crumbs, to prevent the waste of the essence. Put a frill of paper about the knuckle. Send around cabbage or other green vegetables with it.

BAKED HAM.

Soak for twelve hours. Trim away the rusty part from the under side and edges, wipe very dry, cover the bottom with a paste made of flour and hot water, and lay it upside down in the dripping-pan, with water enough to keep it from burning. Bake five hours, or allow fully twenty-five minutes to a pound. Baste now and then, to prevent the crust from cracking and scaling off. When done, peel off this and the skin, and glaze as you would a cold ham.

Put cut paper about the knuckle, and garnish with parsley and sliced red beet—pickled.

ROAST HAM.

Soak for two days in lukewarm water, changing at least six times a day. Take it out, wash very well, scrubbing the under part hard, and trimming away the black and rusty edges. Skin with care, lest you mangle the meat and spoil the symmetry of the shape. Lay in a dish and sponge with a cloth dipped in a mixture of wine, vinegar, sugar, and mustard—about a tablespoonful of white sugar, a saltspoonful of made mustard, and a glass of wine to half a gill of vinegar. Do this at intervals of an hour, washing every part of the ham well, all day and until bed-time. Renew the process next morning until six hours before you need the meat. Put it upon the spit or in the dripping-pan, with a cup of hot water to prevent burning. Add to the mixture—or what is left of it in the dish—a cupful of boiling water. Keep this on the stove and baste continually with it until the liquor flows freely from the ham as it cooks; then substitute the gravy. When done (you must test with a fork), cover with cracker-crumbs, worked to a paste with milk, butter, and a beaten egg, and return to the oven to brown.

Skim the gravy; add a glass of good wine, a tablespoonful of catsup,—walnut, if you have it,—the juice of a lemon, and a little nutmeg. Boil up, and send to table in a boat.

Troublesome as the mode of cooking it may seem, roast ham is so delicious—especially when cold—as fully to recompense the housekeeper who may be tempted to try it.

BROILED HAM.

Cut in slices. Wash well, and soak in scalding water in a covered vessel for half an hour. Pour off the water, and add more boiling water. Wipe dry when the ham has stood half an hour in the second water, and lay in cold for five minutes. Wipe again and broil over (or under) a clear fire.

Cold boiled ham, that is not too much done, is better for broiling than raw. Pepper before serving.

BARBECUED HAM. ✠

If your ham is raw, soak as above directed; then lay the slices flat in a frying-pan; pepper each and lay upon it a quarter of a teaspoonful of made mustard. Pour about them some vinegar, allowing half a teaspoonful to each slice. Fry quickly and turn often. When done to a fine brown, transfer to a hot dish: add to the gravy in the pan half a glass of wine and a very small teaspoonful of white sugar. Boil up and pour over the meat.

Underdone ham is nice barbecued.

FRIED HAM.

If raw, soak as for broiling. Cook in a hot frying-pan turning often until done. Serve with or without the gravy, as you please. In some parts of the country it is customary to take the meat first from the pan, and add to the gravy a little cream, then thicken with flour. Boil up once and pour over the ham. A little chopped parsley is a pleasant addition to this gravy.

Or,

You may dip some slices of cold boiled ham—cut rather thick—in beaten egg, then in cracker-crumbs, and fry them in fat extracted from some bits of salt pork. Take the dry fried pork from the pan before putting in the ham. Garnish with crisped parsley.

HAM SANDWICHES.

Cut some slices of bread in a neat shape, and trim off the crust, unless it is very tender. Butter them and lay between every two some thin slices of cold boiled ham. Spread the meat with a little mustard if you like.

Ground ham makes delicious sandwiches. Cut the bread very thin, and butter well. Put in a good layer of ham, and press the two sides of the sandwiches firmly, but gently, together. Then roll lengthwise, and pile in a plate or basket.

HAM AND CHICKEN SANDWICHES.

Mince some cold roast chicken, and a like quantity of cold boiled ham. Put the mixture into a saucepan, with enough gravy—chicken or veal—to make a soft paste. If you have no gravy, use a little hot water, a few spoonfuls of cream, and a fair lump of butter. Season with pepper to your taste. Stir while it heats almost to boiling, working it very smooth. In about five minutes after it begins to smoke, take from the fire and spread in a dish to cool. With a good-sized cake-cutter, or a plain thin-edged tumbler, cut some rounds of cold bread, and butter one side of each. Sprinkle the buttered sides with grated cheese, and, when the chicken is cold, put a layer between these.

These sandwiches are simple and very good.

HAM AND CHICKEN PIE.

Cut up and parboil a tender young chicken—a year old is best. Line a deep dish with a good pie-crust. Cut some thin slices of cold boiled ham, and spread a layer next the crust; then arrange pieces of the fowl upon the ham. Cover this, in turn, with slices of hard-boiled eggs, buttered and peppered. Proceed in this order until your materials are used up. Then pour in enough veal or chicken gravy to prevent dryness. Unless you have put in too much water for the size of the fowl, the liquor in which the chicken was boiled is best for this purpose. Bake one hour and a quarter for a large pie.

HAM AND EGGS.

Cut your slices of ham of a uniform size and shape. Fry quickly, and take them out of the pan as soon as they are done. Have the eggs ready, and drop them, one at a time, in the hissing fat. Have a large pan for this purpose, that they may not touch and run together. In three minutes they will be done. The meat should be kept hot, and when the eggs are ready, lay one upon each slice of ham, which should have been cut the proper size for this. Do not use the gravy.

PORK AND BEANS.

Parboil a piece of the middling of salt pork, and score the skin. Allow a pound to a quart of dried beans, which must be soaked over night in lukewarm water. Change this twice for more and warmer water, and in the morning put them on to boil in cold. When they are soft, drain off the liquor, put the beans in a deep dish, and half-bury the pork in the middle, adding a very little warm water. Bake a nice brown.

This is a favorite dish with New England farmers and many others. Although old-fashioned, it still makes its weekly appearance upon the tables of hundreds of well-to-do families.

PORK AND PEAS PUDDING.

Soak the pork, which should not be a fat piece, over night in cold water; and in another pan a quart of dried split peas. In the morning put on the peas to boil slowly until tender. Drain and rub through a cullender; season with pepper and salt, and mix with them two tablespoonfuls of butter and two beaten eggs. Beat all well together. Have ready a floured pudding-cloth, and put the pudding into it. Tie it up, leaving room for swelling; put on in warm, not hot water, with the pork, and boil them together an hour. Lay the pork in the centre of the dish, turn out the pudding, slice and arrange about the meat.

COMPANY

LAYING to your conduct the line and plummet of the Golden Rule, never pay a visit (I use the word in contradistinction to "call") without notifying your hostess-elect of your intention thus to favor her.

Perhaps once in ten thousand times, your friend—be she mother, sister, or intimate acquaintance—may be enraptured at your unexpected appearance, travelling-satchel in hand, at her door, to pass a day, a night, or a month; or may be pleasantly surprised when you take the baby, and run in to tea in a social way. But the chances are so greatly in favor of the probability that you will upset her household arrangements, abrade her temper, or put her to undue trouble or embarrassment, by this evidence of your wish to have her feel quite easy with you, to treat you as one of the family, that it is hardly worth your while to risk so much in order to gain so little.

Mrs. Partington has said more silly things than any other woman of her age in this country; but she spoke wisely in declaring her preference for those surprise-parties "when people sent word they were coming." Do not be ashamed to say to your nearest kin, or the confidante of your school-days—"Always let me know when to look for you, that I may so order my time and engagements as to secure the greatest possible pleasure from your visit." If you are the woman I take you to be—methodical, industrious, and ruling your household according to just and firm laws of order and punctuality, you need this notice. If you are likewise social and hospitable, your rules are made with reference to possible and desirable interruptions of this nature. It only requires a little closer packing of certain duties, an easy exchange of times and seasons, and leisure is obtained for the right enjoyment of your friend's society. The additional place is set at table; your spare bed, which yesterday was tossed into a heap that both mattresses might be aired, and covered lightly with a thin spread, is made up with fresh sheets that have not gathered damp and must from lying packed beneath blankets and coverlets for may be a month, for fear somebody might happen in to pass the night, and catch you with the bed in disorder. Towels and water are ready; the room is bright and dustless; the dainty dish so far prepared for dinner or tea as to be like Mrs. Bagnet's greens, "off your mind;" John knows whom he is to see at his home-coming; the children are clean, and on the *qui vive*—children's instincts are always hospitable. The guest's welcome is half given in the air of the house and the family group before you have time to utter a word. It may have appeared to her a useless formality to despatch the note or telegram you insisted upon. She knows you love her, and she would be wounded by the thought that she could ever "come amiss" to your home. Perhaps, as she lays aside her travelling-dress, she smiles at your "ceremonious, old-maidish ways," and marvels that so good a manager should deem such forms necessary with an old friend.

If she had driven to your house at nightfall, to discover that you had gone with husband and children to pass several days with John's mother, in a town fifty miles away, and that the servants were out "a-pleasuring" in the mistress' absence; if she had found you at home, nursing three children through the measles, she having brought her youngest with her; if you were yourself the invalid, bound hand and foot to a Procrustean couch, and utterly unable even to see her—John, meanwhile, being incapacitated from playing the part of agreeable host by worry and anxiety; if, on the day before her arrival, your chambermaid had gone off in a "tiff," leaving you to do her work and to nurse your cook, sick in the third story; if earlier comers than herself had filled every spare mattress in the house;—if any one of these, or a dozen other ills to which housekeepers are heirs, had impressed upon her the idea that her visit was inopportune, she might think better of your "punctilio."

But since unlooked-for visitors will occasionally drop in upon the best regulated families, make it your study to receive them gracefully and cordially. If they care enough for you to turn aside from their regular route to tarry a day, or night, or week with you, it would be churlish not to show appreciation of the favor in which you are held. Make them welcome to the best you can offer at so short a notice, and let no preoccupied air or troubled smile bear token to your perturbation—if you are perturbed. If you respect yourself and your husband, the appointments of your table will never put you to the blush. John, who buys the silver, glass, china, and napery, is entitled to the every-day use of the best. You may have—I hope this is so—a holiday set of each, put away beyond the reach of hourly accidents; but if this is fit for the use of a lord, do not make John eat three hundred and sixty days in the year from such ware as would suit a ditcher's cottage. If your children never see bright silver unless when "there is company," you cannot wonder, although you will be mortified, at their making looking-glasses of the bowls of the spoons, and handling the forks awkwardly. Early impress upon them that what is nice enough for Papa, is nice enough for the President. I have noticed that where there is a wide difference between family and company table furniture, there usually exists a corresponding disparity between every-day and company manners.

Especially, let your welcome be ready and hearty when your husband brings home an unexpected guest. Take care he understands clearly that this is his prerogative: that the rules by which you would govern the visits of your own sex are not applicable to his. Men rarely set seasons for their visits. They snatch an hour or two with an old chum or new friend out of the hurry of business life, as one stoops to pluck a stray violet from a dusty roadside. John must take his chances when he can get them. If he can walk home, arm in arm, with the school-fellow he has not seen before in ten years, not only fearlessly, but gladly, anticipatory of your pleasure at the sight of his; if, when the stranger is presented to you, you receive him as your friend because he is your husband's, and seat him to a family dinner, plain, but nicely served, and eaten in cheerfulness of heart; if the children are well-behaved, and your attire that of a lady who has not lost the desire to look her best in her husband's eyes—you have added to the links of steel that knit your husband's heart to you; increased his affectionate admiration for the best little woman in the world. Many a man has been driven to entertain his friends at hotels and club-rooms, because he dared not take them home without permission from the presiding officer of his household. The majority of healthy men have good appetites and are not disposed to be critical of an unpretending bill of fare. The chance guest of this sex is generally an agreeable addition to the family group, instead of *de trop*—always supposing him to be John's friend.

As to party and dinner-giving, your safest rule is to obey the usage of the community in which you live in minor points, letting common sense and your means guide you in essentials. Be chary of undertaking what you cannot carry through successfully. Pretension is the ruin of more entertainments than ignorance or lack of money. If you know how to give a large evening party (and think it a pleasant and remunerative investment of time and several hundred dollars)—if you understand the machinery of a handsome dinner-party, and can afford these luxuries, go forward bravely to success. But creep before you walk. Study established customs in the best managed houses you visit; take counsel with experienced friends; now and then make modest essays on your own responsibility, and, insensibly, these crumbs of wisdom will form into a comely loaf. There is no surer de-appetizer—to coin a word—to guests than a heated, over-fatigued, anxious hostess, who betrays her inexperience by nervous glances, abstraction in conversation, and, worst of all, by apologies.

A few general observations are all I purpose to offer as hints of a foundation upon which to build your plans for "company-giving." Have an abundance of clean plates, silver, knives, &c., laid in order in a convenient place,—such as an ante-room, or dining-room pantry,—those designed for each course, if your entertainment is a dinner, upon a shelf or stand by themselves, and make your waiters understand distinctly in advance in what order these are to be brought on.

Soup should be sent up accompanied only by bread, and such sauce as may be fashionable or suitable. Before dinner is served, however, snatch a moment, if possible, to inspect the table in person, or instruct a trustworthy factotum to see that everything is in place, the water in the goblets, a slice of bread laid upon a folded napkin at each plate, &c. Unless you have trained, professional waiters, this is a wise precaution. If it is a gentleman's dinner, you can see to it for yourself, since you will not be obliged to appear in the parlor until a few minutes before they are summoned to the dining-room. If there are ladies in the company, you must not leave them.

To return, then, to our soup: It is not customary to offer a second plateful to a guest. When the table is cleared, the fish should come in, with potatoes—no other vegetable, unless it be stewed tomatoes. After a thorough change of plates, &c., come the substantials. If possible, the carving of game and other meats is done before they are brought in. One or more vegetables are passed with each meat course. Salad is a course of itself, unless when it accompanies chicken or pigeon. If wine be used, it is introduced after the fish. Pastry is the first relay of dessert, and puddings may be served from the other end of the table. Next appear creams, jellies, charlotte-russes, cakes, and the like; then fruit and nuts; lastly, coffee, often accompanied with crackers and cheese. Wine, of course, goes around during the dessert—if it flows at all.

Evening parties are less troublesome to a housekeeper, because less ceremonious than dinners. If you can afford it, the easiest way to give a large one is to put the whole business into the hands of the profession, by intrusting your order, not only for supper, but waiters and china, to a competent confectioner. But a social standing supper of oysters, chicken-salad, sandwiches, coffee, ice-cream, jellies, and cake, is not a formidable undertaking when you have had a little practice, especially if your own, or John's mother, or the nice, neighborly matron over the way will assist you by her advice and presence. The "Ladies' Lunch" and afternoon "Kettle-Drum" are social and graceful "modern improvements."

We make this matter of company too hard a business in America; are too apt to treat our friends as the Strasburgers do their geese; shut them up in overheated quarters, and stuff them to repletion. Our rooms would be better for more air, our guests happier had they more liberty, and our hostess would be prettier and more sprightly were she not overworked before the arrivals begin, and full of trepidation after they come,—a woman cumbered with many thoughts of serving, while she is supposed to be enjoying the society of her chosen associates. It is so well understood that company is weariness, that inquiries as to how the principal agent in bringing about an assembly has "borne it," have passed into a custom. The tender sympathies manifested in such queries, the martyr-like air with which they are answered, cannot fail to bring to the satirical mind the Chinaman's comment upon the British officers' dancing on shipboard in warm weather.

"Why you no make your servants do so hard work, and you look at dem?"

We pervert the very name and meaning of hospitality when we pinch our families, wear away our patience, and waste our nervous forces with our husbands' money in getting up to order expensive entertainments for comparative strangers, whose utmost acknowledgment of our efforts in their behalf will consist in an invitation, a year hence it may be, to a party constructed on the same plan, managed a little better or a little worse than ours. This is not hospitality without grudging, but a vulgar system of barter and gluttony more worthy of Abyssinians than Christian gentlefolk.

GAME

VENISON.

I ONCE received a letter from the wife of an Eastern man who had removed to the Great West, in which bitter complaints were made of the scarcity of certain comforts—ice-cream and candy among them—to which she had been accustomed in other days. "My husband shot a fine deer this morning," she wrote, "but I could never endure *venzon*. Can you tell me of any way of cooking it so as to make it tolerably eatible?" I did not think it very singular that one whose chief craving in the goodly land in which she had found a home was for cocoanut cakes and chocolate caramels, should not like the viand the name of which she could not spell. Nor did I wonder that she failed to make it "eatible," or doubt that her cooking matched her orthography. But I am amazed often at hearing really skilful housewives pronounce it an undesirable dish. In the hope of in some measure correcting this impression among Eastern cooks, who, it must be allowed, rarely taste really fresh venison, I have written out, with great care and particularity, the following receipts, most of which I have used in my own family with success and satisfaction.

The dark color of the meat,—I mean now not the black, but rich reddish-brown flesh,—so objectionable to the uninitiated, is to the gourmand one of its chief recommendations to his favor. It should also be fine of grain and well coated with fat.

Keep it hung up in a cool, dark cellar, covered with a cloth, and use as soon as you can conveniently.

HAUNCH OF VENISON. ✠

If the outside be hard, wash off with lukewarm water; then rub all over with fresh butter or lard. Cover it on the top and sides with a thick paste of flour and water, nearly half an inch thick. Lay upon this a large sheet of thin white wrapping-paper well buttered, and above this thick foolscap. Keep all in place by greased pack-thread, then put down to roast with a little water in the dripping-pan. Let the fire be steady and strong. Pour a few ladlefuls of butter and water over the meat now and then, to prevent the paper from scorching. If the haunch is large, it will take at least five hours to roast. About half an hour before you take it up, remove the papers and paste, and test with a skewer to see if it is done. If this passes easily to the bone through the thickest part, set it down to a more moderate fire and baste every few minutes with Claret and melted butter. At the last, baste with butter, dredge with flour to make a light froth, and dish. It should be a fine brown by this time. Twist a frill of fringed paper around the knuckle.

For gravy, put into a saucepan a pound or so of scraps of raw venison left from trimming the haunch, a quart of water, a pinch of cloves, a few blades of mace, half a nutmeg, cayenne and salt to taste. Stew slowly to one-half the original quantity. Skim, strain, and return to the saucepan when you have rinsed it with hot water. Add three tablespoonfuls of currant jelly, a glass of claret, two tablespoonfuls of butter, and thicken with browned flour. Send to table in a tureen.

Send around currant jelly with venison *always*.

NECK.

This is roasted precisely as is the haunch, allowing a quarter of an hour to a pound.

SHOULDER.

This is also a roasting-piece, but may be cooked without the paste and paper. Baste often with butter and water, and toward the last, with Claret and butter. Do not let it get dry for an instant.

TO STEW A SHOULDER,

Extract the bones through the under-side. Make a stuffing of several slices of fat mutton, minced fine and seasoned smartly with cayenne, salt, allspice, and wine, and fill the holes from which the bones were taken. Bind firmly in shape with broad tape. Put in a large saucepan with a pint of gravy made from the refuse bits of venison; add a glass of Madeira or Port wine, and a little black pepper. Cover tightly, and stew very slowly three or four hours, according to the size. It should be very tender. Remove the tapes with care; dish, and when you have strained the gravy, pour over the meat.

This is a most savory dish.

VENISON STEAKS. ✠

These are taken from the neck or haunch. Have your gridiron well buttered, and fire clear and hot. Lay the steaks on the bars and broil rapidly, turning often, not to lose a drop of juice. They will take three or four minutes longer to broil than beef-steaks. Have ready in a hot chafing-dish a piece of butter the size of an egg for each pound of venison, a pinch of salt, a little pepper, a tablespoonful currant-jelly for each pound, and a glass of wine for every four pounds. This should be liquid, and warmed by the boiling water under the dish by the time the steaks are done to a turn. If you have no chafing-dish, heat in a saucepan. Lay each steak in the mixture singly, and turn over twice. Cover closely and let all heat together, with fresh hot water beneath—unless your lamp is burning—for five minutes before serving. If you serve in an ordinary dish, cover and set in the oven for the same time.

Or,

If you wish a plainer dish, omit the wine and jelly; pepper and salt the steaks when broiled, and lay butter upon them in the proportion I have stated, letting them stand between hot dishes five minutes before they go to table, turning them three times in the gravy that runs from them to mingle with the melted butter. Delicious steaks corresponding to the shape of mutton chops are cut from the loin and rack.

VENISON CUTLETS. ✠

Trim the cutlets nicely, and make gravy of the refuse bits in the proportion of a cup of cold water to half a pound of venison. Put in bones, scraps of fat, etc., and set on in a saucepan to stew while you make ready the cutlets. Lard with slips of fat salt pork a quarter of an inch apart, and projecting slightly on either side. When the gravy has stewed an hour, strain and let it cool. Lay the cutlets in a saucepan, with a few pieces of young onion on each. Allow one onion to four or five pounds. It should not be flavored strongly with this. Scatter also a little minced parsley and thyme between the layers of meat, with pepper, and a very little nutmeg. The pork lardoons will salt sufficiently. When you have put in all your meat, pour in the gravy, which should be warm—not hot. Stew steadily twenty minutes, take up the cutlets and lay in a frying-pan in which you have heated just enough butter to prevent them from burning. Fry five minutes very quickly, turning the cutlets over and over to brown, without drying them. Lay in order in a chafing-dish, and have ready the gravy to pour over them without delay. This should be done by straining the liquor left in the saucepan and returning to the fire, with the addition of a tablespoonful of currant jelly, a teaspoonful Worcestershire or other piquant sauce, and half a glass of wine. Thicken with browned flour, boil up well and pour over the cutlets. Let all stand together in a hot dish five minutes before serving. Venison which is not fat or juicy enough for roasting makes a relishable dish cooked after this receipt.

HASHED VENISON. ✠

The remains of cold roast venison—especially a stuffed shoulder—may be used for this dish, and will give great satisfaction to cook and consumers. Slice the meat from the bones. Put these with the fat and other scraps in a saucepan, with a large teacupful of cold water, a small onion—one of the button kind, minced, parsley and thyme, pepper and salt, and three or four whole cloves. Stew for an hour. Strain and return to the saucepan, with whatever gravy was left from the roast, a tablespoonful currant jelly, one of tomato or mushroom catsup, a teaspoonful of anchovy sauce, and a little browned flour. Boil for three minutes; lay in the venison, cut into slices about an inch long, and let all heat over the fire for eight minutes, but do not allow the hash to boil. Stir frequently, and when it is smoking hot, turn into a deep-covered dish.

ROAST FAWN.

Clean, wash thoroughly; stuff with a good force-meat made of bread-crumbs, chopped pork, pepper and salt, a little grated nutmeg, the juice of a lemon. Moisten with water and cream, bind with beaten egg and melted butter. Sew up the fawn, turning the legs under, and binding close to the body. Cover with thin slices of fat pork, bound on with pack-thread, crossing in every direction, and roast at a quick fire. Allow twenty-two minutes to a pound. Twenty minutes before it is dished, remove the pork, and set down the fawn to brown, basting with melted butter. At the last, dredge with flour, let this brown, froth with butter, and serve.

Garnish with abundance of curled parsley, dotted with drops of red currant jelly. A kid can be roasted in the same way—also hares and rabbits.

VENISON PASTY. ✠

This is a name dear to the heart of the Englishman since the days when Friar Tuck feasted the disguised Cœur de Lion upon it in the depths of Sherwood Forest, until the present generation. In this country it is comparatively little known; but I recommend it to those who have never yet been able to make venison "tolerably eatable."

Almost any part of the deer can be used for the purpose, but the neck and shoulders are generally preferred.

Cut the raw venison from the bones, and set aside these, with the skin, fat, and refuse bits, for gravy. Put them into a saucepan with a shallot, pepper, salt, nutmeg and sweet herbs, cover well with cold water, and set on to boil. Meanwhile, cut the better and fairer pieces of meat into squares an inch long, and cook in another saucepan until three-quarters done. Line a deep dish with good puff-paste. That for the lid should be made after the receipt appended to this. Put in the squares of venison, season with pepper, salt, and butter, and put in half a cupful of the liquor in which the meat was stewed, to keep it from burning at the bottom. Cover with a lid of the prepared pastry an inch thick. Cut a round hole in the middle, and if you have not a small tin cylinder that will fit this, make one of buttered paper; stiff writing-paper is best. The hole should be large enough to admit your thumb. Bake steadily, covering the top with a sheet of clean paper so soon as it is firm, to prevent it from browning too fast. While it is cooking prepare the gravy. When all the substance has been extracted from the bones, etc., strain the liquor back into the saucepan; let it come to a boil, and when you have skimmed carefully, add a glass of Port wine, a tablespoonful of butter, the juice of a lemon, and some browned flour to thicken. Boil up once, remove the plug from the hole in the pastry, and pour in through a small funnel, or a paper horn, as much gravy as the pie will hold. Do this very quickly; brush the crust over with beaten egg and put back in the oven until it is a delicate brown, or rather, a golden russet. The pie should only be drawn to the door of the oven for these operations, and everything should be in readiness before it is taken out, that the crust may be light and flaky. If you have more gravy than you need for the dish, serve in a tureen.

CRUST OF PASTY.

- 1½ lb. of flour.

- 12 oz. butter.

- Yolks of 3 eggs.

- Salt.

- Ice-water.

Dry and sift the flour and cut up half the butter in it with a knife or chopper until the whole is fine and yellow; salt, and work up with ice-water, lastly adding the yolks beaten very light. Work out rapidly, handling as little as possible, roll out three times *very* thin, basting with butter, then into a lid nearly an inch thick, reserving a thinner one for ornaments. Having covered in your pie, cut from the second sheet with a cake-cutter, leaves, flowers, stars, or any figures you like to adorn the top of your crust. Bake the handsomest one upon a tin plate by itself, and brush it over with egg when you glaze the pie. After the pasty is baked, cover the hole in the centre with this.

If these directions be closely followed the pasty will be delicious. Bake two or three hours, guiding yourself by the size of the pie. It is good hot or cold.

VENISON HAMS.

These are eaten raw, and will not keep so long as other smoked meats.

Mix together in equal proportions, salt and brown sugar, and rub them hard into the hams with your hand. Pack them in a cask, sprinkling dry salt between them, and let them lie eight days, rubbing them over every day with dry salt and sugar. Next mix equal parts of fine salt, molasses, and a teaspoonful of saltpetre to every two hams. Take the hams out of the pickle, go over them with a brush dipped in cider vinegar, then in the new mixture.

Empty the cask, wash it out with cold water, and repack the hams, dripping from the sticky bath, scattering fine salt over each. Let them lie eight days longer in this. Wash off the pickle first with tepid water, until the salt crystals are removed; then sponge with vinegar, powder them with bran while wet, and smoke a fortnight, or, if large, three weeks. Wrap in brown paper that has no unpleasant odor, stitch a muslin cover over this, and whitewash, unless you mean to use at once. Chip or shave for the table.

VENISON SAUSAGES.

- 5 lbs. lean venison.
- 2 lbs. fat salt pork.
- 5 teaspoonfuls powdered sage.
- 4 teaspoonfuls salt.
- 4 teaspoonfuls black pepper.
- 2 teaspoonfuls cayenne.
- 1 small onion.
- Juice of one lemon.

Chop the meat very small, season, and pack in skins or small stone jars. Hang the skins, and set the jars, tied down with bladders, in a cool, dry place.

Fry as you do other sausages.

RABBITS OR HARES.

The tame rabbit is rarely if ever eaten. The wild hare of the South—in vulgar parlance, "old hare," although the creature may be but a day old—exactly corresponds with the rabbit of the Northern fields, and when fat and tender may be made into a variety of excellent dishes.

Hares are unfit for eating in the early spring. There is thus much significance in "Mad as a March hare." The real English hare is a much larger animal than that which is known in this country by this name. To speak correctly, all our "old field hares" are wild rabbits.

ROAST RABBIT.

Clean, wash, and soak in water slightly salted for an hour and a half, changing it once during this time. It is best to make your butcher or hired man skin it before you undertake to handle it.

Afterward, the task is easy enough. Parboil the heart and liver, chop fine, and mix with a slice of fat pork, also minced. Make a force-meat of bread-crumbs, well seasoned, and working in the minced meat. Stuff the body with this, and sew it up. Rub with butter and roast, basting with butter and water until the gravy flows freely, then with the dripping. It should be done in an hour. Dredge with flour a few minutes before taking it up, then froth with butter. Lay in a hot dish, add to the gravy a little lemon-juice, a young onion minced, a tablespoonful of butter, and thicken with browned flour. Give it a boil up, and serve in a tureen or boat.

Garnish the rabbit with sliced lemon, and put a dot of currant jelly in the centre of each slice. Cut off the head before sending to table.

RABBITS STEWED WITH ONIONS.

Clean a pair of nice rabbits; soak in cold salt and water for an hour, to draw out the blood; put on in a large saucepan with cold water enough to cover them, salt slightly, and stew until tender. Slice into another pot half a dozen young onions, and boil in a very little water until thoroughly done. Drain off the water, and stir the onions into a gill of drawn butter, pepper to taste, and when it simmers, add the juice of a lemon. Cut off the heads of the hares, lay in a hot dish and pour over them the onion-sauce. Let the dish stand in a warm place, closely covered, five minutes before sending to table.

FRICASSEED RABBIT. (*White.*) ✠

Clean two young rabbits, cut into joints, and soak in salt and water an hour. Put into a saucepan with a pint of cold water, a bunch of sweet herbs, an onion finely minced, a pinch of mace, one of nutmeg, pepper, and half a pound of fat salt pork, cut into slips. Cover, and stew until tender. Take out the rabbits and set in a dish where they will keep warm. Add to the gravy a cup of cream (or milk), two well-beaten eggs stirred in a little at a time, and a tablespoonful of butter. Boil up once—when you have thickened with flour wet in cold milk—and take the saucepan from the fire. Squeeze in the juice of a lemon, stirring all the while, and pour over the rabbits. Do not cook the head or neck.

FRICASSEED RABBIT. (*Brown.*)

Cut off the head—joint, and lay in soak for an hour. Season the pieces with pepper and salt, dredge with flour, and fry in butter or nice dripping until brown. Take from the fat, lay in a saucepan, and cover with broth made of bits of veal or lamb. Add a minced onion, a great spoonful of walnut catsup, a bunch of sweet herbs, a pinch of cloves and one of allspice, half a teaspoonful of cayenne. Cover closely, and simmer for half an hour. Lay the pieces of hare in order upon a hot dish and cover to keep warm. Strain the gravy, return to the saucepan, thicken with browned flour, put in a tablespoonful of butter, squeeze in the juice of a lemon, pour over the rabbits, and send to table.

LARDED RABBIT.

Cut off the head and divide the body into joints. Lard with slips of fat pork; put into a clean hot frying-pan and fry until half done. Have ready some strained gravy made of veal or beef—the first is better; put the pieces of rabbit into a saucepan, with a bunch of sweet herbs, a minced onion, and some pepper. Stew, closely covered, half an hour, or until tender; take out the rabbits and lay in a hot covered dish. Strain the gravy, add a tablespoonful of butter, the juice of a lemon, and thicken with flour. Boil up and pour over the meat.

FRIED RABBIT.

They must be very tender for this purpose. Cut into joints; soak for an hour in salt and water; dip in beaten egg, then in powdered cracker, and fry brown in nice sweet lard or dripping. Serve with onion sauce. Garnish with sliced lemon.

BARBECUED RABBIT. ✠

Clean and wash the rabbit, which must be plump and young, and having opened it all the way on the under-side, lay it flat, with a small plate or saucer to keep it down, in salted water for half an hour. Wipe dry and broil whole, with the exception of the head, when you have gashed across the back-bone in eight or ten places that the heat may penetrate this, the thickest part. Your fire should be hot and clear, the rabbit turned often. When browned and tender, lay upon a very hot dish, pepper and salt and butter profusely, turning the rabbit over and over to soak up the melted butter. Cover and set in the oven for five minutes, and heat in a tin cup two tablespoonfuls of vinegar seasoned with one of made mustard. Anoint the hot rabbit well with this, cover and send to table garnished with crisped parsley.

The odor of this barbecue is most appetizing, and the taste not a whit inferior.

RABBIT PIE.

Cut a pair of rabbits into eight pieces each, soak in salted water half an hour, and stew until half done in enough water to cover them. Cut a quarter of a pound of fat pork into slips, and boil four eggs hard. Lay some bits of pork in the bottom of a deep dish and upon these a layer of the rabbit. Upon this spread slices of boiled egg, peppered and buttered. Sprinkle, moreover, with a little powdered mace, and squeeze a few drops of lemon-juice upon each piece of meat. Proceed in this order until the dish is full, the top layer being pork. Pour in the water in which the rabbit was boiled, when you have salted it and added some lumps of butter rolled in flour. Cover with puff-paste, cut a slit in the middle, and bake one hour, laying paper over the top should it brown too fast.

SQUIRRELS.

The large gray squirrel is seldom eaten at the North, but is in great request in Virginia and other Southern States. It is generally barbecued, precisely as are rabbits; broiled, fricasseed, or—most popular of all—made into a Brunswick stew. This is named from Brunswick County, Virginia, and is a famous dish—or was—at the political and social pic-nics known as barbecues. I am happy to be able to give a receipt for this stew that is genuine and explicit, and for which I am indebted to a Virginia housekeeper.

BRUNSWICK STEW. ✠

- 2 squirrels—3, if small.

- 1 quart of tomatoes—peeled and sliced.

- 1 pint butter-beans, or Lima.

- 6 potatoes—parboiled and sliced.

- 6 ears of green corn cut from the cob.

- ½ lb. butter.

- ½ lb. fat salt pork.

- 1 teaspoonful ground black pepper.

- Half a teaspoonful cayenne.

- 1 gallon water.

- 1 tablespoonful salt.

- 2 teaspoonfuls white sugar.

- 1 onion, minced small.

Put on the water with the salt in it, and boil five minutes. Put in the onion, beans, corn, pork or bacon cut into shreds, potatoes, pepper, and the squirrels, which must first be cut into joints and laid in cold salt and water to draw out the blood. Cover closely and stew two and a half hours very slowly, stirring frequently from the bottom. Then add the tomatoes and sugar, and stew an hour longer. Ten minutes before you take it from the fire add the butter, cut into bits the size of a walnut, rolled in flour. Give a final boil, taste to see that it is seasoned to your liking, and turn into a soup-tureen. It is eaten from soup-plates. Chickens may be substituted for squirrels.

RAGOÛT OF SQUIRRELS.

Skin, clean, and quarter a pair of fine young squirrels, and soak in salt and water to draw out the blood. Slice an onion and fry brown in a tablespoonful of butter. Stir into the frying-pan five tablespoonfuls of boiling water, and thicken with two teaspoonfuls of browned flour. Put the squirrels into a saucepan, with a quarter of a pound of bacon cut into slips; season with pepper and salt to taste, add the onion and gravy, and half a cupful of tepid water. Cover and stew for forty minutes, or until tender; pour in a glass of wine and the juice of half a lemon, shake around well, and turn into a deep covered dish.

BROILED SQUIRRELS.

Clean and soak to draw out the blood. Wipe dry and broil over a hot, clear fire, turning often. When done, lay in a hot dish and anoint with melted butter, seasoned with pepper and salt. Use at least a tablespoonful for each squirrel, and let it lie between two hot dishes five minutes before sending to table.

PHEASANTS, PARTRIDGES, QUAILS, GROUSE, ETC.

The real pheasant is never sold in American markets. The bird known as such at the South is called a partridge at the North, and is, properly speaking, the ruffled grouse. The Northern quail is the English and Southern partridge. The wild fowls brought by the hundred dozen from the Far West to Eastern cities, and generally styled prairie-fowls, are a species of grouse. The mode of cooking all these is substantially the same.

ROAST.

Clean, truss, and stuff as you do chickens; roast at a hot fire, and baste with butter and water until brown; sprinkle with salt, dredge lightly at the last with flour to froth the birds, and serve hot. Thicken the gravy with browned flour, boil up, and serve in a boat. Wash the inside of all game—prairie-fowls in particular— with soda and water, rinsing out carefully afterward with fair water.

BROILED.

Clean, wash, and split down the back. Lay in cold water half an hour. Wipe carefully, season with salt and pepper, and broil on a gridiron over a bright fire. When done, lay in a hot dish, butter on both sides well, and serve at once.

Broiled quails are delicious and nourishing fare for invalids.

GROUSE ROASTED WITH BACON. ✠

Clean, truss, and stuff as usual. Cover the entire bird with thin slices of corned ham or pork, binding all with buttered pack-thread. Roast three-quarters of an hour, basting with butter and water three times, then with the dripping. When quite done, dish with the ham laid about the body of the bird. Skim the gravy, thicken with browned flour, season with pepper and the juice of a lemon. Boil up once.

QUAILS ROASTED WITH HAM. ✠

Proceed as with the grouse, but cover the ham or pork with a sheet of white paper, having secured the slices of meat with pack thread. Stitch the papers on, and keep them well basted with butter and water, that they may not burn. Roast three quarters of an hour, if the fire is good. Remove the papers and meat before sending to table, and brown quickly. This is the nicest way of cooking quails.

SALMI OF GAME.

Cut cold roast partridges, grouse, or quails into joints, and lay aside while you prepare the gravy. This is made of the bones, dressing, skin, and general odds and ends, after you have selected the neatest pieces of the birds. Put these—the scraps—into a saucepan, with one small onion, minced, and a bunch of sweet herbs; pour in a pint of water, and whatever gravy you may have, and stew, closely covered, for nearly an hour. A few bits of pork should be added if you have no gravy. Skim and strain, return to the fire, and add a little brown Sherry and lemon-juice, with a pinch of nutmeg; thicken with brown flour, if the stuffing has not thickened it sufficiently, boil up, and pour over the reserved meat, which should be put into another saucepan. Warm until all is smoking-hot, but do not let it boil. Arrange the pieces of bird in a symmetrical heap upon a dish, and pour the gravy over them.

GAME PIE—(*Very fine*).

This may be made of any of the birds named in the foregoing receipts. Grouse and quails together make a delightful Christmas pie. Clean and wash the birds; cut the quails in half, the grouse into four pieces. Trim off bits of the inferior portions, necks, lower ribs, etc., and put them with the giblets into a saucepan, with a pint and a half of water, if your pie requires six birds. While this is stewing make a good puff-paste and line a large pudding-dish, reserving enough for a lid half an inch thick. When the livers are tender, take them out, leaving the gravy to stew in the covered saucepan. Lard the breasts of the birds with tiny strips of salt pork, and mince a couple of slices of the same with the livers, a bunch of parsley, sweet marjoram, and thyme, also chopped fine, the juice of a lemon, pepper, and a very small shallot. Make a force-meat of this, with bread-crumbs moistened with warm milk. Put some thin strips of cold corned (not smoked) ham in the bottom of the pie, next to the crust; lay upon these pieces of the bird, peppered and buttered, then a layer of the force-meat, and so on, until you are ready for the gravy. Strain this, return to the fire, and season with pepper and a glass of wine. Heat to a boil, pour into the pie, and cover with the upper crust, cutting a slit in the middle. Ornament with pastry leaves, arranged in a wreath about the edge, and in the middle a pastry bird, with curled strips of pastry about it. This last should be baked separately and laid on when the pie is done, to cover the hole in the middle.

Bake three hours if your pie be large, covering with paper if it threaten to brown too fast.

QUAIL PIE.

Clean, truss, and stuff the birds. Loosen the joints with a penknife, but do not separate them. Parboil them for ten minutes, while you prepare a puff-paste. Line a deep dish with this; put in the bottom some shreds of salt pork or ham; next, a layer of hard-boiled eggs, buttered and peppered; then the birds, sprinkled with pepper and minced parsley. Squeeze some lemon-juice upon them, and lay upon the breasts pieces of butter rolled in flour. Cover with slices of egg, then with shred ham; pour in some of the gravy in which the quails were parboiled, and put on the lid, leaving a hole in the middle. Bake over an hour.

WILD PIGEONS. (*Stewed.*) ✠

Clean and wash very carefully, then lay in salt and water for an hour. Rinse the inside with soda and water, shaking it well about in the cavity; wash out with fair water and stuff with a force-meat made of bread-crumbs and chopped salt pork, seasoned with pepper. Sew up the birds, and put on to stew in enough cold water to cover them, and allow to each a fair slice of fat bacon cut into narrow strips. Season with pepper and a pinch of nutmeg. Boil slowly in a covered saucepan until tender; take from the gravy and lay in a covered dish to keep warm. Strain the gravy, add the juice of a lemon and a tablespoonful of currant jelly, thickening with browned flour. Boil up and pour over the pigeons.

WILD-PIGEON PIE. ✠

This is made precisely as is quail pie, except that the pigeons are cut into four pieces each, and not stuffed. Parboil and lay in the dish in alternate layers with the bacon and boiled eggs. Make the gravy richer than for the quails, by the addition of a good lump of butter, rolled in flour, stirred in and boiled up to thicken before you put it on the fire. Wild pigeons are usually tougher and leaner than the tame.

WILD DUCKS.

Nearly all wild ducks are liable to have a fishy flavor, and when handled by inexperienced cooks, are sometimes uneatable from this cause. Before roasting them, guard against this by parboiling them with a small carrot, peeled, put within each. This will absorb the unpleasant taste. An onion will have the same effect; but, unless you mean to use onion in the stuffing, the carrot is preferable. In my own kitchen I usually put in the onion, considering a suspicion of garlic a desideratum in roast duck, whether wild or tame.

ROAST DUCK. (*Wild.*)

Parboil as above directed; throw away the carrot or onion, lay in fresh water half an hour; stuff with bread-crumbs seasoned with pepper, salt, sage, and onion, and roast until brown and tender, basting for half the time with butter and water, then with the drippings. Add to the gravy, when you have taken up the ducks, a tablespoonful of currant jelly, and a pinch of cayenne. Thicken with browned flour and serve in a tureen.

WILD DUCKS. (*Stewed.*) ✠

Parboil ten minutes, when you have drawn them, and put in a raw carrot or onion. Lay in very cold water half an hour. Cut into joints, pepper, salt, and flour them. Have ready some butter in a frying-pan, and fry them a light brown. Put them in a saucepan and cover with gravy made of the giblets, necks, and some bits of lean veal. Add a minced shallot, a bunch of sweet herbs, salt, and pepper. Cover closely and stew half an hour, or until tender. Take out the duck, strain the gravy when you have skimmed it; put in a half-cup of cream or rich milk in which an egg has been beaten, thicken with browned flour, add a tablespoonful of wine and the juice of half a lemon, beaten in gradually not to curdle the cream; boil up and pour over the ducks. This is about the best way of cooking wild ducks.

WILD TURKEY.

This stately stalker of Southern forests and Western prairies is eagerly sought after by the lovers of good eating in those regions. The dark meat and game flavor proclaim his birthright of lordly freedom as truly after he is slain and cooked, as did his lithe grace of figure, lofty carriage, and bright eye while he trod his native wilds. I have heard sportsmen declare that when they have inveigled him up to a blind by imitating the call of his harem or younglings, they have stood in covert, gun at shoulder and finger on the trigger, spell-bound by pitying admiration of his beauty. But I have never seen that sensibility curbed appetite while they told the story at the table adorned by the royal bird; have noted, indeed, that their mouths watered rather than their eyes, as he crumbled, like a dissolving view, under the blade of the carver.

Draw and wash the inside very carefully, as with all game. Domestic fowls are, or should be, kept up without eating for at least twelve hours before they are killed; but we must shoot wild when we can get the chance, and of course it often happens that their crops are distended by a recent hearty meal of rank or green food. Wipe the cavity with a dry soft cloth before you stuff. Have a rich force-meat, bread-crumbs, some bits of fat pork, chopped fine, pepper, and salt. Beat in an egg and a couple of tablespoonfuls of melted butter. Baste with butter and water for the first hour, then three or four times with the gravy; lastly, five or six times with melted butter. A generous and able housekeeper told me once that she always allowed a pound of butter for basting a large wild turkey. This was an extravagant quantity, but the meat is drier than that of the domestic fowl, and not nearly so fat. Dredge with flour at the last, froth with butter, and when he is of a tempting brown, serve. Skim the gravy, add a little hot water, pepper, thicken with the giblets chopped fine and browned flour, boil up, and pour into a tureen. At the South the giblets are not put in the gravy, but laid whole, one under each wing, when the turkey is dished. Garnish with small fried sausages, not larger than a dollar, crisped parsley between them.

Send around currant jelly and cranberry sauce with it.

SMALL BIRDS.

ROAST SNIPE OR PLOVERS.

Clean and truss, but do not stuff. Lay in rows in the dripping-pan, or tie upon a spit, sprinkle with salt, and baste well with butter, then with butter and water. When they begin to brown, which will be in about ten minutes, cut as many rounds of bread (without crust) as there are birds. Toast quickly, butter, and lay in the dripping-pan, a bird upon each. When the birds are done, serve upon the toast, with the gravy poured over it. The toast should lie under them while cooking at least five minutes, during which time the birds should be basted with melted butter seasoned with pepper.

The largest snipe will not require above twenty minutes to roast.

WOODCOCK.

This is the most delicious of small birds, and may be either roasted or broiled.

Roast.

The English do not draw woodcock, regarding the *trail* as a *bonne bouche*, and I have known American housekeepers who copied them in this respect. In this case roast precisely as you would snipe or plover, only putting the toast under the birds so soon as they begin to cook, to catch the trail.

To my taste, a better, and certainly to common sense people a less objectionable plan, is to fill the birds with a rich force-meat of bread-crumbs, peppered and salted, shortened with melted butter. Sew them up and roast, basting with butter and water, from twenty minutes to half an hour. When half done, put circular slices of buttered toast beneath, and serve upon these when you take them up.

Broiled.

Split down the back, and broil over a clear fire. Butter, pepper, and salt when done, and let them lie between two hot dishes for five minutes before sending to table. Small snipe are nice broiled in this way; also robins and doves.

SALMI OF WOODCOCK OR SNIPE.

Clean and half-roast the birds; cut in quarters, and put in a saucepan with gravy made of the giblets, necks, and some bits of fat pork, stewed in a little water. Add a minced button onion, salt, and a pinch of cayenne, and stew fifteen minutes or until tender, closely covered. Take out the birds, and pile neatly upon buttered toast in a chafing-dish. Strain the gravy and return to the fire, adding some small pieces of butter rolled in flour, the juice of a lemon and a little wine. Boil up, and pour over the salmi.

ORTOLANS, REED-BIRDS, RAIL, AND SORA

may be roasted or broiled. A good way is to roll an oyster in melted butter, then in bread-crumbs seasoned with pepper and salt, and put into each bird before roasting. Baste with butter and water three times, put the rounds of toast underneath, and baste freely with melted butter. They will require about twenty minutes to cook, and will be found delicious.

TO KEEP GAME FROM TAINTING.

Draw so soon as they come into your possession; rinse with soda and water, then with pure cold water; wipe dry, and rub them lightly with a mixture of fine salt and black pepper. If you must keep them some time, put in the cavity of each fowl a piece of charcoal; hang them in a cool, dark place, with a cloth thrown over them. Small birds, unless there are too many of them, may be kept in a refrigerator after you have drawn, washed, and wiped them.

The charcoal is an admirable preventive of decomposition.

SAUCES FOR MEAT AND FISH.

These are no longer the appendages of the rich man's bill of fare only. A general knowledge of made sauces, as well as the more expensive ones imported from abroad and sold here at high prices, is a part of every intelligent housekeeper's culinary education. Few are so ignorant as to serve a fish sauce with game, or *vice versâ*. From the immense number of receipts which I have collected and examined, I have selected comparatively few but such as I consider "representative" articles. The ingenious housewife is at liberty, as I said before, elsewhere, to modify and improve upon them.

First, *par excellence*, as the most important, and because it is the groundwork of many others, I place

MELTED OR DRAWN BUTTER.

No. 1.

- 2 teaspoonfuls flour.
- 1½ ounce butter.
- 1 teacupful hot water or milk.
- A little salt.

Put the flour and salt in a bowl, and add a little at a time of the water or milk, working it very smooth as you go on. Put into a tin cup or saucepan, and set in a vessel of boiling water. As it warms, stir, and when it has boiled a minute or more, add the butter by degrees, stirring all the time until it is entirely melted and incorporated with the flour and water. Boil one minute.

Mix with milk when you wish to use for puddings, with water for meats and fish.

No. 2.

- 1½ teaspoonful of flour.
- 2 ounces butter.
- 1 teacupful (small) hot water.

Wet the flour to a thin smooth paste with cold water, and stir into the hot, which should be in the inner vessel. When it boils, add the butter by degrees, and stir until well mixed. Boil one minute.

No. 3.

- 3 ounces butter.
- Half-pint water (hot).
- A beaten egg.

- 1 heaping teaspoonful flour.

Wet the flour to a smooth paste with a little cold milk, and add to the hot water in the inner vessel, stirring until thick. Have ready the beaten egg in a cup. Take a teaspoonful of the mixture from the fire, and beat with this until light; then another, and still another. Set aside the cup when this is done, and stir the butter into the contents of the inner saucepan gradually, until thoroughly mixed, then add the beaten egg in the same way. There is no danger of clotting the egg, if it be treated as I have described.

EGG SAUCE. ✠

- 3 hard-boiled eggs.
- A good teacupful drawn butter.
- A little salt.

Chop the yolks only of the eggs very fine, and beat into the hot drawn butter, salting to taste.

This is used for boiled fowls and boiled fish. For the former, you can add some minced parsley; for the latter, chopped pickles, capers, or nasturtium seed. For boiled beef, a small shallot minced fine.

Or,

Omit the boiled eggs, and beat up two raw ones very light, and put into the drawn butter instead, as directed in No. 3. For boiled beef or chicken, you may make the drawn butter of hot liquor taken from the pot in which the meat is cooking, having first carefully skimmed it.

SAUCE FOR BOILED OR BAKED FISH.

- 4 ounces butter.
- 1 tablespoonful flour.
- 2 anchovies.
- 1 teaspoonful chopped capers, or nasturtium seed, or green pickle.
- 1 shallot.

- Pepper and salt to taste.

- 1 tablespoonful vinegar.

- 1 teacupful hot water.

Put the water into the inner saucepan, chop the anchovies and shallot, and put in with the pepper and salt. Boil two minutes, and strain back into the saucepan when you have rinsed with hot water. Now add the flour wet smooth with cold water, and stir until it thickens; put in the butter by degrees, and when it is thoroughly melted and mixed, the vinegar; lastly, the capers and a little nutmeg.

WHITE SAUCE FOR FISH. ✠

Make drawn butter by receipt No. 2, but with double the quantity of flour, and use, instead of water, the liquor in which the fish was boiled. Add four tablespoonfuls of milk, in which a shallot and a head of celery or a pinch of celery-seed has been boiled, then strained out. Boil one minute, and stir in a teaspoonful of chopped parsley.

OYSTER SAUCE. ✠

- 1 pint oysters.

- Half a lemon.

- 2 tablespoonfuls butter.

- 1 tablespoonful flour.

- 1 teacupful milk or cream.

- Cayenne and nutmeg to taste.

Stew the oysters in their own liquor five minutes, and add the milk. When this boils, strain the liquor and return to the saucepan. Thicken with the flour when you have wet it with cold water; stir it well in; put in the butter, next the cayenne (if you like it), boil one minute; squeeze in the lemon-juice, shake it around well, and pour out.

Or,

Drain the oysters dry without cooking at all; make the sauce with the liquor and other ingredients just named. Chop the raw oysters, and stir in when you do the butter; boil five minutes, and pour into the tureen. Some put in the oysters whole, considering that the sauce is handsomer than when they are chopped.

Oyster sauce is used for boiled halibut, cod, and other fish, for boiled turkey, chickens, and white meats generally.

CRAB SAUCE.

- 1 crab, boiled and cold.
- 4 tablespoonfuls of milk.
- 1 teacupful drawn butter.
- Cayenne, mace, and salt to taste.

Make the drawn butter as usual, and stir in the milk. Pick the meat from the crab, chop very fine, season with cayenne, mace, and salt to taste; stir into the drawn butter. Simmer three minutes, but do not boil.

Lobster sauce is very nice made as above, with the addition of a teaspoonful of made mustard and the juice of half a lemon. This is a good fish sauce.

ANCHOVY SAUCE.

- 6 anchovies.
- A teacupful drawn butter.
- A wineglass pale Sherry.

Soak the anchovies in cold water two hours; pull them to pieces, and simmer in just enough water to cover them for half an hour. Strain the liquor into the drawn butter (No. 3), boil a minute, add the wine; heat gradually to a boil, and stew five minutes longer. You may substitute two teaspoonfuls of anchovy paste for the little fish themselves.

Serve with boiled fish.

Sauce for Lobsters.

- 5 tablespoonfuls fresh butter.
- Teacupful vinegar.
- Salt and pepper to taste, with a heaping teaspoonful white sugar.
- 1 teaspoonful made mustard.
- Minced parsley.

Beat the butter to a cream, adding gradually the vinegar, salt, and pepper. Boil a bunch of parsley five minutes, chop small; beat into the butter; lastly the sugar and mustard. The butter must be light as whipped egg.

Bread Sauce.

- 1 pint milk.
- 1 cup bread-crumbs (very fine).
- 1 onion, sliced.
- A pinch of mace.
- Pepper and salt to taste.
- 3 tablespoonfuls butter.

Simmer the sliced onion in the milk until tender; strain the milk and pour over the bread-crumbs, which should be put into a saucepan. Cover and soak half an hour; beat smooth with an egg-whip, add the seasoning and butter; stir in well, boil up once, and serve in a tureen. If it is too thick, add boiling water and more butter.

This sauce is for roast poultry. Some people add some of the gravy from the dripping-pan, first straining it and beating it well in with the sauce.

White Celery Sauce.

- 2 large heads of celery.
- 1 teacupful of broth in which the fowl is boiled.

- 1 teacupful cream or milk.

- Salt and nutmeg.

- Heaping tablespoonful flour, and same of butter.

Boil the celery tender in salted water; drain, and cut into bits half an inch long. Thicken the gravy from the fowl—a teacupful—with the flour; add the butter, salt, and nutmeg, then the milk. Stir and beat until it is smooth; put in the celery; heat almost to boiling, stirring all the while; serve in a tureen, or, if you prefer, pour it over the boiled meat or fowls.

ONION SAUCE.

- 4 white onions.

- 1 teacupful hot milk.

- 3 tablespoonfuls butter.

- Salt and pepper to taste.

Peel the onions, boil tender, press the water from them, and mince fine. Have ready the hot milk in a saucepan; stir in the onions, then the butter, salt, and pepper. Boil up once.

If you want to have it particularly good, make nice melted or drawn butter (No. 3); beat the mashed onion into it; add a teacupful of cream or new milk, season, boil up, and serve.

MAÎTRE D'HÔTEL SAUCE. ✠

- 1 teacupful drawn butter.

- 1 teaspoonful minced parsley.

- 1 lemon.

- Cayenne and salt to taste.

Draw the butter (No. 2); boil the parsley three minutes; take it out and lay in cold water five minutes, to cool; chop and stir into the butter; squeeze in the lemon-juice, the pepper and salt; beat hard with an egg-whip, return to the fire, and boil up once.

This is a "stock" sauce, being suitable for so many dishes, roast or boiled.

MINT SAUCE FOR ROAST LAMB.

- 2 tablespoonfuls green mint, chopped fine.
- 1 tablespoonful powdered sugar.
- Half a teacupful cider vinegar.

Chop the mint, put the sugar and vinegar in a sauce boat, and stir in the mint. Let it stand in a cool place fifteen minutes before sending to table.

MUSHROOM SAUCE.

- 1 teacupful young mushrooms.
- 4 tablespoonfuls butter.
- 1 teacupful cream or milk.
- 1 teaspoonful flour.
- Nutmeg, mace, and salt to taste.

Stew the mushrooms in barely enough water to cover them until tender. Drain, but do not press them, and add the cream, butter, and seasoning. Stew over a bright fire, stirring all the while until it begins to thicken. Add the flour wet in cold milk, boil up and serve in a boat, or pour over boiled chickens, rabbits, etc.

CAULIFLOWER SAUCE.

- 1 small cauliflower.
- 3 tablespoonfuls butter, cut in bits, and rolled in flour.
- 1 onion.
- 1 small head of celery.
- Mace, pepper, and salt.
- 1 teacupful water.
- 1 teacupful milk or cream.

Boil the cauliflower in two waters, changing when about half done, and throwing away the first, reserve a teacupful of the last. Take out the cauliflower, drain and mince. Cook in another saucepan the onion and celery, mincing them when tender. Heat the reserved cupful of water again in a saucepan, add the milk; when warm put in the cauliflower and onion, the butter and seasoning—coating the butter thickly with flour; boil until it thickens.

This is a delicious sauce for boiled corned beef and mutton.

ASPARAGUS SAUCE.

- A dozen heads of asparagus.
- 2 teacupfuls drawn butter.
- 2 eggs.
- The juice of half a lemon.
- Salt and white pepper.

Boil the tender heads in a very little salted water. Drain and chop them. Have ready a pint of drawn butter, with two raw eggs beaten into it; add the asparagus, and season, squeezing in the lemon-juice last. The butter must be hot, but do not cook after putting in the asparagus heads. This accompanies boiled fowls, stewed fillet of veal, or boiled mutton.

APPLE SAUCE.

Pare, core, and slice some ripe tart apples, stew in water enough to cover them until they break to pieces. Beat up to a smooth pulp, stir in a good lump of butter, and sugar to taste.

Apple sauce is the invariable accompaniment of roast pork—or fresh pork cooked in any way. If you wish, you can add a little nutmeg.

PEACH SAUCE.

Soak a quart of dried peaches in water four hours. Wash them, rubbing them against one another by stirring around with a wooden spoon. Drain, and put into a saucepan with just enough water to cover them. Stew until they break to pieces. Rub to a soft smooth pulp, sweeten to taste with white sugar. Send to table cold, with roast game or other meats.

CRANBERRY SAUCE.

Wash and pick a quart of ripe cranberries, and put into a saucepan with a teacupful of water. Stew slowly, stirring often until they are thick as marmalade. They require at least an hour and a half to cook. When you take them from the fire, sweeten abundantly with white sugar. If sweetened while cooking, the color will be bad. Put them into a mould and set aside to get cold.

Or, ✠

And this is a nicer plan—strain the pulp through a cullender or sieve, or coarse mosquito-net, into a mould wet with cold water. When firm, turn into a glass dish or salver. Be sure that it is sweet enough.

Eat with roast turkey, game, and roast ducks.

TO BROWN FLOUR.

Spread upon a tin plate, set upon the stove, or in a *very* hot oven, and stir continually after it begins to color, until it is brown all through.

Keep it always on hand. Make it at odd minutes, and put away in a glass jar, covered closely. Shake up every few days to keep it light and prevent lumping.

TO BROWN BUTTER.

Put a lump of butter into a hot frying-pan, and toss it around over a clear fire until it browns. Dredge browned flour over it, and stir to a smooth batter until it begins to boil. Use it for coloring gravies, such as brown fricassees, etc.; or make into sauce for baked fish and fish-steaks, by beating in celery or onion vinegar, a *very* little brown sugar and some cayenne.

CATSUPS AND FLAVORED VINEGARS.

MADE MUSTARD. ✠

- 4 tablespoonfuls best English mustard.

- 2 teaspoonfuls salt.

- 2 teaspoonfuls white sugar.

- 1 teaspoonful white pepper.

- 2 teaspoonfuls salad oil.

- Vinegar to mix to a smooth paste—celery or Tarragon vinegar if you have it.

- 1 small garlic, minced very small.

Put the mustard in a bowl and wet with the oil, rubbing it in with a silver or wooden spoon until it is absorbed. Wet with vinegar to a stiff paste; add salt, pepper, sugar, and garlic, and work all together thoroughly, wetting little by little with the vinegar until you can beat it as you do cake-batter. Beat five minutes very hard; put into wide-mouthed bottles—empty French mustard bottles, if you have them—pour a little oil on top, cork tightly, and set away in a cool place. It will be mellow enough for use in a couple of days.

Having used this mustard for years in my own family, I can safely advise my friends to undertake the trifling labor of preparing it in consideration of the satisfaction to be derived from the condiment. I mix in a Wedgewood mortar, with pestle of the same; but a bowl is nearly as good. It will keep for weeks.

HORSE-RADISH.

Scrape or grind, cover with vinegar, and keep in wide-mouthed bottles. To eat with roast beef and cold meats.

WALNUT CATSUP.

Choose young walnuts tender enough to be pierced with a pin or needle. Prick them in several places, and lay in a jar with a handful of salt to every twenty-five, and water enough to cover them. Break them with a billet of wood or wooden beetle, and let them lie in the pickle a fortnight, stirring twice a day. Drain off the liquor into a saucepan, and cover the shells with boiling vinegar to extract what juice remains in them. Crush to a pulp and strain through a cullender into the saucepan. Allow for every quart an ounce of black pepper and one of ginger, half an ounce of cloves and half an ounce of nutmeg, beaten fine. Put in a pinch of cayenne, a shallot minced fine for every *two* quarts, and a thimbleful of celery-seed tied in a bag for the same quantity. Boil all together for an hour, if there be a gallon of the mixture. Bottle when cold, putting an equal quantity of the spice in each flask. Butternuts make delightful catsup.

MUSHROOM CATSUP.

- 2 quarts of mushrooms.
- ¼ lb. of salt.

Lay in an earthenware pan, in alternate layers of mushrooms and salt; let them lie six hours, then break into bits. Set in a cool place, three days, stirring thoroughly every morning. Measure the juice when you have strained it, and to every quart allow half an ounce of allspice, the same quantity of ginger, half a teaspoonful of powdered mace, a teaspoonful of cayenne. Put into a stone jar, cover closely, set in a saucepan of boiling water over the fire, and boil five hours *hard*. Take it off, empty into a porcelain kettle, and boil slowly half an hour longer. Let it stand all night in a cool place, until settled and clear. Pour off carefully from the sediment, and bottle, filling the flasks to the mouth. Dip the corks in melted rosin, and tie up with bladders.

The bottles should be very small, as it soon spoils when exposed to the air.

IMITATION WORCESTERSHIRE SAUCE.

- 3 teaspoonfuls cayenne pepper.
- 2 tablespoonfuls walnut or tomato catsup (strained through muslin).
- 3 shallots minced fine.
- 3 anchovies chopped into bits.
- 1 quart of vinegar.
- Half-teaspoonful powdered cloves.

Mix and rub through a sieve. Put in a stone jar, set in a pot of boiling water, and heat until the liquid is so hot you can not bear your finger in it. Strain, and let it stand in the jar, closely covered, two days, then bottle for use.

OYSTER CATSUP.

- 1 quart oysters.
- 1 tablespoonful salt.
- 1 teaspoonful cayenne pepper, and same of mace.
- 1 teacupful cider vinegar.
- 1 teacupful sherry.

Chop the oysters and boil in their own liquor with a teacupful of vinegar, skimming the scum as it rises. Boil three minutes, strain through a hair-cloth; return the liquor to the fire, add the wine, pepper, salt, and mace. Boil fifteen minutes, and when cold bottle for use, sealing the corks.

TOMATO CATSUP. ✠

- 1 peck ripe tomatoes.
- 1 ounce salt.
- 1 ounce mace.
- 1 tablespoonful black pepper.
- 1 teaspoonful cayenne.
- 1 tablespoonful cloves (powdered).
- 7 tablespoonful ground mustard.
- 1 tablespoonful celery seed (tied in a thin muslin bag).

Cut a slit in the tomatoes, put into a bell-metal or porcelain kettle, and boil until the juice is all extracted and the pulp dissolved. Strain and press through a cullender, then through a hair sieve. Return to the fire, add the seasoning, and boil *at least* five hours, stirring constantly for the last hour, and frequently throughout the time it is on the fire. Let it stand twelve hours in a stone jar on the cellar floor. When cold, add a pint of strong vinegar. Take out the bag of celery seed, and bottle, sealing the corks. Keep in a dark, cool place.

Tomato and walnut are the most useful catsups we have for general purposes, and either is in itself a fine sauce for roast meat, cold fowl, game, etc.

LEMON CATSUP.

- 12 large, fresh lemons.
- 4 tablespoonfuls white mustard-seed.
- 1 tablespoonful turmeric.
- 1 tablespoonful white pepper.
- 1 teaspoonful cloves.
- 1 teaspoonful mace.
- 1 saltspoonful cayenne.
- 2 tablespoonfuls white sugar.
- 2 tablespoonfuls grated horse-radish.
- 1 shallot, minced fine.
- Juice of the lemons.
- 2 tablespoonfuls table-salt.

Grate the rind of the lemons; pound or grind the spices, and put all together, including the horse-radish. Strew the salt over all, add the lemon-juice, and let it stand three hours in a cool place. Boil in a porcelain kettle half an hour. Pour into a covered vessel—china or stone—and let it stand a fortnight, stirring well every day. Then strain, bottle, and seal.

It is a fine seasoning for fish sauces, fish soups, and game ragoûts.

"EVER-READY" CATSUP. ✠

- 2 quarts cider vinegar.
- 12 anchovies, washed, soaked, and pulled to pieces.
- 12 small onions, peeled and minced.
- 1 tablespoonful mace.

- 3 tablespoonfuls fine salt.
- 3 tablespoonfuls white sugar.
- 1 tablespoonful cloves.
- 3 tablespoonfuls whole black pepper.
- 2 tablespoonfuls ground ginger.
- 1 tablespoonful cayenne.
- 1 quart mushrooms, minced, *or*
- 1 quart ripe tomatoes, sliced.

Put into a preserving kettle and boil slowly four hours, or until the mixture is reduced to one-half the original quantity. Strain through a flannel bag. Do not bottle until next day. Fill the flasks to the top, and dip the corks in beeswax and rosin.

This catsup will keep for years. Mixed with drawn butter, it is used as a sauce for boiled fish, but is a fine flavoring essence for gravies of almost any kind.

A GOOD STORE SAUCE.

- 2 tablespoonfuls horse-radish (grated).
- 1 tablespoonful allspice.
- A grated nutmeg.
- 3 large pickled onions (minced fine).
- 2 dozen whole black peppers.
- A pinch of cayenne.
- 1 tablespoonful salt.
- 1 tablespoonful white sugar.
- 1 quart vinegar from walnut or butternut pickle.

Mix all the spices well together; crush in a stone jar with a potato-beetle or billet of wood; pour the vinegar upon these, and let it stand two weeks. Put on in a porcelain or clean bell-metal kettle and heat to boiling; strain and set aside until next day to cool and settle. Bottle and cork very tightly. It is an excellent seasoning for any kind of gravy, sauce, or stew.

MOCK CAPERS. ✠

Gather green nasturtium seed when they are full-grown, but not yellow; dry for a day in the sun; put into small jars or wide-mouthed bottles, cover with boiling vinegar, slightly spiced, and when cool, cork closely. In six weeks they will be fit for use. They give an agreeable taste to drawn butter for fish, or boiled beef and mutton.

CELERY VINEGAR.

- A bunch of fresh celery, *or*
- A quarter of a pound of celery seed.
- 1 quart best vinegar.
- 1 teaspoonful salt.
- 1 tablespoonful white sugar.

Cut up the celery into small bits, or pour the seed into a jar; scald the salt and vinegar, and pour over the celery stalks or seed; let it cool, and put away in one large jar tightly corked. In a fortnight strain and bottle in small flasks, corking tightly.

ONION VINEGAR.

- 6 large onions.
- 1 tablespoonful salt.
- 1 tablespoonful white sugar.
- 1 quart best vinegar.

Mince the onions, strew on the salt, and let them stand five or six hours. Scald the vinegar in which the sugar has been dissolved, pour over the onions; put in a jar, tie down the cover, and steep a fortnight. Strain and bottle.

ELDERBERRY CATSUP.

- 1 quart of elderberries.
- 1 quart of vinegar.

- 6 anchovies, soaked and pulled to pieces.

- Half a teaspoonful mace.

- A pinch of ginger.

- 2 tablespoonfuls white sugar.

- 1 teaspoonful salt.

- 1 tablespoonful whole peppers.

Scald the vinegar and pour over the berries, which must be picked from the stalks and put into a large stone jar. Cover with a pane of glass, and set in the hot sun two days. Strain off the liquor, and boil up with the other ingredients, stirring often, one hour, keeping covered unless while stirring. Let it cool; strain and bottle.

This is used for flavoring brown gravies, soups, and ragoûts, and, stirred into browned butter, makes a good piquant sauce for broiled or baked fish.

PEPPER VINEGAR.

- 6 pods red peppers broken up.

- 3 dozen black pepper-corns.

- 2 tablespoonfuls white sugar.

- 1 quart of best vinegar.

Scald the vinegar in which the sugar has been dissolved; pour over the pepper, put into a jar, and steep a fortnight. Strain and bottle.

This is eaten with boiled fish and raw oysters, and is useful in the preparation of salads.

HORSE-RADISH VINEGAR.

- 6 tablespoonfuls scraped or grated horse-radish.

- 1 tablespoonful white sugar.

- 1 quart vinegar.

Scald the vinegar; pour boiling hot over the horseradish. Steep a week, strain and bottle.

SALADS.

"The dressing of the salad should be saturated with oil, and seasoned with pepper and salt before the vinegar is added. It results from this process that there never can be too much vinegar; for, from the specific gravity of the vinegar compared with oil, what is more than useful will fall to the bottom of the bowl. The salt should not be dissolved in the vinegar, but in the oil, by which means it is more equally distributed throughout the salad."— *Chaptal, a French chemist.*

The Spanish proverb says, "that to make a perfect salad, there should be a miser for oil, a spendthrift for vinegar, a wise man for salt, and a madcap to stir the ingredients up and mix them well together."

SYDNEY SMITH'S RECEIPT FOR SALAD DRESSING.

Two boiled potatoes, strained through a kitchen sieve,
Softness and smoothness to the salad give;
Of mordant mustard take a single spoon—
Distrust the condiment that bites too soon;
Yet deem it not, thou man of taste, a fault,
To add a double quantity of salt.
Four times the spoon with oil of Lucca crown,
And twice with vinegar procured from town;
True taste requires it, and your poet begs
The pounded yellow of two well-boiled eggs.
Let onions' atoms lurk within the bowl,
And, scarce suspected, animate the whole;
And lastly, in the flavored compound toss
A magic spoonful of anchovy sauce.
Oh, great and glorious! oh, herbaceous meat!
'Twould tempt the dying anchorite to eat.
Back to the world he'd turn his weary soul,
And plunge his fingers in the salad bowl.

At least twenty-five years ago I pasted the above doggerel in my scrap-book, and committed it to memory. The first salad I was ever trusted to compound was dressed in strict obedience to the directions of the witty divine, and to this day these seem to me pertinent and worthy of note. The anchovy sauce can be omitted if you like, and a spoonful of Harvey's or Worcestershire substituted. This is best suited for chicken or turkey salad.

LOBSTER SALAD. ✠

Pick out every bit of the meat from the body and claws of a cold boiled lobster. Lay aside the coral for the dressing, and mince the rest. For the dressing you will need—

- 4 eggs, boiled hard.

- 2 tablespoonfuls salad oil.

- 1 teaspoonful made mustard.

- 1 teaspoonful salt.

- 2 teaspoonfuls white sugar.

- ½ teaspoonful cayenne pepper. *Vinegar at discretion.*

- 1 teaspoonful of Harvey's, Worcestershire, or anchovy sauce.

Rub the yolks to a smooth paste in a mortar or bowl, with a Wedgewood pestle, a silver or wooden spoon, until *perfectly* free from lumps. Add gradually, rubbing all the while, the other ingredients, the coral last. This should have been worked well upon a plate with a silver knife or wooden spatula. Proceed slowly and carefully in the work of amalgamating the various ingredients, moistening with vinegar as they stiffen. Increase the quantity of this as the mixture grows smooth, until it is thin enough to pour over the minced lobster. You will need a teacupful at least. Toss with a silver fork and do not break the meat. Some mix chopped lettuce with the salad; but unless it is to be eaten within a few minutes, the vinegar will wither the tender leaves. The better plan is to heap a glass dish with the inner leaves of several lettuce-heads, laying pounded ice among them, and pass with the lobster, that the guests may add the green salad to their taste.

When lettuce is out of season, the following dressing, the receipt for which was given me by a French gourmand, may be used.

Prepare the egg and coral as above, with the condiments there mentioned, but mix with the lobster-meat four tablespoonfuls of fine white cabbage, chopped small, with two small onions, also minced into almost invisible bits, a teaspoonful of anchovy or other sauce, and a tablespoonful of celery vinegar.

All lobster salad should be eaten as soon as possible after the dressing is added, else it becomes unwholesome. If you use canned lobster, open and turn out the contents of the can into a china dish several hours before you mix the dressing, that the close, airless smell may pass away.

Garnish the edges of the dish with cool white leaves of curled lettuce, or with a chain of rings made of the whites of the boiled eggs.

EXCELSIOR LOBSTER SALAD WITH CREAM DRESSING. ✠

- 1 fine lobster, boiled and when cold picked to pieces, or two small ones.
- 1 cup of best salad oil.
- ½ cup sweet cream, whipped light to a cupful of froth.
- 1 lemon—the juice strained.
- 1 teaspoonful mustard wet up with vinegar.
- 1 tablespoonful powdered sugar.
- 1 teaspoonful salt.
- A pinch of cayenne pepper.
- 4 tablespoonfuls vinegar.
- Beaten yolks of two eggs.

Beat eggs, sugar, salt, mustard, and pepper until light; then, and very gradually, the oil. When the mixture is quite thick, whip in the lemon. Beat five minutes before putting in the vinegar. Just before the salad goes to table add half the whipped cream to this dressing and stir well into the lobster. Line the salad-bowl with lettuce-leaves; put in the seasoned meat and cover with the rest of the whipped cream.

This salad deserves its name.

CHICKEN SALAD. ✠

- The white meat of a cold boiled or roasted chicken (or turkey).

- Three-quarters the same bulk of chopped celery.

- 2 hard-boiled eggs.

- 1 raw egg, well beaten.

- 1 teaspoonful of salt.

- 1 teaspoonful pepper.

- 1 teaspoonful made mustard.

- 3 teaspoonfuls salad oil.

- 2 teaspoonfuls white sugar.

- ½ teacupful of vinegar.

Mince the meat well, removing every scrap of fat, gristle, and skin; cut the celery into bits half an inch long, *or less*, mix them, and set aside in a cold place while you prepare the dressing.

Rub the yolks of the eggs to a fine powder, add the salt, pepper, and sugar, then the oil, grinding hard, and putting in but a few drops at a time. The mustard comes next, and let all stand together while you whip the raw egg to a froth. Beat this into the dressing, and pour in the vinegar spoonful by spoonful, whipping the dressing well as you do it. Sprinkle a little dry salt over the meat and celery; toss it up lightly with a silver fork; pour the dressing over it, tossing and mixing until the bottom of the mass is as well saturated as the top; turn into the salad-bowl, and garnish with white of eggs (boiled) cut into rings or flowers, and sprigs of bleached celery-tops.

If you cannot get celery, substitute crisp white cabbage, and use celery vinegar in the dressing. You can also, in this case, chop some green pickles, gherkins, mangoes, or cucumbers, and stir in.

Turkey makes even better salad than chicken.

You can make soup of the liquor in which the fowl is cooked, since it need not be boiled in a cloth.

LETTUCE SALAD. ✠

- Two or three heads white lettuce.
- 2 hard-boiled eggs.
- 2 teaspoonfuls salad oil.
- ½ teaspoonful salt.
- 1 teaspoonful white sugar.
- ½ teaspoonful made mustard.
- 1 teaspoonful pepper.
- 4 tablespoonfuls vinegar.

Rub the yolks to a powder, add sugar, pepper, salt, mustard, and oil. Let it stand five minutes, and beat in the vinegar. Cut the lettuce up with a knife and fork,—a chopper would bruise it,—put into a bowl, add the dressing, and mix by tossing with a silver fork.

Or,

You can dress on the table with oil and vinegar only, pulling the heart of the lettuce out with your fingers, and seasoning to taste.

SUMMER SALAD.

- 3 heads of lettuce.
- 2 teaspoonfuls green mustard leaves.
- A handful of water-cresses.
- Four or five very tender radishes.
- 1 cucumber.
- 3 hard-boiled eggs.

- 2 teaspoonfuls white sugar.

- 1 teaspoonful salt.

- 1 teaspoonful pepper.

- 1 teaspoonful made mustard.

- 1 teacupful vinegar.

- 2 tablespoonfuls salad oil.

Mix the dressing as for lettuce salad. Cut up the hearts of the lettuce, the radishes and cucumber, into very small pieces; chop the mustard and cress. Pour over these the dressing, tossing very lightly, not to bruise the young leaves; heap in a salad-bowl upon a lump of ice, and garnish with fennel-heads and nasturtium-blossoms.

This is a delightful accompaniment to boiled or baked fish.

WATER-CRESSES.

Wash and pick over the cresses carefully, pluck from the stems, and pile in the salad bowl, with a dressing of vinegar, pepper, salt, and sugar, well stirred in.

CABBAGE SALAD, OR COLD SLAW. ✠

- 1 head of fine white cabbage, minced fine.

- 3 hard-boiled eggs.

- 2 tablespoonfuls salad oil.

- 2 tablespoonfuls white sugar.

- 1 teaspoonful salt.

- 1 teaspoonful pepper.

- 1 teaspoonful made mustard.

- 1 teacupful vinegar.

Mix as for lettuce and pour upon the chopped cabbage.

Or, ✠

Shred the head of cabbage fine, and dress with—

- 1 cup vinegar.
- 1 tablespoonful butter.
- 1 tablespoonful sugar.
- 2 tablespoonfuls sour cream.
- A pinch of pepper, and the same of salt.

Put the vinegar, with all the ingredients for the dressing, except the cream, in a saucepan, and let them come to a boil. Pour while scalding over the cabbage, and set away until perfectly cold. Add the cream just before serving, stirring in with a silver fork.

This is a very nice preparation of cabbage, and far more wholesome than the uncooked. Try it!

TOMATO SALAD. ✠

- 12 medium-sized tomatoes, peeled and sliced.
- 4 hard-boiled eggs.
- 1 raw egg, well beaten.
- 1 teaspoonful salt.
- ¼ spoonful cayenne pepper.
- 1 teaspoonful white sugar.
- 1 tablespoonful salad oil.
- 2 teaspoonfuls made mustard.
- 1 teacupful vinegar.

Rub the yolks to a smooth paste, adding by degrees the salt, pepper, sugar, mustard, and oil. Beat the raw egg to a froth and stir in—lastly the vinegar. Peel the tomatoes, slice them a quarter of an inch thick, and set the dish on ice, while you are making ready the dressing. Stir a great lump of ice rapidly in this—the dressing—until it is cold; take it out, cover the tomatoes with the mixture, and set back on the ice until you send to table.

This salad is delicious, especially when ice-cold.

CELERY SALAD. ✠

- 1 boiled egg.

- 1 raw egg.

- 1 tablespoonful salad oil.

- 1 teaspoonful white sugar.

- 1 saltspoonful salt.

- 1 saltspoonful pepper.

- 4 tablespoonfuls vinegar.

- 1 teaspoonful made mustard.

Prepare the dressing as for tomato salad; cut the celery into bits half an inch long, and season. Eat at once, before the vinegar injures the crispness of the vegetable.

SALMON SALAD. ✠

- 1½ lb. cold boiled or baked salmon.

- 2 heads white lettuce (or celery).

- 3 hard-boiled eggs.

- 2 tablespoonfuls salad oil.

- 1 teaspoonful salt, and same of cayenne.

- 1 teaspoonful white sugar.

- 1 teaspoonful Worcestershire or anchovy sauce.

- 1 teaspoonful made mustard.

- 1 teacupful vinegar.

Mince three-quarters of the salmon, laying aside four or five pieces half an inch wide and four or five long; cut smoothly and of uniform size. Prepare the dressing in the usual way, and pour over the minced fish. Shred the lettuce, handling as little as possible, and heap in a separate bowl, with pounded ice. This must accompany the salmon, that the guests may help themselves to their liking. Or you may mix the lettuce with the fish, if it is to be eaten immediately. Celery, of course, is always stirred into the salad, when it is used. The reserved pieces of salmon should be laid in the dressing for five minutes before the latter is added to the minced fish, then dipped in vinegar. When you have transferred your salad (or mayonnaise) to the dish in which it is to be served, round it into a mound, and lay the strips upon it in such a manner as to divide it into triangular sections, the bars all meeting at the top and diverging at the base. Between these have subdivisions of chain-work made of the whites of the boiled eggs, each circle overlapping that next to it.

You can dress halibut in the same way.

POTATO SALAD. ✠ (*Very good.*)

- 2 cups of mashed potato, rubbed through a cullender.

- ¾ of a cup of chopped cabbage—white and firm.

- 2 tablespoonfuls cucumber pickle, also chopped.

- Yolks of 2 hard-boiled eggs, pounded fine.

- Mix all well together.

Dressing.

- 1 raw egg, well beaten.

- 1 saltspoonful of celery-seed.

- 1 teaspoonful white sugar.

- 1 tablespoonful of melted butter.

- 1 teaspoonful of flour.

- ½ cupful of vinegar.

- Salt, mustard, and pepper to taste.

Boil the vinegar and pour it upon the beaten egg, sugar, butter, and seasoning. Wet the flour with cold vinegar, and beat into this. Cook the mixture, stirring until it thickens, when pour, scalding hot, upon the salad. Toss with a silver fork, and let it get very cold before eating.

CHEESE SALAD, OR MOCK CRAB.

- ½ lb. pickled shrimps.
- ¼ lb. good old cheese.
- 1 tablespoonful salad oil.
- ½ teaspoonful cayenne pepper.
- 1 teaspoonful salt.
- 1 teaspoonful white sugar.
- 1 teaspoonful made mustard.
- 4 tablespoonfuls celery or onion vinegar.

Mince the shrimps and grate the cheese. Work into the latter, a little at a time, the various condiments enumerated above, the vinegar last. Let all stand together ten minutes before adding the shrimps. When this is done, stir well for a minute and a half and serve in a glass dish, garnished with lemon, or (if you can get one) in a clean crab-shell.

Or, ✠

- ½ lb. old cheese, grated.
- 1 hard-boiled egg.
- ½ teaspoonful cayenne.
- 1 teaspoonful salt.
- 1 teaspoonful white sugar.
- 1 teaspoonful made mustard.
- 1 tablespoonful onion vinegar.

- 1 tablespoonful salad oil.

Rub the yolk of the egg to a paste with the oil, adding in order the salt, pepper, sugar, and mustard, lastly the cheese. Work all well together before putting in the vinegar. Serve in a crab-shell.

These mixtures bear a marvellous resemblance in taste to devilled crab, and make a good impromptu relish at tea or luncheon. Eat with crackers and butter. This is still better if you add a cupful of cold minced chicken.

Use none but the best and freshest olive salad oil (*not* sweet oil, falsely so called) in compounding your salad-dressing. If you cannot obtain this, melted butter is the best substitute I know of.

VEGETABLES
RULES APPLICABLE TO THE COOKING OF ALL VEGETABLES.

1. Have them as fresh as possible. Stale and withered ones are unwholesome and unpalatable. Summer vegetables should be cooked on the same day they are gathered, if possible.

2. Pick over and wash well, cutting out all decayed or unripe parts.

3. Lay them, when peeled, in *cold* water for some time before cooking.

4. If you boil them, put a little salt in the water.

5. Cook them steadily after you put them on.

6. Be sure they are thoroughly done. Rare vegetables are neither good nor fashionable.

7. *Drain well.*

8. Serve hot!

POTATOES.

BOILED POTATOES (*with the skins on.*)

Boil in cold water with a pinch of salt. Have them of uniform size, and cook steadily until a fork will pierce easily to the heart of the largest. Then pour off the water, every drop; sprinkle with salt and set back on the range, a little to one side, with the lid of the pot off. Let them dry three or four minutes; peel very quickly and serve in an uncovered dish.

Without the Skins.

Pare very thin. The glory of a potato is its mealiness, and much of the starch, or meal, lies next the skin—consequently is lost by slovenly paring, which likewise defaces the shape. Lay in cold water for half an hour, have ready a pot of boiling water slightly salted, drop in the potatoes, and keep at a rapid boil until tender. Drain off the water, sprinkle with fine salt, and dry as just described.

And here comes a conflict of authorities. Says my kind friend and neighbor, Mrs. A., an excellent housewife—"I boil my potatoes in cold water always—with a pinch of salt, of course, and when half-done, throw away the boiling water and fill up with cold, then boil again. This makes the potatoes mealy." Mrs. B., whose reputation as a housekeeper and cook is in every kitchen, interposes:—"I have tried both ways. My experience is that potatoes melt into a sort of starchy gruel when boiled in cold water. The philosophy of the operation is to heat quickly and thoroughly, and, the instant they are done, to dry out every drop of water. And—" with a touch of pardonable pride—"we generally have delightful potatoes." This is true, but remembering that Mrs. A.'s are like snow hillocks, ready to crumble at a breath, I come home and try the cold water plan. My cook, unlike most of her tribe, is too sensible to suppose that she knows everything, and willingly abets me. The result of our experiments stands somewhat thus—Garnet, White Mountain, and Early Rose potatoes *are* apt to dissolve in cold water, giving off their starch too readily, perhaps. We boil them in hot water. Peach Blows, Prince Alberts, and other late varieties are best cooked as Mrs. A. recommends—*always* pouring off the water the instant they are done, and letting the potatoes dry for a few minutes. My housewifely friends can decide for themselves which method is preferable.

MASHED POTATOES. ✠

Old potatoes are best mashed. Pare, and let them lie in cold water from half to three-quarters of an hour. A longer time will not hurt them. Boil in hot or cold water, according to the toughness of texture. A coarse, waxy potato is best cooked in cold water. In either case, put in a pinch of salt. Drain thoroughly when done, sprinkle with salt, and mash them in the pot with a potato-beetle, or whip with a split spoon, working in a tablespoonful of butter and enough milk to make the paste about the consistency of soft dough. Leave no lumps in it, and when smooth, dish. Form into a mound with a wooden spoon, and leave dots of pepper here and there on the surface, as large as a half-dime.

Or,

Brown by setting in the oven until a crust is formed. Glaze this with butter, and serve.

TO BOIL NEW POTATOES.

If very young, rub the skin off with a rough towel. If almost ripe, scrape with a blunt knife. Lay in cold water an hour, cover with cold water slightly salted, boil half an hour. Drain, salt, and dry for two or three minutes. Send to table plain.

Or,

You may crack each by pressing lightly upon it with the back of a wooden spoon, lay them in a deep dish, and pour over them a cupful of cream or new milk, heated to a boil, in which a great spoonful of butter has been dissolved.

TO STEW OLD POTATOES. ✠

This is a good way to cook potatoes which are so rank and tough as hardly to be eatable in any other form.

Pare and quarter, if large. Soak in cold water one hour. Put into a pot with enough cold salted water to cover them. When almost done, turn off the water, add a like quantity of milk, and bring to a boil. Before taking up, stir in a heaping tablespoonful of butter, a little salt, a handful of chopped parsley, and thicken slightly with flour previously wet in cold milk. Boil one minute, and pour all into a deep dish.

STEWED POTATOES FOR BREAKFAST. ✠

Pare, cut into dice, and soak in cold water half an hour. Stew in enough hot salted water to cover them. Before taking up, and when they are breaking to pieces, drain off half the water, and pour in a cupful of milk. Boil three minutes, stirring well; put in a lump of butter the size of an egg rolled in flour, a little salt and a pinch of pepper; add a little parsley; boil up well and turn into a covered dish.

This is an excellent family dish. Children are usually fond of it and it is very wholesome.

BAKED POTATOES.

Wash and wipe some large ripe potatoes, and bake in a quick oven until tender, say from three-quarters of an hour to an hour, if of a good size. Serve in a napkin with the skins on. Tear or cut a hole in the top when you eat them, put in a bit of butter with salt and pepper. They are good for boys' cold fingers at supper-time on winter nights.

POTATO PUFF. ✠

Take two cupfuls of cold mashed potato, and stir into it two tablespoonfuls of melted butter, beating to a white cream before adding anything else. Then put with this two eggs whipped very light and a teacupful of cream or milk, salting to taste. Beat all well, pour into a deep dish, and bake in a quick oven until it is nicely browned. If properly mixed, it will come out of the oven light, puffy, and delectable.

POTATOES WARMED OVER—alias au Maître d'Hôtel.

Slice cold boiled potatoes a quarter of an inch thick, and put into a saucepan, with four or five tablespoonfuls of milk, two or three of butter, pepper, salt, and some chopped parsley. Heat quickly, stirring all the time until ready to boil, when stir in the juice of half a lemon. This last ingredient entitles the dish to the foreign title. Pour into a deep dish, and serve very hot.

POTATO CROQUETTES. ✠

Season cold mashed potato with pepper, salt, and nutmeg. Beat to a cream, with a tablespoonful of melted butter to every cupful of potato. Bind with two or three beaten eggs, and add some minced parsley. Roll into oval balls, dip in beaten egg, then in bread-crumbs, and fry in hot lard or drippings.

Pile in a pyramid upon a flat dish, and serve.

FRIED POTATOES. ✠

Pare, wash, and slice some raw potatoes as thin as wafers. This can be done with a sharp knife, although there is a little instrument for the purpose, to be had at the house-furnishing stores, which flutes prettily as well as slices evenly. Lay in ice-water for half an hour, wipe dry in two cloths, spreading them upon one, and pressing the other upon them. Have ready in the frying-pan some boiling lard or nice dripping, fry the potatoes to a light brown, sprinkle with salt, and serve in a napkin laid in a deep dish and folded over them. To dry them of the fat, take from the frying-pan as soon as they are brown, with a perforated skimmer, put into a cullender and shake for an instant. They should be crisp and free from grease.

Or,

Chop cold boiled potatoes into bits, season with pepper and salt, and fry lightly in dripping or butter, turning them constantly until nicely browned.

POTATO RIBBON.

Pare and lay in ice-water for an hour. Choose the largest and soundest potatoes you can get for this dish. At the end of the hour, pare, with a small knife, round and round in one continuous curling strip. There is also an instrument for this purpose, which costs but a trifle, and will do the work deftly and expeditiously. Handle with care, fry—a few at a time, for fear of entanglement— in lard or clarified drippings, drain, and arrange neatly upon a hot flat dish.

POTATOES À LA CRÈME. ✠

Put into a saucepan three tablespoonfuls of butter, a small handful of parsley chopped small, salt and pepper to taste. Stir up well until hot, add a small teacupful of cream or rich milk, thicken with two teaspoonfuls of flour, and stir until it boils. Chop some cold boiled potatoes, put into the mixture, and boil up once before serving.

STUFFED POTATOES. ✠

Take large, fair potatoes, bake until soft, and cut a round piece off the top of each. Scrape out the inside carefully, so as not to break the skin, and set aside the empty cases with the covers. Mash the inside very smoothly, working into it while hot some butter and cream—about half a teaspoonful of each for every potato. Season with salt and pepper, with a good pinch of grated cheese for each; work it very soft with milk, and put into a saucepan to heat, stirring, to prevent burning. When scalding hot, stir in one well-beaten egg for six large potatoes. Boil up once, fill the skins with the mixture, replacing the caps, return them to the oven for three minutes; arrange upon a napkin in a deep dish, the caps uppermost; cover with a fold of the napkin, and eat hot.

Or,

You may omit the eggs and put in a double quantity of cheese. They are very good.

POTATO SCALLOPS.

Boil, and mash the potatoes soft with a little milk. Beat up light with melted butter—a dessertspoonful for every half-pint of the potato—salt and pepper to taste. Fill some patty-pans or buttered scallop shells with the mixture, and brown in an oven, when you have stamped a pattern on the top of each. Glaze, while hot, with butter, and serve in the shells.

If you like, you can strew some grated cheese over the top.

BROWNED POTATOES.—(*Whole.*)

Boil and peel some large, ripe potatoes, and three-quarters of an hour before a piece of roast beef is removed from the fire, skim the fat from the gravy; put the potatoes in the dripping-pan, having dredged them well with flour. Baste them, to prevent scorching, with the gravy, and when quite brown, drain on a sieve. Lay them about the meat in the dish.

BROWNED POTATO.—(*Mashed.*)

This is also an accompaniment to roast beef or mutton. Mash some boiled potatoes smoothly with a little milk, pepper, salt, and a boiled onion (minced); make into small cones or balls; flour well, and put under or beside the meat, half an hour or so before you take it up. Skim off all the fat from the gravy before putting them in. Drain them dry when brown, and lay around the meat when dished.

These are nice with roast spare-rib, or any roast pork that is not *too* fat.

BROILED POTATOES.

Cut whole boiled potatoes lengthwise, into slices a quarter of an inch thick, and lay upon a gridiron over a hot, bright fire. Brown on both sides, sprinkle with pepper and salt, lay a bit of butter upon each, and eat very hot.

POTATO CAKES.

Make cold mashed potato into flat cakes; flour and fry in lard, or good sweet dripping, until they are a light-brown.

ROAST SWEET POTATOES.

Select those of uniform size, wash, wipe, and roast until you can tell, by gently pressing the largest between the finger and thumb, that it is mellow throughout. Serve in their jackets.

Sweet, as well as Irish potatoes, are very good for pic-nic luncheon, roasted in hot ashes. This, it will be remembered, was the dinner General Marion set before the British officer as "quite a feast, I assure you, sir. We don't often fare so well as to have sweet potatoes and salt."

The feast was cleansed from ashes by the negro orderly's shirt-sleeve, and served upon a natural trencher of pine-bark.

BOILED SWEET POTATOES.

Have them all as nearly the same size as possible; put into cold water, without any salt, and boil until a fork will easily pierce the largest. Turn off the water, and lay them in the oven to dry for five minutes. Peel before sending to table.

Or, ✠

Parboil, and then roast until done. This is a wise plan when they are old and watery. Boiling is apt to render them tasteless. Another way still is to boil until they are almost done, when peel and bake brown, basting them with butter several times, but draining them dry before they go to the table.

FRIED SWEET POTATOES ✠

Parboil them, skin, and cut lengthwise into slices a quarter of an inch thick. Fry in sweet dripping or butter.

Cold boiled potatoes may be cooked in this way. Or you can chop them up with an equal quantity of cold Irish potatoes, put them into a frying-pan with a good lump of butter, and stir until they are hot and slightly brown.

CABBAGE.

BOILED CABBAGE.

Pick off the outer green leaves, quarter, examine carefully to be sure there are no insects in it, and lay for an hour in cold water. Then put into a pot with plenty of boiling water, and cook fifteen minutes. Throw away the water, and fill up the pot from the boiling tea-kettle. Cook until tender all through. Three-quarters of an hour will do for a good-sized cabbage when young. Late in the season you must be guided by the tenderness of the stalk. Drain well, chop, and stir in a tablespoonful of butter, pepper, and salt. Serve very hot. If you boil corned beef or pork to eat with cabbage, let the second water be taken from the pot in which this is cooking. It will flavor it nicely.

Always boil cabbage in two waters.

BACON AND CABBAGE.

This, I need hardly say, is a favorite country dish at the South. The old-fashioned way of preparing it was to boil meat and cabbage together, and serve, reeking with fat, the cabbage in quarters, soaking yet more of the essence from the ham or middling about which it lay. In this shape it justly earned a reputation for grossness and indigestibility that banished it, in time, from many tables.

Yet it is a savory and not unwholesome article of food in winter, if the cabbage be boiled in two waters, the second being the "pot liquor" from the boiling meat. Drain thoroughly in a cullender, pressing out every drop of water that will flow, without breaking the tender leaves; and when the meat is dished, lay the cabbage neatly about it, and upon each quarter a slice of hard-boiled egg.

When you eat, season with pepper, salt, and vinegar.

STUFFED CABBAGE.

Choose for this purpose a large, firm cabbage. Take off the outer leaves, and lay in boiling water ten minutes, then in very cold. Do this several hours before you are ready to stuff it. When perfectly cold, bind a broad tape about it, or a strip of muslin, that it may not fall apart when the stalk is taken out. Remove this with a thin sharp knife, leaving a hole about as deep as your middle-finger. Without widening the mouth of the aperture, excavate the centre until you have room for four or five tablespoonfuls of the force-meat—more, if the head be large. Chop the bits you take out very small; mix with some cold boiled pork or ham, or cooked sausage-meat, a *very* little onion, pepper, salt, a pinch of thyme, and some bread-crumbs. Fill the cavity with this, bind a wide strip of muslin over the hole in the top, and lay the cabbage in a large saucepan with a pint of "pot-liquor" from boiled beef or ham. Stew gently until very tender. Take out the cabbage, unbind carefully, and lay in a dish. Keep hot while you add to the gravy, when you have strained it, pepper, a piece of butter rolled in flour, and two or three tablespoonfuls rich milk or cream. Boil up, and pour over the cabbage.

"COLLARDS," OR CABBAGE-SPROUTS.

Pick over carefully, lay in cold water, slightly salted, half an hour; shake in a cullender to drain, and put into boiling water, keeping at a fast boil until tender. A piece of pork seasons them pleasantly. In this case put the meat on first, adding the greens when it is parboiled, and cooking them together. Boil in an uncovered vessel. Drain very well; chop and heap in a dish, laying the meat on top.

LADIES' CABBAGE. ✠

Boil a firm white cabbage fifteen minutes, changing the water then for more from the boiling tea-kettle. When tender, drain and set aside until perfectly cold. Chop fine, and add two beaten eggs, a tablespoonful of butter, pepper, salt, three tablespoonfuls rich milk or cream. Stir all well together, and bake in a buttered pudding-dish until brown. Eat very hot.

I can conscientiously recommend this dish even to those who are not fond of any of the ordinary preparations of cabbage. It is digestible and palatable, more nearly resembling cauliflower in taste than its coarser and commoner cousin—*German.*

FRIED CABBAGE.

Chop cold boiled cabbage, and drain very dry, stirring in a little melted butter, pepper, and salt, with three or four tablespoonfuls of cream. Heat all in a buttered frying-pan, stirring until smoking hot; then let the mixture stand just long enough to brown slightly on the under-side. It is improved by the addition of a couple of beaten eggs. Turn out by putting a flat dish above the pan, upside-down, and reversing the latter. This is a breakfast dish.

SAUERKRAUT.

Shred or chop the cabbage fine. Line a barrel, keg, or jar with cabbage-leaves on the bottom and sides. Put in a layer of the cut cabbage, three inches in depth; press down well and sprinkle with four tablespoonfuls of salt. When you have packed five layers in this way, press hard with a board cut to fit loosely on the inside of the barrel or jar. Put heavy weights on this, or pound with a wooden beetle until the cabbage is a compact mass, when remove the board and put in more layers of salt and shred cabbage, repeating the pounding every four or five layers, until the vessel is full. Cover with leaves, and put the board on the top of these with a heavy weight to keep it down. Set all away to ferment. In three weeks remove the scum, and if need be, cover with water. Keep in a cool, dry cellar. It can be eaten raw or boiled, and seasoned with pork.

This is the mode *simple* if not *pure* of preparing this, to nostrils unaccustomed to it, malodorous compound. Some add to the salt whole black peppers, cloves, garlic, and mace,—"then put it away," as a mild, motherly Teuton dame once told me, "in the cellar to r—"—"Rot!" interpolated a disgusted bystander, anticipating her deliberate utterance. "No, my dear," drawled the placid Frau, "to *ripen.*"

CAULIFLOWER.

BOILED CAULIFLOWER.

Pick off the leaves and cut the stalk close to the bottom of the bunch of flowers. Lay in cold water for half an hour. Unless *very* large, do not cut it; if you do, quarter neatly. Tie a close net of coarse bobbinet lace or tarlatan about it to prevent breaking or bruising; put into boiling water salted, and cook until tender. Undo and remove the net, and lay the cauliflower in a hot dish. Have ready a large cupful of nice drawn butter and pour over it. A little lemon-juice makes of this a *sauce tartare.*

Cut with a silver knife and fork in helping it out, and give a little of the sauce to each person. Take it out of the water as soon as it is done, serve quickly, and eat hot. It darkens with standing.

STEWED CAULIFLOWER.

Use for this dish the smaller and more indifferent cauliflowers. Cut them into small clusters; lay in cold salt and water half an hour, and stew fifteen minutes in boiling water. Turn most of this off, leaving but half a teacupful in the saucepan. Add to this a half-cupful of milk thickened with a very little rice or wheat flour, and two tablespoonfuls of melted butter, pepper, and salt. Shake the saucepan over the fire gently until it boils; take out the cauliflowers with a perforated skimmer, lay in order upon a dish, and pour the sauce over them.

SCALLOPED CAULIFLOWER.

Boil until tender, clip into neat clusters, and pack—the stems downward—in a buttered pudding-dish. Beat up a cupful of bread-crumbs to a soft paste with two tablespoonfuls of melted butter and six of cream or milk; season with pepper and salt, bind with a beaten egg, and with this cover the cauliflower. Cover the dish closely and bake six minutes in a quick oven; brown in five more, and serve very hot in the dish in which they were baked.

BROCCOLI AND BRUSSELS SPROUTS.

Pick over, wash carefully, cut off the lower part of the stems and lay in cold water, slightly salted, half an hour. Cook quickly in boiling water, with a little salt, until tender. This will be in twelve or fifteen minutes. Cook in an uncovered saucepan. Drain well, lay in a neat pile lightly heaped in the centre of a dish, and pour drawn butter over them, or serve this in a tureen.

BROCCOLI AND EGGS.

Boil two or three heads of broccoli until tender. Have ready two cupfuls of butter drawn in the usual way, and beat into it, while hot, four well-whipped eggs. Lay buttered toast in the bottom of a hot dish, and on this the largest head of broccoli whole, as a centre-piece. Arrange close about this the others cut into clusters, the stems downward, and pour the egg-sauce over all.

MASHED TURNIPS.

Peel and lay in cold water, slightly salted, until the water boils in the saucepan intended for them. Put them in and boil until very tender. The time will depend upon their age. Drain and mash in the cullender with a wooden spoon, stirring in at the last a tablespoonful of butter with pepper and salt to taste, and serve hot.

If eaten with boiled corned beef, you may take a little of the liquor from the pot in which the meat is cooking; put it into a saucepan, boil up once to throw off the scum, skim clean, and cook the turnips in this.

Or,

If the turnips are young, rub them when tender *through* the cullender; add a little milk, butter, pepper, and salt; heat to boiling in a clean saucepan and serve.

YOUNG TURNIPS BOILED WHOLE.

Pare smoothly, and trim all into the same size and shape. Lay in cold water half an hour. Put on in boiling water, with a tablespoonful of butter, and stew until tender. Drain dry, without crushing or breaking them; pile in a deep dish, and cover with a white sauce made of butter drawn in milk. Turnips should be eaten very hot always.

BOILED SPINACH.

In respect to quantity, spinach is desperately deceitful. I never see it drained after it is boiled without bethinking myself of a picture I saw many years since, illustrative of the perils of innocent simplicity. A small (lucky) boy and big (unlucky) one have been spending their holiday in fishing. While the former, well satisfied with the result of his day's sport, is busy putting up his rod and tackle, the designing elder dexterously substitutes his own string of minnows for the other's store of fine perch. The little fellow, turning to pick it up, without a suspicion of the cruel cheat, makes piteous round eyes at his fellow, ejaculating, "How they have *swhrunk*!"

A young housekeeper of my acquaintance, ordering a spring dinner for herself and husband, purchased a quart of spinach. When it should have appeared upon the table, there came in its stead a platter of sliced egg, she having given out one for the dressing. "Where is the spinach?" she demanded of the maid of all work. "Under the egg, ma'am!" And it was really all there.

Moral.—Get enough spinach to be visible to the naked eye. A peck is not too much for a family of four or five.

Pick it over very carefully; it is apt to be gritty. Wash in several waters, and let it lie in the last half an hour at least. Take out with your hands, shaking each bunch well, and put into boiling water, with a little salt. Boil from fifteen to twenty minutes. When tender, drain thoroughly, chop *very* fine; put into a saucepan with a piece of butter the size of an egg, and pepper to taste. Stir until very hot, turn into a dish and shape into a flat-topped mound with a silver or wooden spoon; slice some hard-boiled eggs and lay on top.

Or,

Rub the yolks of the eggs to a powder; mix with butter, and when your mound is raised, spread smoothly over the flat top. Four eggs will dress a good-sized dish. Cut the whites into rings and garnish, laying them on the yellow surface. This makes a pleasant dressing for the spinach.

SPINACH À LA CRÈME.

Boil and chop *very* fine, or rub through a cullender. Season with pepper and salt. Beat in, while warm, three tablespoonfuls melted butter (this is for a large dish). Put into a saucepan and heat, stirring constantly. When smoking hot, add three tablespoonfuls of cream and a teaspoonful white sugar. Boil up once, still stirring, and press firmly into a hot bowl or other mould. Turn into a hot dish and garnish with boiled eggs.

GREEN PEAS.

Shell and lay in cold water until you are ready to cook them. Put into salted boiling water, and cook from twenty minutes to half an hour. If young and fresh, the shorter time will suffice. If just gathered from your own vines and tender, season only with salt. Market peas are greatly improved by the addition of a small lump of white sugar. It improves taste and color. The English always put it in, also a sprig of mint, to be removed when the peas are dished. Drain well, and dish, with a great lump of butter stirred in, and a little pepper. Keep hot.

PEA FRITTERS OR CAKES. ✠

Cook a pint or three cups more peas than you need for dinner. Mash while hot with a wooden spoon, seasoning with pepper, salt, and butter. Put by until morning. Make a batter of two whipped eggs, a cupful of milk, quarter teaspoonful soda, a half teaspoonful cream tartar, and half a cup of flour. Stir the pea-mixture into this, beating very hard, and cook as you would ordinary griddle-cakes.

I can testify, from experience, that they make a delightful morning dish, and hereby return thanks to the unknown friend to whom I am indebted for the receipt.

ASPARAGUS (*boiled.*)

Cut your stalks of equal length, rejecting the woody or lower portions, and scraping the white part which remains. Throw into cold water as you scrape them. Tie in a bunch with soft strings— muslin or tape—and put into boiling water slightly salted. If very young and fresh, it is well to tie in a piece of coarse net to protect the tops. Boil from twenty to forty minutes, according to the age. Just before it is done, toast two or three slices of bread, cutting off the crust; dip in the asparagus liquor, butter, and lay in a hot dish. When you take up the asparagus, drain, unbind the bundle, and heap it upon the toast, with bits of butter between the stalks.

ASPARAGUS AND EGGS.

Cut twenty-five or thirty heads of asparagus into bits half an inch long, and boil fifteen minutes. Have a cupful of rich drawn butter in a saucepan, and put in the asparagus when you have drained it dry. Heat together to a boil, seasoning with pepper and salt, and pour into a buttered bake dish. Break five or six eggs carefully over the surface; put a bit of butter upon each; sprinkle with salt, and pepper, and put in the oven until the eggs are set.

Or, ✠

You may beat the eggs—yolks and whites separately—to a froth; season with butter, pepper, and salt; stir them together, with the addition of three tablespoonfuls of milk or cream, and pour evenly over the asparagus mixture in the dish. This is decidedly the better way of the two, although somewhat more troublesome.

ASPARAGUS IN AMBUSH. ✠

Cut off the tender tops of fifty heads of asparagus; boil and drain them. Have ready half a dozen (or more) stale biscuit or rolls, from which you have cut a neat top slice and scraped out the crumb. Set them in the oven to crisp, laying the tops beside them that the cavities may be well dried. Meanwhile, put into a saucepan a sugarless custard made of a pint—if you need so much—of milk, and four well-whipped eggs. Boil the milk first, before beating in the eggs; set over the fire and stir until it thickens, when add a great spoonful of butter, a little salt and pepper; lastly, the asparagus tops, minced fine. Do not let it boil, but take from the fire so soon as the asparagus is fairly in; fill the rolls with the mixture, put on the tops, fitting them accurately; set in the oven three minutes, and arrange on a dish, to be eaten hot.

The number of rolls will depend upon their size. It is better to have them small, so that one can be served to each person. They will be found extremely nice.

BOILED ONIONS.

Cut off tops and tails, and skin them. Lay in cold water half an hour, then put into a saucepan with enough boiling water to cover them. Cook fifteen minutes and drain off the water, re-covering them with more from the boiling tea-kettle. Boil until a straw will pierce them; drain and put into a dish with pepper, salt, and plenty of butter. Send around drawn butter with them. Never cook onions in an iron pot.

STEWED ONIONS. ✠

Young onions should always be cooked in this way. Top, tail, and skin them, lay them in cold water half an hour or more, then put into a saucepan with hot water enough to cover them. When half done, throw off all the water, except a small teacupful—less, if your mess be small; add a like quantity of milk, a great spoonful of butter, with pepper and salt to taste. Stew gently until tender, and turn into a deep dish.

If the onions are strong and large, boil in three waters, throwing away all of the first and second, and reserving a very little of the third to mix with the milk.

It ought to be more generally known that the disagreeable odor left by any of the onion family upon the breath may be removed by chewing and swallowing a few grains of roasted coffee. No more nutritious vegetable ever finds its way to our tables, and it is greatly to be regretted that the unpleasant result just named should deter so many from eating it. It is especially beneficial to brain-workers and nervous invalids—the very people who are least likely to taste it.

BAKED ONIONS.

The large Spanish or Bermuda onions are the only kinds which are usually baked. Wash clean, but do not remove the skins. Boil an hour—the water should be boiling when they are put in, and slightly salt. Change it twice during this time, always replenishing with more, boiling-hot. Turn off the water, take the onions out and lay upon a cloth, that all the moisture may be absorbed or evaporate. Roll each in a round piece of buttered tissue-paper, twisting it at the top to keep it closed, and bake in a slow oven nearly an hour. When tender all through, peel them, put them into a deep dish, and brown slightly, basting with butter freely. This will take perhaps a quarter of an hour more. Serve in a vegetable dish, and pour the melted butter over them when you have sprinkled with pepper and salt.

STUFFED ONIONS.

Wash and skin very large Bermuda onions. Lay in cold water an hour. Parboil in boiling water half an hour. Drain, and while hot extract the hearts, taking care not to break the outer layers. Chop the inside thus obtained very fine, with a little cold fat pork or bacon. Add bread-crumbs, pepper, salt, mace, and wet with a spoonful or two of cream. Bind with a well-beaten egg, and work into a smooth paste. Stuff the onions with this; put into a dripping-pan with a very little hot water, and simmer in the oven for an hour, basting often with melted butter. When done, take the onions up carefully, and arrange the open ends uppermost in a vegetable dish. Add to the gravy in the dripping-pan the juice of half a lemon, four tablespoonfuls of cream or milk, and a little browned flour wet with cold milk. Boil up once, and pour over the onions.

STEWED TOMATOES. ✠

Loosen the skins by pouring scalding water upon them; peel and cut them up, extracting the cores or hard parts of the stem end, and removing all unripe portions. Stew in a saucepan (tin or porcelain) half an hour, when add salt and pepper to taste, a teaspoonful of white sugar, and a tablespoonful of butter. Stew gently fifteen minutes longer, and serve.

Some cooks thicken the tomatoes with a little grated bread. A minced onion—a small one—improves the flavor. Another pleasant variety is to put a quarter as much green corn as you have tomatoes into the saucepan when it is first set on the fire, and stew gently.

STUFFED BAKED TOMATOES. ✠

Choose large, smooth tomatoes, and cut a thin slice from the blossom end of each, laying it aside for further use. Scoop out the inside, and chop fine with a little grated bread, some green corn, salt, pepper, a teaspoonful white sugar, and a tablespoonful butter. Mix well, and stuff the hollowed tomatoes. Fit the tops on neatly, place in circular rows in a deep dish and bake three-quarters of an hour, to a light brown. Fill the interstices with the force-meat if you have any left, before you bake. Do not peel them.

SCALLOPED TOMATOES. ✠

Peel and cut in slices a quarter of an inch thick. Pack in a pudding-dish in alternate layers, with a force-meat made of bread-crumbs, butter, salt, pepper, and a little white sugar. Spread thickly upon each stratum of tomatoes, and when the dish is nearly full, put tomatoes uppermost, a good bit of butter upon each slice. Dust with pepper and a little sugar. Strew with dry bread-crumbs, and bake covered half an hour; remove the lid and bake brown.

SCALLOP OF TOMATOES AND GREEN CORN. ✠

This is made as above, substituting for the bread-crumbs in the force-meat, green corn cut from the cob, and seasoning with some fat pork chopped very fine, a minced shallot, pepper, salt, and sugar. Let the top layer be tomatoes, butter and season, and sift grated bread-crumbs over it to brown the scallop. Bake covered half an hour; uncover and leave in the oven as much longer. This time is for a large dishful.

BROILED TOMATOES.

Select large, firm ones, and do not peel. Slice half an inch thick, and broil upon an oyster gridiron. A few minutes will suffice to cook them. Have ready in a cup some hot butter, seasoned with pepper, salt, a little sugar, and a half a teaspoonful of made mustard. As soon as the tomatoes are done, dip each piece in this mixture and lay upon a hot chafing-dish. When all are dished, heat what remains of the seasoning to a boil, pour upon them, and serve at once.

Broiled tomatoes are much liked by those who have eaten them cooked in this manner.

BAKED TOMATOES (*Plain.*)

Peel and slice a quarter of an inch thick. Pack in a pudding-dish, seasoning each layer with salt, pepper, butter, and a very little white sugar. Bake covered half an hour, remove the lid, and brown for fifteen minutes. Five minutes before taking from the oven, pour over the top three or four tablespoonfuls of cream whipped up for a few minutes with melted butter.

RAW TOMATOES.

Do not loosen the skins with scalding water. It impairs the flavor and destroys the crispness. Pare with a keen knife, slice and lay in a glass dish. Season with pepper, salt, and vinegar, stirring a piece of ice rapidly around in the dressing before pouring it over the tomatoes, and setting the dish in the refrigerator until wanted.

There is no salad, excepting, perhaps, lettuce and cucumbers, that is more improved by the use of ice than tomatoes.

RAW CUCUMBERS.

Pare neatly from end to end, and lay in ice-water one hour. Wipe them and slice thin. Season with pepper, salt and vinegar— and oil, if you wish—laying some bits of ice among them, with thin slices of onion. Cucumbers should be gathered while the dew is on them, and eaten the same day. Leave them in a cool place until you are ready to pare them.

FRIED CUCUMBERS. ✠

Pare and lay in ice-water half an hour. Cut lengthwise, into slices *nearly* half an inch thick, and lay in ice-water ten minutes longer. Wipe each piece dry with a soft cloth, sprinkle with pepper and salt, and dredge with flour. Fry to a delicate brown in sweet clarified dripping, nice lard, or butter.

Many declare that cucumbers are never fit to eat unless fried, and they are assuredly far more wholesome than when served raw.

STEWED CUCUMBERS.

Pare, lay in ice-water an hour; then, slice a quarter of an inch thick. Pick out the seeds with a penknife, and put into a saucepan with enough boiling water to cover them. Stew fifteen minutes, and drain off the water. Add enough from the boiling tea-kettle to keep them from burning; season with salt and pepper, and stir carefully in a tablespoonful of butter—or two, should the quantity of cucumber be large. Stew gently ten minutes, and add half a cupful of rich milk; thicken with a little flour, boil up, and serve in a deep dish, squeezing some lemon-juice in at the last.

This is a popular English dish, although it seems a strange one to American ideas.

BOILED GREEN CORN.

Choose young sugar-corn, full grown, but not hard; test with the nail. When the grain is pierced, the milk should escape in a jet, and not be thick. Clean by stripping off the outer leaves, turn back the innermost covering carefully, pick off every thread of silk, and recover the ear with the thin husk that grew nearest it. Tie at the top with a bit of thread, put into boiling water salted, and cook fast from twenty minutes to half an hour, in proportion to size and age. Cut off the stalks close to the cob, and send whole to table wrapped in a napkin.

Or, you can cut from the cob while hot, and season with butter, pepper and salt. Send to table in a vegetable dish.

CORN AND TOMATOES.

Take equal quantities of green corn cut from the cob, and tomatoes sliced and peeled. Stew together half an hour; season with pepper, salt, and a *very* little sugar. Stew fifteen minutes longer, and stir in a great lump of butter. Five minutes later, pour out and serve.

SUCCOTASH.

This is made of green corn and Lima beans, although you can substitute for the latter string or butter beans. Have a third more corn than beans, when the former has been cut from the cob and the beans shelled. Put into boiling water enough to cover them— no more—and stew gently together until tender—perhaps half an hour—stirring now and then. Pour off nearly all the water, and add a large cupful of milk. Stew in this, watching to prevent burning, for an hour; then stir in a great lump of butter, a teaspoonful of flour wet with cold milk, pepper and salt to taste. Boil up once, and pour into a deep vegetable-dish. If you use string-beans, string and cut up into half-inch lengths before cooking.

GREEN CORN PUDDING. ✠

- 1 quart milk.
- 5 eggs.
- 2 tablespoonfuls melted butter.
- 1 tablespoonful white sugar.
- 1 dozen ears of corn—large ones.

Grate the corn from the cob; beat the whites and yolks of the eggs separately. Put the corn and yolks together, stir *hard*, and add the butter; then the milk gradually, beating all the while; next the sugar and a little salt; lastly the whites. Bake slowly at first, covering the dish, for an hour. Remove the cover, and brown finely.

This is a most delicious accompaniment to a meat course, when properly mixed and baked. Warm up what is left from dinner for breakfast, by moistening it with a little warm milk, and stirring in a saucepan until smoking hot. You can make this pudding from canned corn in winter, chopping the corn fine.

GREEN CORN FRITTERS OR CAKES. ✠

Grate the corn, and allow an egg and a half for every cupful, with a tablespoonful of milk or cream. Beat the eggs well, add the corn by degrees, beating very hard; salt to taste; put a tablespoonful of melted butter to every pint of corn; stir in the milk, and thicken with just enough flour to hold them together—say a tablespoonful for every two eggs. You may fry in hot lard, as you would fritters, but a better plan is to cook upon a griddle, like batter cakes. Test a little first, to see that it is of the right consistency.

Eaten at dinner or breakfast, these always meet with a cordial welcome.

STEWED GREEN CORN.

Cut from the cob, and stew fifteen minutes in boiling water. Turn off most of this, cover with cold milk, and stew until very tender, adding, before you take it up, a large lump of butter cut into bits and rolled in flour. Season with pepper and salt to taste. Boil five minutes, and serve.

Cold corn left from dinner should be cut from the cob and stewed a few minutes in a little milk, adding seasoning as above. Or, you can mix it with chopped cold potatoes—Irish or sweet; heat a piece of butter or beef-dripping in a frying-pan, and stir in the mixture until smoking-hot. Never throw away a good ear of sweet corn.

ROASTED GREEN CORN.

Turn back the husks upon the stalk, pick off the silk, recover with the husks as closely as possible, and roast in the hot ashes of a wood-fire. Eat with butter, salt, and pepper, out of doors, in the forest, or on the beach.

SALSIFY OR OYSTER-PLANT. (*Stewed.*) ✠

Scrape the roots, dropping each into cold water as soon as it is cleaned. Exposure to the air blackens them. Cut in pieces an inch long, put into a saucepan with hot water enough to cover them, and stew until tender. Turn off nearly all the water, and add a cupful of cold milk. Stew ten minutes after this begins to boil; put in a great lump of butter, cut into bits, and rolled in flour; pepper and salt to taste. Boil up once, and serve. The taste is curiously like that of stewed oysters.

FRIED SALSIFY, OR MOCK OYSTERS. ✠

Scrape the roots thoroughly, and lay in cold water ten or fifteen minutes. Boil whole until tender, drain, and when cold, mash with a wooden spoon to a smooth paste, picking out all the fibres. Moisten with a little milk; add a tablespoonful of butter, and an egg and a half for every cupful of salsify. Beat the eggs light. Make into round cakes, dredge with flour, and fry brown.

FRIED EGG-PLANT. ✠

Slice the egg-plant at least half an inch thick; pare each piece carefully, and lay in salt and water, putting a plate upon the topmost to keep it under the brine, and let them alone for an hour or more. Wipe each slice, dip in beaten egg, then in cracker-crumbs, and fry in hot lard until well done and nicely browned.

STUFFED EGG-PLANT. ✠

Parboil for ten minutes. Slit each down the side, and extract the seeds. Prop open the cut with a bit of clean wood or china, and lay in cold salt and water while you prepare the force-meat. Make this of bread-crumbs, minute bits of fat pork, salt, pepper, nutmeg, parsley, and a *very* little onion, chopped up together. Moisten with cream, and bind with a beaten egg. Fill the cavity in the egg-plant with this; wind soft pack-thread about them to keep the slit shut, and bake, putting a little water in the dripping-pan. Baste with butter and water when they begin to cook. Test with a straw when they are tender, and baste twice at the last with butter. Lay the egg-plants in a dish, add two or three tablespoonfuls of cream to the gravy, thicken with a little flour, put in a teaspoonful of chopped parsley, boil up once, and pour over the vegetable.

BOILED CARROTS.

Wash and scrape well, and lay in cold water half an hour. If large, split them, or cut across in two or three pieces. Put into boiling water, slightly salted, and boil until tender. Large ones will require nearly an hour and a half to cook. Young carrots should only be washed before they are boiled, and the skin be rubbed off with a cloth afterward. Butter well, and serve hot.

STEWED CARROTS.

Scrape, and lay in cold water half an hour or more. Boil whole three-quarters of an hour, drain, and cut into round slices a quarter of an inch thick. Put on in a saucepan with a teacupful of broth— veal, or beef, or mutton; pepper and salt to taste, and stew gently half an hour. Just before they are done, add four tablespoonfuls cream or milk, and a good lump of butter cut into bits, and rolled in flour. Boil up and serve.

If you have not the broth, use water, and put in a tablespoonful of butter when the saucepan is set on the fire, in addition to the quantity I have specified.

Another Way.

Scrape and boil until nearly done. Cut into small squares, and put into a saucepan, with two small onions, minced; a little chopped parsley, pepper and salt to taste, and half a cup of rather thin drawn butter. They will require half an hour's simmering. Serve hot.

MASHED CARROTS.

Wash, scrape, and lay in cold water a while. Boil very tender in hot water, slightly salted. Drain, and mash with a beetle or wooden spoon, working in a large spoonful of butter, with pepper and salt. A little cream will improve them. Mound as you would mashed potatoes, and stamp a figure upon them, or mark in squares with a knife.

FRENCH, OR STRING OR "SNAP" BEANS.

Break off the tops and bottoms and "string" carefully. *Then* pare both edges with a sharp knife, to be certain that no remnant of the tough fibre remains. Not one cook in a hundred performs this duty as deftly and thoroughly as it should be done. I have heard several gentlemen say that they could always tell, after the first mouthful, whether the mistress or the hireling had "strung" the beans. It is a tedious and disagreeable business, this pulling bits of woody thread out of one's mouth when he wants to enjoy his dinner.

Cut the beans thus cleared of their troublesome *attachés*, in pieces an inch long, and lay in cold water with a little salt for fifteen or twenty minutes. Drain them, and put into a saucepan of boiling water. Boil quickly, twenty minutes if well-grown—less if small—at any rate, until tender. Drain in a cullender until the water ceases to drip from them. Dish with a great spoonful of butter stirred in.

To my taste, beans *need* to have a bit of bacon boiled with them—whole, or chopped into bits that dissolve in the boiling. It mellows the rank taste you seek to remove by boiling.

LIMA AND BUTTER BEANS.

Shell into cold water; let them lie a while; put into a pot with plenty of boiling water and a little salt, and cook fast until tender. Large ones sometimes require nearly an hour's boiling. The average time is forty minutes. Drain and butter well when dished, peppering to taste.

KIDNEY AND OTHER SMALL BEANS.

Shell into cold water, and cook in boiling until tender. A small piece of fat bacon boiled with them is an advantage to nearly all. If you do this, do not salt them.

DRIED BEANS.

Wash and soak over night in lukewarm water, changing it several times for warmer. If this is done they will require but two hours' boiling. Drain very thoroughly, pressing them firmly, but lightly, in the cullender with a wooden spoon; salt, pepper and mix in a great lump of butter when they are dished.

BOILED BEETS.

Wash, but do not touch with a knife before they are boiled. If cut while raw, they bleed themselves pale in the hot water. Boil until tender—if full-grown at least two hours. When done, rub off the skins, slice round if large, split if young, and butter well in the dish. Salt and pepper to taste.

A nice way is to slice them upon a hot dish, mix a great spoonful of melted butter with four or five of vinegar, pepper and salt, heat to boiling, and pour over the beets.

Instead of consigning the cold ones "left over" to the swill pail, pour cold vinegar upon them and use as pickles with cold or roast meat.

STEWED BEETS.

Boil young, sweet beets, until nearly done; skin and slice them. Put into a saucepan with a minced shallot and parsley, two tablespoonfuls melted butter, a like quantity of vinegar, some salt and pepper. Set on the fire and simmer twenty minutes, shaking the saucepan now and then. Serve with the gravy poured over them.

BOILED PARSNIPS.

If young, scrape before cooking. If old, pare carefully, and if large, split. Put into boiling water, salted, and boil, if small and tender, from half to three-quarters of an hour, if full-grown, more than an hour. When tender, drain and slice lengthwise, buttering well when you dish.

FRIED PARSNIPS. ✠

Boil until tender, scrape off the skin, and cut in thick lengthwise slices. Dredge with flour and fry in hot dripping or lard, turning when one side is browned. Drain off every drop of fat; pepper, and serve hot.

PARSNIP FRITTERS. ✠

Boil tender, mash smooth and fine, picking out the woody bits. For three large parsnips allow two eggs, one cup rich milk, one tablespoonful butter, one teaspoonful salt, three tablespoonfuls flour. Beat the eggs light, stir in the mashed parsnips, beating hard; then the butter and salt, next the milk, lastly the salt. Fry as fritters, or as griddle-cakes.

MASHED PARSNIPS.

Boil and scrape them, mash smooth with the back of a wooden-spoon, or a potato beetle, picking out the fibres; mix in three or four spoonfuls of cream, a great spoonful of butter, pepper and salt to taste. Heat to boiling in a saucepan, and serve. Heap in a mound as you would potato cooked in the same way.

BUTTERED PARSNIPS.

Boil tender and scrape. Slice a quarter of an inch thick lengthwise. Put into a saucepan with three tablespoonfuls melted butter, pepper and salt, and a little chopped parsley. Shake over the fire until the mixture boils. Lay the parsnips in order upon a dish, pour the sauce over them, and garnish with parsley. It is a pleasant addition to this dish to stir a few spoonfuls of cream into the sauce after the parsnips are taken out; boil up, and pour upon them.

BOILED SEA-KALE.

Tie up in bunches when you have picked it over carefully, and lay in cold water for an hour. Put into salted boiling water, and cook twenty or thirty minutes until tender. Lay some slices of buttered toast in the bottom of a dish, clip the threads binding the stems of the sea-kale, and pile upon the toast, buttering it abundantly. Or, you can send around with it a boat of drawn butter.

STEWED SEA-KALE.

Clip off the stems, wash well, tie in neat bunches, and when it has lain in cold water an hour or so, put into a saucepan of boiling water, slightly salted. Boil fifteen minutes, drain well, clip the threads, and return to the saucepan, with a little rich gravy if you have it. If not, pour in three or four tablespoonfuls of butter drawn in milk, pepper and salt, and simmer eight or ten minutes.

ARTICHOKES.

Strip off the outer leaves, and cut the stalks close to the bottom. Wash well and lay in cold water two hours. Immerse in boiling water, the stalk-ends uppermost, with an inverted plate upon them to keep them down. Boil an hour and a half, or until very tender. Arrange in circles upon a dish, the tops up, and pour drawn butter over them.

SUMMER SQUASH OR CYMBLING.

There are many varieties of this vegetable, but the general rules for cooking them are the same. Unless they are extremely tender, it is best to pare them, cutting away as little as possible besides the hard outer rind. Take out the seeds, when you have quartered them, and lay the pieces in cold water. Boil until tender throughout. Drain well, pressing out all the water; mash soft and smooth, seasoning with butter, pepper, and salt. Do this quickly, that you may serve up hot.

WINTER SQUASH.

Pare, take out the seeds, cut into small pieces, and stew until soft and tender. Drain, press well, to rid it of all the water, and mash with butter, pepper, and salt. It will take much longer to cook than the summer squash, and before you put it into hot water, should lie in cold at least two hours.

STEWED PUMPKIN.

Cut in two, extract the seeds, slice, and pare. Cover with cold water for an hour; put over the fire in a pot of boiling water and stew gently, stirring often, until it breaks to pieces. Drain and squeeze, rub through a cullender, then return to the saucepan with a tablespoonful of butter, pepper, and salt to taste. Stir rapidly from the bottom until very hot, when dish, rounding into a mound, with "dabs" of pepper on the top.

BAKED PUMPKIN.

Choose the richest pumpkin you can find; take out the seeds, cut in quarters or eighths, pare, and slice lengthwise half an inch thick. Arrange in layers—not more than two or three slices deep—in a shallow but broad baking-dish. Put a *very* little water in the bottom, and bake very slowly until not only done, but dry. It requires a long time, for the heat should be gentle. Butter each strip on both sides when you dish, and eat hot with bread and butter for tea.

I have been assured, by people who have tried it, that this is a palatable dish to those who are fond of the flavor of pumpkin. I insert it here upon their recommendation—not my own.

POKE STALKS.

When the young stalks are not larger than a man's little finger, and show only a tuft of leaves at top a few inches above ground, is the time to gather them. They are unfit for table-use when larger and older. Scrape the stalks, but do not cut off the leaves. Lay in cold water, with a little salt, for two hours. Tie in bundles, as you do asparagus, put into a saucepan of boiling water, and cook fast three-quarters of an hour. Lay buttered toast in the bottom of a dish, untie the bundles, and pile the poke evenly upon it, buttering very well, and sprinkling with pepper and salt. This is a tolerable substitute for asparagus.

MUSHROOMS.

Imprimis.—Have nothing to do with them until you are an excellent judge between the true and false. That sounds somewhat like the advice of the careful mother to her son, touching the wisdom of never going near the water until he learned how to swim—but the caution can hardly be stated too strongly. Not being ambitious of martyrdom, even in the cause of gastronomical enterprise, especially if the instrument is to be a contemptible, rank-smelling fungus, I never eat or cook native mushrooms; but I learned, years ago, in hill-side rambles, how to distinguish the real from the spurious article. Shun low, damp, shady spots in your quest. The good mushrooms are most plenty in August and September, and spring up in the open, sunny fields or commons, after low-lying fogs or soaking dews. The top is a dirty white,—*par complaisance*, pearl-color,—the under side pink or salmon, changing to russet or brown soon after they are gathered. The poisonous sport all colors, and are usually far prettier than their virtuous kindred. Those which are dead-white above and below, as well as the stalk, are also to be let alone.

Cook a peeled white onion in the pot with your mushrooms. If it turn black, throw all away, and be properly thankful for your escape. It is also deemed safe to reject the mess of wild pottage, if in stirring them, your silver spoon should blacken. But I certainly once knew a lady who did not discover until hers were eaten and partially digested, that the silver had come to grief in the discharge of duty. It was very dark, and required a deal of rubbing to restore cleanliness and polish; but the poison—if death were, indeed, in the pot—was slow in its effects, since she lived many years after the experiment. It is as well perhaps, though, not to repeat it too often.

To re-capitulate.—The eatable ones are round when they first show their heads in a critical world. As they grow, the lower part unfolds a lining of salmon fringe, while the stalk and top are dirty white. When the mushroom is more than twenty-four hours old, or within a few hours after it is gathered, the salmon changes to brown. The skin can also be more easily peeled from the edges than in the spurious kinds.

STEWED MUSHROOMS.

Choose button mushrooms of uniform size. Wipe clean and white with a wet flannel cloth, and cut off the stalks. Put into a porcelain saucepan, cover with cold water, and stew very gently fifteen minutes. Salt to taste; add a tablespoonful of butter, divided into bits and rolled in flour. Boil three or four minutes; stir in three or four tablespoonfuls of cream whipped up with an egg, stir two minutes without letting it boil, and serve.

Or,

Rub them white, stew in water ten minutes; strain partially, and cover with as much warm milk as you have poured off water; stew five minutes in this; salt and pepper, and add some veal or chicken gravy, or drawn butter. Thicken with a little flour wet in cold milk, and a beaten egg.

BAKED MUSHROOMS.

Take fresh ones,—the size is not very important,—cut off nearly all the stalks, and wipe off the skin with wet flannel. Arrange neatly in a pie-dish, pepper and salt, sprinkle a little mace among them, and lay a bit of butter upon each. Bake about half an hour, basting now and then with butter and water, that they may not be too dry. Serve in the dish in which they were baked, with *maître d'hôtel* sauce poured over them.

BROILED MUSHROOMS.

Peel the finest and freshest you can get, score the under side, and cut the stems close. Put into a deep dish and anoint well, once and again, with melted butter. Salt and pepper, and let them lie in the butter an hour and a half. Then broil over a clear, hot fire, using an oyster-gridiron, and turning it over as one side browns. Serve hot, well buttered, pepper and salt, and squeeze a few drops of lemon-juice upon each.

CELERY.

Wash and scrape the stalks when you have cut off the roots. Cut off the green leaves and reject the greenest, toughest stalks. Retain the blanched leaves that grow nearest the heart. Keep in cold water until you send to table. Serve in a celery glass, and let each guest dip in salt for himself. (*See Celery Salad.*)

STEWED CELERY. ✠

- 1 bunch of celery—scraped, trimmed, and cut into inch lengths.

- 1 cup milk.

- 1 great spoonful of butter, rolled in flour.

- Pepper and salt.

Stew the celery in clear water until tender. Turn off the water, add the milk, and as soon as this boils, seasoning and butter. Boil up once and serve very hot.

RADISHES.

A friend of mine, after many and woful trials with "the greatest plague of life," engaged a supercilious young lady who "only hired out in the best of families as a professed cook." She arrived in the afternoon, and was told that tea would be a simple affair—bread-and-butter, cold meat, cake, and a dish of radishes, which were brought in from the garden as the order was given. The lady was summoned to the parlor at that moment, and remarked in leaving—"You can prepare those now, Bridget." Awhile later she peeped into the kitchen, attracted by the odor of hot fat. The frying-pan hissed on the fire, the contents were a half-pound of butter, and the "professional" stood at the table with a radish topped and tailed in one hand, a knife in the other. "I'm glad to see ye," thus she greeted the intruder. "Is it paled or *on*paled ye'll have them radishes? Some of the quality likes 'em fried wid the skins on—some widout. I thought I'd wait and ask yerself."

My readers can exercise their own choice in the matter of peeling, putting the frying out of the question. Wash and lay them in ice-water so soon as they are gathered. Cut off the tops when your breakfast or supper is ready, leaving about an inch of the stalks on; scrape off the skin if you choose, but the red ones are prettier if you do not; arrange in a tall glass or a round glass saucer, the stalks outside, the points meeting in the centre; lay cracked ice among them and send to table. Scrape and quarter the large white ones.

Good radishes are crisp to the teeth, look cool, and taste hot.

OKRA.

Boil the young pods, in enough salted hot water to cover them, until tender. Drain thoroughly, and when dished pour over them a sauce of three or four spoonfuls melted (not drawn) butter, a tablespoonful of vinegar, pepper, and salt to taste. Heat to boiling before covering the okras with it.

BOILED HOMINY.

The large kind, made of cracked, not ground corn, is erroneously termed "samp" by Northern grocers. This is the Indian name for the fine-grained. To avoid confusion, we will call the one large, the other small. Soak the large over night in cold water. Next day put it into a pot with at least two quarts of water to a quart of the hominy, and boil slowly three hours, or until it is soft. Drain in a cullender, heap in a root-dish, and stir in butter, pepper, and salt.

Soak the small hominy in the same way, and boil in as much water, slowly, stirring very often, almost constantly at the last. It should be as thick as mush, and is generally eaten at breakfast with sugar, cream, and nutmeg. It is a good and exceedingly wholesome dish, especially for children. The water in which it is boiled should be slightly salt. If soaked in warm water, and the same be changed once or twice for warmer, it will boil soft in an hour. Boil in the last water.

FRIED HOMINY.

If large, put a good lump of butter or dripping in the frying-pan, and heat. Turn in some cold boiled hominy, and cook until the under-side is browned. Place a dish upside down on the frying-pan and upset the latter, that the brown crust may be uppermost.

Eat with meat.

Cut the small hominy in slices and fry in hot lard or drippings. Or, moisten to a soft paste with milk; beat in some melted butter, bind with a beaten egg, form into round cakes with your hands, dredge with flour and fry a light brown.

HOMINY CROQUETTES. ✠

To a cupful of cold boiled hominy (small-grained) add a tablespoonful melted butter and stir hard, moistening, by degrees, with a little milk, beating to a soft light paste. Put in a teaspoonful of white sugar, and lastly, a well-beaten egg. Roll into oval balls with floured hands, dip in beaten egg, then cracker-crumbs, and fry in hot lard.

Very good!

BAKED HOMINY. ✠

To a cupful of cold boiled hominy (small kind) allow two cups of milk, a heaping teaspoonful of butter, a teaspoonful of white sugar, a little salt, and three eggs. Beat the eggs very light, yolks and whites separately. Work the yolks first into the hominy, alternately with the melted butter. When thoroughly mixed, put in sugar and salt, and go on beating while you soften the batter gradually with the milk. Be careful to leave no lumps in the hominy. Lastly stir in the whites, and bake in a buttered pudding-dish, until light, firm, and delicately browned.

This can be eaten as a dessert, but it is a delightful vegetable, and the best substitute that can be devised for green corn pudding.

RICE CROQUETTES. ✠

- Half a cup of rice.
- 1 pint milk.

- 2 tablespoonfuls sugar.
- 3 eggs.
- A little grated lemon-peel.
- 1 tablespoonful melted butter.
- A saltspoonful salt.

Soak the rice three hours in warm water enough to cover it. Drain *almost* dry, and pour in the milk. Stew in a farina-kettle, or one saucepan set in another of hot water, until the rice is very tender. Add the sugar, butter and salt, and simmer ten minutes. Whisk the eggs to a froth, and add cautiously, taking the saucepan from the fire while you whip them into the mixture. Return to the range or stove, and stir while they thicken, not allowing them to boil. Remove the saucepan, and add the grated lemon-peel; then turn out upon a well-greased dish to cool. When cold and stiff, flour your hands and roll into oval or pear-shaped balls; dip in beaten egg, then in fine cracker-crumbs, and fry in nice lard.

Or,

You can make a plainer dish of cold boiled rice, moistened with milk and a little melted butter to a smooth paste. Add sugar and salt, bind with two or three beaten eggs; make into cakes or balls, and proceed as directed above. Eat hot with roast or boiled fowls. If you shape like a pear, stick a clove in the small end for the stem.

BOILED RICE.

Pick over carefully and wash in two waters, letting it stand in the last until you are ready to boil. Have ready some boiling water slightly salted, and put in the rice. Boil it just twenty minutes, and do not put a spoon in it, but *shake* up hard and often, holding the cover on with the other hand. When done, drain off the water, and set the saucepan uncovered upon the range, where the rice will dry, not burn, for five minutes.

Eat with boiled mutton or fowls.

BAKED MACARONI. ✠

Break half a pound of pipe macaroni in pieces an inch long, and put into a saucepan of boiling water slightly salted. Stew gently twenty minutes. It should be soft, but not broken or split. Drain well and put a layer in the bottom of a buttered pie or pudding-dish; upon this grate some mild, rich cheese, and scatter over it some bits of butter. Spread upon the cheese more macaroni, and fill the dish in this order, having macaroni at the top, buttered well, without the cheese. Add a few spoonfuls of cream or milk, and a very little salt. Bake covered half an hour, then brown nicely, and serve in the bake-dish.

STEWED MACARONI—ITALIAN STYLE.

Break the macaroni into inch lengths, and stew twenty minutes, or until tender. Prepare the sauce beforehand. Cut half a pound of beef into strips and stew half an hour. The water should be cold when the meat is put in. At the end of that time, add a minced onion and a pint of tomatoes peeled and sliced. Boil for an hour, and strain through a cullender when you have taken out the meat. The sauce should be well boiled down by this time. You do not want more than a pint for a large dish of macaroni. Return the liquid to the saucepan, add a good piece of butter, with pepper and salt, and stew until you are ready to dish the macaroni. Drain this well, sprinkle lightly with salt, and heap upon a chafing-dish or in a root-dish. Pour the tomato-sauce over it; cover and let it stand in a warm place ten minutes before sending to table. Send around grated cheese with it. The Italians serve the meat also in a separate dish as a ragoût, adding some of the sauce, highly seasoned with pepper and other spices.

MACARONI À LA CRÈME. ✠

Cook the macaroni ten minutes in boiling water. Drain this off, and add a cupful of milk, with a little salt. Stew until tender. In another saucepan heat a cup of milk to boiling, thicken with a teaspoonful of flour, stir in a tablespoonful of butter, and lastly, a beaten egg. When this thickens, pour over the macaroni after it is dished.

This is a simple and good dessert, eaten with butter, sugar, and nutmeg, or sweet sauce. If set on with meat, grate cheese thickly over it, or send around a saucer of grated cheese with it.

Eggs

To guess (I do not say determine) whether an egg is good, shut one eye; frame the egg in the hollow of the hand, telescope-wise, and look at the sun through it with the open eye. If you can distinctly trace the outline of the yolk and the white looks clear around it, the chances are in favor of the egg and the buyer. Or, shake it gently at your ear. If addled, it will gurgle like water; if there is a chicken inside, you may distinguish a slight "thud" against the sides of the egg. Or, still again, you may try eggs from your own poultry-yard by putting them into a pan of cold water. The freshest sink first. Those that float are questionable—generally worse.

The best plan is to break them. In making cake, or anything that requires more than one, break each over a saucer, that it may be alone in its condemnation, if bad. Reject doubtful ones without hesitation. Yield implicit trust, or none at all.

Keep eggs in a cool, not cold place. Pack in bran or salt, with the small end downward, if you wish to use within two or three weeks; and furthermore, take the precaution to grease them well with linseed oil, or wash them over with a weak solution of gum tragacanth or varnish. This excludes the air. Another way is to make some pretty strong lime-water, allowing a pound of lime to a gallon of boiling water. When perfectly cold, fill a large jar with it in which you have packed the eggs, small end downward; lay a light saucer upon the top to keep them under water, and keep in a cool place. Renew the lime-water every three weeks. You may add an ounce of saltpetre to it.

Eggs for boiling may be "canned" as follows: So soon as they are brought in from the nests, put two or three dozen at a time in a deep pan; pour scalding water over them; let it stand thirty seconds, and turn it all off. Cover immediately with more scalding water, and repeat the process yet the third time. Wipe dry, and pack in bran or salt when they cool. This hardens the albumen into an air-tight case for the yolk. Of course, you cannot use these eggs for cake or syllabubs, or anything that is prepared with whipped eggs. Pack with the small end down.

BOILED EGGS.

Put into a saucepan of *boiling* water with a tablespoon, not to break or crack them. Only a slovenly cook, or a careless one, drops them in with her fingers. Boil steadily three minutes, if you want them soft—ten, if hard.

Another way is to put them on in cold water, and let it come to a boil, which will be in ten minutes. The inside, white and yolk, will be then of the consistency of custard. Many gourmands like them best thus. Still another is to put them in one of the silver egg-boilers used on the breakfast-table (a covered bowl will do as well); cover them with boiling water, and let them stand three minutes. Pour this off, and refill with more, also boiling hot, and leave them in it five minutes longer. Wrap in a napkin in a deep dish, if you have not a regular egg-dish.

DROPPED OR POACHED EGGS.

Strain some boiling water into a frying-pan, which must also be perfectly clean. The least impurity will mar the whiteness of the eggs. When the water boils, break the eggs separately into a saucer. Take the frying-pan off, and slip the eggs, one by one, carefully upon the surface. When all are in, put back over the fire and boil gently three minutes. Take out with a perforated skimmer, drain, and lay upon slices of buttered toast in a hot dish. Garnish with parsley, and dust with pepper and salt.

POACHED EGGS À LA CRÈME. ✠

Nearly fill a clean frying-pan with strained water boiling hot; strain a tablespoonful of vinegar through double muslin, and add to the water with a little salt. Slip your eggs from the saucer upon the top of the water (first taking the pan from the fire.) Boil three minutes and a half, drain, and lay on buttered toast in a hot dish. Turn the water from the pan and pour in half a cupful of cream or milk. If you use the latter, thicken with a very little corn-starch. Let it heat to a boil, stirring to prevent burning, and add a great spoonful of butter, some pepper and salt. Boil up once, and pour over the eggs. A better way still is to heat the milk in a separate saucepan, that the eggs may not have to stand. A little broth improves the sauce.

HAM AND EGGS.

Fry the eggs in a little very nice salted lard; drain off every drop of grease, and lay them upon a hot dish, with neat slices of fried ham around the edges, half the size of the slice as first carved from the ham. Trim off the rough edges of the eggs, and cut the ham evenly in oblong pieces before dishing. Garnish with parsley.

FRIED EGGS.

Melt some butter in a frying-pan, and when it hisses drop in the eggs carefully. Fry three minutes; dust with pepper and salt, and transfer to a hot dish.

FRICASSEED EGGS. ✠

Boil the eggs hard, cut in half crosswise, and take out the yolks. Chop these fine, or rub to a paste, with a little ground tongue or ham or cold fowl, some minced parsley, some melted butter, and a *very* little made mustard. Work well together and fill the whites with it, setting them close together in a deep covered dish, the open ends up. Have ready some veal gravy or chicken broth; heat to boiling in a saucepan with a half teaspoonful chopped parsley, salt, pepper, and lastly three tablespoonfuls of cream to a cup of broth. Boil up; pour smoking hot over the eggs, let them stand five minutes, closely covered, and send to table.

This is not an expensive dish. Eggs are always a cheaper breakfast-dish for a small family than meat, even at fifty cents a dozen. Six will make a nice quantity of the fricassee, and it is a delicious relish. Always drop hard-boiled eggs into cold water as soon as they are done, to prevent the yolks from turning black.

BREADED EGGS. ✠

Boil hard, and cut in round thick slices. Pepper and salt; dip each in beaten raw egg, then in fine bread-crumbs or powdered cracker, and fry in nice dripping or butter, hissing hot. Drain off every drop of grease, and serve on a hot dish for breakfast, with sauce, like that for fricasseed eggs, poured over them.

BAKED EGGS.

Break six or seven eggs into a buttered dish, taking care that each is whole, and does not encroach upon the others so much as to mix or disturb the yolks. Sprinkle with pepper and salt, and put a bit of butter upon each. Put into an oven and bake until the whites are well set. Serve very hot, with rounds of buttered toast, or sandwiches.

SCRAMBLED EGGS. ✠

Put a good piece of butter in a frying-pan, and when it is hot drop in the eggs, which should be broken whole into a bowl. Stir in with them a little chopped parsley, some pepper and salt, and keep stirring to and fro, up and down, without cessation, for three minutes. Turn out at once into a hot dish, or upon buttered toast and eat without delay.

CHINESE BIRD'S-NEST OF EGGS.

Make a white sauce as follows: Stew half a pound of lean veal, cut into strips, with a large sprig of parsley, in a quart of water, until the meat is in rags, and the liquor reduced one-half. Strain through tarlatan or lace, and return to the saucepan with half a cupful of milk. When it boils, thicken with a little rice or wheat flour, season with white pepper and salt, and the juice of half a lemon. Set in the corner to keep hot. Have ready six, or eight, or ten hard-boiled eggs. Take out the yolks carefully, and cut the whites into thin shreds. Pile the yolks in the centre of a round, shallow dish, arrange the shreds of white about them in the shape of a bird's nest; give a final stir to the sauce, and pour carefully over the eggs. It should not rise higher in the dish than half way to the top of the nest, when it flows down to its level. Garnish with parsley.

SCALLOPED EGGS. ✠

Make a force-meat of chopped ham—ground is better—fine bread-crumbs, pepper, salt, a little minced parsley, and some melted butter. Moisten with milk to a soft paste, and half fill some patty-pans or scallop-shells with the mixture. Break an egg carefully upon the top of each, dust with pepper and salt, and sift some very finely powdered cracker over all. Set in the oven, and bake until the eggs are *well* set—about eight minutes. Eat hot. They are very nice. You can substitute ground tongue for the ham.

POACHED EGGS, WITH SAUCE. ✠

Make the sauce by putting half a cupful of hot water in a saucepan, with a teaspoonful of lemon-juice, three tablespoonfuls of veal or chicken broth (strained), pepper, salt, mace, and a tablespoonful of butter, with a little minced parsley. Boil slowly ten minutes, and stir in a well-whipped egg carefully, lest it should curdle. Have ready some poached eggs in a deep dish, and pour the sauce over them.

EGGS UPON TOAST. ✠

Put a good lump of butter into the frying-pan. When it is hot, stir in four or five well-beaten eggs, with pepper, salt, and a little parsley. Stir and toss for three minutes. Have ready to your hand some slices of buttered toast (cut round with a tin cake-cutter before they are toasted); spread thickly with ground or minced tongue, chicken, or ham. Heap the stirred egg upon these in mounds, and set in a hot dish garnished with parsley and pickled beets.

EGGS AU LIT (*in bed*). ✠

Mince some cold fowl—chicken, turkey, or duck (or some cold boiled veal and ham in equal quantities)—very fine, and rub in a Wedgewood mortar, adding by degrees some melted butter, pepper, salt, minced parsley, and two beaten eggs. Warm in a frying-pan when it is well mixed, stirring in a little hot water should it dry too fast. Cook five minutes, stirring to keep it from scorching or browning. Form, on a hot platter or flat dish, into a mound, flat on top, with a ridge of the mixture running all around. It is easily moulded with a broad-bladed knife. In the dish thus formed, on the top of the mince-meat, lay as many poached eggs as it will hold, sprinkling them with pepper and salt. Arrange triangles of buttered toast in such order, at the base of the mound, that they shall make a pointed wall against it.

DEVILLED EGGS.

Boil six or eight eggs hard; leave in cold water until they are cold; cut in halves, slicing a bit off the bottoms to make them stand upright, *à la* Columbus. Extract the yolks, and rub to a smooth paste with a very little melted butter, some cayenne pepper, a touch of mustard, and just a dash of vinegar. Fill the hollowed whites with this, and send to table upon a bed of chopped cresses, seasoned with pepper, salt, vinegar, and a little sugar. The salad should be two inches thick, and an egg be served with a heaping tablespoonful of it. You may use lettuce or white cabbage instead of cresses.

EGG-BASKETS. ✠

Make these for breakfast the day after you have had roast chicken, duck, or turkey for dinner. Boil six eggs hard, cut neatly in half and extract the yolks. Rub these to a paste with some melted butter, pepper, and salt, and set aside. Pound the minced meat of the cold fowl fine in the same manner, and mix with the egg-paste, moistening with melted butter as you proceed, or with a little gravy, if you have it to spare. Cut off a slice from the bottoms of the hollowed whites of the egg, to make them stand; fill with the paste; arrange close together upon a flat dish, and pour over them the gravy left from yesterday's roast, heated boiling hot, and mellowed by a few spoonfuls of cream or rich milk.

OMELETTE (*plain*). ✠

Beat six eggs very light, the whites to a stiff froth that will stand alone, the yolks to a smooth thick batter. Add to the yolks a small cupful of milk, pepper, and salt; lastly stir in the whites lightly. Have ready in a hot frying-pan a good lump of butter. When it hisses, pour in your mixture gently and set over a clear fire. It should cook in ten minutes at most. Do not stir, but contrive, as the eggs "set," to slip a broad-bladed knife under the omelette to guard against burning at the bottom. The instant "hiss" of the butter as it flows to the hottest part of the pan will prove the wisdom and efficacy of the precaution. If your oven is hot, you may put the frying-pan into it as soon as the middle of the omelette is set. When done, lay a hot dish bottom upward on the top of the pan, and dexterously upset the latter to bring the browned side of the omelette uppermost. Eat soon, or it will fall.

I *know* these directions to be worthy of note. I have never seen lighter or better omelettes anywhere than in households where these have been the rule for years in the manufacture of this simple and delightful article of food.

OMELETTE WITH HAM, TONGUE, OR CHICKEN. ✠

Make precisely as above; but when it is done, scatter thickly over the surface some minced ham, tongue, or seasoned chicken, slip your broad knife under one side of the omelette and double in half, enclosing the meat. Then upset the frying-pan upon a hot dish.

Or,

You can stir the minced meat into the omelette after all the ingredients are put together, adding, if you like, some chopped parsley.

CAULIFLOWER OMELETTE.

Chop some cold cauliflower very fine, and mix in when your omelette is ready to go into the pan. Season highly with cayenne pepper and salt.

ASPARAGUS OMELETTE. ✠

Is made of the tops only, minced and seasoned, and stirred in as is the cauliflower. *Tomato omelette* has stewed tomato spread over the surface, and is then doubled in half.

EGG-BALLS FOR SOUP. ✠

Rub the yolks of three or four hard-boiled eggs to a smooth paste with a *very* little melted butter, pepper, and salt. To these add two raw ones, beaten light, and enough flour to hold the paste together. Mince into balls with floured hands and set in a cool place until just before your soup comes off, when put in carefully and boil one minute.

OMELETTE AUX FINES HERBES.

After the yolks and whites are mixed together with the milk, stir in, with two or three strokes of the spoon or whisk, two tablespoonfuls of chopped parsley, green thyme, and sweet marjoram, with pepper and salt. Fry instantly.

CHEESE OMELETTES.

Grate some rich old cheese, and having mixed the omelette as usual, stir in the cheese with a swift turn or two of the whisk, and at the same time some chopped parsley and thyme. If you beat long the cheese will separate the milk from the eggs. Cook at once.

Or,

Make the omelette in the usual way; grate cheese upon it and fold it over.

SWEET OMELETTES.

Omelette Soufflée—(Fried.)

- 6 eggs.
- 4 tablespoonfuls sugar (powdered.)
- 1 teaspoonful of vanilla.
- 2 tablespoonfuls butter.

Beat the whites and yolks separately. Add the sugar to the yolks, a little at a time, beating very thoroughly, until they are smooth and thick. The whites should stand alone. Put two tablespoonfuls of butter in a frying-pan, heat to boiling, and when you have added the vanilla to the omelette, pour it in and cook very quickly, as you would a plain one. Slip the knife frequently under it, to loosen from the sides and bottom. It is more apt to scorch than an omelette without sugar. Turn out upon a *very* hot dish, sift powdered sugar over the top, and serve instantly, or it will fall and become heavy.

Omelette Soufflée—(Baked.)

- 6 eggs.
- 6 tablespoonfuls of powdered sugar.
- Juice of a lemon and half the peel, grated.

Beat yolks and whites separately and very well. Add to the yolks by degrees the powdered sugar, and beat until it ceases to froth, and is thick and smooth. The whites should be stiff enough to cut with a knife. Stir together lightly with the seasoning, pour into a well-buttered dish, and bake in a quick oven five or six minutes. The dish should be warmed when it is buttered, not to chill the eggs. Send around with a spoon, and let each one help himself before it can fall.

APPLE OMELETTE. ✠

- 6 large pippins.
- 1 tablespoonful butter.
- 8 eggs.
- 5 or 6 tablespoonfuls sugar.
- Nutmeg to taste.
- 1 teaspoonful rose-water.

Stew the apples, when you have pared and cored them, as for apple-sauce. Beat them very smooth while hot, adding the butter, sugar, and nutmeg. When perfectly cold, put with the eggs, which should be whipped light, yolks and whites separately. Put in the yolks first, then the rose-water, lastly the whites, and pour into a deep bake-dish, which has been warmed and buttered. Bake in a moderate oven until it is delicately browned. Eat warm—not hot—for tea, with Graham bread. It is better for children—I say nothing of their elders—than cake and preserves.

OMELETTE WITH JELLY.

- Currant or other tart jelly.
- 5 eggs.
- 4 tablespoonfuls cream, or the same of milk, thickened with a teaspoonful of rice-flour or arrow-root.
- 2 tablespoonfuls powdered sugar.
- 1 teaspoonful bitter almond or vanilla flavoring.

Beat whites and yolks separately, adding to the latter the sugar and milk after they are thick and smooth. Next, chop in the seasoning; lastly, stir in the whites with a few swift strokes. Put a large spoonful of butter in the frying-pan, and, when it is hot, pour in the omelette. Spread upon it when done, which will be in a very few minutes, some nice jelly. Take the pan from the fire to do this, spread quickly, slip your knife or tin spatula under one-half of the omelette, and double it over. Turn over on a hot platter, sift powdered sugar upon it, and eat at once.

MILK, BUTTER, CHEESE, ETC.

A cool cellar is the best place in which to keep milk, if you have no dairy or milk-room. Strain it into broad shallow pans, which are lukewarm from recent scalding. You can get them made in one piece, with no seams in which sour cream or dirt may lurk unsuspected. Set upon swing shelves, to avoid the possibilities of drowned mice, and keep the cellar dark to save it from flies. In twelve hours skim for the table, and, unless you have need of the milk, let it stand twelve hours more for the second rising of cream. Put this into the stone jar or crock in which the cream is kept for churning. Even in butter-making, I have found it a good plan to take off at night the cream clean from the morning churning, instead of letting it stand twenty-four hours, as is the usual custom. The "second rising" will repay one for the additional trouble. Churn as soon as convenient after the cream "loppers" or thickens. If it stands too long, it becomes bitter or musty. The churn should be well scalded and aired between the churnings. Scrupulous cleanliness should be the unbending rule of dairy arrangements. All strongly-flavored substances must be kept from the neighborhood of milk and butter. They are ready absorbents, and when they contract odor or taste, never get rid of it. Have earthen and tin milk vessels, and never allow them to be put to any other use.

Scald the churn, and cool with ice or spring water; pour in the thick cream. Churn rather fast, until the butter-flakes, left by the dasher upon the top, show that the end to be gained is near—then more slowly. The motion should always be regular. In warm weather pour a little cold water into the churn, should the butter come slowly. Take it up with the perforated dasher, turning it dexterously just below the surface of the butter-milk, to catch every stray bit. Have ready some clean, *very* cold water, in a deep wooden tray, and into this plunge the dasher when you draw it from the churn. The butter will float off, leaving the dasher free. Having collected every particle, gather behind a wooden butter-shovel and drain off the water, squeezing and pressing the butter with the shovel. Set in a cool place for an hour to harden—a necessary measure in summer—then work and knead it with a wooden ladle until not another drop of water exudes, and the butter is like yellow marble in polish and closeness of pores. When you have worked out the butter-milk, add by degrees fine salt in the proportion of a dessertspoonful to every pound. Then set aside for some hours, *always* in a cool place. The last working is a slight affair, comparatively. Still using the paddle, and never, from beginning to end of the operation, touching with your hands, mould into rolls or pound "pats." Mark with grooves or checkers with the ladle, or stamp with a print. Wrap each roll in a clean wet linen cloth, which has no touch of soap or starch about it, and pack in a stone jar, sprinkling a little salt between the layers.

If you wish to keep it a long time, work with especial care, and pack down *hard* in a perfectly clean stone jar. Do not, above all things, take one that has ever been used for pickles. You may not detect the faintest odor lingering about it, but the butter will, and absorb it, too. Some cover the butter with strong brine, but a better way is to press a fine linen cloth closely to the surface, and cover this with a thick layer of clean fine salt. Set in a cool, dry place, and keep the cloth over it all the time; also a tightly-fitting lid. When you begin to use it, take out enough to last a week, and re-cover. If you admit the air every day, it is apt to grow strong. A pretty plate of butter for the table is made of balls half the size of an egg, rolled in the little fluted paddles sold for the purpose.

BONNY-CLABBER, OR LOPPERED-MILK. ✠

Set a china or glass dish of skimmed milk away in a warm place, covered. When it turns—*i. e.*, becomes a smooth, firm, but not tough cake, like blanc-mange—serve in the same dish. Cut out carefully with a large spoon, and put in saucers, with cream, powdered sugar, and nutmeg to taste. It is better, if set on the ice for an hour before it is brought to table. Do not let it stand until the whey separates from the curd.

Few people know how delicious this healthful and cheap dessert can be made, if eaten before it becomes tart and tough, with a liberal allowance of cream and sugar. There are not many jellies and creams superior to it.

RENNET.

Clean the stomach of a calf (or have your butcher do it for you) as soon as it is killed, scouring inside and out with salt. When perfectly clean, tack upon a frame to dry in the sun for a day. Cut in squares, and pack down in salt, or keep in wine or brandy. When you wish to use the salted, soak half an hour in cold water, wash well, and put into the milk to be turned, tied to a string, that it may be drawn out without breaking the curd. The liquor rennet sold by druggists is sometimes good, quite as often worthless. You can, however, get the dried or salted in the markets, and often in the drug-stores.

MOUNTAIN CUSTARD, OR JUNKET. ✠

Take a piece of rennet an inch long, or a teaspoonful of the wine in which rennet is kept, to each quart of milk. Season with vanilla or lemon, a little nutmeg, and a tablespoonful of sugar to each part. More will retard the formation. Set in a warm place— near the fire, or on the kitchen table—closely covered. Look at it from time to time, and if, in the course of an hour, there are no signs of stiffening, add more rennet. When it is firm, like blanc-mange, and before the whey separates from the curd, remove the rennet, and set upon ice until it is wanted. Serve with powdered sugar and cream.

THICKENED MILK.

Boil a quart of milk, add a very little salt, and two tablespoonfuls of rice or wheat flour wet in cold milk. Stir in smoothly, and let it thicken in a vessel of boiling water, keeping the outer saucepan at a hard boil for half an hour. Eat with butter and sugar, or with cream and sugar. For invalids, or children who are suffering with summer disorders, boil at least an hour, stirring very often.

CHEESE

I have doubted the utility of inserting a receipt for regular cheese-making. The apparatus necessary for the manufacture is seldom, if ever, found in a private family, while cheese can be had in every country store at one-third the expense to an amateur of making it. But, remembering that it may be a pleasant, if not profitable experiment, for the mistress of many cows to make at her odd moments, I have secured what purports to be an exact description of "cheese-making on a small scale."

To each gallon of milk warm from the cow, add a piece of rennet six inches long and three wide, or two tablespoonfuls rennet water—*i. e.*, water in which rennet has been boiled. Cover, and set in a warm place until it becomes a firm curd; this should be, at the most, not more than three-quarters of an hour. When the whey has separated entirely, and looks clear and greenish, wash your hands very clean, and with them gently press all the curd to one side of the pan or tub, while an assistant dips out the whey. Have ready a stout linen bag, pour the curd into it, and hang it up to dry until not another drop of whey can be pressed out; then put the curd into a wooden dish, and chop it fine. Empty into a finer bag, and put into a small cheese-box, or other circular wooden box with a perforated bottom, and a lid that slides down easily but closely on the inside. Your bag should be as nearly as possible the same shape and size as this box. Lay heavy weights upon the top, in lack of a cheese-press, and let it stand an hour. The cloth should be wet *inside* as well as out, before you put the curds in. At the end of the hour, take out the cheese and chop again, adding salt this time. Have ready a fresh wet cloth; pack in the curd hard. There should be a circular cover for this bag, which must be basted all around, and very smooth on top. Scald the box and cover, then rinse with cold water, and put the cheese again under press for twelve hours. Next day, take it out, rub all over with salt, and fit on a clean wet cloth. Look at it sixteen hours later, pare off the rough edges, and scrape the sides of inequalities before returning to the press for the last time. Let it remain under the weights for twenty-four hours. Strip off the cloth, rub the cheese well with butter, and lay upon a clean cloth spread on a shelf in a cool, dry place. A wire-safe is best. Wipe clean; then rub every day with butter for a week, and turn also every twenty-four hours. At the end of the week, omit the greasing, and rub hard with a coarse cloth. Do this every day for a month. Your cheese will then be eatable, but it will be much finer six months later.

Stilton cheeses—renowned over the world—are buried in dry heather when they are firm enough to remove from the shelves, and kept there a month. This is called "ripening."

COTTAGE CHEESE.

Heat sour milk until the whey rises to the top. Pour it off, put the curd in a bag and let it drip six hours, without squeezing it. Put in a wooden bowl, chop fine with a wooden spoon, salt to taste, and work to the consistency of soft putty, adding a little cream and butter as you proceed. Mould with your hands into round "pats" or balls, and keep in a cool place. It is best when fresh.

CREAM CHEESE.

Stir a little salt into a pan of "loppered" cream. Pour into a linen bag, and let it drain three days, changing the bag every day. Then pack into a wooden cup or mould with holes in the bottom, and press two hours. Wet the mould with cold water before putting in the cream-curd. Wrapped in soft white paper—two or three folds of tissue paper will do—to exclude the air, they will keep in a cool place for a week.

This is the cheese sold in this country under the name of *Neufchatel.*

BREAD

If eminence of importance entitled a subject to pre-eminence of position, that of which we are now about to speak should have stood foremost in this work. It is not a pleasant thing to think or write about, but it is a stubborn fact, that upon thousands of tables, in otherwise comfortable homes, *good* bread is an unknown phenomenon. I say phenomenon, because it would indeed be a marvellous estrangement of cause and effect were indifferent flour, unskillfully mixed with flat yeast, badly risen and negligently baked, to result in that pride of the notable housekeeper—light, sweet, wholesome bread. I know a household where sour, stiff bread is the rule, varied several times during the week by muffins scented and colored with soda, clammy biscuit, and leathery griddle-cakes; another where the bread is invariably over-risen, and consequently tasteless, sometimes slightly acid; yet another in which home-made bread is not used at all because it is "so troublesome and uncertain," the mistress preferring to feed her family, growing children and all, upon the vari-colored sponges bought at the bakers—sponges inflated with sal volatile, flavorless, and dry as chips when a day old, and too often betraying, in the dark streaks running through the interior of the loaf, want of cleanliness in the kneader. Yet these are all well-to-do people, who submit to these abominations partly because they do not know how badly off they are—chiefly because it is their way of doing, and they see no reason for changing. "I have been a housekeeper for thirty years, and have always mixed my bread just so," retorted a mistress once, when I mildly set forth the advantages of "setting a sponge" over-night. "I put in flour, yeast, and milk if I have it, and give them a good stir; then set the dough down to rise. Our folks don't fancy very light bread. There don't seem to be any substance in it—so to speak. Mine generally turns out pretty nice. It's all luck, after all, about bread."

"I'm told you have a receipt for making bread," laughed another to me; "I never heard of such a thing in my life, and I've been keeping house eighteen years. So I thought I'd call and ask you for it—just as a curiosity, you know. I want to see what it is like."

I wisely kept *my* thoughts to myself, and dictated the receipt, which she jotted down in a memorandum-book laughing all the while at the "excellent joke."

"You really use this?" she demanded, when this was done.

"I do. I have used no other for many years."

"And the bread I ate upon your table, the other night, was made according to this?"

Again an affirmative answer.

"I guess your cook could tell another story," rejoined the skeptic. "You can't make me believe that bread is made by rule. I put my materials together anyhow, and I have as good luck as most of my neighbors."

I regarded my visitor as an impertinent simpleton; but I have been amazed, in subsequent years, at finding that her creed is that of hundreds of housewives more or less sensible. "Luck" rules the baking, and upon the shoulders of this Invisible are laid the deficiencies of the complacent cook. Cheap flour and laziness are at the bottom of more mishaps in the bread line than any other combination of circumstances. From the inferior grades of flour, it is possible to make tolerable biscuit, crumpets, and muffins, plain pastry, and very good griddle-cakes. You cannot, by any stretch of art, produce excellent bread from poor flour. It is no economy to purchase it for this purpose. It *is* judicious to lay in two barrels at a time, and to use the best only for the semi- or tri-weekly baking.

Chiefest then among the conditions to good bread, I place good "family" flour—dry, elastic, and odorless. Whiteness is a secondary consideration, although, to American eyes, this is a recommendation. A little experience will teach you to detect the signs that foretell satisfactory baking-days, and *vice versâ*. If in handling the flour you discern a heaviness like that of ground plaster; if in squeezing a handful tightly you discover that it retains the imprint of palm and fingers, and rolls back into the tray a compact ball or roll; if it is in the least musty, or sour, use it very sparingly in your trial-baking, for the chances are as ten to one that you will head the barrel up again and return it to your grocer.

Sometimes new flour can be ripened for use by sifting enough for each baking into a large tray, and exposing it to the hot sun for some hours, or by setting it upon the kitchen hearth for the same time. And it not unfrequently happens that flour improves greatly after the barrel has been open for several days or weeks. It dries out and becomes lighter, more elastic. Next in importance to the quality of the flour is that of the yeast. This should be light in color and lively, effervescing easily when shaken, and emitting an odor like weak ammonia. If dull or sour, it is bad. In cities it is easiest, perhaps cheapest, to buy yeast from a brewery or bakery, exercising your discrimination as to quality. Unless you can satisfy yourself in this regard, you had better make your own. I can confidently recommend the receipts given in this work as easy and safe, having tried them in my own family.

Novices in bread-making, and many who should have learned better by long experience, fall into a sad mistake in the consistency of the dough. It should be mixed as *soft as it can be handled*. Bread will rise sooner and higher, be lighter and more digestible, and keep fresh much longer, if this rule be followed. Stiff bread is close in texture, often waxy to the teeth, and after a day or so becomes very hard.

Set the dough to rise in a moderately warm place, and keep it in an even temperature. There is force in the old lament—"My bread took cold, last night." Cold arrests the process of fermentation. There is a chance, should this occur, that a removal to a more genial atmosphere and careful nursing may cure the congestion, should it be only partial. Too much heat carries forward the work too rapidly. In this case, you will find your dough puffy and sour. Correct the latter evil by dissolving a little soda or saleratus in hot water, and working it well in.

Knead your bread faithfully and from all sides, until it rebounds like india-rubber after a smart blow of the fist upon the centre of the mass.

The oven should not be too hot. If you cannot hold your bare arm within it while you count thirty, it is too quick. Keep the heat steady after the bread goes in. Too much fire at first, and rapidly cooling, produce the effect upon the bread which is technically called "slack-baked," *i. e.*, the inside of the loaf is never properly done. Practice and intelligent observation will, in time, make you an adept in the management of your ovens. If the bread rises rapidly while baking, and the crust begins to form before the lower part of the loaf is baked, cover the top with clean paper until you are ready to brown it.

Grate away the burned portions of the crust, should there be such. This is better than chipping with a knife. One of the best bread-makers I know bakes in round pans, each loaf by itself, and grates the whole outer surface, top, bottom, and sides, quickly and lightly, toning down the brown to a uniform and pleasing tint. Tilt your loaves upon the edge, the lower part resting upon the table, the upper supported by the wall or other upright object, and throw a coarse dry cloth over them until they cool. This position allows the air to get at all sides, and prevents "sweating." A tin bread-box is best, with a cloth at bottom and enwrapping the loaves.

YEAST (*Hop.*) ✠

- 4 large potatoes, or six small.

- 2 quarts cold water.

- Double handful hops, tied in a coarse muslin bag.

- 4 tablespoonfuls flour.

- 2 tablespoonfuls white sugar.

Peel the potatoes, and put them with the hop-bag into a saucepan containing two quarts cold water. Cover and boil until the potatoes break and fall apart. Take these out with a perforated skimmer, leaving the water still boiling, mash them fine with a potato-beetle, and work in the flour and sugar. Moisten this gradually with the *boiling* hop tea, stirring it to a smooth paste. When all the tea has been mixed in, set it aside to cool. While still slightly warm, add four tablespoonfuls of lively yeast, and turn all into a large open vessel to "work." Keep this in a warm place until it ceases to bubble up, or until next day. In summer it will work well in a few hours. When quite light, put in earthen jars with small mouths, in which fit corks, or bottle it, and remove to ice-house or cellar. It will keep good for a fortnight—longer in winter.

When you wish to use it for baking, send a small vessel to the cellar for the desired quantity, and re-cork at once. A half-hour in a hot kitchen may spoil it.

YEAST (*Self-working*).

- 8 potatoes.

- 2 ounces hops.

- 4 quarts cold water.

- 1 lb. flour.

- ½ lb. white sugar.

- 1 tablespoonful salt.

Tie the hops in a coarse muslin bag, and boil one hour in four quarts of water. Let it cool to lukewarmness before removing the bag. Wet with the tepid liquor—a little at a time—the flour, making to a smooth paste. Put in the sugar and salt, beat up the batter three minutes before adding the rest of the tea. Set it away for two days in an open bowl covered with a thin cloth, in a closet which is moderately and evenly warm.

On the third day peel, boil, and mash the potatoes, and when entirely free from lumps and specks, stir in gradually the thickened hop-liquor. Let it stand twelve hours longer in the bowl, stirring often, and keeping it in the warm kitchen. Then bottle or put away in corked jars, which must be perfectly sweet and freshly scalded. This will keep a month in a cool cellar. It is more troublesome to make it than other kinds of yeast, but it needs no other "rising" to excite fermentation, and remains good longer than that made in the usual way.

YEAST (*Potato.*) ✠

- 6 potatoes.

- 2 quarts cold water.

- 4 tablespoonfuls flour.

- 2 tablespoonfuls white sugar.

Peel and boil the potatoes until they break. Leaving the water on the fire, take them out and mash fine with the flour and sugar, wetting gradually with the hot water until it is all used. When lukewarm, add a gill of good yeast, and set aside in an open vessel and warm place to ferment. When it ceases to effervesce, bottle and set in ice-house.

This yeast is very nice and white, and is preferred by many who dislike the bitter taste of hops. It is also convenient to make when hops cannot be obtained.

YEAST CAKES. ✠

- 2 quarts water (cold.)
- 1 quart pared and sliced potatoes.
- Double-handful hops, tied in coarse muslin bag.
- Flour to make stiff batter.
- 1 cup Indian meal.

Boil the potatoes and hop-bag in two quarts of water for three-quarters of an hour. Remove the hops, and while boiling hot, strain the potatoes and water through a cullender into a bowl. Stir into the scalding liquor enough flour to make a stiff batter. Beat all up well; add two tablespoonfuls lively yeast and set in a warm place to rise. When light, stir in a cup of Indian meal, roll into a sheet a quarter of an inch thick, and cut into round cakes. Dry these in the hot sun, or in a *very* moderate oven, taking care they do not heat to baking. It is best to put them in after the fire has gone down for the night, and leave them in until morning. When entirely dry and cold, hang them up in a bag in a cool, dry place.

Use one cake three inches in diameter for a loaf of fair size; soak in tepid water until soft, and add a pinch of soda or saleratus, then mix.

These cakes will remain good a month in summer, two in winter.

BAKING POWDERS.

- 1 ounce super-carbonate soda.

- 7 drachms tartaric acid—(in powder.)

Roll smoothly and mix thoroughly. Keep in a tight glass jar or bottle. Use one teaspoonful to a quart of flour.

Or,

- 12 teaspoonfuls carb. soda.

- 24 teaspoonfuls cream tartar.

Put as above, and use in like proportion.

BREAD SPONGE (*Potato.*) ✠

- 6 potatoes, boiled and mashed fine while hot.

- 6 tablespoonfuls baker's yeast.

- 2 tablespoonfuls white sugar.

- 2 tablespoonfuls lard.

- 1 even teaspoonful soda.

- 1 quart warm—*not* hot—water.

- 3 cups flour.

Mash the potatoes, and work in the lard and sugar. Stir to a cream, mixing in gradually a quart of the water in which the potatoes were boiled, which should have been poured out to cool down to blood warmth. *Beat* in the flour, already wet up with a little potato-water to prevent lumping, then the yeast, lastly the soda. Cover lightly if the weather is warm, more closely in winter, and set to rise over night in a warm place.

BREAD SPONGE (*Plain.*) ✠

- 1 quart warm water.

- 6 tablespoonfuls baker's yeast.

- 2 tablespoonfuls lard.

- 2 tablespoonfuls white sugar.

- 1 teaspoonful soda.

- Flour to make a soft batter.

Melt the lard in the warm water, add the sugar, then the flour by degrees, stirring in smoothly. A quart and a pint of flour will usually be sufficient if the quality is good. Next comes the yeast, lastly the soda. Beat up hard for several minutes, and set to rise as above.

Bread mixed with potato-sponge is more nutritious, keeps fresh longer, and is sweeter than that made with the plainer sponge, But there are certain seasons of the year when good *old* potatoes cannot be procured, and new ones will not do for this purpose.

The potato-sponge is safer, because surer for beginners in the important art of bread-making. After using it for fifteen years, I regard it as almost infallible—given the conditions of good flour, yeast, kneading, and baking.

FAMILY BREAD (*White.*) ✠

Having set your sponge over night, or, if you bake late in the afternoon, early in the morning, sift dry flour into a deep bread-tray, and strew a few spoonfuls of fine salt over it. The question of the quantity of flour is a delicate one, requiring judgment and experience. Various brands of flour are so unequal with respect to the quantity of gluten they contain, that it is impossible to give any invariable rule on this subject. It will be safe, however, to sift two quarts and a pint, if you have set the potato-sponge; two quarts for the plain. This will make two good-sized loaves. Make a hole in the middle of the heap, pour in the risen sponge (which should be very light and seamed in many places on the top), and work down the flour into it with your hands. If too soft, add more flour. If you can mould it at all, it is not too soft. If stiff, rinse out the bowl in which the sponge was set with a little lukewarm water, and work this in. When you have it in manageable shape, begin to knead. Work the mass into a ball—your hands having been well floured from the first; detach it from the tray, and lift it in your left hand, while you sprinkle flour with the right thickly over the bottom and sides of the tray. Toss back the ball into this, and knead hard—always toward the centre of the mass, which should be repeatedly turned over and around, that every portion may be manipulated. Brisk and long kneading makes the pores fine and regular. Gaping holes of diverse sizes are an unerring tell-tale of a careless cook. Spend at least twenty minutes—half an hour is better—in this kind of useful gymnastics. It is grand exercise for arms and chest. This done, work the dough into a shapely ball in the centre of the tray, sprinkle flour over the top; throw a cloth over all and leave it on the kitchen-table to rise, taking care it is not in a draught of cold air. In summer, it will rise in four or five hours—in winter, six are often necessary. It should come up steadily until it at least trebles its original bulk and the floured surface cracks all over. Knead again for ten or fifteen minutes. Then, divide it into as many parts as you wish loaves, and put these in well-greased pans for the final rising. In a large household baking, it is customary to mould the dough into oblong rolls, three or four, according to the number of loaves you desire, and to lay these close together in one large pan. The second kneading is done upon a floured board, and should be thorough as the first, the dough being continually shifted and turned. Set the pans in a warm place for an hour longer, with a cloth thrown over them to keep out the air and dust. Then bake, heeding the directions set down in the article upon bread in general. If your ovens are in good condition, one hour should bake the above quantity of bread. But here again experience must be your guide. Note carefully for yourself how long a time is required for your first successful baking, as also how much dry flour you have worked into your sponge, and let these data regulate future action. I have known a variation of two quarts in a large baking, over the usual measure of flour. I need not tell you that you had better shun a brand that requires such an excessive quantity to bring the dough to the right consistency. It is neither nutritious nor economical. When you make out the loaves, prick the top with the fork.

Do not make your first baking too large. Practice is requisite to the management of an unwieldy mass of dough. Let your trial-loaf be with say half the quantity of sponge and flour I have set down, and increase these as skill and occasion require, carefully preserving the proportions. Seven or eight quarts of flour will be needed for the semi-weekly baking of a family of moderate size.

If I have seemed needlessly minute in the directions I have laid down, it is because I wish to be a guide, not a betrayer, and because I am deeply impressed with the worth of such advice as may tend to diminish the number of those who know not for themselves the comfort and delight of eating from day to day, and year to year, good family bread.

FAMILY BREAD (*Brown.*) ✠

I wish it were in my power, by much and earnest speaking and writing, to induce every housekeeper to make brown bread—that is, bread made of unbolted, usually called Graham flour—a staple article of diet in her family. I only repeat the declaration of a majority of our best chemists and physicians when I say that our American fondness for fine white bread is a serious injury to our health. We bolt and rebolt our flour until we extract from it three-quarters of its nutritive qualities, leaving little strength in it except what lies in gluten or starch, and consign that which makes bone and tissue, which regulates the digestive organs, and leaves the blood pure, the brain clear, to the lower animals. Growing children especially should eat brown bread daily. It supplies the needed phosphate to the tender teeth and bones. If properly made, it soon commends itself to their taste, and white becomes insipid in comparison. Dyspeptics have long been familiar with its dietetic virtues, and, were the use of it more general, we should have fewer wretches to mourn over the destroyed coats of their stomachs. It is wholesome, sweet, honest, and should be popular.

Prepare a sponge as for white bread, using potatoes or while flour. My rule is to take out a certain quantity of the risen sponge on baking day, and set aside for brown bread. Put into a tray two parts Graham flour, one-third white, and to every quart of this allow a handful of Indian meal, with a teaspoonful of salt. Wet this up with the sponge, and when it is mixed, add, for a loaf of fair size, half a teacupful of molasses. The dough should be *very* soft. If there is not enough of the sponge to reduce it to the desired consistency, add a little blood-warm water. Knead it diligently and long. It will not rise so rapidly as the white flour, having more "body" to carry. Let it take its time; make into round, comfortable loaves, and set down again for the second rising, when you have again kneaded it. Bake steadily, taking care it does not burn, and do not cut while hot. The result will well repay you for your trouble. It will take a longer time to bake than white bread. Brown flour should not be sifted.

BOSTON BROWN BREAD.

Set a sponge over night, with potatoes or white flour, in the following proportions:—

- 1 cup yeast.
- 6 potatoes, mashed fine with three cups of flour.
- 1 quart warm water.
- 2 tablespoonfuls lard (*or*, if you leave out the potatoes, one quart of warm water to three pints of flour).
- 2 tablespoonfuls brown sugar.

Beat up well and let it rise five or six hours.

When light, sift into the bread-tray—

- 1 quart rye-flour.
- 2 quarts Indian meal.
- 1 tablespoonful salt.
- 1 teaspoonful soda, or saleratus.

Mix this up very soft with the risen sponge, adding warm water, if needed, and working in gradually

- Half a teacupful of molasses.

Knead well, and let it rise from six to seven hours. Then work over again, and divide into loaves, putting these in well-greased, round, deep pans. The second rising should last an hour, at the end of which time bake in a moderate oven about four hours. Rapid baking will ruin it. If put in late in the day, let it stay in the oven all night.

RYE BREAD.

Set a sponge, as above, but with half the quantity of water.

In the morning mix with this:

- 1 quart warm milk.
- 1 tablespoonful salt.
- 1 cup Indian meal.
- And enough rye flour to make it into pliable dough.

Proceed as with wheat bread, baking it a little longer.

It is a mistake to suppose that acidity, greater or less, is the normal state of rye bread. If you find your dough in the slightest degree sour, correct by adding a teaspoonful of soda dissolved in warm water. It is safest to add this always in warm weather.

MILK BREAD.

- 1 quart of milk.
- ½ teacupful of yeast.
- ¼ lb. butter, one tablespoonful white sugar.

Stir into the milk, which should be made blood-warm, a pint of flour, the sugar, lastly the yeast. Beat all together well, and let them rise five or six hours. Then melt the butter, and add with a little salt. Work in flour enough to make a stiff dough; let this rise four hours, and make into small loaves. Set near the fire for half an hour, and bake.

In warm weather, add a teaspoonful of soda, dissolved in warm water, to the risen sponge, as all bread mixed with milk is apt to sour.

BUTTERMILK BREAD.

- 1 pint buttermilk heated to scalding.

Stir in, while it is hot, enough flour to make a tolerably thick batter. Add half a gill of yeast, and let it rise five or six hours. If you make it over night you need not add the yeast, but put in, instead, a tablespoonful of white sugar. In the morning, stir into the sponge a tablespoonful of soda, dissolved in hot water, a little salt, and two tablespoonfuls melted butter. Work in just flour enough to enable you to handle the dough comfortably; knead well, make into loaves, and let it rise until light.

This makes very white and wholesome bread.

RICE BREAD.

Make a sponge of—

- 1 quart warm water.
- 1 teacupful yeast.
- 1 tablespoonful white sugar.
- 2 tablespoonfuls lard.
- 1 quart wheat flour.

Beat well together, and when it has risen, which will be in about five hours, add three pints of warm milk and three teacupfuls rice-flour wet to a thin paste with cold milk, and boiled four minutes as you would starch. This should be a little more than blood-warm when it is stirred into the batter. If not thick enough to make out into dough, add a little wheat-flour. Knead thoroughly, and treat as you would wheat bread in the matter of the two risings and baking.

This is nice and delicate for invalids, and keeps well. If you cannot procure the rice-flour, boil one cup of whole rice to a thin paste, mashing and beating it smooth.

FRENCH ROLLS. (*No. 1.*) ✠

In kneading dough for the day's baking, after adding and working in the risen sponge, set aside enough for a loaf of tea-rolls. Work into this a heaping tablespoonful of lard or butter, and let it stand in a tolerably cool place (not a cold or draughty one) for four hours. Knead it again, and let it alone for three hours longer. Then make into rolls, by rolling out, *very* lightly, pieces of the dough into round cakes, and folding these, not quite in the centre, like turn-overs. The third rising will be for one hour, then bake steadily half an hour or less, if the oven is quick.

Having seen these rolls, smoking, light, and delicious, upon my own table, at least twice a week for ten years, with scarcely a failure in the mixing or baking, I can confidently recommend the receipt and the product. You can make out part of your Graham dough in the same manner.

FRENCH ROLLS. (*No. 2.*)

- 1 quart milk; new, warm milk is best.
- 1 teacup yeast.
- 1 quart and a pint of flour.

When this sponge is light, work in a well-beaten egg and two tablespoonfuls melted butter, with a teaspoonful of salt, half a teaspoonful soda dissolved in hot water, one tablespoonful white sugar and enough white flour to make a soft dough. Let this stand four or five hours, roll out into round cakes and fold as in No. 1, or shape with your hands into balls. Set these closely together in the baking-pan; let them rise one hour, and just before putting them into the oven, cut deeply across each ball with a sharp knife. This will make the cleft roll, so familiar to us in French restaurants. Bake half an hour.

RISEN BISCUIT. ✠

- 1 quart milk.
- ¾ cup lard or butter—half-and-half is a good rule.
- ¾ cup of yeast.
- 2 tablespoonfuls white sugar.
- 1 teaspoonful salt.
- Flour to make a soft dough.

Mix over night, warming the milk slightly and melting the lard or butter. In the morning, roll out into a sheet three-quarters of an inch in thickness; cut into round cakes, set these closely together in a pan, let them rise for twenty minutes, and bake twenty minutes.

These delightful biscuits are even better if the above ingredients be set with half as much flour, in the form of a thin sponge, and the rest of the flour be worked in five hours later. Let this rise five hours more, and proceed as already directed. This is the best plan if the biscuits are intended for tea.

SALLY LUNN. (*No. 1.*) ✠

- 1 quart of flour.

- 4 eggs.

- ½ cup melted butter.

- 1 cup warm milk.

- 1 cup warm water.

- 4 tablespoonfuls yeast.

- 1 teaspoonful salt.

- ½ teaspoonful soda, dissolved in hot water.

Beat the eggs to a stiff froth, add the milk, water, butter, soda, and salt; stir in the flour to a smooth batter, and beat the yeast in well. Set to rise in a buttered pudding-dish, in which it must be baked and sent to table. Or, if you wish to turn it out, set to rise in a *well*-buttered mould. It will not be light under six hours. Bake steadily three-quarters of an hour, or until a straw thrust into it comes up clean. Eat while hot.

This is the genuine old-fashioned Sally Lunn, and will hardly give place even yet to the newer and faster compounds known under the same name.

SALLY LUNN. (*No. 2.*) ✠

- 1 scant quart flour.

- 4 eggs.

- 1 teacupful milk.

- 1 teacupful lard and butter mixed.

- 1 teaspoonful cream-tartar.

- ½ teaspoonful soda, dissolved in hot water.

- 1 teaspoonful salt.

Beat the eggs very light, yolks and whites separately, melt the shortening, sift the cream-tartar into the flour; add the whites the last thing.

POTATO BISCUIT.

- 8 potatoes of medium size, mashed very fine.

- 4 tablespoonfuls butter, melted.

- 2 cups milk, blood-warm.

- 1 cup yeast.

- Flour to make a thin batter.

- 2 tablespoonfuls white sugar.

Stir all the above ingredients together except the butter, and let the sponge rise until light—four or five hours will do; then add the melted butter with a little salt and flour, enough to make soft dough. Set aside this for four hours longer, roll out in a sheet three-quarters of an inch thick, cut into cakes; let these rise one hour, and bake.

MRS. E——'S BISCUIT (*Soda.*) ✠

- 1 quart flour.

- 2 heaping tablespoonfuls of lard.

- 2 cups sweet—if you can get it—*new* milk.

- 1 teaspoonful soda.

- 2 teaspoonful cream-tartar.

- 1 saltspoonful of salt.

Rub the soda and cream-tartar into the flour, and sift all together before they are wet; then put in the salt; next the lard, rubbed into the prepared flour quickly and lightly; lastly, pour in the milk. Work out the dough rapidly, kneading with as few strokes as possible, since handling injures the biscuit. If properly prepared the dough will have a rough surface and the biscuit be flaky. The dough should also be *very* soft. If the flour stiffen it too much, add more milk. Roll out lightly, cut into cakes at least half an inch thick, and bake in a quick oven. The biscuit made by the friend from whom I had this receipt were marvels of lightness and sweetness. I have often thought of them since with regretful longing, when set down to so-called "soda-biscuit," marbled with greenish-yellow streaks, and emitting, when split, an odor which was in itself an eloquent dissuasive to an educated appetite. Few cooks make really good, quick biscuit—why, I am unable to say, unless upon the principle of "brains will tell." I have had more than one in my kitchen, who, admirable in almost every other respect, were absolutely unfit to be intrusted with this simple yet delicate manufacture. The common fault is to have too "heavy a hand" with soda, and to "guess at" the quantities, instead of measuring them. Eat while warm.

GRAHAM BISCUIT. ✠

- 3 cups Graham flour.
- 1 cup white flour.
- 3 cups milk.
- 2 tablespoonfuls lard.
- 1 heaping tablespoonful white sugar.
- 1 saltspoonful of salt.
- 1 teaspoonful of soda.
- 2 teaspoonfuls cream-tartar.

Mix and bake as you do the white soda-biscuit (Mrs. E——'s). They are good cold as well as hot.

MINUTE BISCUIT.

- 1 pint sour, or buttermilk.
- 1 teaspoonful soda.
- 2 teaspoonfuls melted butter.

Flour to make soft dough—just stiff enough to handle. Mix, roll, and cut out rapidly, with as little handling as may be, and bake in a quick oven.

GRAHAM WHEATLETS.

- 1 pint Graham flour.
- Nearly a quart of boiling water or milk.
- 1 teaspoonful salt.

Scald the flour, when you have salted it, into as soft dough as you can handle. Roll it nearly an inch thick, cut in round cakes, lay upon a hot buttered tin or pan, and bake them in the hottest oven you can get ready. Everything depends upon heat in the manufacture of these. Some cooks spread them on a hot tin, and set this upon a red-hot stove. Properly scalded and cooked, they are light as puffs, and very good; otherwise they are flat and tough. Split and butter while hot.

SWEET RUSK. ✠

- 1 pint warm milk.
- ½ cup of butter.
- 1 cup of sugar.
- 2 eggs.
- 1 teaspoonful of salt.
- 2 tablespoonfuls yeast.

Make a sponge with the milk, yeast, and enough flour for a thin batter, and let it rise over night. In the morning add the butter, eggs, and sugar, previously beaten up well together, the salt, and flour enough to make a soft dough. Mould with the hands into balls of uniform size, set close together in a pan, and let them rise until very light. After baking, wash the tops with a clean soft cloth dipped in molasses and water.

DRIED RUSK. ✠

- 1 pint of warm milk.
- 2 eggs.

- ½ teacup of butter.
- Half a cup of yeast.
- 1 teaspoonful salt.

Set a sponge with these ingredients, leaving out the eggs, and stirring in flour until you have a thick batter. Early next morning add the well-beaten eggs, and flour enough to enable you to roll out the dough. Let this rise in the bread-bowl two hours. Roll into a sheet nearly an inch thick, cut into round cakes, and arrange in your baking-pan two deep, laying one upon the other carefully. Let these stand for another half-hour, and bake.

These are now very nice for eating, and you may, if you like, reserve a plateful for tea; but the rule for the many, handed down through, I am afraid to say how many generations, in the family where I first ate this novel and delightful biscuit, is to divide the twins, thus leaving one side of each cake soft, and piling them loosely in the pan, set them in the oven when the fire is declining for the night, and leave them in until morning. Then, still obeying the traditions of revered elders, put them in a clean muslin bag, and hang them up in the kitchen. They will be fit to eat upon the third day. Put as many as you need in a deep dish, and pour over them iced milk, or water, if you cannot easily procure the former. Let them soak until soft, take them out, drain them for a minute in a shallow plate, and eat with butter. Invalids and children crave them eagerly. Indeed, I have seen few refuse them who had ever tasted them before. There is a pastoral flavor about the pleasant dish, eaten with the accompaniment of fresh berries, on a summer evening, that appeals to the better impulses of one's appetite.

Try my soaked rusk—not forgetting to ice the milk—and you will find out for yourself what I mean, but cannot quite express.

Dried rusk will keep for weeks, and grow better every day. The only risk is in their being eaten up before they attain maturity.

BUTTER CRACKERS.

- 1 quart of flour.
- 3 tablespoonfuls butter.

- ½ teaspoonful soda, dissolved in hot water.

- 1 saltspoonful salt.

- 2 cups sweet milk.

Rub the butter into the flour, or, what is better, cut it up with a knife or chopper, as you do in pastry; add the salt, milk, and soda, mixing well. Work into a ball, lay upon a floured board, and beat with a rolling-pin half an hour, turning and shifting the mass often. Roll into an even sheet, a quarter of an inch thick, or less, prick deeply with a fork, and bake hard in a moderate oven. Hang them up in a muslin bag in the kitchen for two days to dry.

WAFERS. ✠

- 1 pound of flour.

- 2 tablespoonfuls butter.

- A little salt.

Mix with sweet milk into a stiff dough, roll out very thin, cut into round cakes, and again roll these as thin as they can be handled. Lift them carefully, lay in a pan, and bake very quickly.

These are extremely nice, especially for invalids. They should be hardly thicker than writing-paper. Flour the baking-pan instead of greasing.

CRUMPETS (*Sweet.*)

- 1 pint raised dough.

- 3 eggs.

- 3 tablespoonfuls butter.

- ½ cup white sugar.

When your bread has passed its second rising, work into the above-named quantity the melted butter, then the eggs and sugar, beaten together until very light. Bake in muffin-rings about twenty minutes.

CRUMPETS (*Plain.*) ✠

- 3 cups warm milk.
- ½ cup yeast.
- 2 tablespoonfuls melted butter.
- 1 saltspoonful salt, and the same of soda, dissolved in hot water.
- Flour to make good batter.

Set these ingredients—leaving out the butter and soda—as a sponge. When very light, beat in the melted butter, with a *very* little flour, to prevent the butter from thinning the batter too much; stir in the soda hard, fill pattypans or muffin-rings with the mixture, and let them stand fifteen minutes before baking.

This is an excellent, easy, and economical receipt.

GRAHAM MUFFINS. ✠

- 3 cups Graham flour.
- 1 cup white flour.
- 1 quart of milk.
- ¾ cup yeast.
- 1 tablespoonful lard or butter.
- 1 teaspoonful salt.
- 2 tablespoonfuls sugar.

Set to rise over night, and bake in muffin-rings twenty minutes in a quick oven. Eat hot.

QUEEN MUFFINS. ✠

- 1 quart of milk.
- ¾ cup of yeast.
- 2 tablespoonfuls white sugar.
- 1 tablespoonful of lard or butter.

- 1 teaspoonful salt.

- Flour to make a good batter.

- 4 eggs.

Set the batter—leaving out the eggs—to rise over night. In the morning beat the eggs very light, stir into the batter, and bake in muffin-rings twenty minutes in a quick oven.

CREAM MUFFINS. ✠

- 1 quart sweet milk (half-cream, if you can get it).

- 1 quart flour—heaping.

- 6 eggs.

- 1 tablespoonful butter, and the same of lard—melted together.

Beat the eggs light—the yolks and whites separately; add the milk, with a little salt, then the shortening, lastly the flour, stirring in lightly. Bake immediately in well-greased rings half-filled with the batter. Your oven should be hot, and the muffins sent to table so soon as they are taken up.

BUTTERMILK MUFFINS.

- 1 quart buttermilk, or "loppered" sweet milk.

- 2 eggs.

- 1 teaspoonful soda, dissolved in hot water.

- 1 teaspoonful salt.

- Flour to make good batter.

Beat the eggs well and stir them into the milk, beating hard all the while; add the flour and salt, and at the last the soda. Bake at once in a quick oven.

"Mother's" Muffins. ✠

- 1 pint milk.
- 1 egg.
- 1 tablespoonful lard.
- ½ cup yeast.
- Flour for stiff batter.
- 1 teaspoonful salt.

Set to rise over night.

Charlotte Muffins. ✠

- 1 quart of flour.
- 3 eggs—the whites and yolks beaten separately and until stiff.
- 3 cups of milk. If sour, no disadvantage, if soda be added.
- A little salt.

The excellence of these depends upon thorough beating and quick baking.

Rice Muffins. ✠

- 1 cup cold boiled rice.
- 1 pint of flour.
- 2 eggs.
- 1 quart of milk, or enough to make thin batter.
- 1 tablespoonful lard or butter.
- 1 teaspoonful salt.

Beat hard and bake quickly.

HOMINY MUFFINS. ✠

- 2 cups fine hominy—boiled and cold.

- 3 eggs.

- 3 cups sour milk. If sweet, add one teaspoonful cream tartar.

- ½ cup melted butter.

- 2 teaspoonfuls salt.

- 2 tablespoonfuls white sugar.

- 1 large cup flour.

- 1 teaspoonful soda.

Beat the hominy smooth; stir in the milk, then the butter, salt, and sugar; next the eggs, which should first be well beaten; then the soda, dissolved in hot water; lastly the flour.

There are no more delicious or wholesome muffins than these, if rightly mixed and quickly baked.

BELLE'S MUFFINS.

- 3 pints of flour.

- 1 quart of milk.

- 2 eggs.

- 2 tablespoonfuls cream tartar.

- 1 tablespoonful soda.

- 1 tablespoonful salt.

Sift the cream tartar with the flour. Beat the eggs very light. Dissolve the soda in hot water. Bake in rings in a quick oven.

CORN BREAD.

There is a marked difference between the corn-meal ground at the South, and that which is sent out from Northern mills. If any one doubts this, it is not she who has perseveringly tried both kinds, and demonstrated to her own conviction that the same treatment will not do for them. An intelligent lady once told me that the shape of the particles composing the meal was different—the one being round and smooth, the other angular. I am inclined to believe this. The Southern meal is certainly coarser, and the bread made from it less compact. Moreover, there is a partiality at the North for yellow meal, which the Southerners regard as only fit for chicken and cattle-feed. The yellow may be the sweeter, but I acknowledge that I have never succeeded in making really nice bread from it.

Indian meal should be purchased in small quantities, except for a very large family. It is apt to heat, mould, and grow musty, if kept long in bulk or in a warm place. If not sweet and dry, it is useless to expect good bread or cakes. As an article of diet, especially in the early warm days of spring, it is healthful and agreeable, often acting as a gentle corrective to bile and other disorders. In winter, also, it is always acceptable upon the breakfast or supper table, being warming and nutritious. In summer the free use of it is less judicious, on account of its laxative properties. As a kindly variation in the routine of fine white bread and baker's rolls, it is worth the attention of every housewife. "John and the children" will like it, if it approximates the fair standard of excellence; and I take it, my good friend—you who have patiently kept company with me from our prefatory talk until now—that you love them well enough to care for their comfort and likings.

"My husband is wild about corn bread," a wife remarked to me not a hundred years ago, "but I won't make it for him; it is such a bother! And if I once indulge him, he will give me no peace."

Beloved sister, I am persuaded better things of you. Good husbands cannot be spoiled by petting. Bad ones cannot be made worse—they may be made better. It seems a little thing, so trifling in its consequences, you need not tire further your aching back and feet to accomplish it—the preparation of John's favorite dish when he does not expect the treat—to surprise him when he comes in cold and hungry, by setting before him a dish of hot milk-toast, or a loaf of corn bread, brown and crisp without, yellow and spongy within, instead of the stereotyped pile of cold slices, brown or white. If he were consulted, he would say, like the generous soul he is—"Don't take one needless step for me, dear." And he would mean it. But for all that, he will enjoy your little surprise—ay! and love you the better for it. It is the "little by little" that makes up the weal and woe of life.

May I make this digression longer yet, by telling you what I overheard a husband say to a wife the other day when he thought no one else was near enough to hear him. He is no gourmand, but he is very partial to a certain kind of cruller which nobody else can make, he thinks, so well as his little wife. It so chanced that in frying some of them, she scalded her hand badly. After it was bandaged, she brought up a plate of the cakes for luncheon. He looked at them, then at her, with a loving, mournful smile.

"I can understand now," said he, "how David felt when his men-of-war brought him the water from the well of Bethlehem."

Then he stooped and kissed the injured fingers. Yet he has been married twenty years. I was not ashamed that my eyes were moist. I honored him the more that his were dim.

This is my lesson by the wayside *apropos* to corn-bread.

And now again to business.

Receipts for Bread made of Northern Indian Meal.

NONPAREIL CORN BREAD. ✠

- 2 heaping cups of Indian meal.
- 1 cup of flour.
- 3 eggs.
- 2½ cups milk.
- 1 tablespoonful lard.
- 2 tablespoonfuls white sugar.
- 1 teaspoonful soda.
- 2 tablespoonfuls cream-tartar.
- 1 tablespoonful salt.

Beat the eggs very thoroughly—whites and yolks separately—melt the lard, sift the cream-tartar and soda into the meal and flour while yet dry, and stir this in at the last. Then, to borrow the direction scribbled by a rattle-tongued girl upon the above receipt, when she sent it to me—"*beat like mad!*" Bake quickly and steadily in a buttered mould. Half an hour will usually suffice. In cutting corn bread *hold the knife perpendicularly* and cut toward you.

CORN MEAL MUFFINS.

Mix according to the foregoing receipt, only a little thinner, and bake in rings or small pattypans. All kinds of corn bread should be baked quickly and eaten while hot.

RISEN CORN BREAD.

- 1 pint Indian meal.
- 2 cups risen sponge, taken from your regular baking of wheat bread.
- ½ cup molasses, *or*, what is better, 4 tablespoonfuls white sugar.
- 1 teaspoonful soda, dissolved in hot water.
- 1 tablespoonful lard, melted.
- 1 cup flour, or enough for stiff batter.

Mix well, put to rise in a buttered mould until very light. Bake one hour. It is well to scald the meal and stir in while blood-warm.

STEAMED CORN BREAD. ✠

- 2 cups Indian meal.
- 1 cup flour.
- 2 tablespoonfuls white sugar.
- 2½ cups "loppered" milk, or buttermilk.
- 1 teaspoonful soda.
- 1 teaspoonful salt.
- 1 heaping tablespoonful lard, melted.

Beat very hard and long, put in buttered mould, tie a coarse cloth tightly over it, and if you have no steamer, fit the mould in the top of a pot of boiling water, taking care it does not touch the surface of the liquid. Lay a close cover over the cloth tied about the mould, to keep in all the heat. Steam one hour and a half, and set in an oven ten minutes. Turn out upon a hot plate, and eat while warm.

This will do for a plain dessert, eaten with pudding-sauce.

CORN-MEAL CRUMPETS.

- 1 quart Indian meal.
- 1 quart boiled milk.
- 4 tablespoonfuls yeast.
- 2 tablespoonfuls white sugar.
- 2 heaping tablespoonfuls lard, or butter, or half-and-half.
- 1 saltspoonful salt.

Scald the meal with the boiling milk, and let it stand until lukewarm. Then stir in the sugar, yeast, and salt, and leave it to rise five hours. Add the melted shortening, beat well, put in greased muffin-rings, set these near the fire for fifteen minutes, and bake. Half an hour in a quick oven ought to cook them.

Never cut open a muffin or crumpet of any kind, least of all one made of Indian meal. Pass the knife lightly around it to pierce the crust, then break open with the fingers.

Receipts for Corn Bread made of Southern Indian Meal.

JOHNNY CAKE.

- 1 teacupful sweet milk.
- 1 teacupful buttermilk.
- 1 teaspoonful salt.
- 1 teaspoonful soda.
- 1 tablespoonful melted butter.

Enough meal to enable you to roll it into a sheet half an inch thick. Spread upon a buttered tin, or in a shallow pan, and bake forty minutes. As soon as it begins to brown, baste it with a rag tied to a stick and dipped in melted butter. Repeat this five or six times until it is brown and crisp. Break—not cut it up—and eat for luncheon or tea, accompanied by sweet or buttermilk.

AUNT JENNY'S JOHNNY CAKE.

Mix as above; knead well, and bake upon a perfectly clean and sweet board, before a hot fire, with something at the back to keep it up. Incline at such an angle as will prevent the cake from slipping off, until it is hardened slightly by baking, then place upright. Baste frequently with butter until nicely crisped.

BATTER BREAD, OR "EGG BREAD." ✠

- Half a cup cold boiled rice.
- 2 eggs.
- 2 cups Indian meal.
- 1 tablespoonful lard or butter.
- 1 teaspoonful salt.
- 1 pint milk.

Beat the eggs light, and the rice to a smooth batter in the milk. Melt the shortening. Stir all together very hard, and bake in shallow tins very quickly.

RISEN CORN BREAD.

Mix a tolerably stiff dough of corn-meal and boiling water, a little salt, and a tablespoonful butter. Let it stand four or five hours until light; make into small loaves and bake rather quickly.

CORN-MEAL PONE.

- 1 quart Indian meal.
- 1 teaspoonful salt.
- A little lard, melted.
- Cold water to make a soft dough.

Mould with the hands into thin oblong cakes, lay in a well-greased pan, and bake very quickly.

The common way is to mould into oval mounds, higher in the middle than at the ends, shaping these rapidly and lightly with the hands, by tossing the dough over and over. This is done with great dexterity by the Virginia cooks, and this corn-meal pone forms a part of every dinner. It is broken, not cut, and eaten very hot.

ASH CAKE

is mixed as above. A clean spot is swept upon the hot hearth, the bread put down and covered with hot wood ashes. It must be washed and wiped dry before it is eaten. A neater way is to lay a cabbage-leaf above and below the pone. The bread is thus steamed before it is baked, and is made ready for eating by stripping off the leaves.

FRIED PONE.

Instead of moulding the dough with the hands, cut into slices with a knife. Try out some fat pork in a frying-pan, and fry the slices in the gravy thus obtained to a light-brown.

GRIDDLE-CAKES, WAFFLES, ETC.

If you have not used your griddle or waffle-iron for some time, wash it off hard with hot soap and water; wipe and rub well with dry salt. Heat it and grease with a bit of fat salt pork on a fork. It is a mistake, besides being slovenly and wasteful, to put on more grease than is absolutely necessary to prevent the cake from sticking. A piece of pork an inch square should last for several days. Put on a great spoonful of butter for each cake, and before filling the griddle test it with a single cake, to be sure that all is right with it as well as the batter.

The same rules apply to waffles. Always lay hot cakes and waffles upon a hot plate as soon as baked.

BUCKWHEAT CAKES. ✠

- 1 quart buckwheat flour.
- 4 tablespoonfuls yeast.

- 1 teaspoonful salt.

- 1 handful Indian meal.

- 2 tablespoonfuls molasses—*not* syrup.

Warm water enough to make a thin batter. Beat very well and set to rise in a warm place. If the batter is in the least sour in the morning, stir in a very little soda dissolved in hot water.

Mix in an earthen crock, and leave some in the bottom each morning—a cupful or so—to serve as sponge for the next night, instead of getting fresh yeast. In cold weather this plan can be successfully pursued for a week or ten days without setting a new supply. Of course you add the usual quantity of flour, &c., every night, and beat up well.

Do not make your cakes too small. Buckwheats should be of generous size. Some put two-thirds buckwheat, one-third oat-meal, omitting the Indian.

FLANNEL CAKES. ✠

- 1 quart milk.

- 3 tablespoonfuls yeast.

- 1 tablespoonful butter, melted.

- 2 eggs, well beaten.

- 1 teaspoonful salt.

Flour to make a good batter. Set the rest of the ingredients as a sponge over night, and in the morning add the melted butter and eggs.

CORN-MEAL FLAPJACKS.

- 1 quart sour buttermilk.

- 2 eggs, beaten light.

- 1 teaspoonful salt.

- 1 teaspoonful soda dissolved in hot water.

- 2 tablespoonfuls molasses.

- 1 tablespoonful lard, melted.
- ½ cup flour.

Meal to make a batter a trifle thicker than flannel cakes.

GRAHAM CAKES. ✠

- 2 cups brown flour.
- 1 cup white flour.
- 3 cups sour or buttermilk.
- 1 full teaspoonful soda, dissolved in hot water.
- 1 teaspoonful salt.
- 1 heaping tablespoonful lard.
- 3 eggs, beaten very light.

If you use sweet milk, add two teaspoonfuls cream-tartar. Bake as soon as they are mixed.

AUNTIE'S CAKES (*without eggs*). ✠

- 1 quart sour or buttermilk.
- 2 teaspoonfuls soda (small ones).
- 1 teaspoonful salt.
- Flour to make a tolerably thick batter.

Stir until smooth—no longer—and bake immediately.

EGGLESS FLANNEL CAKES.

- 1 quart milk.
- ½ teacupful yeast.
- 2 cups white flour.
- 1 cup Indian meal.
- 1 tablespoonful lard, melted.
- 1 teaspoonful salt.

Set over night, adding the lard in the morning.

GRANDPA'S FAVORITES. ✠

- 1 quart milk.
- 2 cups stale bread-crumbs.
- 1 good handful of flour.
- 1 tablespoonful melted butter.
- 3 eggs, well beaten.
- 1 teaspoonful salt.

Work the bread and milk smooth, stir in the butter and eggs, then the salt, lastly just enough flour to bind the mixture. If too thick, add milk. These are wholesome and good. Take care they do not stick to the griddle.

RISEN BATTER-CAKES.

- 3 cups white Indian meal.
- 1 cup white flour.
- 1 tablespoonful butter, melted and added in the morning.
- 1 quart milk.
- 4 tablespoonfuls of yeast.
- 1 teaspoonful soda, dissolved in hot water, and added in the morning.
- 1 teaspoonful salt.

Mix over night.

RICE CAKES. ✠

- One cup cold boiled rice.
- One pint flour.
- One teaspoonful salt.
- Two eggs, beaten light.

- Milk to make a tolerably thick batter.

Beat all together well.

HOMINY CAKES. ✠

- 2 cups fine hominy, boiled and cold.
- 1 cup white flour.
- 1 quart milk.
- 3 eggs, very well beaten.
- 1 teaspoonful salt.

Beat smooth the hominy, work in the milk and salt, then the flour, lastly the eggs. Bake at once, and keep the mixture well stirred.

CREAM CAKES. ✠

- 1 pint cream and same quantity of milk, slightly sour.
- 4 eggs, whites and yolks whipped separately.
- 1 teaspoonful soda dissolved in boiling water.
- 1 teaspoonful salt.
- Flour to make a good batter, well beaten in.

VELVET CAKES.

- 1 quart new unskimmed milk—half cream and half milk is preferable.
- 3 eggs, whites and yolks beaten separately, and very stiff.
- 1 teaspoonful salt.
- Rice flour.

Mix the beaten yolks with the milk, add the salt, then rice flour to make a batter as thick as that for flannel cakes; lastly, whip in the stiffened whites very lightly, and bake immediately.

RISEN WAFFLES.

- 1 quart milk.
- 1 heaping quart flour.
- 5 tablespoonfuls yeast.
- 2 eggs.
- 1 tablespoonful melted butter.
- 1 teaspoonful salt.

Set the mixture—minus the eggs and butter—over night as a sponge; add these in the morning, and bake in waffle-irons.

"MOTHER'S" WAFFLES. ✠

- 2 cups milk.
- 2 eggs.
- 3 cups flour.
- 1 teaspoonful cream-tartar.
- ½ teaspoonful soda.
- 1 saltspoonful salt.
- 1 tablespoonful melted butter.

Sift the cream-tartar into the flour with the salt. Dissolve the soda in a little hot water. Beat the eggs very well. Add the flour the last thing. If the batter is too stiff, put in more milk.

RICE WAFFLES (*No. 1.*) ✠

- 1 cup boiled rice.
- 1 pint milk.
- 2 eggs.
- Lard, the size of a walnut.

- ½ teaspoonful soda.

- 1 teaspoonful cream-tartar.

- 1 teaspoonful salt.

- Flour for a thin batter.

RICE WAFFLES (*No. 2.*)

- 1 quart milk.

- 1 cup cold boiled rice.

- 3 cups rice flour, or enough for thin batter.

- 1 tablespoonful melted butter.

- 3 eggs.

- 1 teaspoonful salt.

QUICK WAFFLES.

- 1 pint milk.

- 3 eggs, beaten very light.

- 1 tablespoonful melted butter.

- 1 teaspoonful cream-tartar sifted in the flour.

- ½ teaspoonful soda.

- 1 teaspoonful salt.

- A heaping pint of flour, or enough to make soft batter.

RICE AND CORN-MEAL WAFFLES.

- 1 cup cold boiled rice.

- ½ cup white flour, and same of corn-meal.

- 2 eggs well whipped, and milk to make soft batter.

- 1 tablespoonful melted butter.

- ½ teaspoonful soda, dissolved in hot water.

- 1 teaspoonful of salt.

Beat the mixture smooth before baking.

Be especially careful in greasing your irons for these waffles, as for all which contain rice.

SHORTCAKE, &C.

Sunnybank Shortcake (for fruit.) ✠

- 2 scant quarts flour.

- 2 tablespoonfuls lard.

- 3 tablespoonfuls butter.

- 2½ cups sour or buttermilk. "Loppered" cream is still better.

- 2 eggs, well beaten.

- 1 teaspoonful soda, dissolved in hot water.

- 1 teaspoonful salt.

Chop up the shortening in the salted flour, as for pastry. Add the eggs and soda to the milk; put all together, handling as little as may be. Roll lightly and quickly into two sheets, the one intended for the upper crust half an inch thick, the lower less than this. Lay the latter smoothly in a well-greased baking-pan, strew it *thickly* with raspberries, blackberries, or, what is better yet, huckleberries; sprinkle four or five tablespoonfuls of sugar over these, cover with the thicker crust, and bake from twenty to twenty-five minutes, until nicely browned, but not dried. Eat hot for breakfast with butter and powdered sugar.

If sweet milk be used, add two teaspoonfuls cream-tartar sifted into the dry flour. It should be mixed as soft as can be rolled. This shortcake is very nice made with the common "black-caps" or wild raspberries.

STRAWBERRY SHORTCAKE. ✠

- 1 quart flour.

- 3 tablespoonfuls butter.

- 1 *large* cup sour cream or very rich "loppered" milk.

- 1 egg.

- 4 tablespoonfuls white sugar.

- 1 teaspoonful soda, dissolved in hot water.

- 1 saltspoonful salt.

Proceed, in mixing and baking, as with the huckleberry short-cake, except that, instead of putting the berries between the crust, you lay one sheet of paste smoothly upon the other, and bake until done. While warm—not hot—separate these. They will come apart easily, just where they were joined. Lay upon the lower a thick coating several deep, of strawberries; sprinkle powdered sugar among and over them; cover with the upper crust. It is best to bake strawberry shortcake in round jelly-cake tins, or round pans a little deeper than these, as they should be sent to table whole, while the hot short-cake is generally cut into square slices, and piled upon a plate.

Strawberry shortcake is esteemed a great delicacy in its season. It is eaten at tea, cut into triangles like pie, and sweet cream poured over each slice, with more sugar sifted over it, if desired.

SCOTCH SHORT-BREAD.

- 2 lbs. flour.

- 1 lb. best butter.

- ½ lb. powdered sugar.

Chop the flour and butter together, having made the latter quite soft by setting it near the fire. Knead in the sugar, roll into a sheet half an inch thick, and cut in shapes with a cake-cutter. Bake upon buttered paper in a shallow tin until crisp and of a delicate yellowish brown.

GRANDMA'S SHORTCAKE.

- 1 lb. flour, dried and sifted.
- ¼ lb. butter, and half as much lard.
- 1 saltspoonful salt.
- A pinch of soda, thoroughly dissolved in just enough vinegar to cover it, and well worked in.

Enough ice-water to enable you to roll out into paste half an inch thick. Cut into squares, prick with a fork, and bake light brown. Split, butter, and eat while hot.

EASTER BUNS (*"Hot Cross."*) ✠

- 3 cups sweet milk.
- 1 cup yeast.
- Flour to make thick batter.

Set this as a sponge over night. In the morning add—

- 1 cup sugar.
- ½ cup butter, melted.
- ½ nutmeg.
- 1 saltspoonful salt.

Flour enough to roll out like biscuit. Knead well, and set to rise for five hours. Roll half an inch thick, cut into round cakes, and lay in rows in a buttered baking-pan. When they have stood half an hour, make a cross upon each with a knife, and put instantly into the oven. Bake to a light brown, and brush over with a feather or soft bit of rag, dipped in the white of an egg beaten up stiff with white sugar.

These are the "hot cross-buns" of the "London cries."

PLAIN BUNS

Are made as above, but not rolled into a sheet. Knead them like biscuit-dough, taking care not to get it too stiff, and after the five-hour rising, work in two or three handfuls of currants which have been previously well washed and dredged with flour. Mould with your hands into round balls, set these closely together in a pan, that they may form a loaf—"one, yet many"—when baked. Let them stand nearly an hour, or until very light; then bake from half to three-quarters of an hour until brown. Wash them over while hot with the beaten egg and sugar.

These are generally eaten cold, or barely warm, and are best the day they are baked.

CAKE.

Use none but the best materials for making cake. If you cannot afford to get good flour, dry white sugar, and the best family butter, make up your mind to go without your cake, and eat plain bread with a clear conscience.

There are no intermediate degrees of quality in eggs. I believe I have said that somewhere else, but it ought to be repeated just here. They should be, like Cæsar's wife, above suspicion. A tin whisk or whip is best for beating them. The "Dover Egg-beater" is the best in the market. All kinds of cake are better for having the whites and yolks beaten separately. Beat the former in a large shallow dish until you can cut through the froth with a knife, leaving as clear and distinct an incision as you would in a solid substance. Beat the yolks in an earthenware bowl until they cease to froth, and thicken as if mixed with flour. Have the dishes *cool*—not too cold. It is hard to whip whites stiff in a warm room.

Stir the butter and sugar to a cream. Cakes often fail because this rule is not followed. Beat these as faithfully as you do the eggs, warming the butter very slightly if hard. Use only a silver or wooden spoon in doing this.

Do not use fresh and stale milk in the same cake. It acts as disastrously as a piece of new cloth in an old garment. Sour milk makes a spongy cake; sweet, one closer in grain.

Study the moods and tenses of your oven carefully before essaying a loaf of cake. Confine your early efforts to tea-cakes and the like. Jelly-cake, baked in shallow flat tins, is good practice during the novitiate. Keep the heat steady, and as good at bottom as top.

Streaks in cake are caused by unskilful mixing, too rapid or unequal baking, or a sudden decrease in heat before the cake is quite done.

Don't delude yourself, and maltreat those who are to eat your cake, by trying to make soda do the whole or most of the duty of eggs. Others have tried it before, with unfortunate results. If curiosity tempt you to the experiment, you had better allay it by buying some sponge-cake at the corner bakery.

Test whether a cake is done by running a clean straw into the thickest part. It should come up clean.

Do not leave the oven-door open, or change the cake from one oven to the other, except in extreme cases. If it harden too fast on the top, cover with paper. It should rise to full height before the crust forms.

Except for gingerbread, use none but white sugar.

Always sift the flour.

Be accurate in your weights and measures.

There is no royal road to good fortune in cake-making. What is worth doing at all is worth doing well. There is no disgrace in not having time to mix and bake a cake. You may well be ashamed of yourself if you are too lazy, or careless, or hurried to beat your eggs, cream your butter and sugar, or measure your ingredients.

Yet, sometimes, when you believe you have left no means untried to deserve success, failure is your portion. What then?

If the cake be uneatable, throw it away upon the first beggar-boy who comes for broken meat, and say nothing about it. If streaky or burned, cut out the best parts, make them presentable as possible, and give them to John and the children as a "second-best" treat. Then keep up a brave heart and try again. You *may* not satisfy yourself in a dozen trials. You certainly *will* not, if you never make another attempt.

Cake should be wrapped in a thick cloth as soon as cool, and kept in tight tin boxes. Do not cut more at a time than you are likely to use, as it is not good when dry. Jelly-cakes are best set away upon plates, cloths wrapped closely about them, and a box enclosing all.

Cream your sugar and butter, measure milk, spices, etc., before beginning work. For fruit-cake it is best to prepare the materials the day before. Let your icing dry thoroughly before wrapping up the cake.

Sift your flour before measuring, as all the following receipts are for sifted flour.

ICING. ✠

- Whites of 4 eggs.

- 1 pound powdered white sugar.

- Lemon, vanilla, or other seasoning.

Break the whites into a broad, clean, cool dish. Throw a small handful of sugar upon them, and begin whipping it in with slow, steady strokes of the beater. A few minutes later, throw in more sugar, and keep adding it at intervals until it is all used up. Beat perseveringly until the icing is of a smooth, fine, and firm texture. Half an hour's beating should be sufficient, if done well. If not stiff enough, put in more sugar. A little practice will teach you when your end is gained. If you season with lemon-juice, allow, in measuring your sugar, for the additional liquid. Lemon-juice or a very little tartaric acid whitens the icing. Use *at least* a quarter of a pound of sugar for each egg.

This method of making icing was taught me by a confectioner, as easier and surer than the old plan of beating the eggs first and alone. I have used no other since my first trial of it. The frosting hardens in one-fourth the time required under the former plan, and not more than half the time is consumed in the manufacture. I have often iced a cake but two hours before it was cut, and found the sugar dry all through.

Pour the icing by the spoonful on the top of the cake and near the centre of the surface to be covered. If the loaf is of such a shape that the liquid will settle of itself to its place, it is best to let it do so. If you spread it, use a broad-bladed knife, dipped in cold water. If it is as thick with sugar as it should be, you need not lay on more than one coat. You may set it in a moderate oven for three minutes, if you are in great haste. The better plan is to dry in a sunny window, where the air can get at it, and where there is no dust.

Color icing yellow by putting the grated peel of a lemon or orange in a thin muslin bag, straining a little juice through it, and squeezing it hard into the egg and sugar.

Strawberry-juice colors a pretty pink, as does also cranberry-syrup.

ALMOND ICING.

- Whites of four eggs.
- 1 pound sweet almonds.
- 1 pound powdered sugar.
- A little rose-water.

Blanch the almonds by pouring boiling water over them and stripping off the skins. When dry, pound them to a paste, a few at a time, in a Wedgewood mortar, moistening it with rose-water as you go on. When beaten fine and smooth, beat gradually into icing, prepared according to foregoing receipt.

Put on very thick, and, when nearly dry, cover with plain icing.

This is very fine.

Or,

Mingle a few bitter almonds with the sweet. The blended flavor of these and the rose-water is very pleasant.

MARTHA'S CAKE (*For Jelly.*) ✠

- 3 eggs.
- 1 cup sugar.

- Butter, the size of an egg.

- 1 cup flour.

- 1 teaspoonful cream-tartar, sifted in the flour.

- ½ teaspoonful soda, dissolved in a tablespoonful milk.

Bake in jelly-cake tins, and spread, when cold, with fruit-jelly.

This is, although so simple and inexpensive, an admirable foundation for the various kinds of jelly, cream, and *méringue* cake, which are always popular. It seldom fails, and when well mixed and baked, is very nice. If prepared flour be used leave out soda and cream-tartar.

MRS. M.'S CUP CAKE. ✠

- 1 cup butter.

- 2 cup sugar.

- 3 cups *prepared* flour.

- 4 eggs.

- 1 cup sweet milk.

Bake in a loaf, or as jelly-cake.

CREAM-CAKE. ✠

- 2 cups powdered sugar.

- ⅔ cupful butter.

- 4 eggs.

- ½ cupful milk.

- ½ teaspoonful soda.

- 1 teaspoonful cream-tartar.

- 3 cups flour.

Bake in thin layers as for jelly-cake, and spread between them, when cold, the following mixture:—

- ½ pint of milk.

- 2 small teaspoonfuls corn-starch.

- 1 egg.

- 1 teaspoonful vanilla.

- ½ cup sugar.

Heat the milk to boiling, and stir in the corn-starch, wet with a little cold milk; take out a little and mix gradually with the beaten egg and sugar; return to the rest of the custard, and boil, stirring constantly until quite thick. Let it cool before you season, and spread on cake. Season the icing also with vanilla.

JELLY-CAKE.

- 1 lb. sugar.

- 1 lb. flour.

- ½ lb. butter.

- 6 eggs.

- 1 cup milk.

- ½ teaspoonful soda.

- 1 teaspoonful cream-tartar.

Bake in shallow tins, and when cold put jelly between.

COCOANUT-CAKE. ✠

- 2 cups powdered sugar.

- ½ cup butter.

- 3 eggs.

- 1 cup milk.

- 3 cups flour.

- 2 teaspoonfuls cream-tartar.

- 1 teaspoonful soda.

Bake as for jelly-cake.

Filling.

- 1 grated cocoanut.

- To one half of this add whites of three eggs, beaten to a froth, and one cup of powdered sugar. Lay this between the layers.

Mix with the other half of the grated cocoanut four tablespoonfuls powdered sugar, and strew thickly on top of cake.

ROSIE'S COCOANUT-CAKE.

- 2 cups flour.

- 1½ cups sugar.

- ½ cup butter.

- ½ cup sweet milk.

- 3 eggs.

- 1 teaspoonful cream-tartar.

- ¼ teaspoonful soda.

Sift cream-tartar and soda into the dry flour; cream the butter and sugar; add the beaten eggs, then the milk; lastly the flour. Bake in jelly-cake tins.

Grate one cocoanut; mix with it a cup and a half of white sugar, also the milk of the cocoanut. Set the mixture in the oven until the sugar melts; then spread between the cakes.

LOAF COCOANUT-CAKE.

- 1 lb. sugar.

- ½ lb. butter.

- 6 eggs.

- ½ lb. prepared flour.

- 1 lb. finely grated cocoanut, stirred lightly in the last thing.

Bake immediately.

"ONE, TWO, THREE, FOUR" COCOANUT-CAKE.

- 1 cup butter.
- 2 cups sugar.
- 3 cups flour.
- 4 eggs (the whites only).
- 1 cup milk.
- 1 teaspoonful cream-tartar, }
- ½ teaspoonful soda, } sifted into the flour.
- ½ small cocoanut, stirred in at the last.

COCOANUT-CAKES (*Small.*)

- 1 cocoanut, carefully skinned and grated.
- Milk of the same.
- 1½ lb. powdered sugar.
- As much water as you have cocoanut milk.
- Whites of three eggs.

Dissolve one pound of sugar in the milk and water. Stew until it becomes a "ropy" syrup, and turn out into a buttered dish. Have ready the beaten white of egg, with the remaining half-pound of sugar whipped into it; mix with this the grated cocoanut, and little by little—beating all the while—the boiled syrup, so soon as it cools sufficiently not to scald the eggs. Drop in tablespoonfuls upon buttered papers. Try one first, and if it runs, beat in more sugar. Bake in a very moderate oven, watching to prevent scorching. They should not be suffered to brown at all.

These will keep some time, but are best quite fresh.

COCOANUT CONES.

- 1 lb. powdered sugar.

- ½ lb. grated cocoanut.

- Whites of 5 eggs.

- 1 teaspoonful best arrowroot.

Whip the eggs as for icing, adding the sugar as you go on, until it will stand alone, then beat in the cocoanut and arrowroot.

Mould the mixture with your hands into small cones, and set these far enough apart not to touch one another upon buttered paper in a baking-pan. Bake in a very moderate oven.

LEE CAKE. ✠

- 10 eggs.

- 1 lb. sugar.

- ½ lb. flour.

- 2 lemons.

- 1 orange.

Beat whites and yolks separately; add to all the yolks and the whites of seven eggs the sugar, the rind of two lemons, and juice of one. Bake as for jelly-cake.

To the whites of three eggs allow a pound and a quarter of powdered sugar; beat stiff as for icing, take out enough to cover the top of the cake and set aside. Add to the rest the juice and half the grated rind of a large orange. When the cake is nearly cold, spread this between the layers. Beat into the icing reserved for the top a little lemon-juice, and, if needed, more sugar. It should be thicker than that spread between the cakes.

You can make a very delightful variation of this elegant cake, by spreading the orange icing between layers made according to the receipt given for "Martha's Jelly-Cake" several pages back, and frosting with lemon *méringue*, as above.

WHITE-MOUNTAIN CAKE.

- 3 cups sugar.

- 1 cup butter.

- ½ cup sweet milk.

- Whites of ten eggs.

- ½ teaspoonful soda, }

- 1 teaspoonful cream tartar,} sifted with the flour.

- 4 cups flour.

- Flavor with essence of bitter almond.

Icing, whites of three eggs, 1 lb. powdered sugar. Flavor with lemon-juice. Bake in jelly-cake tins, and fill with grated cocoanut, sweetened with a quarter of its weight of powdered sugar, or with icing such as is made for Lee cake, only flavored with lemon entirely.

FRENCH CAKE.

- 1 lb. sugar.

- ½ lb. butter.

- 1 lb. currants, washed clean and dredged with flour.

- 3 cups flour.

- 4 eggs.

- Nutmeg and cinnamon to taste.

- ½ teaspoonful soda dissolved in three tablespoonfuls milk.

LEMON CAKE (*No. 1.*)

- 1 lb. sugar.

- 12 eggs, whites and yolks beaten separately.

- ¾ lb. flour.

- Juice and rind of a lemon.

- Icing flavored with same.

Baked in small square tins, and iced on sides and top, these are sometimes called biscuits *glacés*.

LEMON-CAKE (*No. 2.*)

- 1 cup of butter (packed).
- 2 scant cups of sugar.
- 10 eggs, yolks and whites beaten separately.
- 1 small cup of milk.
- Juice and rind of a lemon.
- 1 small teaspoonful soda.

Flour to make tolerably thin batter (a little over three cups). Of some qualities of flour four cups will be needed.

Bake in a quick oven.

LADY-CAKE (*No. 1.*)

- ½ lb. butter.
- 1 lb. flour.
- 8 eggs.
- 1 teaspoonful cream-tartar,
- ½ teaspoonful soda.
- 1 lb. sugar.
- ½ pint milk.

LADY-CAKE (*No. 2.*) ✠

- 1 lb. sugar.
- ¾ lb. sifted flour.
- 6 oz. butter.
- The whipped *whites* of ten eggs.

Flavor with bitter almond, and bake in square, not very deep tins. Flavor the frosting with vanilla. The combination is very pleasant.

SISTER MAG'S CAKE. ✠

- 2½ cups powdered sugar.
- ¾ cup of butter.
- 1 cup sweet milk.
- 3 cups flour.
- 4 eggs.
- 1 lemon, juice and rind.
- 1 small teaspoonful soda.

Bake in a square or oblong tin, and frost with whites of two eggs beaten stiff with powdered sugar.

DOVER CAKE. ✠

- 1 lb. flour.
- 1 lb. white sugar.
- ½ lb. butter, rubbed with the sugar to a *very* light cream.
- 6 eggs.
- 1 cup sweet milk.
- 1 teaspoonful soda dissolved in vinegar.
- 1 teaspoonful powdered cinnamon.
- 1 tablespoonful rose-water.

Flavor the frosting with lemon-juice.

CHOCOLATE CAKE. ✠

- 2 cups of sugar.
- 1 cup butter.

- The yolks of five eggs and whites of two.

- 1 cup of milk.

- 3½ cups flour.

- ⅓ teaspoonful soda.

- 1 teaspoonful cream-tartar, sifted into the flour.

Bake in jelly-cake tins.

Mixture for filling.

- Whites of three eggs.

- 1½ cup sugar.

- 3 tablespoonfuls grated chocolate.

- 1 teaspoonful vanilla.

Beat well together, spread between the layers and on top of cake.

CARAMEL CAKE. ✠

- 3 cups sugar.

- 1½ cups butter.

- 1 cup milk.

- 4½ cups prepared flour.

- 5 eggs.

Caramel for Filling.

- 1½ cup brown sugar.

- ½ cup milk.

- 1 cup molasses.

- 1 teaspoonful butter.

- 1 tablespoonful flour.

- 2 tablespoonfuls cold water.

Boil this mixture five minutes, add half a cake Baker's chocolate (grated), boil until it is the consistency of rich custard. Add a pinch of soda, stir well, and remove from fire.

When cold, flavor with a large teaspoonful vanilla, and spread between the layers of cake, which should be baked as for jelly-cake. Cover the top with the same, and set in an open, sunny window to dry.

The above quantity will make two large cakes.

MARBLE CAKE.

Light.

- 1 cup white sugar.
- ½ cup butter.
- ½ cup milk.
- Whites of three eggs.
- 2 cups prepared flour.

Dark.

- ½ cup brown sugar.
- ¼ cup butter.
- ½ cup molasses.
- ¼ cup milk.
- ½ cup nutmeg.
- 1 teaspoonful cinnamon.
- ½ teaspoonful allspice.
- ½ teaspoonful soda.
- 2 cups flour.
- Yolks of three eggs.

Butter your mould, and put in the dark and light batter in alternate tablespoonfuls.

MARBLED CAKE. ✠

- 1 cup butter.

- 2 cups powdered sugar.

- 3 cups flour.

- 4 eggs.

- 1 cup sweet milk.

- ½ teaspoonful soda.

- 1 teaspoonful cream-tartar sifted with flour.

When the cake is mixed take out about a teacupful of the batter, and stir into this a great spoonful of grated chocolate, wet with a *scant* tablespoonful of milk. Fill your mould about an inch deep with the yellow batter, and drop upon this, in two or three places, a spoonful of the dark mixture. Give to the brown spots a slight stir with the tip of your spoon, spreading it in broken circles upon the lighter surface. Pour in more yellow batter, then drop in the brown in the same manner as before, proceeding in this order until all is used up. When cut, the cake will be found to be handsomely variegated.

Or,

You may color the reserved cupful of batter with enough prepared cochineal to give it a fine pink tint, and mix as you do the brown.

CHOCOLATE ICING (*Simple.*)

- ¼ cake chocolate.

- ½ cup sweet milk.

- 1 tablespoonful corn-starch.

- 1 teaspoonful vanilla.

Mix together these ingredients, with the exception of the vanilla; boil it two minutes (after it has fairly come to a boil), flavor, and then sweeten to taste with powdered sugar, taking care to make it sweet enough.

CARAMELS (*Chocolate.*)

- 2 cups brown sugar.
- 1 cup molasses.
- 1 tablespoonful (heaping) of butter.
- 3 tablespoonfuls flour.

Boil twenty-five minutes; then stir in half a pound of grated chocolate wet in half a cup of sweet milk, and boil until it hardens on the spoon, with which you must stir it frequently. Flavor with a teaspoonful of vanilla.

CHOCOLATE ÉCLAIRS.

- 4 eggs.
- The weight of the eggs in sugar.
- Half their weight in flour.
- ¼ teaspoonful soda, }
- ½ teaspoonful cream-tartar,} sifted *well* with the flour.

If you bake these often, it will be worth your while to have made at the tinner's a set of small tins, about five inches long and two wide, round at the bottom, and kept firm by strips of tin connecting them. If you cannot get these, tack stiff writing-paper into the same shape, stitching each of the little canoes to its neighbor after the manner of a pontoon bridge. Have these made and buttered before you mix the cake; put a spoonful of batter in each, and bake in a steady oven. When nearly cold, cover the rounded side with a caramel icing, made according to the foregoing receipt.

These little cakes are popular favorites, and with a little practice can be easily and quickly made.

ELLIE'S CAKE. ✠

- 1 cup of sugar.
- ½ cup of butter.

- 3 eggs.
- ½ cup sweet milk.
- 2½ cups prepared flour.

Bake in jelly-cake tins, and fill with jelly or chocolate. A simple and excellent cake.

SPONGE CAKE.

- 1 teacup powdered sugar.
- 3 eggs.
- ½ teaspoonful cream-tartar.
- ¼ teaspoonful soda.
- 1 teacupful flour.

Flavor with lemon—half the juice and half the rind of one. Bake twenty minutes in shallow tins.

MRS. M.'S SPONGE-CAKE. ✠

- 12 eggs.
- The weight of the eggs in sugar.
- Half their weight in flour.
- 1 lemon, juice and rind.

Beat yolks and whites *very* light, the sugar into the former when they are smooth and stiff; next, the juice and grated peel of the lemon, then the beaten whites; lastly, the flour, *very* lightly.

The lady from whom I had this admirable receipt was celebrated among her acquaintances for her beautiful and delicious sponge-cake.

"Which should always be baked in tins like these," she said to me once, sportively, "or it does not taste just right."

The moulds were like a large brick in shape, with almost perpendicular sides. I instantly gave an order for a couple precisely like them, and really fancied that cake baked in them was a little better than in any other form. But you can hardly fail of success if you prepare yours precisely as I have directed, bake in whatever shape you will. Be careful that your oven is steady, and cover the cake with paper to prevent burning.

It is a good plan to line the pans in which sponge-cake is baked with buttered paper, fitted neatly to the sides and bottom.

POUND CAKE (*No. 1.*)

- 1 lb. sugar.
- 1 lb. flour.
- ¾ lb. butter.
- 9 eggs.
- 2 teaspoonfuls cream-tartar.
- 1 teaspoonfuls soda.

Cream the butter and sugar with great care; beat the yolks and whites separately; sift the cream-tartar well through the flour. Add the flour last.

POUND CAKE (*No. 2.*)

- 1 lb. flour.
- 1 lb. eggs.
- 1 lb. sugar.
- ¾ lb. butter.
- 1 glass brandy.
- 1 nutmeg.
- 1 teaspoonful mace.

Cream half the flour with the butter, and add brandy and spice. Beat the yolks until light, add the sugar, then the beaten whites and the rest of the flour alternately. When this is thoroughly mixed, put all together and beat steadily for half an hour.

If properly made and baked this is a splendid cake.

WASHINGTON CAKE.

- 3 cups sugar.
- 2 cups butter.
- 5 eggs.
- 1 cup milk.
- 4 cups flour.
- 2 teaspoonfuls cream-tartar.
- 1 teaspoonful soda.

Mix as usual and stir in, at the last—

- ½ lb. currants well washed and dredged.
- ¼ lb. raisins seeded and chopped fine, then floured.
- A handful of citron sliced fine.
- Cinnamon and nutmeg to taste.

Fruit-cake takes longer to bake than plain, and the heat must be kept steady.

LINCOLN CAKE.

- ¾ lb. butter.
- 1 lb. sugar.
- 1 lb. flour.
- 6 eggs.
- 2 cups sour cream or milk.
- 1 grated nutmeg.
- 1 teaspoonful powdered cinnamon.
- ¼ lb. citron.
- 1 tablespoonful rose-water.

- 1 teaspoonful soda dissolved in hot water, and stirred into the milk just before adding the latter to the cake.

Cream the butter and sugar, put with them the yolks whipped light, then the cream and spice, next the flour, then the rose-water, and a double-handful of citron cut in slips and dredged; finally, the beaten whites of the eggs. Stir all well, and bake in a loaf or in a "card," using a square shallow baking-pan.

This is a good cake, and keeps well.

BLACK OR WEDDING CAKE.

- 1 lb. powdered sugar.

- 1 lb. butter.

- 1 lb. flour.

- 12 eggs.

- 1 lb. currants well washed and dredged.

- 1 lb. raisins seeded and chopped.

- ½ lb. citron cut into slips.

- 1 tablespoonful cinnamon.

- 2 teaspoonfuls nutmeg.

- 1 teaspoonful cloves.

- 1 wineglass brandy.

Cream the butter and sugar, add the beaten yolks of the eggs, and stir all *well* together before putting in half of the flour. The spice should come next, then the whipped whites stirred in alternately with the rest of the flour, lastly the brandy.

The above quantity is for two large cakes. Bake at least two hours in deep tins lined with well-buttered paper.

The icing should be laid on stiff and thickly. This cake, if kept in a cool, dry place, will not spoil in two months.

I have eaten wedding-cake a year old.

Test the cakes well, and be sure they are quite done before taking them from the oven.

FRUIT-CAKE (*plainer.*)

- 1 lb. powdered sugar.

- 1 lb. flour.

- ¾ lb. butter.

- 7 eggs.

- ½ lb. currants—washed, picked over, and dredged.

- ½ lb. raisins—seeded and chopped, then dredged.

- ¼ lb. citron cut into slips.

- 1 teaspoonful nutmeg.

- 1 teaspoonful cinnamon.

- 1 glass brandy.

Cream butter and sugar; add the beaten yolks, then the spice and the whipped whites alternately with the flour; the fruit and brandy last.

ALMOND CAKE.

- 1 lb. powdered sugar.

- 1 lb. flour.

- ¼ lb. butter.

- 8 eggs.

- 1 coffee-cupful sweet almonds, blanched by putting them into hot water, and, when stripped of their skins and perfectly cold, beaten to a smooth paste in a Wedgewood mortar, with a little rose-water and half a teaspoonful essence of bitter almonds.

Beat whites and yolks separately; stir butter and sugar to a cream; add to this the yolks; beat very hard before putting in the flour; stir in the almond-paste alternately with the whites. Put in the brandy last.

Season the icing with rose-water.

NUT-CAKE. ✠

- 2 cups sugar.
- 1 cup butter.
- 3 cups flour.
- 1 cup cold water.
- 4 eggs.
- 1 teaspoonful soda.
- 2 teaspoonfuls cream-tartar.
- 2 cupfuls kernels of hickory-nuts or white walnuts, carefully picked out, and added last of all.

GOLD CAKE. ✠

- 1 lb. sugar.
- ½ lb. butter.
- 1 lb. flour.
- Yolks of ten eggs—well beaten.
- Grated rind of one orange, and juice of two lemons.
- 1 teaspoonful soda dissolved in hot water.

Cream the butter and sugar, and stir in the yolks. Beat very hard for five minutes before putting in the flour. The soda next, and lastly the lemon-juice, in which the grated orange-peel should have been steeped and strained out in a piece of thin muslin, leaving the flavoring and coloring matter in the juice.

Flavor the icing also with lemon.

SILVER CAKE. ✠

- 1 lb. sugar.

- ¾ lb. flour.

- ½ lb. butter.

- Whites of ten eggs—whipped very stiff.

- 1 large teaspoonful essence bitter almonds.

Cream butter and sugar; put next the whites of the eggs; then the flour, lastly the flavoring.

Make gold and silver cake on the same day; bake them in tins of corresponding size, and lay them in alternate slices in the cake-basket. Flavor the icing of silver cake with rose-water.

ALMOND MACAROONS.

Prepare the almonds the day before you make the cakes, by blanching them in boiling water, stripping off the skins, and pounding them when *perfectly* cold—a few at a time—in a Wedgewood mortar, adding from time to time a little rose-water. When beaten to a smooth paste, stir in, to a pound of the sweet almonds, a generous tablespoonful of essence of bitter almonds; cover closely, and set away in a cold place until the morrow. Then to a pound of the nuts allow:—

- 1 lb. powdered sugar.

- The beaten whites of eight eggs.

- 1 teaspoonful nutmeg.

- 1 teaspoonful arrowroot.

Stir the sugar and white of egg lightly together; then whip in gradually the almond-paste.

Line a broad baking-pan with buttered white paper; drop upon this spoonfuls of the mixture at such distances apart as shall prevent their running together. Sift powdered sugar thickly upon each, and bake in a quick oven to a delicate brown.

Try the mixture first, to make sure it is of the right consistency, and if the macaroons run into irregular shapes, beat in more sugar. This will hardly happen, however, if the mixture is already well beaten.

HUCKLEBERRY CAKE. ✠

- 1 cup butter.
- 2 cups sugar.
- 3 cups flour.
- 5 eggs.
- 1 cup sweet milk.
- 1 teaspoonful soda dissolved in hot water.
- 1 teaspoonful nutmeg, and the same of cinnamon.
- 1 qt. ripe, fresh huckleberries, thickly dredged with flour.

Stir the butter and sugar to a cream, add the beaten yolks; then the milk, the flour, and spice, the whites whipped stiff, and the soda. At the last stir in the huckleberries with a wooden spoon or paddle, not to bruise them. Bake in a loaf or card, in a moderate but steady oven, until a straw comes out clean from the thickest part.

This is a delicious cake, and deserves to be better known. It is best on the second day after baking.

CORN-STARCH CAKE. ✠

- 2 cups sugar,}
- 1 cup butter,} rubbed to a cream.
- 1 cup milk.
- 2 cups flour.

- 3 eggs, whites and yolks beaten separately.

- ½ cup corn-starch.

- 2 teaspoonfuls cream-tartar, sifted well through the flour.

- 1 teaspoonful soda, dissolved in hot water.

Sift the corn-starch with the flour, and add the last thing. Bake in small tins and eat while fresh. They dry in two or three days and become insipid, but are very nice for twenty-four hours after they are baked.

WHITE CAKE. ✠

- 1 cup butter.

- 2 cups sugar.

- 1 cup sweet milk.

- Whites of five eggs.

- 3 cups prepared flour.

COOKIES, ETC.

MRS. B.'S COOKIES. ✠

- 6 eggs, whites and yolks separately.
- 1 cup butter.
- 3 cups sugar.

Flour to make batter *just* stiff enough to be moulded with well-floured hands.

Flavor with lemon.

Make into round cakes and bake in a quick oven.

SMALL SUGAR CAKES.

- 1 heaping teacup of sugar.
- ¾ teacup of butter.
- ¼ teacup sweet milk.
- 2 eggs, well beaten.
- 2 teaspoonfuls cream-tartar.
- 1 teaspoonful soda dissolved in hot water.
- Flour sufficient to enable you to roll out the dough.
- 1 saltspoonful salt.
- Nutmeg and cinnamon to taste.

Cut in round cakes and bake quickly.

NEW YEAR'S CAKES. (*Very nice.*) ✠

- 1¼ lb. sugar.

- 1 lb. butter.

- ½ pint cold water.

- 3 eggs.

- 3 lbs. flour.

- 1 teaspoonful soda dissolved in hot water.

- 4 tablespoonfuls caraway seed sprinkled through the flour.

Rub the butter, or, what is better, chop it up in the flour; dissolve the sugar in the water; mix all well with the beaten eggs, cut in square cakes, or with oval mould, and bake quickly.

"MOTHER'S" COOKIES.

- 1 cup butter.

- 2 cups sugar.

- 3 eggs, well beaten.

- ¼ teaspoonful soda dissolved in boiling water.

- 1 teaspoonful nutmeg.

- 1 teaspoonful cloves.

Flour to make soft dough, just stiff enough to roll out. Try two cups to begin with, working it in gradually. Cut in round cakes, stick a raisin or currant in the top of each, and bake quickly.

CORIANDER COOKIES. ✠

- 1 cup butter.

- 3 cups sugar.

- 1 cup "loppered" milk or cream.

- 4 eggs.

- 6 cups flour, or just enough to stiffen into a *rollable* paste.

- 2 tablespoonfuls coriander seed (ground or beaten).

- 1 tablespoonful soda, dissolved in boiling water.

If you use sweet milk, add two teaspoonfuls cream-tartar. You may substitute caraway for the coriander-seed.

RICE-FLOUR COOKIES.

- ½ lb. ground rice.

- 1 lb. rice-flour, dried and sifted.

- 1 lb. powdered sugar.

- ½ lb. butter.

- 4 eggs.

- Juice and half the grated rind of a lemon.

- 1 tablespoonful orange-flower water.

Beat yolks and whites *very* light; then put the sugar with the yolks. Beat ten minutes, add the orange-flower water and lemon; lastly, the flour and whites alternately. Beat the mixture half an hour. Bake immediately in patty-pans. Eat while fresh.

MOLASSES COOKIES (*Good.*)

- 1 cup butter.

- 2 cups molasses.

- 1 teaspoonful cloves.

- 1 tablespoonful ginger.

Sufficient flour to make *soft* dough. Mould with the hands into small cakes, and bake in a steady rather than quick oven, as they are apt to burn.

GINGER-SNAPS. (*No. 1.*)

- 1 cup butter.

- 1 cup molasses.

- 1 cup sugar.

- ¾ cup sweet milk.

- 1 teaspoonful saleratus.

- 2 teaspoonfuls ginger.

Flour for tolerably stiff dough.

GINGER-SNAPS (*No. 2.*)

- 1 large cup butter and lard mixed.

- 1 coffee-cup sugar.

- 1 cup molasses.

- ½ cup water.

- 1 tablespoonful ginger.

- 1 tablespoonful cinnamon.

- 1 teaspoonful cloves.

- 1 teaspoonful soda dissolved in hot water.

- Flour for pretty stiff dough.

Roll out rather thinner than sugar cakes, and bake quickly. These ginger-snaps will keep for weeks, *if locked up.*

GINGER-SNAPS (*No. 3.*)

- 1 pint molasses.

- 1 teacup sugar.

- 1 teaspoonful ginger.

- 1 teaspoonful allspice.

- 1 cup butter.

- 5 cups flour.

Roll thin and cut into small cakes. Bake in quick oven.

AUNT MARGARET'S JUMBLES.

- 1 cup butter.

- 2 cups sugar.

- 1 teacup milk.

- 5 eggs.

- ½ teaspoonful soda dissolved in boiling water.

- 1 teaspoonful nutmeg.

Sufficient flour to make *soft* dough. Roll out, cut into shapes and sift sugar over them before they go into the oven.

LEMON JUMBLES.

- 1 egg.

- 1 teacupful sugar.

- ½ teacupful butter.

- 3 teaspoonfuls milk.

- 1 teaspoonful cream-tartar.

- ½ teaspoonful soda.

- 2 small lemons, juice of two and grated rind of one.

Mix rather stiff. Roll and cut out with a cake-cutter.

RING JUMBLES.

- 1 lb. butter.

- 1 lb. sugar.

- 4 eggs.

- 1 lb. flour, or enough to make out a soft dough.

- Wineglass (small) rose-water.

Cream the butter and sugar, add the beaten yolks, then the rose-water, next half the flour, lastly the whites, stirred in very lightly, alternately with the remaining flour. Have ready a pan, broad and shallow, lined on the bottom with buttered paper. With a tablespoon form regular rings of the dough upon this, leaving a hole in the centre of each. Bake quickly, and sift fine sugar over them as soon as they are done.

You may substitute lemon or vanilla for the rose-water.

MRS. M.'S JUMBLES.

- 1 cup sugar.
- 1 cup butter.
- ½ cup sour cream.
- 1 egg.
- 1 teaspoonful soda, dissolved in hot water.
- Nutmeg to taste.
- Flour for soft dough.

Bake in rings, as directed in previous receipt.

ALMOND JUMBLES.

- 1 lb. sugar.
- ½ lb. flour.
- ¼ lb. butter.
- 1 teacup "loppered" milk.
- 5 eggs.
- 2 tablespoonfuls rose-water.
- ¾ lb. almonds, blanched and chopped small, but not pounded.
- 1 teaspoonful soda dissolved in boiling water.

Cream butter, and sugar; stir in the beaten yolks, the milk, the flour, and the rose-water, the almonds, lastly the beaten whites very lightly and quickly. Drop in rings or round cakes upon buttered paper, and bake immediately.

You may substitute grated cocoanut, or the chopped kernels of white walnuts, for the almonds, in which case add a little salt.

CURRANT CAKES.

- 1 lb. flour.
- ½ lb. butter.
- ¾ lb. sugar.
- 4 eggs.
- ½ lb. currants, well washed and dredged.
- ½ teaspoonful soda dissolved in hot water.
- ½ lemon, grated rind and juice.
- 1 teaspoonful cinnamon.

Drop from a spoon upon well buttered paper, lining a baking-pan. Bake quickly.

DROP SPONGE-CAKES.

- ½ lb. powdered sugar.
- ¼ lb. flour.
- 4 eggs—yolks and whites separate, and beaten very stiff.
- 1 lemon—all the juice, and half the grated rind.

Drop upon buttered paper, not too near together. Try one, and if it runs, beat the mixture some minutes longer *hard*, adding a very little flour. Your oven should be very quick, and the cakes a delicate yellow brown.

LADY'S FINGERS

Are mixed like drop sponge-cakes, but disposed upon the paper in long, narrow cakes. They are very nice dipped in chocolate icing, or caramel.

AUNT MARGARET'S CRULLERS. ✠

- 1 lb. butter.
- 1½ lb. powdered sugar.
- 12 eggs.
- Mace and nutmeg to taste.
- Flour to roll out stiff.

This is for a large quantity of crullers. Roll out in a thin sheet, cut into shapes with a jagging-iron, and fry in *plenty* of boiling lard. Test the heat first by dropping in one. It should rise almost instantly to the surface. Crullers and doughnuts soak in fat at the bottom of the kettle. These should be a fine yellow.

The most delicious and the nicest-looking crullers I have ever seen were made by the dear old lady from whom I had this receipt. They were as pretty and perfect a picture of their kind as she was of hers.

Crullers are better the second day than the first. If the fat becomes so hot that the crullers brown before they puff out to their full dimensions, take the kettle from the fire for a few minutes. Have enough cut out before you begin to fry them, to keep a good supply all the while on the fire. If you undertake the task alone, cut out all before cooking one.

KATIE'S CRULLERS.

- 1 lb. sugar.
- ¼ lb. butter.
- 6 eggs.
- 1 tablespoonful sweet milk.
- 1 small teaspoonful soda.
- 1 nutmeg.

- Sufficient flour to roll out stiff.

"MOTHER'S" CRULLERS.

- 1½ teacup sugar.

- ½ teacup sour cream or milk.

- ⅓ teacup butter.

- 1 egg.

- 1 small teaspoonful soda dissolved in hot water.

- Flour to roll out a tolerably stiff paste.

ANNIE'S CRULLERS.

- 2 cups sugar.

- 1 cup butter.

- 2 eggs.

- 2 cups sour milk.

- 1 teaspoonful soda dissolved in hot water.

- Flour to roll out tolerably stiff.

RISEN DOUGHNUTS.

- 1 lb. butter.

- 1¾ lb. sugar.

- 1 quart sweet milk.

- 4 eggs.

- 1 large cup yeast.

- 1 tablespoonful mace or nutmeg.

- 2 teaspoonfuls cinnamon.

- Flour to make all stiff as bread dough.

- 1 teaspoonful salt.

Cream the butter and sugar, add the milk, yeast, and one quart and a pint of flour. Set to rise over night. In the morning beat the eggs very light, and stir into the batter with the spice and rest of the flour. Set to rise three hours, or until light; roll into a pretty thick sheet, cut out, and fry in boiling lard. Sift powdered sugar over them while hot.

QUICK DOUGHNUTS.

- 1 cup butter.
- 2 cups sugar.
- 4 eggs.
- 1 cup sour milk or cream.
- 1 teaspoonful soda dissolved in hot water.
- 1 teaspoonful nutmeg.
- ½ teaspoonful cinnamon.
- Flour to roll out in pretty soft dough.

Cut into shapes and fry in hot lard.

SOFT GINGERBREAD. ✠

- 1 cup butter.
- 1 cup molasses.
- 1 cup sugar.
- 1 cup sour or buttermilk.
- 1 teaspoonful soda dissolved in boiling water.
- 1 tablespoonful ginger.
- 1 teaspoonful cinnamon.
- 2 eggs.

About five cups of flour—enough to make it thick as cup-cake batter, perhaps a trifle thicker. Work in four cups first, and add very cautiously.

Stir butter, sugar, molasses, and spice together to a light cream, set them on the range until slightly warm; beat the eggs light; add the milk to the warmed mixture, then the eggs, the soda, and lastly the flour. Beat very hard ten minutes, and bake at once in a loaf, or in small tins. Half a pound raisins, seeded and cut in half, will improve this excellent gingerbread. Dredge them well before putting them in. Add them at the last.

SPONGE GINGERBREAD (*eggless*.) ✠

- 5 cups flour.
- 1 heaping tablespoonful butter.
- 1 cup molasses.
- 1 cup sugar.
- 1 cup milk (sour is best).
- 2 teaspoonfuls saleratus, *not* soda, dissolved in hot water.
- 2 teaspoonfuls ginger.
- 1 teaspoonful cinnamon.

Mix the molasses, sugar, butter, and spice together; warm them slightly, and beat until they are lighter in color by many degrees than when you began. Add the milk, then the saleratus, and having mixed all well, put in the flour. Beat very hard five minutes, and bake in a broad, shallow pan, or in *pâté*-tins. Half a pound of seeded raisins cut in pieces will be a pleasant addition.

Try this gingerbread warm for tea or luncheon, with a cup of hot chocolate to accompany it, and you will soon repeat the experiment.

PLAIN GINGERBREAD.

- 2 cups molasses.
- ½ cup lard.

- ½ cup butter.

- 2 tablespoonfuls soda dissolved in hot water.

- 2 tablespoonfuls ginger.

- 1 cup sour milk.

- Thicken with flour to a soft dough.

Warm the molasses, lard, butter, and ginger, and beat them ten minutes before adding the milk, soda, and flour. Roll out, cut into shapes, and bake in a quick, but not too hot oven. Keep in a tight tin box. Brush over with white of egg while hot.

GINGERBREAD LOAF (*No. 1.*)

- 1 cup butter.

- 1 cup molasses.

- 1 cup sugar.

- ½ cup cold water.

- 1 tablespoonful ginger.

- 1 teaspoonful cinnamon.

- 1 teaspoonful soda, dissolved in boiling water.

- Flour to make stiff batter.

Melt the butter, slightly warm the molasses, spice, and sugar, and beat together ten minutes. Then put in the water, soda, and flour. Stir very hard, and bake in three small loaves. Brush them over with syrup while hot, and eat fresh.

LOAF GINGERBREAD (No. 2.)

- 1 cup butter.

- 2 cups molasses.

- 1 tablespoonful ginger.

- 2 eggs, very well beaten.

- 1 teaspoonful saleratus.

- 1 cup milk, sweet or sour. If sour, heap your spoon with saleratus.

- Flour to the consistency of pound cake.

SPICED GINGERBREAD.

- 1 lb. flour.

- 1 lb. sugar.

- ⅛ lb. butter.

- 5 eggs.

- ½ teaspoonful soda dissolved in hot water.

- 1 teaspoonful cream-tartar.

- 3 tablespoonfuls sweet milk.

- 1 large tablespoonful ginger.

- 1 teaspoonful cloves.

- 1 teaspoonful nutmeg.

- 1 teaspoonful cinnamon.

Cream the sugar and butter, stir in the beaten yolks, the milk and spice, the soda, and when these are well mixed, the flour. Bake in two square or round loaves.

SUGAR GINGERBREAD.

- 1 cup of butter.

- 2 cups of sugar.

- 1 cup sour cream or milk.

- 3 eggs.

- 1 teaspoonful soda dissolved in hot water.

- 2 teaspoonfuls ginger.

- 1 teaspoonful cinnamon.

- 5 cups of flour, or enough to roll out *soft*.

Cut in shapes, brush over with white of egg while hot, and bake.

BREAD CAKE.

On baking-day, take from your dough, after its second rising— 2 cups risen dough. Have ready, also—

- 2 cups white sugar.

- 1 cup butter, creamed with the sugar.

- 3 eggs.

- 1 even teaspoonful soda, dissolved in hot water.

- 2 tablespoonfuls sweet milk—cream is better.

- ½ lb. currants, well washed and dredged.

- 1 teaspoonful nutmeg.

- 1 teaspoonful cloves.

Beat the yolks very light, add the creamed butter and sugar, the spice, milk, soda, and dough. Stir until all are well mixed; put in the beaten whites, lastly the fruit. Beat hard five minutes, let it rise twenty minutes in two well-buttered pans, and bake half an hour or until done.

FRUIT GINGERBREAD.

- 2 lbs. flour.

- ¾ lb. butter.

- 1 lb. sugar.

- 1 lb. raisins, seeded and chopped.

- 1 lb. currants, well washed.

- 2 cups molasses.

- ½ cup sour cream.

- 6 eggs.

- 1 heaping teaspoonful soda dissolved in hot water.

- 2 tablespoonfuls ginger.

- 1 teaspoonful cinnamon.

- 1 teaspoonful cloves.

Cream the butter and sugar, warm the molasses slightly, and beat these together; then the beaten yolks, next the milk and spice, the soda, the flour and whites well whipped; lastly, the fruit, which must be thickly dredged. Beat well before baking.

A little citron, shred fine, is an improvement. Bake in two broad pans, in a moderate oven. This cake will keep a long time.

SWEET WAFERS.

- 6 eggs.

- 1 pint flour.

- 2 oz. melted butter.

- 1½ cup powdered sugar.

- 1 cup milk.

- 1 teaspoonful nutmeg.

Beat whites and yolks separately and very stiff, rub the sugar and butter together, and work in first the yolks, then the milk, then the flour and whites. Bake in well-buttered wafer or waffle-irons, very quickly, browning as little as possible. Roll them while hot upon a smooth, round stick, not larger than your little finger, slipping it out carefully when the cake takes the right shape.

These little cakes are an acceptable addition to any tea or supper table, and look well among fancy cakes in a basket.

BOSTON CREAM CAKES. ✠

- ½ lb. butter.
- ¾ lb. flour.
- 8 eggs.
- 1 pint water.

Stir the butter into the water, which should be warm, set it on the fire in a saucepan, and slowly bring to a boil, stirring it often. When it boils, put in the flour, boil one minute, stirring all the while; take from the fire, turn into a deep dish, and let it cool. Beat the eggs very light, and whip into this cooled paste, first the yolks, then the whites.

Drop, in great spoonfuls, upon buttered paper, taking care not to let them touch or run into each other, and bake ten minutes.

Cream for filling.

- 1 quart milk.
- 4 tablespoonfuls corn-starch.
- 2 eggs.
- 2 cups sugar.

Wet the corn-starch with enough milk to work it into a smooth paste. Boil the rest of the milk. Beat the eggs, add the sugar and corn-starch to these, and so soon as the milk boils pour in the mixture gradually, stirring all the time until smooth and thick. Drop in a teaspoonful of butter, and when this is mixed in, set the custard aside to cool. Then add vanilla or lemon seasoning; pass a sharp knife lightly around the puffs, split them, and fill with the mixture.

The best cream cakes I have ever tasted were made by this somewhat odd receipt. Try it.

NOUGAT.

- 1 lb. sweet almonds.
- ¾ lb. fine white sugar.

- 1 tablespoonful rose-water.

Blanch the almonds in boiling water. When stripped of their skins, throw them into ice-water for five minutes. Take them out and dry between two cloths. Shave with a small knife into thin slips. Put them into a slow oven until they are *very* slightly colored. Meanwhile, melt the sugar—*without adding water*—in a farina kettle over the fire, stirring it all the while. When it bubbles up and is quite melted take off the kettle and instantly stir in the hot almonds. Have ready a tin pan or mould, well buttered and slightly warmed. Pour in the nougat; press it thin and flat to the bottom of the pan if you mean to cut into strips; to all sides of the mould if you intend to fill it with syllabub or macaroons. Let it cool in the mould, for the latter purpose, withdrawing it carefully when you want it. If you cut it up, do it while it is still warm—not hot.

The syrup should be a bright yellow before putting in the almonds.

PIES

Use none but the best butter in pastry.

"Cooking butter is a good thing," said a grave epicure to me once, "an admirable thing—in its place, which is in the soap-fat kettle or upon wagon-wheels!"

It is certainly out of place in biscuits, cake, or in any substance destined for human palates and stomachs. It is never less in place than in pastry; never betrays its vileness more surely and odiously.

Butter intended for pastry should be washed carefully in several clear, cold waters, and kneaded while under water, to extract the salt. Then wipe it dry and lay it in a cold place until you are ready to work it in.

"Keep cool," is a cardinal motto for pastry-makers. A marble slab is a good thing to roll out paste upon. Next to this, the best article is a *clean* board of hard wood, which is never used for any other purpose. It is harder to make good pastry in warm weather than cold, on account of the tendency of the butter to oil, and thus render the crust heavy and solid.

Few people know what really good pastry is. Fewer still can make it. It has no inevitable resemblance either to putty or leather. It *is* light, crisp, flaky, goodly to behold—goodlier to the taste.

"Pork fat and pies kill more people yearly in the United States than do liquor and tobacco," said a popular lecturer upon conservatism.

Perhaps so; but I incline to the belief that bad pastry is answerable for a vast majority of the murders. Not that I recommend pies of any description as healthful daily food—least of all for children. But since they are eaten freely all over our land, let us make them as wholesome and palatable as possible.

FAMILY PIE-CRUST (No. 1.) ✠

- 1 quart flour.
- ⅓ lb. lard, sweet and firm.
- ½ lb. butter.
- 1 small teacup ice-water.

Sift the flour into a deep wooden bowl. With a broad-bladed knife, or a small keen "chopper," cut up the lard into the flour until it is fine as dust. Wet with ice-water into a stiff dough, working it with a wooden spoon until obliged to make it into a roll or ball with your hands. Flour these, and knead the paste into shape with as few strokes as will effect your end. Lay the lump upon a floured kneading-board and roll it out into a thin sheet, always rolling from you with quick, light action. When thin enough, stick bits of butter in regular close rows all over the sheet, using a knife for this purpose rather than your hands. Roll up the paste into close folds as you would a sheet of music. Flatten it that your rolling-pin can take hold, and roll out again as thin as before. Baste, roll up and then out, until your butter is gone. It is a good plan to sprinkle the inside of each sheet with a little flour after buttering it, before making it into a roll. Finally, make out your crust; butter your pie-plates, lay the paste lightly within them, cut it off evenly about the edges after fitting it neatly; gather up the scraps left from cutting, and make into another sheet. If the pies are to have a top crust, fill the plates with fruit or whatever you have ready, lay the paste on this, cut it to fit, and press down the edges to prevent the escape of the juice, with a spoon, knife, or jagging-iron, ornamenting it in a regular figure.

Bake in a moderate oven until a light brown. Be particularly careful to have your heat as great at the bottom as at the top, or the lower crust will be clammy and raw.

Pastry is always best when fresh.

It is well, when you can spare the time, to lay the roll, when all the butter is used up, in a very cold place for fifteen minutes or so before rolling it into crust. Indeed, some good housewives let it stand on the ice an hour in hot weather. They say it tends to make it flaky as well as firm.

Touch as little with your hands as may be practicable.

FAMILY PIE-CRUST (No. 2.) ✠

- 1 lb. flour.
- ¾ lb. butter.
- 1 teaspoonful soda.
- 2 teaspoonfuls cream-tartar.
- Ice-water to make into a stiff dough.

Chop half the butter into the flour until it looks like yellow sand (sift the soda and cream-tartar with the flour, passing it through the sieve twice to make sure it is well mixed); work with ice-water into stiff dough; roll into a thin sheet, baste with one-third the remaining butter, fold up closely into a long roll, flatten and re-roll, then baste again. Repeat this operation three times, until the butter is gone, when make out your crust.

This is an easy and sure receipt, and the paste very fine.

FRENCH PUFF PASTE. ✠

- 1 lb. flour.
- ¾ lb. butter.
- 1 egg; use the yolk only.
- Ice-water.

Chop half the butter into the flour; stir the beaten egg into half a cup ice-water, and work the flour into a stiff dough; roll out *thin*, baste with one-third the remaining butter, fold closely, roll out again, and so on until the butter is used up. Roll very thin, and set the last folded roll in a very cold place ten or fifteen minutes before making out the crust. Wash with beaten egg while hot. This paste is very nice for oyster-*pâtés* as well as for fruit-pies.

PUFF-PASTE.

- 1 pint flour.
- ½ lb. butter.

- 1 egg, well beaten. Use the yolk only.

- 1 gill ice-water.

Mix the flour, a tablespoonful of butter, the beaten egg and ice-water into a paste with a wooden spoon. Flour your pastry-board, and roll out the crust very thin. Put the rest of the butter, when you have washed it, in the centre of this sheet, in a flat cake. Turn the four corners of the paste over it, and roll out carefully, not to break the paste. Should it give way, flour the spot, that it may not stick to the roller. When very thin, sprinkle lightly with flour, fold up, and roll out four times more. Set in a cool place for an hour, roll out again, and cut into tartlet-shells or top crust for pies.

The bottom crust of pies may often be made of plainer pastry than the upper.

TRANSPARENT CRUST. (*Very rich.*)

- 1 lb. flour.

- 1 lb. butter.

- 1 egg—the yolk only.

Wash the butter, dry, and then melt it in a vessel set in another of boiling water, stirring gently all the while to prevent oiling. Take off the salty scum from the top, and when almost cold beat up the butter little by little with the egg, which should be previously whipped light. When these are thoroughly incorporated, work in the flour, roll out twice, sprinkling lightly with flour before you fold it up; let it stand folded five minutes in a cold place, and make out for tartlets or *pâtés*. It is not suitable for large pies. Bake before you fill them, and brush over with a beaten egg while hot.

MINCE PIES (*No. 1.*)

- 4 lbs. meat—*i. e.*, two-thirds apple, one-third meat.

- 3 lbs. raisins, seeded and chopped.

- 2 lbs. currants, washed, picked over, and dried.

- 3 quarts cider.

- 1 pint brandy.

- 1 heaping teaspoonful cinnamon.

- 1 heaping teaspoonful nutmeg.

- The same of cloves, and half the quantity of mace.

- Make very sweet with brown sugar.

The meat should be a good piece of lean beef, boiled the day before it is needed. Half a pound of raw suet, chopped fine, may be added. Chop the meat, clean out bits of skin and gristle, and mix with twice the quantity of fine juicy apples, also chopped; then put in the fruit, next the sugar and spice, lastly the liquor. Mix very thoroughly, cover closely, and let all stand together for twenty-four hours before making the pies.

MINCE PIES (*No. 2.*) ✠

- 2 lbs. lean fresh beef, boiled, and when cold, chopped fine.

- 1 lb. beef-suet, cleared of strings and minced to powder.

- 5 lbs. apples, pared and chopped.

- 2 lbs. raisins, seeded and chopped.

- 1 lb. sultana raisins, washed and picked over.

- 2 lbs. currants, washed and *carefully* picked over.

- ¾ lb. citron, cut up fine.

- 2 tablespoonfuls cinnamon.

- 1 teaspoonful powdered nutmeg.

- 2 tablespoonfuls mace.

- 1 tablespoonful cloves.

- 1 tablespoonful allspice.

- 1 tablespoonful fine salt.

- 2½ lbs. brown sugar.

- 1 quart brown Sherry.

- 1 pint best brandy.

Mince-meat made by this receipt will keep all winter in a cool place. Keep in stone jars, tied over with double covers. Add a little more liquor (if it should dry out), when you make up a batch of pies. Let the mixture stand at least twenty-four hours after it is made before it is used.

Lay strips of pastry, notched with a jagging-iron, in a cross-bar pattern, upon the pie, instead of a top-crust.

I take this opportunity of warning the innocent reader against placing any confidence whatever in dried currants. I years ago gave over trying to guess who put the dirt in them. It is always there! Gravel-stones lurking under a specious coating of curranty-looking paste, to crucify grown people's nerves and children's teeth; mould that changes to mud in the mouth; twigs that prick the throat, not to mention the legs, wings, and bodies of tropical insects—a curious study to one interested in the entomology of Zante. It is all *dirt!* although sold to us at *currant* prices.

Wash your currants, therefore, first in warm water, rolling up your sleeves, and rubbing the conglomerate masses apart, as you would scrub a muddy garment. Drain them in a cullender, and pass them through three more waters—cold now, but cleansing. Then spread them upon a large dish, and enter seriously upon your geological and entomological researches. "Sultanas"—sweet and seedless—are nearly as troublesome, but their specialty is more harmless, being stickiness and stems.

Nevertheless, since John has a weakness for mince-pies (I never saw an un-dyspeptic man who had not), it is worth your while to make them, having this consolation, that if you are wise you need not engage in the manufacture oftener than once, or at most, twice a winter. But let the children taste them sparingly, and never at night, if you value their health and your own sound slumbers.

APPLE MINCE-MEAT.

- 2 lbs. apples—pared and chopped.
- ¾ lb. beef suet—cleared of strings and powdered.
- 1 lb. currants.
- ½ lb. raisins, seeded and chopped.
- ½ lb. sultana raisins.
- ¼ lb. citron, cut into shreds.
- 1 lemon—juice and grated rind.
- 1 tablespoonful cinnamon.
- 1 teaspoonful cloves.
- 1 teaspoonful mace.
- 1 tablespoonful allspice.
- 2 lbs. brown sugar.
- Half-pint best brandy.
- A glass of wine.
- 2 teaspoonfuls salt.

Pack down in a stone jar, with close cover, and keep in a cool place.

MOCK MINCE-MEAT. ✠

- 6 soda crackers—rolled fine.
- 2 cups cold water.
- 1 cup molasses.
- 1 cup brown sugar.
- 1 cup *sour* cider.
- 1½ cup melted butter.
- 1 cup raisins—seeded and chopped.
- 1 cup currants.

- 2 eggs—beaten light.

- 1 tablespoonful cinnamon and allspice mixed.

- 1 teaspoonful nutmeg.

- 1 teaspoonful cloves.

- 1 teaspoonful salt.

- 1 teaspoonful black pepper.

- 1 wineglass of brandy.

"Mince-pie in summer is a pleasant rarity," was the remark of a party of hungry travellers, in semi-apology for the fact that every plate made a return journey to the comely landlady, who was dispensing generous triangles of pie. She smiled gratifiedly, but said nothing in reply, until, when the gentlemen had strolled off to the woods with their cigars, she came upon me, seated alone on the piazza, and grew confidential under the influence of that sort of free-masonic understanding housekeepers have with one another, almost at sight.

"I had to laugh," said the good soul, "when they praised my mince-pies. They're healthfuller in summer time than the real thing."

I took down the receipt on the spot from her lips. If any one doubts the merits of the counterfeit, let her do as I did—try it.

APPLE PIE (*No. 1.*) ✠

Pare, core, and slice ripe, tart winter apples—Pippins, Greenings, or Baldwins—line your dish with a good crust, put in a layer of fruit, then sprinkle light-brown sugar thickly over it, scatter half a dozen whole cloves upon this, lay on more apples, and so on, until the dish is well filled. Cover with crust and bake. Sift powdered sugar over the top before sending to table.

APPLE PIE (*No. 2.*) ✠

Stew green or ripe apples, when you have pared and cored them. Mash to a smooth compote, sweeten to taste, and, while hot, stir in a teaspoonful butter for each pie. Season with nutmeg. When cool, fill your crust, and either cross-bar the top with strips of paste, or bake without cover.

Eat cold, with powdered sugar strewed over it.

APPLE CUSTARD PIE. ✠

- 3 cups stewed apple.
- Nearly a cup white sugar.
- 6 eggs.
- 1 quart milk.

Make the stewed apple very sweet, and let it cool. Beat the eggs light, and mix the yolks well with the apple, seasoning with nutmeg only. Then stir in gradually the milk, beating as you go on; lastly add the whites; fill your crust and bake without cover.

APPLE MÉRINGUE PIES. ✠

Stew and sweeten ripe, juicy apples, when you have pared and sliced them. Mash smooth, and season with nutmeg. If you like the flavor, stew some lemon-peel with the apple, and remove when cold. Fill your crust, and bake until just done. Spread over the apple a thick méringue, made by whipping to a stiff froth the whites of three eggs for each pie, sweetening with a tablespoonful of powdered sugar for each egg. Flavor this with rose-water or vanilla; beat until it will stand alone, and cover the pie three-quarters of an inch thick. Set back in the oven until the méringue is well "set." Should it color too darkly, sift powdered sugar over it when cold. Eat cold.

They are very fine.

Peach pies are even more delicious, made in this manner.

PIPPIN PIES.

- 12 fine ripe pippins, pared and grated.
- 1 lb. white sugar.
- ½ lb. butter.

- 6 eggs—whites and yolks separately beaten.

- 1 lemon—grated peel and juice, with nutmeg.

Cream the butter and sugar, stir in the beaten yolks, then the lemon, nutmeg, and apple; lastly the whites, very lightly. Bake in paste, with cross-bars of the same on top.

PUMPKIN PIE (No. 1.) ✠

- 1 quart stewed pumpkin—pressed through a sieve.

- 9 eggs—whites and yolks beaten separately.

- 2 scant quarts milk.

- 1 teaspoonful mace.

- 1 teaspoonful cinnamon, and the same of nutmeg.

- 1½ cup white sugar, or very light brown.

Beat all well together, and bake in crust without cover.

PUMPKIN PIE (No. 2.)

- 1 quart pumpkin—stewed and strained.

- 1 quart milk.

- 1 cup sugar.

- 7 eggs—beaten very light.

- 1 teaspoonful ginger, and same of mace and cinnamon each.

SQUASH PIE

Is made precisely like pumpkin pie, except that, being less rich, it requires one more egg for each pie.

SWEET-POTATO PIE (No. 1.)

Parboil, skin, and slice crosswise firm sweet potatoes. Line a dish with paste, put in a layer of sliced potato, sprinkle thickly with sugar, scatter among them a few whole cloves, and cover with more slices. Fill the dish in this order; put a tablespoonful of melted butter in each pie; pour in a little water; cover with crust, and bake.

Eat cold.

SWEET POTATO PIE (No. 2.) ✠

- 1 lb. mealy sweet potatoes. The firm yellow ones are best.

- ½ cup butter.

- ¾ cup white sugar.

- 1 tablespoonful cinnamon.

- 1 teaspoonful nutmeg.

- 4 eggs—whites and yolks beaten separately.

- 1 cup of milk.

- 1 lemon, juice and rind, and glass of brandy.

Parboil the potatoes, and grate them when quite cold. If grated hot, they are sticky and heavy. Cream the butter and sugar; add the yolk, the spice, and lemon; beat the potato in by degrees and until all is light; then the milk, then the brandy, and stir in the whites. Bake in dishes lined with good paste—without cover.

You may make a pudding of this by baking in a deep dish—well buttered, without paste. Cool before eating.

IRISH POTATO PIE (*or pudding.*) ✠

- 1 lb. mashed potato, rubbed through a cullender.

- ½ lb. butter—creamed with the sugar.

- 6 eggs—whites and yolks separately.

- 1 lemon—squeezed into the potato while hot.

- 1 cup of milk.

- 1 teaspoonful nutmeg, and same of mace.

- 2 cups white sugar.

Mix as you do sweet potato pudding, and bake in open shells of paste. To be eaten cold.

LEMON PIE (*or Transparent Pudding.*) ✠

- ½ lb. butter.

- 1 lb. sugar.

- 6 eggs—whites and yolks separately.

- Juice of one lemon.

- Grated rind of two.

- 1 nutmeg.

- ½ glass brandy.

Cream butter and sugar, beat in the yolks, the lemon, spice, and brandy, stirring in the whites at the last.

Bake in pie-crust, open.

You may, if you wish to have these very nice, beat up the whites of but four eggs in the mixture, and whip the whites of four more into a méringue with four tablespoonfuls sugar and a little lemon-juice, to spread over the top of each pie.

Eat cold. They are very nice baked in pattypans.

LEMON PIE (No. 2.) ✠

- 1 apple, chopped fine.

- 1 egg.

- 1 lemon, chop the inside very fine and grate the rind.

- 1 cup sugar.

- Butter, the size of a walnut.

This is just enough for one pie. Take the thick white rind off the lemon before you chop it. Take out the seeds carefully.

LEMON CREAM PIE. ✠

- 1 teacup powdered sugar.

- 1 tablespoonful butter.

- 1 egg.

- 1 lemon—juice and grated rind, removing the seeds with care.

- 1 teacupful boiling water.

- 1 tablespoonful corn-starch, dissolved in cold water.

Stir the corn-starch into the water, cream the butter and sugar, and pour over them the hot mixture. When quite cool, add lemon and the beaten egg. Take the inner rind off the lemon and mince very small.

Bake in open shell.

LEMON PIE (No. 3.)

- 3 eggs.

- 1 great spoonful butter.

- ¾ cup white sugar.

- Juice and grated peel of lemon.

- Bake in open shells of paste.

Cream the sugar and butter, stir in the beaten yolks and the lemon, and bake. Beat the whites to a stiff méringue with three tablespoonfuls powdered sugar and a little rose-water. When the pies are done, take from the oven just long enough to spread the méringue over the top, and set back for three minutes. This mixture is enough for two small, or one good-sized pie.

Eat cold.

ORANGE PIE. ✠

- 3 eggs.
- ¾ cup of white sugar.
- 2 tablespoonfuls butter.
- 1 orange—juice and half the grated rind.
- ½ lemon—juice and grated peel.
- Nutmeg to taste.

Cream the butter and sugar, beating in the orange and lemon until very light; add the beaten yolks, fill two pastry shells and bake. Beat the whites stiff with two tablespoonfuls powdered sugar, and when the pies are done, spread over them, returning to the oven for three or four minutes.

LEMON TART.

- 1 cup sugar.
- 2 lemons—all the juice, and a teaspoonful grated peel.
- 1 teaspoonful corn-starch, dissolved in a little cold water.
- A dozen raisins stewed, cut in two and seeded.

Beat up well, and bake with upper and lower crust.

ORANGE TARTLETS.

- 2 fine Havana oranges, juice of both, and grated peel of one.
- ¾ cup of sugar-½ cup if the oranges are very sweet.

- 1 tablespoonful of butter.
- ½ lemon—juice only, to wet 1 teaspoonful corn-starch.

Beat all well together, and bake in tartlet shells without cover.

CHOCOLATE TARTS. ✠

- 4 eggs, whites and yolks.
- ½ cake of Baker's chocolate, grated.
- 1 tablespoonful corn-starch dissolved in water.
- 3 tablespoonfuls milk.
- 4 tablespoonfuls white sugar.
- 2 teaspoonfuls vanilla.
- 1 saltspoonful salt.
- ½ teaspoonful cinnamon.
- 1 teaspoonful butter, melted.

Rub the chocolate smooth in the milk and heat to boiling over the fire, then stir in the corn-starch. Stir five minutes until well thickened, remove from the fire, and pour into a bowl. Beat all the yolks and the whites of two eggs well with the sugar, and when the chocolate mixture is almost cold, put all together with the flavoring, and stir until light. Bake in open shells of pastry. When done, cover with a méringue made of the whites of two eggs and two tablespoonfuls of sugar flavored with a teaspoonful of lemon-juice. Eat cold.

These are nice for tea, baked in pattypans.

COCOA-NUT PIE (No. 1.) ✠

- ½ lb. grated cocoa-nut.
- ¾ lb. white sugar (powdered.)
- 6 oz. butter.

- 5 eggs—the whites only.

- 1 glass white wine.

- 2 tablespoonfuls rose-water.

- 1 tablespoonful nutmeg.

Cream the butter and sugar, and when well mixed, beat very light, with the wine and rose-water. Add the cocoanut with as little and as light beating as possible; finally, whip in the stiffened whites of the eggs with a few skillful strokes, and bake at once in open shells. Eat cold, with powdered sugar sifted over them.

These are very pretty and delightful pies.

COCOA-NUT PIE (No. 2.)

- 1 lb. grated cocoa-nut.

- ½ lb. butter.

- ½ lb. powdered sugar.

- 1 glass of brandy.

- 2 teaspoonfuls lemon-juice.

- 4 eggs—white and yolks separated.

- 2 teaspoonfuls vanilla.

Rub the butter and sugar together; beat light with the brandy and lemon-juice; stir in the beaten yolks; lastly the cocoa-nut and the whites, alternately. Bake in open shells.

Eat cold, with powdered sugar sifted over it.

COCOA-NUT CUSTARD PIE. ✠

- 1 lb. cocoa-nut, grated.

- ½ lb. powdered sugar.

- 1 quart milk, *unskimmed.*

- 6 eggs beaten to a froth.

- 1 teaspoonful nutmeg.

- 2 teaspoonfuls vanilla or rose-water.

Boil the milk, take it from the fire, and whip in gradually the beaten eggs. When nearly cold, season; add the cocoa-nut, and pour into paste-shells. Do not boil the egg and milk together. Bake twenty minutes.

Some put the custard quite raw into the pie-dishes, but the cocoa-nut is apt, in that case, to settle at the bottom.

You may, however, pour the raw mixture into cups, and bake by setting in a pan of boiling water, stirring well once, as they begin to warm. This is cocoa-nut cup-custard, and is much liked.

CHOCOLATE CUSTARD-PIE.

- 1 quarter-cake of Baker's chocolate, grated.
- 1 pint boiling water.
- 6 eggs.
- 1 quart milk.
- ½ cup white sugar.
- 2 teaspoonfuls vanilla.

Dissolve the chocolate in a very little milk, stir into the boiling water, and boil three minutes. When nearly cold, beat up with this the yolks of all the eggs and the whites of three. Stir this mixture into the milk, season, and pour into shells of good paste. When the custard is "set"—but not more than half done—spread over it the whites, whipped to a froth, with two tablespoonfuls sugar.

You may bake these custards without paste, in a pudding-dish or cups set in boiling water.

CORN-STARCH CUSTARD PIE. ✠

- 6 eggs.
- 3 pints milk.
- 6 tablespoonfuls white sugar.
- 2 tablespoonfuls corn-starch.

- 2 teaspoonfuls essence bitter almonds.

Boil the milk, stir in the corn-starch wet in a little cold milk, and boil one minute. When nearly cold, stir in the sugar, the yolks of all the eggs, and the whites of two; flavor, and pour into your paste-shells. Whip the remaining whites to a méringue, with two tablespoonfuls white sugar and a teaspoonful of vanilla, and when the custard is just "set," draw your pies to the edge of the oven to spread this over them. Do it quickly, lest the custard fall by exposure to the air.

You may bake this as a pudding by omitting the pastry. Eat cold.

If you have not corn-starch, substitute arrow-root or rice-flour.

CUSTARD PIE.

- 4 eggs.
- 1 quart of milk.
- 4 tablespoonfuls white sugar.
- Flavor with vanilla or other essence.

Beat the yolks and sugar light, and mix with the milk; flavor, whip in the whites, which should be already a stiff froth, mix well, and pour into shells. Grate nutmeg upon the top.

Bake this as cup-custard, or a custard pudding, in cups or a deep dish set in a pan of boiling water.

PEACH PIE. ✠

Peel, stone, and slice the peaches. Line a pie-plate with a good crust, and lay in your fruit, sprinkling sugar liberally over them in proportion to their sweetness. Very ripe peaches require comparatively little. Allow three peach-kernels, chopped fine, to each pie; pour in a very little water, and bake with an upper crust, or with cross-bars of paste across the top.

Some simply pare the peaches and put in whole, packing them well, and sweetening freely. In this case they should be covered entirely with crust.

For one of the most delightful pies that can be made of any fruit, look for *apple méringue pie*, and substitute peaches. Peach méringue pie may be made in winter from canned peaches.

CHERRY PIE.

Line the dish with a good crust, and fill with ripe cherries, regulating the quantity of sugar you scatter over them by their sweetness. Cover and bake.

Eat cold, with white sugar sifted over the top.

BLACKBERRY, RASPBERRY, AND PLUM PIES

Are made in the same manner.

CURRANT AND RASPBERRY TART. ✠

To three cups of currants allow one of raspberries. Mix well together before you fill the crust, and sweeten abundantly. Cover with crust and bake.

Eat cold, with white sugar sifted over it.

CURRANT TART

Is made as above, with more sugar. The most common fault of currant pie is extreme sourness. Small fruits should be looked over carefully before they are cooked. Currants are troublesome, but they must nevertheless be looked after warily on account of their extreme stemminess.

GREEN GOOSEBERRY TART. ✠

Top and tail the gooseberries. Put into a porcelain kettle with enough water to prevent burning, and stew slowly until they break. Take them off, sweeten *well*, and set aside to cool. When cold pour into pastry shells, and bake with a top crust of puff-paste. Brush all over with beaten egg while hot, set back in the oven to glaze for three minutes.

Eat cold.

RIPE GOOSEBERRY PIE.

Top and tail the berries. Line your dish with crust, and fill with berries, strewing white sugar among them. Cover and bake.

DAMSON TART.

Pick over the fruit, put in a dish lined with pastry, sweeten very freely, cover and bake. Brush with beaten egg when done, and return to the oven for a few minutes to glaze.

CRANBERRY TART.

Wash and pick over the berries. Put into a porcelain saucepan with a very little water, and simmer until they burst open and become soft. Run through a cullender to remove the skins, and sweeten to taste. Bake in pastry shells, with a cross-bar of pastry over the top.

STRAWBERRY PIE.

Cap and pick over the berries, arrange in layers, besprinkle with a good coating of sugar, in a shell of pastry. Fill it very full, as strawberries shrink very much in cooking. Cover with crust and bake.

Huckleberry pie is made in the same way.

CREAM RASPBERRY TART. ✠

Line a dish with paste and fill with raspberries, made very sweet with powdered sugar. Cover with paste, but do not pinch it down at the edges. When done, lift the top crust, which should be thicker than usual, and pour upon the fruit the following mixture:—

- 1 small cup of milk—half cream, if you can get it, heated to boiling.
- Whites of two eggs, beaten light and stirred into the boiling milk.
- 1 tablespoonful white sugar.
- ½ teaspoonful corn-starch wet in cold milk.

Boil these ingredients three minutes; let them get perfectly cold before you put them into the tart. Replace the top crust, and set the pie aside to cool. Sprinkle sugar over the top before serving.

You can make strawberry cream tart in the same manner.

RHUBARB TART. (*Open.*)

Skin the stalks with care, cut into small pieces; put into a saucepan with very little water, and stew slowly until soft. Sweeten while hot, but do not cook the sugar with the fruit. It injures the flavor, by making it taste like preserves. Have ready some freshly-baked shells. Fill up with the fruit and they are ready to serve.

Or— ✠

You may, after sweetening the stewed rhubarb, stir in a lump of butter the size of a hickory-nut for each pie, also a well-beaten egg for each, and bake in pastry. Lay cross-bars of pastry over the top.

RHUBARB PIE (*Covered.*)

Skin the stalks, cut in lengths of half an inch; strew lavishly with sugar, and fill the crusts with the raw fruit. Some scatter seedless raisins among the rhubarb. Cover, and bake nearly three-quarters of an hour. Brush with egg while hot, and return to the oven to glaze.

Eat cold, as you do all fruit-pies.

SERVANTS

SOME years ago—more than I care to count over—I read a lively little book entitled, "The Greatest Plague of Life." I have forgotten who wrote it, if I ever knew. It was in the form of an autobiography; the heroine called herself, with an amusing affectation of disguise, Mrs. S-k-n-s-t-n," and it was illustrated by George Cruikshank. I read it aloud in my home-circle, and many a hearty laugh we had over the poor lady's perplexities and calamities.

Regarding the history as a clever burlesque, I suffered no appreciable draught upon my sympathies until time and experience brought me in contact with so many who echoed her plaint, that I could not but recur, now and then, with a half-sad smile, to her sufferings under the rule of Norah, who chased her up-stairs with a carving-knife; with Mary, who drank up the cherry-brandy, filled the bottle with cold weak tea, and kept her pitying employers up all night to pull her through an epileptic fit; with John, who never answered the parlor bell "unless they persevered;" whose stomach could not bear cold meat at dinner, but rallied bravely under a couple of pounds at supper. There was one nursery-maid who whipped Mrs. S-k-n-s-t-n's child, and another who upset the perambulator in the park, and, too much absorbed in the suit of a whiskered Guardsman to note what had happened, went on dragging the carriage upon its side until the baby's cheek was cruelly scarified by the gravel—besides a host of other *un*worthies set for the distress of Mrs. S-k-n-s-t-n's mind, body, and estate.

"Douglas Jerrold wrote that book," interrupts a friend at my elbow. "And, *apropos de bottes*, have you seen Punch's recent article, 'Servantgalism; or, What Shall Be Done With the Missusses?'"

"The malady in America must bear another name," remarks a lady, gayly. "We have no servants—at least in this region. My cook is forty-seven years old, and my chambermaid a widow, who has buried two children; yet they would be highly affronted were I to speak of them except as 'girls.' It is a generic term that belongs to the class 'who live out,' from sixteen up to sixty. I had a lesson on this head not a month since. My laundress, who has lived with me six years, was thanking me for a service I had done her brother.

"'I'll never forget you for it, mem,' she sobbed. 'I'll bless you for it, on me knees, night and morning.'

"I am glad I have been able to help your friends, Katy," I said. "You have been a faithful servant to me——"

She cut my sentence in the middle by walking out of the room—I supposed, to conceal her emotions. I was undeceived, five minutes later, when her angry tones reached me from the kitchen, the door of which she had left open.

"'I'll never believe a person has a good heart, or deserves to be called a Christian, who names an honest, respectable girl, who tries to do her duty, a *servant!* 'A faithful servant!' says she; 'as if she was a queen, and meself a beggar!'"

"What did you say to the ungrateful wretch?" asks a listener, indignantly.

"Nothing. I went quietly out of hearing, reminded, for the hundredth time, of Solomon's warning, 'Take no heed unto all words that are spoken, lest thou hear thy servant curse thee.' I recalled, too, the saying of a mightier than the Royal Preacher: 'Whosoever will be greatest among you, let him be your *servant.*'"

"I thought you were one of the favored few who had no trouble with them," says another housekeeper, sighingly. "There is real comfort,—excuse me, my dear Mrs. Sterling—but it is refreshing to a wearied soul to know that you have felt some of our tribulations. It seems to me, at times, that there is no other affliction worthy the name when compared with what we endure from the 'Necessary Evil.' I have tried all sorts—the representatives from every nation under heaven, I verily believe—and *they are all alike!* They will wear me into an untimely grave yet."

"I wouldn't let them, my dear Martha," replies Mrs. Sterling, with her sunny smile. "If evils, they are surely minor afflictions. And, after all, I imagine 'they' are a good deal like the rest of man and womankind—pretty much as you choose to take them. The truth is, there is no justice in wholesale denunciation of any class.

You recollect the Western orator's truism, 'Human nature, Mr. President, nine cases out of ten, is human nature.' When I consider the influences under which a majority of our servants have been reared—ignorance, poverty, superstition, often evil example in their homes—my wonder is, not at the worthlessness of some, but that so many are virtuous, honest, and orderly. You will allow that, as a general thing, they are quite as industrious as their mistresses, and control their tempers almost as well. And we make so many mistakes in our dealings with them!"

My old friend does not often lecture, but she has something to say now, and forgets herself in her subject.

"We err so grievously in our management, that a sense of our failures should teach us charity. Do we understand, ourselves, what is the proper place of a hired 'help' in our families? If it is the disposition of Mrs. Shoddy to trample upon them as soulless machines, Mrs. Kindly makes a sort of elder daughter of her maid; indulges, consults, and confides in her, and wonders, by-and-by, to find herself under Abigail's thumb—her husband and children subject to the caprices of a pampered menial. I never hear a lady say of a valued domestic, 'I could not get along without her,' without anticipating as a certainty the hour when she shall announce, 'There *is* such a thing as keeping a servant too long.' The crisis comes, then, to Mrs. Kindly. In a moment of desperation she frees her neck from the yoke. Abigail packs her six trunks, having entered Mrs. Kindly's service, seven years before, with her worldly all done up in a newspaper, shakes the dust off the neat Balmoral boots which have replaced her brogans, against the heartless tyrant who sits crying, in her own room up-stairs, over thoughts of how Abigail has been so clean, quick, and devoted to her interests; how she has nursed her through a long and dangerous illness, and had the charge of Emma and Bobby from their birth. She has prepared a handsome present for her in memory of all this, and is hurt more than by anything else when she learns that the girl has taken her final departure without even kissing the baby.

"It is not strange that the deceived mistress should, from that day, write down Abigail a monster of ingratitude, and forget the faithful service of years in the smart of wounded feeling; when the truth is that she did the maid more injury by injudicious petting, than the latter could do her mistress had she absconded with all the plate in the house. She has, as might have been expected, proved Abigail's unfitness to be her confidante and co-adviser; but, at the same time, she has filled her brain with notions of her superiority to her fellow-servants, her heart with burnings for the higher station she can never occupy.

"I speak feelingly upon this subject," continues Mrs. Sterling, with a laugh; "for I was once led into this very mistake myself, by the attractive qualities of a young woman who lived with me nine years as seamstress and chambermaid. She was so even-tempered, so sensible, industrious, and respectful, that she gained upon the esteem of us all. One day, while we sat together at work, I told her of some family changes in prospect, prefacing the communication by the remark, 'I want to speak to you of something, Eliza, which you must not mention to any one else at present. The interests of an employer and a servant should be the same.'

"Then, very foolishly, I opened up my mind freely on the subject that engaged it. She answered modestly, but intelligently, entering into my plans with such cordial interest and pledges of co-operation, that I went to prepare for a walk, feeling really strengthened and cheered by the talk. At the front door I was met by a letter requiring an immediate reply. Returning to my chamber to lay off my hat and shawl, I heard Eliza talking loudly and gleefully in the adjoining sewing-room, with the cook, whom she must have called up-stairs through the speaking-tube. You cannot imagine, nor I describe, my sensations at listening, against my will, to an exaggerated account of the interview which had just taken place. Not only my language, but my tones were mimicked with great gusto and much laughter by my late confidante—the phrase 'The interests of the employer and the servant should be the same' occurring again and again, and forming, apparently, the cream of the joke. I was very angry. But for the rule adopted early in my married life, never to reprove a servant when out of humor, I should instantly have ordered the treacherous creature—as I named her—from the house. I sat down instead, to cool off and to think. With reflection, common sense rallied to my aid.

"'The girl does well enough in her place, which is that of a hired chambermaid and seamstress,' said this monitor. 'She knew her position, and would have kept it, but for your folly in dragging her up to temporary equality with yourself. You made yourself ridiculous, and she was shrewd enough to see it. Take the lesson to heart; write it out in full for future guidance, and keep your own counsel.'

"Eliza never suspected my discovery. She remained with me until her marriage a year afterward, and we parted upon good terms."

I have quoted from my friend at length, because I honor her excellent judgment and mature experience, and because I agree so fully with her touching the evil of so-called confidential servants. The principle of acknowledged favoritism is ruinous to domestic comfort, let who may be the object thus distinguished. Rely upon it, my dear lady, at least one third of home-wrangles and social scandal arises from this cause. Be assured, also, that if you do not perceive the impropriety of lowering yourself to the level of your subordinates, *they* will, and gauge their behaviour accordingly. The connection is an unnatural one, and, like all others of the kind, must terminate disastrously in time. Then the discarded favorite, aggrieved and exasperated, leaves your house to tattle in the ears of some other indiscreet mistress, of your sayings and doings. Show your servant that you respect yourself and her too truly to forget what is due to both. Be kind, pleasant, always reasonable and attentive to her needs, willing to hearken to and meet any lawful request. Make her comfortable, and, so far as you can, happy.

Excuse one more quotation from Mrs. Sterling, whom, when I was much younger than I am now, I consulted with regard to the just medium between familiarity and austerity.

"Remember they are human beings, and treat them as such," she said. "Not that you are likely to reap a large reward in their gratitude, but because it is right, and because you find no exceptions to the practice of the Golden Rule laid down in the Bible. Be faithful in your obedience to the law of kindness. With the return tide you have nothing to do. This is a safe and straight path. I believe it to be also the smoothest. You will be better and more cheerfully served than your neighbor, who, recognizing in every hireling a natural enemy, is always on the defensive."

I have found the most serious obstacle to a comfortable pursuance of her safe path, to lie in this same prejudice—rooted by centuries of misunderstandings and caste-wars—the belief of necessary antagonism between employers and employed. Mrs. Sterling's Eliza only expressed the prevailing sentiment of her class, when she ridiculed her mistress' proposition that their interests ought to be identical. I have failed so often and so signally in the endeavor to impress the merits of this policy upon domestics, that I rarely attempt it now. There is always a suspicion—more or less apparent—that you have a single eye to self-interest in all your regulations and counsels. "What does she hope to gain? What am I in danger of losing?" are the queries that invariably present themselves to the subordinate's mind. The arguments by which your plans are supported are thrown away upon ignorant and illogical listeners—your array of facts totally disbelieved. Your auditor does not say this, but in divers and ingenious ways she contrives to let you know that she is not so silly as to be imposed upon by the specious array of evidence.

For how much of this are mistresses responsible? Has this creed of distrust been learned by experience of injustice or exaction, or is it one of the popular prejudices, which are harder to overthrow than sound and well-established principle? Of one thing I am certain: Mistresses and maids would more speedily come to a right understanding of oneness of interest but for the influence exerted over the former by Mrs. Jones, Mrs. Robinson, and Mrs. Brown, who don't allow this, and couldn't think of that, and never heard of the other privilege or immunity being granted to servants. Before they would yield such a point, or submit to one syllable of dictation, they would do all their own work, etc., etc. Poor Mrs. Pliable, listening dumbly and meekly, goes home with a low-spirited sense of her own pusillanimity upon her, and tries to assert her authority and redeem past faults by a sudden tightening of the reins, that results in a runaway and general smash-up.

Cannot we remember—you and I, my dear reader—that we may sometimes be as nearly right as those who talk more loudly and strongly than we upon domestic economy, laying down rules we never thought of suggesting; splitting into ninths a hair our short-sighted eyes cannot make out when whole, and annihilating our timid objections with a lordly "*I* always do so," which is equal to a decree of infallibility? Cannot we make up our minds, once and for all, to be a law unto ourselves in all matters pertaining to our households? Mrs. Jones' rule may be good for her; Mrs. Robinson's better than any other in her particular case, and Mrs. Brown's best of all for one in her peculiar circumstances; yet any one or all of them be unsuitable for our use.

Avoid talking about your domestic affairs with people whose gossip on these topics is incessant. You are angry when a whiff of some such discussion as enlightened Mrs. Sterling, with regard to her mistake, is wafted to you through the dumb-waiter or register, an accident that will occur while the tones of the plaintiffs are loud and untrained by education or policy. It is mean and unkind— traitorous, in fact, you say, for them so to misrepresent and revile you—after all the kindness you have showed to them, too! Bridget, Chloe, or Gretchen, passing the parlor-door and catching the sound of her name as roughly handled, may have her own sensations, and draw her own inferences—*being human like yourself.* It is tiresome and vulgar, this everlasting exchange of experiences about "my girl," and "your girl," and everybody else's "girl." It is time sensible women ceased, in this respect, to imitate the fashion of the class they censure, and put down the bootless tattle with a strong will. Order your household, then, so far aright as you can by the help of common sense and grace from on high, and let Mesdames Jones, Robinson, and Brown look to the ways of their own, and expend their surplus energies upon their neighbors' concerns—counting you out.

(I believe that is slang, but let it stand!)

These worthy and fussy housewives act upon the supposition that all "girls" are cast in the same mould. Being human (do not let us forget that!), the probability is, that there are varieties of the species.

But, if the mistresses are led by their associates, the "girl's" "acquaintances" sway her yet more powerfully. Every conscientious, well-meaning housewife knows what a brake is this informal, but terrible "Union" upon her endeavors to improve and really benefit those under her direction. I have been amazed and disgusted at the tyranny exercised by this irresponsible body over the best servants I have ever seen.

"We would be hooted at, ma'am, if we didn't give in to them," said one, when I represented how senseless and almost suicidal was the course recommended by these evil advisers. "There's not a girl in the town would speak to us if we didn't join in with the rest. It's like a strike, you see—awful upon them as holds back."

Do not, then, my discouraged fellow-laborer, imagine that I am ignorant of your trials, your doubts, your disheartening experiences. If I disagree with Mrs. S-k-n-s-t-n and do not pronounce our servants to be the greatest plague of life, inclining rather to the belief that—always allowing for human nature and the drawbacks I have enumerated—good mistresses are apt to make good servants, it is in consequence of long and careful study and observation of the practical working of Mrs. Sterling's rule. Like begets like. Pleasant words are more likely to be answered by pleasant than are tart or hasty ones. If you would have your servants respectful to you, be respectful to them. The best way to teach them politeness is by example. It should not cost you an effort to say, "Thank you," or "If you please." The habit exerts an unconscious refining influence upon them, and you dignify instead of degrading your ladyhood by being pitiful and courteous to all. If you can only maintain your position by haughtiness and chilling disregard of the feelings of inferiors, your rank is false, or you unfit to hold it.

To begin, then: Be mistress of yourself. Amid all your temptations to angry or sarcastic speech (and how many and how strong these are, you and I know), curb yourself with the recollection that it is despicable, no less than useless, to say cutting things to one who has no right to retort upon you in kind.

"Ma'," says Miss Aurelia in Miss Sedgwick's admirable story, "Live and let Live"—"how can you let your help be so saucy to you?"

Master Julius, who was standing by, took a different view of the matter.

"If Ma' doesn't want her help to be *sarcy* to her," he said, "she hadn't ought to be *sarcy* to them."

Teach your children the like forms of kindly speech and habits of consideration for the comfort and happiness of your domestics, checking with equal promptness undue freedom and the arrogance of station. It is as graceful to bend as it is mean to grovel.

Learn not to see everything, and, so soon as you can, put far from you the delusive hope that anybody else—unless it be dear old John—will ever serve you as well as you would serve yourself. This failure is attributable to some one of the nine-tenths we spoke of just now. She is a prudent housekeeper who can wink at trifling blemishes without effort or parade. There is one text which has come into my troubled mind hundreds of times on such occasions, calming perturbation into solemnity, and bringing, I hope, charity with humility—

"If *Thou*, Lord, shouldst mark iniquities, O Lord, who shall stand?"

But if your hold of the rein be gentle, let it also be firm. Never forget that the house is yours, and that you—not hirelings—are responsible for the disposition of the stores purchased with John's money.

"I was much amused the other day," said an easy-tempered lady to me, "at a talk that passed under my window between my new cook and one of her visitors.

"'And how are ye gitting along?' asked the guest.

"'Oh! pretty well-ish, now,' was the reply. 'I was a-feard, when I first come, that *she* would bother me a-trotting down into the kitchen so constant. But I give her a hint as how that wasn't the trick of a raal lady, and she's kep' out nicely sence then. You've got to stand up for your own rights in this wurrld, or you'll be trod upon.'"

Now, it would be throwing away words to reason with a woman like that cook, or a mistress might show that in no other department of labor would such a principle be tolerated—that from the Secretary of State down to the scavenger who empties your ash-pan, every employé who draws wages has an overlooker, to whom he is accountable for the manner in which his work is done and his money earned; and that the fact that she is an ignorant, high-tempered woman is no just cause of exemption. Yet in how many families is this point tacitly yielded, and the mistress admitted upon sufferance to her own kitchen—the room furnished with her money, and in which she hardly dare touch or look at the articles intended for the consumption of her own family?

One often hears such remarks as, "It isn't every girl who will stand having the mistress popping in and out while she is at work." When, in any other situation, the very fact of this unwillingness to have the owner of the materials used in that work present, would be strong presumptive proof of negligence or dishonesty. The principle is pernicious from beginning to end, and should not be tolerated for an instant.

It gives me pleasure to state here, that I know nothing personally of this curious reversal of the rights of employer and domestic. I am inclined to believe, if one-half I hear of other housewives' trials be true, that I have been highly favored among American women. My authority in the kitchen, as in other parts of the household, has never been disputed—in my hearing or presence, that is. I have always met with a cheerful reception below-stairs when I appeared there to direct or share the labors of my cooks; have found them willing to undertake new dishes, and ready to learn my "way," however unlike it might be to their own. As a rule, also,—to which the exceptions have been few and very far between—those employed by me have been cleanly, industrious, kind-hearted, and respectful; patient under inconveniences, and attentive in sickness. I should not, therefore, do my duty, did I not lift my voice in a plea for charitable judgment, just and generous treatment of a class which, however faulty, have much to do and to endure. Mrs. Skinflint's grocer's account may be less than yours, if you adopt this policy—Mrs. Sharp's coal-cellar be better dusted, and the paint in her attic scrubbed oftener; but I believe, in the long run, you will be the most comfortable in body, as in conscience. Your machinery will move with fewer jerks and less friction. Your servants will remain with you longer, and be better-tempered while they stay, if you show that you appreciate the fact of a common humanity; that you owe them duties you are resolved to fulfil during their sojourn under your roof, however mercenary may be their performance of those devolving upon them.

Finally, dear sister, do not add to the real miseries of life by regarding the annoyance of a careless, slothful, or impertinent domestic as a real trouble. Class it with petty vexations which are yet curable as well as endurable, and live above it—a noble, beneficent existence in the love of your fellow-creatures and the fear of GOD—a life that can not suffer perceptible disturbance from such a contemptible rootlet of bitterness as this. It is only the feeble, the inefficient, or the indolent mistress whose peace of mind is dependent upon such casualties as a breeze, a hurricane, or a sudden vacancy in the department of the interior.

Recollect, when the infliction is sharpest, that brier-pricks are disagreeable, but never serious, unless the blood be *very* impure.

PUDDINGS

I have, for convenience sake, classed among pies all preparations baked *in crust* in a pie-dish. Many of these, however, are called puddings, such as custards of various kinds, lemon, cocoa-nut, and orange puddings. The reader will have no trouble in finding the receipts for these, if she will bear the above remark in mind.

BAKED PUDDINGS.

Beat your eggs very light—and, if you put in only one or two, whip white and yolk separately, beating the latter into the sugar before adding the whites.

Fruit, rice, corn-starch, and bread puddings require a steady, moderate oven in baking. Custard and batter puddings should be put into the dish, and this into the oven, the instant they are mixed, and baked quickly. *No* pudding, unless it be raised with yeast, should be allowed to stand out of the oven after the ingredients are put together. Give one final hard stir just before it goes in, and be sure the mould is well greased.

APPLE MÉRINGUE PUDDING.

- 1 pint stewed apples.

- 3 eggs—whites and yolks separate.

- ½ cup white sugar, and one teaspoonful butter.

- 1 teaspoonful nutmeg and cinnamon mixed.

- 1 teaspoonful essence bitter almond (for the méringue.)

Sweeten and spice, and, while the apple is still very hot, stir in the butter, and, a little at a time, the yolks. Beat all light, pour into a buttered dish, and bake ten minutes. Cover, without drawing from the oven, with a méringue made of the beaten whites, two tablespoonfuls white sugar, and the bitter almond seasoning. Spread smoothly and quickly, close the oven again, and brown very slightly.

Eat cold, with white sugar sifted over the top, and send around cream to pour over it instead of sauce.

BAKED APPLE PUDDING.

- 6 large firm pippins (grated.)
- 3 tablespoonfuls butter.
- ½ cup sugar.
- 4 eggs—whites and yolks separate.
- Juice of one lemon, and half the peel.

Beat butter and sugar to a cream, stir in the yolks, the lemon, the grated apple, lastly the whites. Grate nutmeg over the top, and bake until nicely browned.

Eat cold with cream.

SWEET APPLE PUDDING. ✠

- 1 quart milk.
- 4 eggs.
- 3 cups chopped apple.
- 1 lemon—all the juice and half the rind.
- Nutmeg and cinnamon.
- ¼ teaspoonful of soda dissolved in a little vinegar.
- Flour for a stiff batter.

Beat the yolks very light, add the milk, seasoning, and flour. Stir hard five minutes, and beat in the apple, then the whites, lastly the soda, well mixed in.

Bake in two square shallow pans one hour, and eat hot, with sweet sauce. Much of the success of this pudding depends upon the mixing—almost as much upon the baking. Cover with paper when half done, to prevent hardening.

PIPPIN PUDDING. ✠

- 8 fine pippins, pared, cored, and sliced, breaking them as little as possible.

- ½ cup very fine bread-crumbs.

- 2 teaspoonfuls butter—melted.

- 5 eggs—whites and yolks separate.

- ¾ cup sugar.

- 1 oz. citron, shred finely.

- 1 teaspoonful nutmeg, and a dozen whole cloves.

- 1 cup milk or cream.

Soak the bread-crumbs in the milk, cream the butter and sugar, and beat into this the yolks. Next, adding the milk and soaked bread, stir until very smooth and light. Put in the nutmeg and citron, and whip in the whites lightly. Butter a deep dish, and put in your sliced apple, sprinkling each piece well with sugar, and scattering the cloves among them. Pour the custard you have prepared over them, and bake three-quarters of an hour.

Sift powdered sugar over the top, and eat cold.

BROWN BETTY. ✠

- 1 cup bread-crumbs.

- 2 cups chopped apples—tart.

- ½ cup sugar.

- 1 teaspoonful cinnamon.

- 2 tablespoonfuls butter cut into small bits.

Butter a deep dish, and put a layer of the chopped apple at the bottom; sprinkle with sugar, a few bits of butter, and cinnamon; cover with bread-crumbs; then more apple. Proceed in this order until the dish is full, having a layer of crumbs at top. Cover closely, and steam three-quarters of an hour in a moderate oven; then uncover and brown quickly.

Eat warm with sugar and cream, or sweet sauce.

This is a homely but very good pudding, especially for the children's table. Serve in the dish in which it is baked.

APPLE BATTER PUDDING. ✠

- 1 pint rich milk.
- 2 cups flour.
- 4 eggs.
- 1 teaspoonful salt.
- ¼ teaspoonful soda, dissolved in hot water.

Peel and core eight apples carefully, and range them closely together in a deep dish. Beat the batter very light and pour over them. Unless the apples are very ripe and sweet (for tart apples), fill the centre of each with white sugar. Bake an hour, and eat hot with sweet sauce.

APPLE AND PLUM PUDDING.

- ¾ lb. fine tart apples, pared and chopped.
- ¾ lb. sugar.
- ¾ lb. flour.
- ½ lb. beef suet, rubbed fine.
- ¾ lb. raisins, seeded and chopped.
- 6 eggs.

- 1 teaspoonful nutmeg and the same powdered cloves.

- 1 teaspoonful salt.

- ½ glass brown Sherry and the same of brandy.

Stir the beaten yolks and sugar very light, add the suet and apples with the spice; then the raisins, well dredged with flour; next the flour, and when this is all in, the liquor; lastly the whites beaten *very* stiff. Bake in two buttered moulds, in a moderate oven, an hour and a half at least. Eat hot, with sauce.

You may boil this pudding if you like.

APPLE AND TAPIOCA PUDDING. ✠

- 1 teacupful tapioca.

- 6 apples—juicy and well-flavored pippins—pared and cored.

- 1 quart water.

- 1 teaspoonful salt.

Cover the tapioca with three cups of lukewarm water, and set it in a tolerably warm place to soak five or six hours, stirring now and then. Pack your apples in a deep dish, adding a cup of lukewarm water; cover closely and steam in a moderate oven until soft all through, turning them as they cook at bottom. If the dish is more than a quarter full of liquid, turn some of it out before you pour the soaked tapioca over all. Unless your apples are *very* sweet fill the centre with sugar and stick a clove in each, just before you cover with the tapioca. Indeed, I always do this. It softens the hard acid of the fruit. Bake, after the tapioca goes in, one hour.

Eat warm, with sweet hard sauce.

BAKED APPLE DUMPLINGS. ✠

- 1 quart flour.

- 2 tablespoonfuls lard—or half butter is better.

- 2 cups of milk.

- 1 teaspoonful soda, dissolved in hot water.

- 2 teaspoonfuls cream-tartar sifted into the dry flour.

- 1 saltspoonful salt.

Chop the shortening into the flour after you have sifted this and the cream-tartar together; put in the soda and wet up quickly—just stiff enough to roll into a paste less than half an inch thick. Cut into squares, and lay in the centre of each a juicy, tart apple, pared and cored; bring the corners of the square neatly together and pinch them slightly. Lay in a buttered baking-pan, the joined edges downward, and bake to a fine brown. When done, brush over with beaten egg, and set back in the oven to glaze for two or three minutes. Sift powdered sugar over them, and eat hot with rich sweet sauce.

I greatly prefer the above simple crust for all kinds of dumplings, to the rich paste which becomes heavy so soon as it begins to cool. It is also more quickly and easily made, and far more wholesome than pastry.

TAPIOCA PUDDING. ✠

- 1 cup tapioca.

- 1 quart milk.

- 5 eggs—whites and yolks beaten separately.

- 2 tablespoonfuls butter, melted.

- 2 tablespoonfuls sugar.

Soak the tapioca, in enough cold water to cover it, two hours; drain off the water, if it be not all absorbed; soak two hours longer in the milk, which should be slightly warmed. When the tapioca is quite soft, beat the sugar and butter together; add the yolks, the milk and tapioca, lastly the whites. Stir very well, and bake in a buttered dish. Eat warm with sweet sauce.

You may make a sago pudding in the same way.

CORN-STARCH PUDDING. ✠

- 4 tablespoonfuls corn-starch.

- 1 quart milk.

- 4 eggs—whites and yolks separate.

- ¾ cup sugar.

- Nutmeg and cinnamon.

- 1 tablespoonful butter.

Dissolve the corn-starch in a little cold milk, and having heated the rest of the milk to boiling, stir this in and boil three minutes, stirring all the time. Remove from the fire, and while still very hot, put in the butter. Set away until cold; beat the eggs very light—the sugar and seasoning with them, and stir into the corn-starch, beating thoroughly to a smooth custard. Turn into a buttered dish, and bake half an hour. Eat cold, with powdered sugar sifted over it.

CORN-STARCH MÉRINGUE. ✠

- 5 eggs.

- 1 quart of milk.

- ¾ cup sugar.

- 4 teaspoonfuls corn-starch.

- ½ cup fruit-jelly or jam.

Heat the milk to boiling, and stir in the corn-starch, which has previously been dissolved in a little cold milk. Boil fifteen minutes, stirring all the while. Remove from the fire, and while still hot, add gradually the yolks of the eggs beaten up with the sugar and seasoned with vanilla, lemon, or bitter almond. Pour this into a buttered pudding-dish and bake fifteen minutes, or until the custard begins to "set." Without withdrawing it further than the door of the oven, spread lightly and *quickly* upon this a méringue of the whites whipped up stiff with a half-cup jelly—added gradually. Use crab-apple jelly, if bitter almond has been put into the custard; currant, for vanilla; strawberry or other sweet conserve, if you season the custard with lemon. Bake, covered, for five minutes. Then remove the lid, and brown the méringue *very* slightly.

Eat cold, with powdered sugar sifted thickly over the top.

ARROW-ROOT PUDDING

Is made according to either of the foregoing receipts, substituting arrow-root for corn-starch. Farina pudding also.

BREAD PUDDING. ✠

- 1 quart of milk.

- 2 cups of fine bread crumbs—*always* stale and dry.

- 4 eggs.

- 2 tablespoonfuls melted butter.

- Nutmeg to taste.

- ¼ teaspoonful soda dissolved in hot water.

Beat the yolks very light, and having soaked the bread-crumbs well in the milk, stir these together; then the butter and seasoning, with the soda; lastly the whites. Bake to a fine brown, and eat hot with pudding-sauce.

This, if well mixed and baked, is quite a different dish from the traditional and much-despised bread-pudding of stingy housekeepers and boarding-house landladies. "Which," says an English Josh. Billings, "nothing can be more promiskus than a boarding-house bread-pudding." Try mine instead, putting all the sugar into the sauce, and enough there, and you will cease to sneer.

You may boil this pudding, if you like, in a floured cloth or buttered mould.

FRUIT BREAD PUDDING. ✠

- 1 quart milk.

- 5 eggs.

- 2 tablespoonfuls melted butter.

- 2 tablespoonfuls (heaping) sugar.

- ¼ lb. raisins, seeded and chopped.

- ¼ lb. currants, well washed and picked over.

- Handful of shred citron, and 1 teaspoonful soda, dissolved in hot water.

- 2 *scant* cups fine bread-crumbs, from a stale loaf.

Beat the yolks light with the sugar, add the bread-crumbs when they have been well soaked in the milk, and stir until smooth. Next put in the fruit, well dredged with flour, the soda, and finally the whites, whipped to a stiff froth.

This will require longer and steadier baking than if the fruit were not in. Cover it if it threatens to harden too soon on top. Send to table hot in the dish in which it was baked, or turn out very carefully upon a hot plate. Eat warm, with pudding-sauce.

BREAD-AND-BUTTER PUDDING.

- 4 eggs.

- 3 cups milk.

- ¾ cup sugar.

- Vanilla or other extract.

- Nutmeg to taste.

- Bread and butter.

Cut thin slices of bread (stale), spread thickly with butter, and sprinkle with sugar. Fit them neatly and closely into a buttered pudding-dish until it is half full. Lay a small, heavy plate upon them to prevent them from floating, and saturate them gradually with a hot custard made of the milk, heated almost to boiling, then taken from the fire, and the beaten eggs and sugar stirred in with the seasoning. Let the bread soak in this fifteen minutes or so, adding by degrees all the custard. Just before you put the pudding in the oven, take up the plate gently. If the bread still rise to the top, keep down with a silver fork or spoon, laid upon it from the side of the dish, until the custard thickens, when slip it out. Eat cold.

BREAD-AND-MARMALADE PUDDING ✠

Is made precisely as above, except that each slice is spread with marmalade or jam besides the butter.

Either of these puddings is good boiled.

ALICE'S PUDDING. ✠

- 1 quart of milk.
- 4 eggs.
- 1 cup very fine dry bread-crumbs.
- ½ cup strawberry or other sweet jam.
- ½ cup sugar.

Butter a pudding-dish; sprinkle the bottom with bread-crumbs; pour over these half a cup jam, and cover this well with the rest of the crumbs, wet with a very little milk. Heat the quart of milk until *near* boiling, take it from the fire and add, gradually, the beaten yolks and sugar, stirring in the beaten whites lightly at the last. Heat this by degrees, stirring constantly until it begins to thicken; put it, spoonful by spoonful, upon the layer of bread-crumbs, taking care not to disturb these, and when all is in, bake until well "set" and very slightly browned.

Eat cold. Cream is a delicious accompaniment to it.

THE QUEEN OF PUDDINGS. ✠

- 1½ cup white sugar.
- 2 cups fine dry bread-crumbs.
- 5 eggs.
- 1 tablespoonful of butter.
- Vanilla, rose-water, or lemon seasoning.
- 1 quart fresh rich milk, and one half cup jelly or jam.

Rub the butter into a cup of sugar; beat the yolks very light, and stir these together to a cream. The bread-crumbs, soaked in milk, come next, then the seasoning. Bake this in a buttered pudding-dish—a large one and but two-thirds full—until the custard is "set." Draw to the mouth of the oven, spread over with jam or other nice fruit-conserve. Cover this with a méringue made of the whipped whites and half a cup of sugar. Shut the oven and bake until the méringue begins to color.

Eat cold, with cream.

You may, in strawberry season, substitute the fresh fruit for preserves. It is then truly delightful.

CRACKER PUDDING. ✠

- 1 quart milk.
- 1 cup powdered cracker.
- 5 eggs.
- 2 tablespoonfuls melted butter.
- ½ teaspoonful soda—dissolved in boiling water.

Heat the milk slightly, and pouring it over the cracker, let them stand together fifteen minutes. Stir into this first the beaten yolks, then the butter and soda; beat all smooth and add the whipped whites.

Eat hot, with pudding sauce.

DORCHESTER CRACKER PLUM PUDDING.

- 2 quarts milk.
- 6 Boston crackers—split and buttered.
- 8 eggs—beaten very light.
- 2 cups sugar. Nutmeg, cloves, and cinnamon to taste.
- 1 teaspoonful of salt.
- 1 lb. raisins, seeded and cut in two.

Make a custard of the milk, eggs, and sugar, seasoned with the spices, by heating the milk *almost* to boiling, then taking it from the fire and adding gradually the yolks, sugar, seasoning, and whites. Do not boil it again. Butter a pudding-dish; put a layer of crackers in the bottom, moistening with a few spoonfuls of the hot custard. On this lay some of the raisins—a thick stratum; cover with crackers—the buttered side downward; moisten with the custard, and proceed in this order until your crackers and fruit are used up. Pour in custard until only the top of the upper layer is visible, but not enough to float them; cover closely and set in the cellar over night. In the morning add the rest of the custard, at intervals of five or six minutes between the cupfuls.

Bake two hours in a moderate oven. Cover with paper if it should seem likely to harden too fast.

Eat hot, with sauce.

CRACKER SUET PUDDING. ✠

- ¼ lb. beef suet, freed from strings, and powdered.
- 1 cup fine cracker-crumbs.
- 2 tablespoonfuls sugar.
- 4 eggs.
- 3 cups milk.
- Pinch of soda.
- 1 teaspoonful salt.

Beat the yolks with the sugar; add to these the milk in which the cracker has been soaked for half an hour; work into a smooth paste before putting in the suet and soda. Whip the whites in last, and bake nearly, if not quite an hour. Cover, should the crust form too rapidly. Eat hot, with wine sauce.

You may also steam or boil this pudding.

FRUIT CRACKER PUDDING.

- 1 cup powdered cracker soaked in one pint of milk.

- ¼ lb. beef suet, cleared from strings and powdered.

- ½ lb. raisins, seeded and cut in two.

- ¼ lb. currants, washed and dried.

- 3 oz. almonds.

- 5 eggs.

- ½ cup sugar.

- 1 teaspoonful nutmeg, and same of cinnamon. Rose-water to taste.

Blanch the almonds and cut with a sharp knife into thin shavings. Beat the yolks with the sugar until light and thick; mix in the cracker and milk; the suet and the fruit well dredged; the spice and rose-water; then the whipped whites, finally the almonds.

Bake in a buttered mould one hour and a half. Turn out and eat with wine sauce.

Or,

Boil in a well-buttered mould. In this case, blanch, but do not cut the almonds, and do not stone the raisins. Butter the mould so thickly that you can stick the almonds to the sides in regular rows, alternately with rows of whole raisins. Put in the mixture gently, not to disturb these; cover the mould and boil or steam three hours. Treated in this way, it makes a pretty-looking pudding. It is palatable in any shape.

CRACKER AND JAM PUDDING.

- 3 eggs.

- ½ cup cracker-crumbs.

- ½ cup sugar.

- 1 tablespoonful butter.

- 1 teacup milk.

- ½ lemon—juice and grated rind.

- 3 tablespoonfuls jam.

Soak the cracker in the milk; rub the butter and sugar together, adding the lemon, and beating to a cream; then stir in the beaten yolks; next the cracker and milk; lastly, the whites. Butter a deep dish, and put the jam, which should be pretty stiff, at the bottom. Fill up with the mixture, and bake about half an hour.

Eat cold, with sugar sifted over the top.

RICE PUDDING (*Plain.*) ✠

- 1 coffee-cup rice.
- 2 quarts milk.
- 8 tablespoonfuls sugar.
- 1 teaspoonful salt.
- Butter the size of an egg—melted.
- Nutmeg and cinnamon to taste.

Wash and pick over the rice, and soak in one pint of the milk two hours. Then add the rest of the milk, the sugar, salt, butter and spice. Bake two hours, and eat cold.

RICE AND TAPIOCA PUDDING. ✠

- ½ cup rice.
- ½ cup tapioca.
- ¾ cup sugar.
- 3 pints milk.
- Cinnamon to taste.

Soak the tapioca in a cup of the milk three hours; wash the rice in several waters, and soak in another cup of milk as long as you do the tapioca. Sweeten the remaining quart of milk; put all the ingredients together, and bake two hours in a slow oven. Eat cold.

RICE PUDDING WITH EGGS. ✠

- 1 quart milk.
- 4 eggs.

- ½ cup rice.

- ¾ cup sugar.

- 1 tablespoonful butter.

- Handful of raisins, seeded and cut in two.

Soak the rice in a pint of the milk an hour, then set the saucepan containing it where it will slowly heat to a boil. Boil five minutes; remove and let it cool. Beat the yolks, add the sugar and butter, the rice and the milk in which it was cooked, with the pint of unboiled; the beaten whites, and finally the raisins. Grate nutmeg on the top, and bake three-quarters of an hour, or until the custard is well set and of a light brown. Eat cold.

RICE-FLOUR PUDDING.

- 2 quarts of milk.

- ½ lb. rice flour.

- 1 cup sugar.

- 6 eggs.

- 1 tablespoonful butter.

- 1 small teaspoonful nutmeg.

- 2 teaspoonfuls vanilla or rose-water.

- 1 lemon—juice of the whole, and half the grated rind.

Heat the milk to a boil, and stir in the rice-flour wet to a smooth paste with a little cold milk; boil until well thickened, stirring all the time. Take from the fire, and while still hot stir in the butter, the yolks beaten light with the sugar, the lemon, nutmeg, and the whites of three eggs. Mix well, and bake in a buttered dish three-quarters of an hour. Just before you take it up, draw to the mouth of the oven and cover with a méringue of the remaining whites, beaten stiff with two tablespoonfuls powdered sugar, and flavored with vanilla or rose-water. Bake until the méringue begins to brown. Sift sugar on the top and eat cold.

BATTER PUDDING. ✠

- 1 pint of milk.
- 4 eggs—whites and yolks beaten separately.
- 2 even cups flour.
- 1 teaspoonful salt.
- 1 pinch of soda.

Bake in a buttered dish three-quarters of an hour. Serve in the pudding-dish as soon as it is drawn from the oven, and eat with rich sauce.

Or,

You may boil it in a buttered mould or floured bag, flouring it *very* thickly. Boil two hours, taking care the boiling does not cease for a moment until the pudding is done.

BATTER PUDDING (*No. 2.*)

- 1 quart milk.
- 10 tablespoonfuls flour.
- 7 eggs.
- 1 teaspoonful salt.
- ½ teaspoonful soda, dissolved in hot water.
- 1 teaspoonful cream-tartar, sifted into the flour.

Wet the flour gradually with the milk to a very smooth paste; next add the beaten yolks, then the salt and soda, lastly the whites, whipped to a stiff froth. Bake in a buttered dish for an hour, and serve at once. Eat hot, with sauce.

If you boil it, leave plenty of room to swell in the bag, and boil two hours.

COTTAGE PUDDING. ✠

- 1 cup of sugar.

- 1 tablespoonful of butter.

- 2 eggs.

- 1 cup sweet milk.

- 3 cups flour, or enough to make a tolerably stiff batter.

- ½ teaspoonful of soda.

- 1 teaspoonful cream-tartar, sifted with the flour.

- 1 teaspoonful salt.

Rub the butter and sugar together, beat in the yolks, then the milk and soda, the salt, and the beaten whites, alternately with the flour. Bake in a buttered mould; turn out upon a dish; cut in slices, and eat with liquid sauce.

This is a simple but very nice pudding.

GERMAN PUFFS. ✠

- 3 cups flour.

- 3 cups milk.

- 3 eggs—whites and yolks beaten separately and *very* light.

- 3 teaspoonfuls melted butter.

- 1 saltspoonful salt.

Pour in nine well-buttered cups of same size as that used for measuring, and bake to a fine brown. Eat as soon as done, with sauce.

CUP PUDDINGS.

- 4 eggs.

- The weight of the eggs in sugar and in flour.

- Half their weight in butter.

- 2 tablespoonfuls milk.

- ¼ teaspoonful soda, dissolved in hot water.

Rub the sugar and butter together; beat the yolks light, and add then the milk and soda; lastly the flour and beaten whites alternately. Fill six small cups, well buttered, and bake twenty minutes, or until a nice brown. Eat warm.

LEMON PUDDING. ✠

- 1 cup of sugar.

- 4 eggs.

- 2 tablespoonfuls corn-starch.

- 2 lemons—juice of both and rind of one.

- 1 pint milk.

- 1 tablespoonful butter.

Heat the milk to boiling, and stir in the corn-starch, wet with a few spoonfuls of cold water. Boil five minutes, stirring constantly. While hot, mix in the butter, and set it away to cool. Beat the yolks light, and add the sugar, mixing very thoroughly before putting in the lemon juice and grated rind. Beat this to a stiff cream, and add gradually to the corn-starch milk, when the latter is cold. Stir all smooth, put in a buttered dish, and bake. Eat cold.

LEMON MÉRINGUE PUDDING (*very nice.*)

- 1 quart milk.

- 2 cups bread-crumbs.

- 4 eggs.

- ½ cup butter.

- 1 cup white sugar.

- 1 large lemon—juice and half the rind, grated.

Soak the bread in the milk; add the beaten yolks, with the butter and sugar rubbed to a cream, also the lemon. Bake in a buttered dish until firm and slightly brown. Draw to the door of the oven and cover with a méringue of the whites whipped to a froth with three tablespoonfuls of powdered sugar, and a little lemon-juice. Brown very slightly; sift powdered sugar over it, and eat cold.

You may make an orange pudding in the same way.

COCOANUT PUDDING.

- ½ lb. grated cocoanut.
- ½ cup stale sponge cake, crumbed fine.
- 1 cup sugar.
- 1 *large* cup rich milk—cream, if you can get it.
- 6 eggs.
- 2 teaspoonfuls vanilla, or rose-water.

Cream the butter and sugar, and add the beaten yolks. When these are well mixed, put in the cocoanut; stir well before adding the milk, cake-crumbs, flavoring; and lastly, the whites of three eggs. Whip the other whites stiff with three tablespoonfuls of powdered sugar; flavor with vanilla, and just before taking the pudding from the oven, spread this méringue over the top, and close the oven until the icing is slightly browned.

Bake in all three-quarters of an hour.

ORANGE MARMALADE PUDDING. ✠

- 1 cup fine bread-crumbs.
- ½ cup sugar.
- 1 cup milk or cream.
- 4 eggs.
- 2 teaspoonfuls butter.

- 1 cup orange or other sweet marmalade.

Rub the butter and sugar together; add the yolks well beaten, the milk, bread-crumbs, and the whites whipped to a froth. Put a layer of this in the bottom of a well-buttered mould, spread thickly with some pretty stiff marmalade—orange is nicest—then another layer of the mixture, and so on until the mould is full, having the custard mixture at top. Bake in a moderate oven about an hour, turn out of the mould upon a dish and serve, with sweetened cream or custard.

MACARONI PUDDING. ✠

- 1 cup macaroni broken into inch lengths.

- 1 quart milk.

- 4 eggs.

- ½ lemon—juice and grated peel.

- 2 tablespoonfuls butter.

- ¾ cup sugar.

Simmer the macaroni in half the milk until tender. While hot stir in the butter, the yolks, well beaten up with the sugar, the lemon, and lastly the whipped whites. Bake in a buttered mould about half an hour, or until nicely browned.

VERMICELLI PUDDING

May be made according to the foregoing receipt.

NEAPOLITAN PUDDING.—(*Very fine.*) ✠

- 1 large cup fine bread-crumbs soaked in milk.

- ¾ cup sugar.

- 1 lemon—juice and grated rind.

- 6 eggs.

- ½ lb. stale sponge-cake.

- ½ lb. macaroons—almond.

- ½ cup jelly or jam, and one small tumbler of Sherry wine.

- ½ cup milk poured upon the bread-crumbs.

- 1 tablespoonful melted butter.

Rub the butter and sugar together; put the beaten yolks in next; then the soaked bread-crumbs, the lemon, juice, and rind, and beat to a smooth, light paste before adding the whites. Butter your mould *very* well, and put in the bottom a light layer of dry bread-crumbs; upon this one of macaroons, laid evenly and closely together. Wet this with wine, and cover with a layer of the mixture; then with slices of sponge-cake, spread thickly with jelly or jam; next macaroons, wet with wine, more custard, sponge-cake, and jam, and so on until the mould is full, putting a layer of the mixture at the top. Cover closely, and steam in the oven three-quarters of an hour; then remove the cover to brown the top. Turn out carefully into a dish, and pour over it a sauce made of currant jelly warmed, and beaten up with two tablespoonfuls melted butter and a glass of pale Sherry.

A plain round mould is best for the pudding, as much of its comeliness depends upon the manner in which the cake and macaroons are fitted in.

It is a pretty and good pudding, and will well repay the trifling trouble and care required to manage it properly.

It is also nice boiled in a buttered mould.

RHUBARB PUDDING.

Prepare the stalks as for pies; cover the bottom of a buttered pudding-dish with slices of bread and butter; cover with the rhubarb cut into short pieces; sprinkle abundantly with sugar; then put on another layer of bread and butter, and so on until your dish is full. Cover and steam, while baking, for half an hour. Remove the lid and bake ten minutes, or until browned.

Eat with hot sauce.

GOOSEBERRY PUDDING. ✠

- 1 pint ripe or nearly ripe gooseberries.

- 6 or 8 slices toasted stale bread.

- 1 cup milk.

- ½ cup sugar.

- 1 tablespoonful butter, melted.

Stew the gooseberries ten minutes—very slowly, not to break them. Cut your slices of bread to fit your pudding-dish, and toast to a light brown on both sides. (Cut off all the crust before toasting.) Dip each slice, while hot, in milk, and spread with the melted butter. Cover the bottom of the dish with them; put next a layer of the gooseberries, sprinkled thickly with sugar; more toast, more berries, and so on, until the dish is full. Cover closely and steam in a moderate oven twenty or twenty-five minutes. Turn out upon a hot dish and pour over it a good pudding-sauce.

This is considered a wholesome breakfast dish, and is certainly good. In this case omit the sauce, sift powdered sugar over the top, and eat with the same.

NEWARK PUDDING.

- 1 cup fine bread-crumbs soaked in a pint of the milk.

- 1 quart of milk.

- 5 eggs.

- 2 tablespoonfuls rice-flour.

- ½ lb. raisins seeded, cut in two, and dredged with flour.

- Vanilla or bitter almond extract.

- 2 tablespoonfuls melted butter, and a half-teaspoonful soda.

Beat the yolks light; add the soaked bread-crumbs and milk; stir to a smooth batter, put in the rice-flour, wet up first with cold milk; the reserved pint of milk, the seasoning, butter, the fruit, lastly the whites whipped stiff. Bake an hour in a buttered mould; turn out and pour sauce over it, serving hard sauce also with it.

Or,

You may boil the mixture two hours in a floured cloth or buttered mould.

BAKED PLUM PUDDING.

- 1¼ lb. of flour.

- 1 lb. raisins seeded, cut in two, and dredged with flour.

- ½ lb. suet, freed from strings and powdered.

- 1 cup sugar.

- 2 oz. citron, shred fine.

- 5 eggs—whites and yolks beaten separately.

- Nutmeg, cinnamon, and cloves—one teaspoonful each.

- Milk to make a thick batter of the flour. Begin with two cups, and add more if necessary.

Beat the yolks and sugar together; add the suet and spice, then the flour, moistening the mixture gradually with milk until you can move the spoon in it. Dredge the fruit and put in by degrees; finally, stir in the beaten whites. Beat all very hard and long before baking in a buttered mould. It will require *at least* an hour and a half in a moderate oven.

Turn out, and eat with rich sweet sauce.

BELLE'S DUMPLINGS.

- 1 quart *prepared* flour.

- 2½ tablespoonfuls lard and butter mixed.

- 2 cups of milk, or enough to make a soft dough.

Roll out a quarter of an inch thick, cut into oblong pieces, rounded at the corners; put a great spoonful damson, cherry, or other tart preserve in the middle and roll into a dumpling. Bake three-quarters of an hour, brush over with beaten egg while hot, set back in the oven three minutes to glaze.

Eat hot with brandy or wine sauce.

Or,

You may make a roll-pudding of it by rolling out the paste into an oblong sheet, spreading thickly with the preserves, folding it up as one would a travelling-shawl to be put into a strap, pinching the ends together that the juice may not escape, and boiling in a floured cloth fitted to the shape of the "roley-poley." Boil an hour and a half.

BOILED PUDDINGS.

You can boil puddings in a bowl, a mould, or a cloth. The mould should have a closely-fitting top, and be buttered well—top and all—before the batter or dough is put in. These moulds are usually made with hasps or other fastening. In lack of this, you had better tie down the cover securely. I once boiled a pudding in a tin pail, the top of which I made more secure by fitting it over a cloth floured on the inside, lest the pudding should stick. The experiment succeeded admirably, and I commend the suggestion to those who find, after the pudding is mixed, that their mould leaks, or the bowl that did duty as a substitute has been broken, and nothing said to "the mistress" about it. If you use a bowl, butter it, and tie a floured cloth tightly over the top. If a cloth, have it clean and sweet, and flour bountifully on the inside. In all, leave room for batter, bread, rice, and cracker puddings to swell. Tie the string very tightly about the mouth of the bag, which must be made with *felled* seams at sides and bottom, the better to exclude the water.

The water must be boiling when the pudding goes in, and not stop boiling for one instant until it is done. If it is in a bag, this must be turned several times, *under water*, to prevent sticking or scorching to the sides of the pot. The bag must also be entirely covered, while the water should not quite reach to the top of a mould. If you use a basin, dip the cloth in boiling water before dredging with flour on the inside.

When the time is up, take mould, basin, or cloth from the boiling pot, and plunge *instantly* into cold water; then turn out without the loss of a second. This will prevent sticking, and leave a clearer impression of the mould upon the contents.

Boiled puddings should be served as soon as they are done, as they soon become heavy.

Many of the baked puddings I have described are quite as good boiled. As a safe rule, *double the time of baking if you boil.*

BERRY PUDDING.

- 1 pint of milk.
- 2 eggs.
- 1 saltspoonful salt.
- ¼ teaspoonful soda, dissolved in hot water.
- ½ teaspoonful cream-tartar, sifted through a cup of flour, and added to enough flour to make a thick batter.
- 1 pint blackberries, raspberries, currants, or huckleberries, well dredged with flour—stirred in at the last.

HUCKLEBERRY PUDDING. ✠

- 1 pint milk.
- 2 eggs.
- 1 quart flour—or enough for thick batter.
- 1 gill baker's yeast.
- 1 saltspoonful salt.

- 1 teaspoonful soda, dissolved in boiling water.

- Nearly a quart of berries—well dredged with flour.

Make a batter of eggs, milk, flour, yeast, salt, and soda, and set it to rise in a warm place about four hours. When you are ready to boil it, stir in the dredged fruit quickly and lightly. Boil in a buttered mould or a floured cloth for two hours.

This will be found lighter and more wholesome than boiled pastry.

Eat hot with sweet sauce.

FRUIT VALISE PUDDING. ✠

- 1 quart flour.

- 1 tablespoonful lard, and same of butter.

- 1 teaspoonful soda, dissolved in hot water.

- 2 teaspoonful cream-tartar—sifted through the flour.

- 1 saltspoonful salt.

- 2 cups milk, or enough to make the flour into soft dough.

- 1 quart berries, chopped apples, sliced peaches, or other fruit; jam, preserves, canned fruit, or marmalade may be substituted for the berries.

Roll out the crust less than half an inch thick—indeed, a quarter of an inch will do—into an oblong sheet. Cover thickly with the fruit and sprinkle with sugar. Begin at one end and roll it up closely, the fruit inside. In putting this in, leave a narrow margin at the other end of the roll, which should be folded down closely like the flap of a pocket-book. Pinch the ends of the folded roll together, to prevent the escape of the fruit, and baste up in a bag, the same size and shape as the "valise." Flour the bag well before putting in the pudding, having previously dipped it—the cloth—into hot water, and wring it out.

Boil an hour and a half. Serve hot with sauce, and cut crosswise in slices half an inch thick.

BOILED APPLE DUMPLINGS. (No. 1.) ✠

Make a paste according to the above receipt; cut in squares, and put in the centre of each an apple, pared and cored. Bring the corners together; enclose each dumpling in a small square cloth, tied up bag-wise, leaving room to swell. Each cloth should be dipped in hot water, wrung out and floured on the inside before the apple is put in.

Boil one hour.

APPLE DUMPLINGS. (No. 2.) ✠

- 1 quart flour.
- ¼ lb. suet.
- 1 teaspoonful salt.
- ½ teaspoonful soda dissolved in hot water.
- 1 teaspoonful cream-tartar sifted in the flour.
- Cold water enough to make into a tolerably stiff paste.

Roll out, cut into squares, put in the middle of each a fine, juicy apple, pared and cored. Fill the hole left by the core with marmalade, or with sugar wet with lemon-juice. Stick a clove in the sugar. Close the paste, tie up in the cloths, when you have wet them with hot water and floured them, and boil one hour.

A pleasing idea for dumpling cloths is to crochet them in a close stitch with stout tidy cotton. They are easily done, wash and wear well, and leave a very pretty pattern upon the paste when they are opened. Crochet them round, with a cord for drawing run into the outer edge.

BOILED FRUIT PUDDING.

Prepare a paste in accordance with either of the foregoing receipts, but roll into one sheet. Lay apples, peaches, or berries in the centre, paring and slicing the fruit; sprinkle with sugar, and close the paste over them as you would a dumpling. Dip a stout cloth in hot water, flour the inside, put in the pudding, tie tightly, and boil two hours and a half.

Eat hot with sauce.

RICE DUMPLINGS. ✠

- 1 lb. rice boiled without stirring, until soft, and at the top dry.
- 12 pippins, pared and cored.
- Strawberry marmalade or crab-apple jelly.

Let the rice cool upon a sieve or coarse cloth, that it may dry at the same time. Dip your dumpling cloths in hot water; wring them out and flour well inside. Put a handful of the cold rice upon each, spreading it out into a smooth sheet. Lay in the centre an apple; fill the hole left by the core with marmalade or jelly; draw up the cloth carefully to enclose the apple with a coating of rice; tie, and boil one hour.

Turn over with care; pour sweet sauce or rich sweetened cream over them, and send around more in a boat with them.

SUET DUMPLINGS (*plain.*)

- 2 cups fine bread-crumbs, soaked in a very little milk.
- 1 cup beef suet, freed from strings, and powdered.
- 4 eggs, whites and yolks separated, and beaten very light.
- 1 tablespoonful sugar.
- 1 teaspoonful cream-tartar, sifted into the flour.

- • ½ teaspoonful soda dissolved in boiling water

- • 1 teaspoonful salt.

- • Enough milk to mix into a stiff paste.

Make into large balls with floured hands; put into dumpling cloths dipped into hot water and floured inside; leave room to swell, and tie the strings very tightly.

Boil three-quarters of an hour. Serve hot with wine sauce.

FRUIT SUET DUMPLINGS

Are made as above, with the addition of ½ lb. raisins, seeded, chopped, and dredged with flour, and ¼ lb. currants, washed, dried, and dredged.

Boil one hour and a quarter.

BOILED INDIAN MEAL PUDDING.

- • 1 quart milk.

- • 1 quart Indian meal.

- • 3 eggs.

- • 3 heaping tablespoonfuls sugar, and 1 teaspoonful salt.

- • ½ lb. beef suet, chopped into powder.

Scald the milk, and while boiling hot stir in the meal and suet with the salt. When cold add the yolks, beaten light with the sugar, then the whites. Dip your bag in hot water, flour it, and fill half-full with the mixture, as it will swell very much. Boil five hours.

Eat very hot with butter and sugar.

CABINET PUDDING.

- ½ lb. flour.
- ¼ lb. butter.
- 5 eggs,
- 1½ lb. sugar.
- ½ lb. raisins, seeded and cut in three pieces each.
- ¼ lb. currants, washed and dried.
- ½ cup cream or milk.
- ½ lemon—juice and rind grated.

Cream the butter and sugar; add the beaten yolks, then the milk and the flour, alternately, with the whites. Lastly, stir in the fruit, well dredged with flour, turn into a buttered mould, and boil two hours and a half at least.

Serve hot, with cabinet pudding sauce over it. (*See Sweet Sauces.*)

EVE'S PUDDING.

- 1 heaping cup of fine dry bread-crumbs.
- ½ lb. pared and chopped apples.
- ½ lb. raisins, seeded and chopped.
- 6 oz. currants, washed and dried.
- 6 eggs.
- 1 teaspoonful nutmeg, and same of allspice.
- 1 glass brandy.
- 1 cup sugar, and 1 teaspoonful salt.
- ½ lb. suet, chopped to powder.

Work the sugar into the beaten yolks; then the suet and crumbs, with the chopped apples; next the brandy and spice, then the whipped whites; lastly the fruit, well dredged with flour.

Boil in a buttered bowl or mould three hours. Eat hot with sauce.

THE QUEEN OF PLUM PUDDINGS.

- 1 lb. butter.
- 1 lb. of suet, freed from strings and chopped fine.
- 1 lb. of sugar.
- 2½ lbs. of flour.
- 2 lbs. of raisins, seeded, chopped, and dredged with flour.
- 2 lbs. of currants, picked over carefully after they are washed.
- ¼ lb. of citron, shred fine.
- 12 eggs, whites and yolks beaten separately.
- 1 pint of milk.
- 1 cup of brandy.
- ½ oz. of cloves.
- ½ oz. of mace.
- 2 grated nutmegs.

Cream the butter and sugar; beat in the yolks when you have whipped them smooth and light; next put in the milk; then the flour, alternately with the beaten whites; then the brandy and spice; lastly the fruit, well dredged with flour. Mix all thoroughly; wring out your pudding-cloth in hot water; flour well inside, pour in the mixture, and boil five hours.

I can confidently recommend this as the best plum pudding I have ever tasted, even when the friend at whose table I had first the pleasure of eating it imitated the example of "good King Arthur's" economical spouse, and what we "couldn't eat that night," "next *day* fried," by heating a little butter in a frying-pan, and laying in slices of her pudding, warmed them into almost their original excellence. It will keep a long time—in a *locked* closet or safe.

ORANGE ROLEY-POLEY. ✠

Make a light paste as for apple dumplings or valise pudding, roll in an oblong sheet, and lay oranges (sweet ones), peeled, sliced, and seeded, thickly all over it. Sprinkle with white sugar; scatter a teaspoonful or two of the grated yellow peel over all and roll up closely, folding down the end to secure the syrup. Boil in a pudding-cloth one hour and a half.

Eat with lemon sauce.

CHERRY OR CURRANT PYRAMID. ✠

Wash and stone the cherries, or pick the currants from their stems. Make some good light crust, roll it out a quarter of an inch thick, and cut for the bottom a round piece about the size of a tea-plate. You can use the top of a tin pail for a cutter. Spread your fruit upon this, and sprinkle with sugar, leaving a half inch margin all around. Roll out a second sheet an inch less in diameter than the first, lay it carefully upon the fruit, and turn up the margin of the lower piece over the edge of this. Spread this, in turn, with fruit and sugar, and cover with a third and lessening round; proceeding in this order until the sixth and topmost cover is not more than three inches across. Have ready a conical cap of stout muslin adapted to the proportions and dimensions of your pile; dip it in boiling water, flour inside, and draw gently over all. It should be large enough to meet and tie under the base without cramping the pyramid.

Boil two hours, and eat with sweet sauce.

FRITTERS, PANCAKES, ETC.

Have plenty of nice sweet lard in which to fry fritters, and test the heat by dropping in a teaspoonful before you risk more. If right, the batter will rise quickly to the surface in a puff-ball, spluttering and dancing, and will speedily assume a rich golden-brown. Take up, as soon as done, with a skimmer, shaking it to dislodge any drops of lard that may adhere; pile in a hot dish, sift sugar over them, and send instantly to the table. Fry as many at a time as the kettle will hold, and send in hot fresh ones while the batter lasts. A round-bottomed saucepan or kettle, rather wide at top, is best for frying them.

Use a frying-pan for pancakes; heat it; put in a teaspoonful or two of lard and run it quickly over the bottom; then pour in a large ladleful of batter—enough to cover the bottom of the pan with a thin sheet. Turn with a tin spatula, very carefully, to avoid tearing it. The frying-pan should be a small one. Have ready a hot dish; turn out the pancake upon it, cover with powdered sugar, and roll up dexterously like a sheet of paper. Send half a dozen to table at once, keeping them hot by setting the dish in the oven until enough are baked.

I am thus explicit in these general instructions to save myself the trouble, and the reader the tedium, of a repetition under each receipt.

In olden times it was a boast of notable cooks that they could toss a pancake from the pan out of the top of the chimney with such accuracy of calculation, that it would turn itself on the way back, and settle in its place, ready, like St. Lawrence, to have the other side fried. *I* never saw a pancake tossed, although in my childish days I saw hundreds fried by the honorable tribe—now so fast passing away—of Old Virginia cooks. I do not advise this acrobatic system of culinary exploit, especially for beginners. Indeed, I doubt if the pancakes would be found equal to the journey in these days of tight chimney-throats and cooking stoves.

They must be out of practice as well as their manufacturers. Be careful not to have too much grease in the pan.

FRITTERS (*No. 1.*) ✠

- 1 pint flour.
- 4 eggs.
- 1 teaspoonful salt.
- 1 pint boiling water.

Stir the flour into the water by degrees, and stir until it has boiled three minutes. Let it get almost cold, when beat in the yolks, then the whites of the eggs, which must be previously whipped *stiff.*

FRITTERS (*No. 2.*)

- 6 eggs.
- 1 quart milk.
- 3 cups flour.
- ½ teaspoonful soda dissolved in hot water.
- 1 teaspoonful cream-tartar sifted into the flour.
- A little salt.

Beat the yolks and whites separately, of course; stir the milk in with the former, then the soda, the flour, and salt, finally the whites. Beat very hard, and fry *at once*, in great ladlefuls.

APPLE FRITTERS. ✠

- A batter according to the preceding receipt.
- 3 large juicy apples, pared and quartered.
- 1 glass brandy.
- 1 tablespoonful white sugar.
- 1 teaspoonful cinnamon.

Put the brandy, a very little water, the sugar, and the spice into a covered saucepan with the apples. Stir gently until half done; drain off the liquor, every drop; mince the apple when cold, and stir into the batter.

Or,

You may parboil the apples in clear water, with a very little sugar, and proceed as just directed.

JELLY FRITTERS.

- 1 scant cup sponge-cake crumbs—very fine and dry.

- 1 cup boiling milk.

- 4 eggs.

- 2 tablespoonfuls powdered sugar.

- 1 teaspoonful corn-starch, wet in a little cold milk.

- 2 tablespoonfuls currant or cranberry jelly.

Soak the cake-crumbs in the boiling milk, and stir in the corn-starch. Heat all together to a boil, stirring all the time. Beat the yolks light, and add to this as it cools, with the sugar. Whip in the jelly, a little at a time, and put in the whites—beaten to a stiff froth—at the last.

Fry immediately.

BREAD FRITTERS.

- 1 quart milk—boiling-hot.

- 2 cups fine bread-crumbs (aërated bread is best).

- 3 eggs.

- 1 teaspoonful nutmeg.

- 1 tablespoonful butter—melted.

- 1 saltspoonful salt, and the same of
  soda, dissolved in hot water.

Soak the bread in the boiling milk ten minutes, in a covered bowl. Beat to a smooth paste; add the whipped yolks, the butter, salt, soda, and finally the whites, whipped stiff.

QUEEN'S TOAST. ✠

Fry slices of stale baker's bread—aërated, if you can get it—in boiling lard to a fine brown. Dip each slice quickly in boiling water to remove the grease. Sprinkle with powdered sugar and pile upon a hot plate. Before toasting, cut the slices with a round cake-cutter, taking off all the crust. They look better when piled up. Pour sweet wine sauce over them when hot, and serve at once.

JELLY-CAKE FRITTERS (*very nice*). ✠

- Some stale sponge, or *plain* cup cake,
  cut into rounds with a cake-cutter.

- Hot lard.

- Strawberry or other jam, or jelly.

- A little boiling milk.

Cut the cake carefully and fry a nice brown. Dip each slice for a second in a bowl of boiling milk, draining this off on the side of the vessel; lay on a hot dish and spread thickly with strawberry jam, peach jelly, or other delicate conserve. Pile them neatly and send around hot, with cream to pour over them.

This is a nice way of using up stale cake, and if rightly prepared, the dessert is almost equal to Neapolitan pudding.

PANCAKES.

- 1 pint of flour.

- 6 eggs.

- 1 saltspoonful salt, and same of soda
  dissolved in vinegar.

Milk to make a *thin* batter. Begin with two cups and add until the batter is of the right consistency. Beat the yolks light, add the salt, soda, and two cups of milk, then the flour and beaten whites alternately, and thin with more milk.

JELLY OR JAM PANCAKES.

A batter as above. When the pancakes are fried, lay upon a hot plate, spread quickly with nice jam or jelly, and roll up neatly upon the preserves. Sprinkle lightly with powdered sugar, and send around with wine sauce or sweetened cream.

SWEET, OR PUDDING SAUCES

HARD SAUCE. ✠

Stir to a cream 1 cup of butter.

3 cups of powdered sugar.

When light, beat in ¾ teacup wine.

Juice of a lemon.

2 teaspoonfuls nutmeg.

Beat long and hard until several shades lighter in color than at first, and creamy in consistency. Smooth into shape with a broad knife dipped in cold water, and stamp with a wooden mould, first scalded and then dipped in cold water. Set upon the ice until the pudding is served.

BEE-HIVE SAUCE. ✠

Mix a hard sauce according to the previous receipt, and when light, set aside three or four tablespoonfuls in a plate. To the larger quantity left add gradually, cherry, currant, or cranberry juice enough to color it a good pink. Red jelly will do if berries are out of season. Beat the coloring matter in thoroughly, and shape into a conical mound. Roll half a sheet of note-paper into a long, narrow funnel, tie a string about it to keep it in shape, and fill with the uncolored sauce. Squeeze it out gently through the small end in a ridge, beginning at the base of the cone and winding about it to the top, filling your funnel as it is emptied, and guiding it carefully. The effect of the alternate white-and pink lines is very pretty.

If the pudding is one to which chocolate would be a pleasant addition, color with grated chocolate, rubbed smooth in a little of the wine, and ridge with white. Set upon the ice or upon the cellar-floor until firm. Stick a colored almond or other ornamental candy upon the top.

This bee-hive is easily made, and will set off even a plain pudding handsomely.

BRANDY SAUCE (*hard.*) ✠

- ½ cup butter.

- 2 cups powdered sugar.

- 1 wineglass brandy.

- 1 teaspoonful mixed cinnamon and mace.

Warm the butter very slightly, work in the sugar, and, when this is light, the brandy and spice. Beat hard—shape into a mould and set in a cold place until wanted.

WHITE WINE SAUCE (*liquid.*) ✠

- ½ cup butter.

- 2½ cups powdered sugar.

- 2 wineglasses pale Sherry or white wine.

- ½ cup boiling water.

- 1 teaspoonful nutmeg.

Work the butter into the sugar, moistening, as you go on, with boiling water. Beat long and hard until your bowl is nearly full of a creamy mixture. Then add gradually the wine and nutmeg, still beating hard. Turn into a tin pail, set within a saucepan of boiling water, and stir frequently until the sauce is hot, but *not* until it boils. Take the saucepan from the fire and leave the pail standing in the water, stirring the contents now and then, until you are ready to serve the pudding.

If rightly made, this sauce will be nearly as white as milk.

LEMON SAUCE. ✠

- 1 *large* cup of sugar.

- Nearly half a cup of butter.

- 1 egg.

- 1 lemon—all the juice and half the grated peel.

- 1 teaspoonful nutmeg.

- 3 tablespoonfuls boiling water.

Cream the butter and sugar and beat in the egg whipped light; the lemon and nutmeg. Beat hard ten minutes, and add, a spoonful at a time, the boiling water. Put in a tin pail and set within the uncovered top of the tea-kettle, which you must keep boiling until the steam heats the sauce very hot, but not to boiling. Stir constantly.

MILK PUDDING SAUCE. ✠

- 2 eggs, beaten stiff.

- 1 large cup of sugar.

- 5 tablespoonfuls boiling milk.

- ½ teaspoonful arrow-root or corn-starch, wet with cold milk.

- 1 teaspoonful nutmeg, or mace.

- 1 tablespoonful butter.

Rub the butter into the sugar, add the beaten eggs, and work all to a creamy froth. Wet the corn-starch and put in next with the spice—finally, pour in by the spoonful the boiling milk, beating well all the time. Set within a saucepan of boiling water five minutes, stirring all the while, but do not let the sauce boil.

This is a good sauce for bread and other simple puddings.

CABINET PUDDING SAUCE. ✠

- Yolks of four eggs, whipped very light.

- 1 lemon—juice and half the grated peel.

- 1 good glass of wine.

- 1 teaspoonful of cinnamon.

- 1 cup of sugar.

- 1 tablespoonful of butter.

Rub the butter into the sugar, add the yolks, lemon, and spice. Beat ten minutes and put in the wine, still stirring hard. Set within a saucepan of boiling water, and beat while it heats, but do not let it boil.

Pour over the pudding.

FRUIT PUDDING SAUCE. ✠

- ½ cup butter.

- 2½ cups sugar.

- 1 dessert spoonful corn-starch wet in a little cold milk.

- 1 lemon—juice and half the grated peel.

- 1 glass of wine.

- 1 cup boiling water.

Cream the butter and sugar well; pour the corn-starch into the boiling water and stir over a clear fire until it is well thickened; put all together in a bowl and beat five minutes before returning to the saucepan. Heat once, almost to the boiling point, add the wine, and serve.

CUSTARD SAUCE.

- 1 pint of milk.

- 2 eggs, beaten very light.

- ½ wineglass of brandy.

- 1 cup powdered sugar, stirred into the eggs.

- Nutmeg to taste.

- 1 teaspoonful vanilla.

Heat the milk to boiling, and add by degrees to the beaten eggs and sugar; put in the nutmeg, and set within a saucepan of boiling water. Stir until it begins to thicken. Take it off and add the brandy gradually. Set, until it is wanted, within a pan of boiling water.

Pour over the pudding when it comes from the mould.

JELLY SAUCE. ✠

- ½ cup currant jelly.
- 1 tablespoonful butter, melted.
- ½ dessert spoonful arrowroot or corn-starch; wet with cold water.
- 1 glass pale Sherry.
- 3 tablespoonfuls boiling water.

Stir the arrowroot into the boiling water and heat, stirring all the time, until it thickens; add the butter, and set aside until almost cool, when beat in, spoonful by spoonful, the jelly to a smooth pink paste. Pour in the wine, stir hard, and heat in a tin vessel, set within another of boiling water, until very hot.

Pour over and around Neapolitan, bread-and-marmalade puddings, cake fritters, and Queen's toast.

SWEETENED CREAM (*cold.*)

- 1 pint of cream.
- 4 tablespoonfuls powdered sugar.
- 1 teaspoonful of nutmeg.
- 1 teaspoonful vanilla.

Mix all well together, stirring until the sugar is dissolved. Eat with jam puddings, queen of all puddings, Alice's pudding, and peach roley-poley.

CREAM SAUCE (*hot.*) ✠

- 1 pint cream.
- 4 tablespoonfuls powdered sugar.

- Whites of two eggs, beaten stiff.

- Extract of vanilla or bitter almonds, one teaspoonful.

- 1 teaspoonful nutmeg.

Heat the cream slowly in a vessel set in a saucepan of boiling water, stirring often. When scalding, but not boiling hot, remove it from the fire, put in the sugar and nutmeg; stir three or four minutes and add the whites. Mix thoroughly and flavor, setting the bowl containing it in a pan of hot water until the pudding is served, stirring now and then.

JELLY SAUCE. (*No. 2*). ✠

- ½ cup currant jelly.

- 2 tablespoonfuls melted butter.

- 1 lemon—juice and half the grated peel.

- ½ teaspoonful nutmeg.

- 2 glasses wine, and a tablespoonful powdered sugar.

Heat the butter a little more than blood-warm; beat the jelly to a smooth batter and add gradually the butter, the lemon, and nutmeg. Warm almost to a boil, stirring all the while; beat hard, put in the sugar, lastly the wine. Set in a vessel of hot water stirring now and then, until it is wanted. Keep it covered to hinder the escape of the wine flavor. Stir well before pouring out.

This is a very fine sauce, particularly for cabinet and Neopolitan puddings.

CUSTARDS, BLANC-MANGE, JELLIES, AND CREAMS.

A good rule for custard is five eggs to a quart of milk, and a tablespoonful of sugar to each egg, although a good plain custard can be made with an egg for each cup of milk and four tablespoonfuls of sugar to the quart. Creams and custards that are to be frozen must have at least one-third more sugar than those which are not to undergo this process.

In heating the milk for custard, do not let it quite boil before adding the yolks. My plan, which has proved a safe one thus far, is to take the scalding milk from the fire, and instead of pouring the beaten eggs into it, to put a spoonful or two of the milk to *them*, beating well all the while, adding more and more milk as I mix, until there is no longer danger of sudden curdling. Then, return all to the fire and boil gently until the mixture is of the right consistency. From ten to fifteen minutes should thicken a quart. Stir constantly. A pinch of soda added in hot weather will prevent the milk from curdling.

Always boil milk and custard in a vessel set within another of boiling water. If you have not a custard or farina kettle, improvise one by setting a tin pail inside of a pot of hot water, taking care it does not float, also that the water is not so deep as to bubble over the top. Custards are better and lighter if the yolks and whites are beaten separately, the latter stirred in at the last.

BOILED CUSTARD. ✠

- 1 quart of milk.
- Yolks of five eggs and the whites of seven—(two for the méringue).
- 6 tablespoonfuls sugar.
- Vanilla flavoring—1 teaspoonful to the pint.

Heat the milk almost to boiling; beat the yolks light and stir in the sugar. Add the milk in the manner described in "general directions" at head of this section; stir in five whites whipped stiff; return to the fire and stir until thick, but not until it breaks. Season it with vanilla, pour into glass cups; whip the whites of two eggs to a méringue with a heaping tablespoonful of powdered sugar, and when the custard is cold, pile a little of this upon the top of each cup. You may lay a preserved strawberry or cherry, or a bit of melon sweetmeat, or a little bright jelly upon each.

ALMOND CUSTARDS.

- 1 pint milk (half cream).

- ¼ lb. almonds, blanched and pounded to a paste, a few at a time in a Wedgewood mortar, adding gradually—

- 2 tablespoonfuls of rose-water.

- Yolks of three eggs and whites of four—(two for méringue).

- 4 tablespoonfuls sugar.

- 1 teaspoonful extract bitter almond in méringue.

Scald the milk, add the beaten yolks, the sugar, the almond paste, and the whites of two eggs. Boil, stirring constantly until it thickens. Stir up well when almost cold and pour into cups. Make a méringue of the whites of two eggs and two tablespoonfuls powdered sugar, flavored with bitter almond, and heap upon each cup.

QUAKING CUSTARD. ✠

- 3 cups milk.

- Yolks of four eggs—reserving the whites for méringue.

- ½ package Cooper's or Coxe's gelatine.

- 6 tablespoonfuls sugar.

- Vanilla or lemon flavoring. Juice of a lemon in méringue.

Soak the gelatine in a cup of the cold milk two hours. Then heat the rest of the milk to boiling, add that in which the gelatine is, and stir over the fire until the latter is quite dissolved. Take from the fire, and let it stand five minutes before putting in the beaten yolks and sugar. Heat slowly until it begins to thicken perceptibly, not boil—say seven or eight minutes, stirring constantly. When nearly cold, having stirred it every few minutes during the time, flavor it, wash out your mould in cold water, and without wiping it, pour in the custard and set on the ice or in a cold place to harden. When quite firm, turn into a cold dish, loosening it by wrapping about the mould a cloth wrung out in hot water, or dipping the mould for an instant in warm, not boiling water. Have ready the whites whipped to a froth with three tablespoonfuls powdered sugar and juice of a lemon. Heap neatly about the base of the moulded custard, like snow-drifts. If you like, you may dot this with minute bits of currant jelly.

This is a pleasing dish to the eye and taste,

FLOATING ISLAND. ✠

- 1 quart of milk.

- 5 eggs—whites and yolks beaten separately.

- 4 tablespoonfuls (heaping) white sugar.

- 2 teaspoonfuls extract bitter almond or vanilla.

- ½ cup currant jelly.

Beat the yolks well, stir in the sugar, and add the hot, not boiling milk, a little at a time. Boil until it begins to thicken. When cool, flavor and pour into a glass dish, first stirring it up well. Heap upon it a méringue of the whites into which you have beaten, gradually, half a cup of currant, cranberry, or other bright tart jelly. Dot with bits of jelly cut into rings or stars, or straight slips laid on in a pattern.

SPANISH CREAM. ✠

- ½ box of gelatine.

- 1 quart of milk.

- Yolks of three eggs.

- 1 small cup of sugar.

Soak the gelatine an hour in the milk; put on the fire and stir well as it warms. Beat the yolks very light with the sugar, add to the scalding milk, and heat to boiling point, stirring all the while. Strain through thin muslin or tarlatan, and when almost cold, put into a mould wet with cold water. Flavor with vanilla or lemon.

BAVARIAN CREAM (*Very fine.*) ✠

- 1 quart sweet cream.
- Yolks only of four eggs.
- ½ oz. of gelatine or isinglass.
- 1 cup (small) of sugar.
- 2 teaspoonfuls vanilla or bitter almond extract.

Soak the gelatine in just enough cold water to cover it, for an hour. Drain, and stir into a pint of the cream made boiling hot. Beat the yolks smooth with the sugar, and add the boiling mixture, beaten in a little at a time. Heat until it begins to thicken, but do not actually boil; remove it from the fire, flavor, and while it is still hot stir in the other pint of cream, whipped or churned in a syllabub churn to a stiff froth. Beat in this "whip," a spoonful at a time, into the custard until it is the consistency of sponge-cake batter. Dip a mould in cold water, pour in the mixture, and set on the ice to form.

SNOW CUSTARD. ✠

- ½ package Coxe's gelatine.
- 3 eggs.
- 1 pint milk.
- 2 cups of sugar.
- Juice of one lemon.

Soak the gelatine one hour in a teacupful of cold water. To this, at the end of this time, add one pint boiling water. Stir until the gelatine is thoroughly dissolved; add two-thirds of the sugar and the lemon-juice. Beat the whites of the eggs to a stiff froth, and when the gelatine is quite cold, whip it into the whites, a spoonful at a time, for an hour. Whip steadily and evenly, and when all is stiff, pour into a mould, previously wet with cold water, and set in a cold place. In four or five hours turn into a glass dish.

Make a custard of the milk, eggs, and remainder of the sugar, flavor with vanilla or bitter almond, and when the méringue is turned out of the mould, pour this around the base.

BAKED CUSTARD. ✠

- 1 quart of milk.

- 5 eggs, beaten light—whites and yolks separately.

- 5 tablespoonfuls sugar, mixed with the yolks.

- Nutmeg and vanilla.

Scald but not boil the milk; add by degrees to the beaten yolks, and when well mixed, stir in the whites. Flavor, and pour into a deep dish, or custard-cups of white stone-china. Set these in a pan of hot water, grate nutmeg upon each, and bake until firm. Eat cold from the cups.

FRENCH TAPIOCA CUSTARD. ✠

- 5 dessert spoonfuls tapioca.

- 1 quart of milk.

- 1 pint of cold water.

- 3 eggs.

- 1 teaspoonful vanilla, or other essence.

- 1 heaping cup of sugar.

- A pinch of salt.

Soak the tapioca in the water five hours. Let the milk come to a boil; add the tapioca, the water in which it was boiled, and a good pinch of salt. Stir until boiling hot, and add gradually to the beaten yolks and sugar. Boil again (*always* in a vessel set within another of hot water), stirring constantly. Let it cook until thick, but not too long, as the custard will break. Five minutes after it reaches the boil will suffice. Pour into a bowl, and stir gently into the mixture the whites of the eggs, beaten to a stiff froth. Flavor, and set aside in a glass dish until very cold.

Eat with an accompaniment of light cake and brandied, or canned peaches or pears. This will be found a very delightful dessert.

Tapioca Blanc-Mange. ✠

- ½ lb. tapioca, soaked in a cup of cold water four hours.
- 1 pint rich new milk.
- ¾ cup of sugar.
- 2 teaspoonfuls bitter almond or vanilla essence.
- A little salt.

Heat the milk, and stir in the soaked tapioca. When it has dissolved, add the sugar. Boil slowly fifteen minutes, stirring all the time; take from the fire, and beat until nearly cold. Flavor and pour into a mould dipped in cold water. Turn out, and pour cold sweetened cream around it.

Sago Blanc-Mange.

May be made in the same way as tapioca.

Corn-Starch Blanc-Mange. ✠

- 1 quart of milk.
- 4 tablespoonfuls corn-starch, wet in a little cold water.
- 3 eggs, well beaten—whites and yolks separately.
- 1 cup of sugar.
- Vanilla, lemon, or other essence.
- 1 saltspoonful salt.

Heat the milk to boiling; stir in the corn-starch and salt, and boil together five minutes (in a farina-kettle), then add the yolks, beaten light, with the sugar; boil two minutes longer, stirring all the while; remove the mixture from the fire, and beat in the whipped whites while it is boiling hot. Pour into a mould wet with cold water, and set in a cold place. Eat with sugar and cream.

FARINA BLANC-MANGE

Is made according to the above receipt, but boiled fifteen minutes before the eggs are added. You may omit the eggs if you like, and only want a plain dessert.

ARROWROOT BLANC-MANGE. ✠

- 3 cups of new milk.

- 2½ tablespoonfuls of arrowroot, wet up with cold milk.

- ¾ cup of sugar.

- Vanilla, lemon, or bitter almond flavoring, with a little white wine.

Mix the arrowroot to a smooth batter with one cup of the milk. Heat the remainder to boiling; add the arrowroot, stirring constantly. When it begins to thicken put in the sugar, and cook ten minutes longer, still stirring it well from the sides and bottom. Take it off; beat well five minutes; flavor with the essence and a small wineglass of white wine. Give a hard final stir before putting it into a mould wet with cold water.

This is very nourishing for invalids and young children. For the latter you may omit the wine.

ALMOND BLANC-MANGE. ✠

- 1 quart of milk.

- 1 oz. Cooper's gelatine.

- 3 ozs. of almonds, blanched and pounded in a mortar, with

- 1 tablespoonful of rose-water, added to prevent oiling.

- ¾ cup sugar.

Heat the milk to boiling, having previously soaked the gelatine in a cup of it for an hour. Turn in this when the milk is scalding hot; add the pounded almond-paste, and stir all together ten minutes before putting in the sugar. When the gelatine has dissolved, remove the blanc-mange from the vessel of boiling water in which you have cooked it, and strain through a thin muslin bag, pressing it well to get out the flavor of the almonds. There should be three or four bitter ones among them. Wet a mould with cold water, put in the blanc-mange, and set in a cold place until firm.

You may make blanc-mange without the almonds, although it will not be so nice—and substitute vanilla for the rose-water.

NEAPOLITAN BLANC-MANGE. ✠

Make according to the foregoing receipt, and, after straining, separate into four different portions, allowing about a cupful of the mixture for each. Have ready

- 1 great tablespoonful chocolate, wet with a very little boiling water, and rubbed to a smooth paste, for the brown coloring.

- Yolk of an egg beaten light for the yellow.

- 1 great tablespoonful of currant jelly for the pink.

Beat the chocolate into one portion, mixing it well; the jelly into another, the egg into a third, returning this and that flavored with chocolate, to the fire, and stirring until very hot, but not boiling. Leave the fourth uncolored. When quite cold and a little stiff, pour carefully into a wet mould—the white first; then the pink; next the yellow; and the chocolate last. Of course, when the blanc-mange is turned out, this order of colors will be reversed. Set in a cold place. Loosen, when firm, by dipping the mould for a moment in warm water, and working the top free from the edge with a few light touches of your fingers. This is a handsome dish and easily managed. Currant juice or cranberry color a finer pink than jelly, but are apt to thin the blanc-mange, unless used cautiously. A little vanilla improves the chocolate.

JAUNE-MANGE. ✠

- 1 oz. Coxe's gelatine, soaked in half a cup cold water one hour.

- 1 cup of boiling water.

- Yolks of four eggs beaten very light.

- 1 orange, juice and half the grated peel.

- 1 lemon, juice and one-third the grated peel.

- 1 cup white wine or clear pale Sherry.

- 1 cup powdered sugar and a good pinch cinnamon.

Stir the soaked gelatine in the boiling water until dissolved; take from the fire and beat, a little at a time, into the yolks; return to the inner saucepan with the sugar, orange, lemon and cinnamon. Stir over a clear fire until it is boiling hot; put in the wine and strain through a hair-sieve or a piece of tarlatan. Set away in a mould wet with cold water.

The success of this dish depends much upon the stirring and the watchfulness of the cook. The mixture should not be allowed to boil at any moment.

VELVET BLANC-MANGE. ✠

- 2 cups of sweet cream.

- ½ oz. Cooper's gelatine, soaked in a very little cold water one hour.

- ½ cup white sugar (powdered.)

- 1 teaspoonful extract of bitter almonds.

- 1 glass white wine.

Heat the cream to boiling, stir in the gelatine and sugar, and, so soon as they are dissolved, take from the fire. Beat ten minutes, or, what is better, churn in a syllabub-churn until very light; flavor, and add by degrees the wine, mixing it in well. Put into moulds wet with cold water.

CHOCOLATE BLANC-MANGE.

- 1 quart of milk.

- 1 oz. Cooper's gelatine, soaked in a cup of the milk one hour.

- 4 heaping tablespoonfuls of grated chocolate, rubbed up with a little milk.

- 3 eggs, whites and yolks beaten separately.

- ¾ cup sugar and 2 teaspoonfuls of vanilla.

Heat the milk to boiling; pour in the gelatine and milk, and stir until it is dissolved; add the sugar to the beaten yolks and stir until smooth; beat the chocolate into this, and pour in, spoonful by spoonful, the scalding milk upon the mixture, stirring all the while until all is in. Return to the inner saucepan and heat gently, stirring faithfully until it almost boils. Remove from fire, turn into a bowl, and whip in lightly and briskly the beaten whites with the vanilla. Set to form in moulds wet with cold water.

CHARLOTTE RUSSE. ✠

- 1 lb. of lady's-fingers.

- 1 quart of rich sweet cream.

- ¾ cup powdered sugar.

- 2 teaspoonfuls vanilla or other extract.

Split and trim the cakes, and fit neatly in the bottom and sides of two quart moulds. Whip the cream to a stiff froth in a syllabub-churn when you have sweetened and flavored it; fill the moulds, lay cakes closely together on the top, and set upon the ice until needed.

Or,

You may use for this purpose a loaf of sponge-cake, cutting strips from it for the sides and leaving the crust for the bottom and top, each in one piece.

A TIPSY CHARLOTTE. ✠

- 1 large stale sponge-cake.
- 1 pint rich sweet cream.
- 1 cup Sherry wine.
- ½ oz. Cooper's gelatine, soaked in a cup of cold water two hours.
- 1 teaspoonful vanilla or bitter almond extract.
- 3 eggs, whites and yolks beaten together, but very light.
- 1 pint milk.
- 1 cup sugar.

Heat the cream almost to boiling; put in the soaked gelatine and half a cup of sugar, and stir until dissolved. Remove from the fire, flavor, and when cool, beat or churn to a standing froth. Cut off the top of the cake in one piece, and scoop out the middle, leaving the sides and bottom three-quarters of an inch thick. Over the inside of these pour the wine in spoonfuls, that all may be evenly moistened. Fill with the whipped cream, replace the top, which should also be moistened with wine and set in a cold place until needed.

Serve with it, or pour around it, a custard made of the eggs, milk, and the other half cup of sugar.

CHOCOLATE CHARLOTTE RUSSE. ✠

- ½ oz. Cooper's gelatine, soaked in a very little cold water.
- 3 tablespoonfuls grated chocolate rubbed smooth in a little milk.

- ½ cup powdered sugar.

- 4 eggs.

- ½ lb. sponge-cake.

- 1 teaspoonful vanilla.

- 1 pint cream.

Heat the cream to boiling, slowly, stirring frequently; add the sugar, chocolate, and gelatine, and, when these are dissolved, add, a spoonful at a time, to the beaten yolks. Set back in the saucepan of boiling water, and stir five minutes, until very hot, but do not let it boil. Take it off, flavor, and whip or churn to a standing froth, adding the beaten whites toward the last. Line a mould with cake, fill with the mixture, and set upon the ice.

FLUMMERY.

- 2 oz. almonds—a few bitter among them.

- 1 tablespoonful orange-flower or rose-water.

- 1 pint cream.

- 1 oz. Cooper's gelatine, soaked one hour in one cup cold water.

- 1 cup milk.

- ½ cup sugar.

Blanch the almonds, and, when cold, pound them to a paste in a Wedgewood mortar, adding orange-flower or rose-water to prevent oiling. Heat the *milk* to boiling, put in the gelatine, the sugar and almonds, and stir five minutes, or until they are thoroughly dissolved. Strain through thin muslin, pressing the cloth well. When cool, beat in the cream, a little at a time, with an egg-whip, or churn in a syllabub-churn until thick and stiff. Wet your mould, put in the mixture, and let it stand seven or eight hours in a cold place.

GELATINE CHARLOTTE RUSSE. (*Very nice.*) ✠

- 1 pint of cream, whipped light.

- ½ oz. gelatine, dissolved in 1 gill of hot milk.

- Whites of 2 eggs, beaten to a stiff froth.

- 1 small teacup of powdered sugar.

- Flavor with bitter almond and vanilla.

Mix the cream, eggs, and sugar; flavor, and beat in the gelatine and milk last. It should be quite cold before it is added.

Line a mould with slices of sponge-cake, or with lady's fingers, and fill with the mixture.

Set upon the ice to cool.

WHIPPED SYLLABUBS.

- 1 pint of cream, rich and sweet.

- ½ cup sugar, powdered.

- 1 glass of wine.

- Vanilla or other extract, 1 large teaspoonful.

Sweeten the cream, and, when the sugar is thoroughly dissolved, churn to a strong froth. Lastly, stir in wine and seasoning, carefully. Serve at once.

Heap in glasses, and eat with cake.

GOOSEBERRY FOOL.

- 1 quart of gooseberries, ripe.

- 1 tablespoonful butter.

- 1 cup of sugar.

- Yolks of four eggs.

- Méringue of whites, and 3
  tablespoonfuls sugar.

Stew the gooseberries in just water enough to cover them. When soft and broken, rub them through a sieve to remove the skins. While still hot beat in the butter, sugar, and the whipped yolks of the eggs. Pile in a glass dish, or in small glasses, and heap upon the top a méringue of the whipped whites and sugar.

CREAM MÉRINGUES.

- 4 eggs (the whites only), whipped stiff, with 1 lb. powdered sugar.

- Lemon or vanilla flavoring.

- 1 teaspoonful arrowroot.

When *very* stiff, heap in the shape of half an egg upon stiff letter-paper lining the bottom of your baking-pan. Have them half an inch apart. Do not shut the oven-door closely, but leave a space through which you can watch them. When they are a light yellow-brown, take them out and cool quickly. Slip a thin-bladed knife under each; scoop out the soft inside, and fill with cream whipped as for Charlotte Russe.

They are very fine. The oven should be very hot.

CALF'S-FOOT JELLY.

- 4 calf's feet, cleaned carefully.

- 4 quarts of water.

- 1 pint of wine.

- 3 cups of sugar—or sweeten to taste.

- Whites of 3 eggs, well beaten.

- 2 teaspoonfuls of nutmeg.

- Juice of 1 lemon, and half the grated peel.

Boil the calf's feet in the water until it is reduced one half; strain the liquor, and let it stand ten or twelve hours. Skim off every particle of the fat, and remove the dregs; melt slowly in a porcelain or bell-metal kettle, add the seasoning, sugar, and the whipped whites of the eggs, and boil fast about twelve minutes, skimming well. Strain through a double flannel bag suspended between the four legs of an upturned high stool or backless chair, the bowl set beneath. Do not squeeze or shake it, until the jelly ceases to run freely; then slip out the bowl, and put under another, into which you may gently press what remains. The first will be the clearer jelly, although the second dripping will taste quite as well. Wet your moulds, put in the jelly, and set in a cool place.

There are still some housekeepers who insist that the jellies made from the modern gelatine are not comparable in beauty and flavor to those prepared from the genuine feet. Seeing means taste as well as belief with them, and when they handle and behold the beloved feet, they know what they are about. Gelatine, they will darkly and disgustfully assert, is made of horn-shavings and hoofs and the like, and no more fit to be used for cooking purposes than so much glue.

Nevertheless, while gelatine is so clean, bright, and convenient, housewives who find the days now but half as long as did their mothers, despite labor-saving machines, will turn a deaf ear to these alarmists, and escape the tedious process above-described by using the valuable substitute.

WINE JELLY. ✠

- 3 cups of sugar.
- 1 pint of wine—pale Sherry or White.
- 1 cup of cold water.
- 1 package Coxe's gelatine.
- Juice of two lemons and grated peel of one.
- 1 quart of boiling water.
- 1 good pinch of cinnamon.

Soak the gelatine in the cold water one hour. Add to this the sugar, lemons, and cinnamon; pour over all a quart of boiling water, and stir until the gelatine is thoroughly dissolved. Put in the wine, strain through a double flannel bag, without squeezing, wet your moulds with cold water, and set the jelly away in them to cool.

CIDER JELLY. ✠

May be made by the receipt just given, substituting a pint of clear, sweet cider for the wine.

Fever patients may use cider jelly when wine is forbidden, and they will find this both refreshing and nutritious.

BIRD'S NEST IN JELLY. ✠

- 1 quart of jelly, made according to either of the receipts just given, but with a cup less of boiling water, that it may be very firm.
- 3 cups of white blanc-mange.
- 9 empty eggshells.
- Fresh rinds of two oranges.
- 1 cup of sugar.

Cut the rind from the oranges in long narrow strips, and stew these gently in enough water to cover them until they are tender. Add to them a cup of sugar, and simmer fifteen minutes longer in the syrup. Lay them out upon a dish to cool, taking care not to break them. If you have preserved orange-peel in the house, it will save you the trouble of preparing this.

The blanc-mange should be made the day before you want it, and the eggshells filled. The original contents, yolk and white, should be poured out through a hole, not larger than a half-dime, in the small end, and the interior washed with pure water, shaken around well in them. Then fill with blanc-mange and set in a pan of flour or sugar—the open end up—that they may not be jostled or overturned.

Next morning fill a glass dish two-thirds full of the jelly, which should be very clear, reserving a large cupful. Break the shells from about the blanc-mange, and lay the artificial eggs upon the jelly so soon as the latter is firm enough to bear them. Pile them neatly, but not too high in the middle, bearing in mind that what is the top now will be the bottom when the jelly is turned out. Lay the orange peel which represents *straw*, over these and around them. Warm the reserved jelly, so that it will flow readily, but do not get it hot; pour over the straw and eggs, and set away in a cold place to form. When firm, turn out upon a glass dish or salver.

This pretty and fanciful dish is yet easily made. The materials are so simple and inexpensive, and the effect of the work, if deftly done, so pleasing, that I have no hesitation in calling the attention even of novices to it.

WINE JELLY (*boiled.*)

- 1 box Coxe's gelatine, soaked in 1 pint of cold water one hour.

- 1 quart of boiling water poured over this, and stirred until the gelatine is dissolved.

- 1½ lb. white sugar.

- 2 lemons—juice and peel.

- 1 pint of wine.

Put all over the fire, boil up once well, and strain through a double flannel bag into moulds.

ORANGE JELLY. ✠

- 2 oranges—juice of both and grated rind of one.

- 1 lemon—juice and peel.

- 1 package Coxe's gelatine, soaked in a very little water, one hour.

- 1 quart boiling water.

- 1½ cup sugar, and 1 small cup of wine.

- 1 good pinch of cinnamon.

Squeeze the juice of the fruit into a bowl, and put with them the grated peel and the cinnamon. Pour over them the boiling water, cover closely, and let them stand half an hour. Strain, add the sugar, let it come to a boil, stir in the gelatine, and, when this is well dissolved, take the saucepan from the fire. Strain through a double flannel bag into moulds.

VARIEGATED JELLY. ✠

- 1 quart of clear jelly.
- ½ teaspoonful prepared cochineal or red currant juice.
- 1 cup white blanc-mange.

Divide the jelly into two equal portions, and color one with a *very* little prepared cochineal, leaving the other as it is, of a pale amber. Wet a mould with cold water and pour in a little of the latter. Set the mould in the ice, that the jelly may harden quickly, and so soon as it is firm pour in carefully some of the red. Set back upon the ice to get ready for the amber, adding the two colors in this order until you are ready for the base, which should be wider than the other stripes, and consist of the white blanc-mange. Keep both jelly and blanc-mange near the fire until you have filled the mould—I mean, of course, that intended for the latest layers. Let all get very firm before you turn it out.

You may vary two moulds of this jelly by having the blanc-mange base of one colored with chocolate, a narrow white stripe above relieving the grave effect of the brown.

ICE-CREAM AND OTHER ICES.

If you wish to prepare ice-cream at an hour's notice, you cannot do better than to purchase the best patent freezer you can procure. I had one once which would freeze cream admirably in half an hour. I have forgotten the patentee's name, and perhaps this is well for him, since truth would oblige me to record an unlucky habit his machine had of getting out of order just when I wanted it to do its best. My earliest recollections of ice-cream are of the discordant grinding of the well-worn freezer among the blocks of ice packed about it—a monotone of misery, that, had it been unrelieved by agreeable associations of the good to which it was "leading up," would not have been tolerated out of Bedlam. For one, two, three, sometimes four hours, it went on without other variety than the harsher sounds of the fresh ice and the rattling "swash" as the freezer plunged amid the icy brine when these were nearly melted; without cessation save when the unhappy operator nodded over his work, or was relieved by another predestined victim of luxury and ennui—a battalion of the laziest juveniles upon the place being detailed for this purpose. I verily believed in those days that the freezing could not be facilitated by energetic action, and used to think how fortunate it was that small darkies had a predilection for this drowsy employment. I shall never forget my amazement at seeing a brisk Yankee housewife lay hold of the handle of the ponderous tin cylinder, and whirl it with such will and celerity, back and forth, back and forth, that the desired end came to pass in three-quarters of an hour.

That day has gone by. Time has grown too precious now even to juvenile contrabands for them to sit half the day shaking a freezer under the locust-tree on the old plantation lawn. Machines that will do the work in one-tenth of the time, with one-fiftieth of the labor, are sold at every corner. But, so far as I know, it was reserved for a nice old lady up in the "Jersey" mountains—the tidiest, thriftiest, most cheerful bee I ever knew—to show her neighbors and acquaintances that ice-cream could be made to freeze itself. For twelve years I have practised her method, with such thankfulness to her, and such satisfaction to my guests and family, that I eagerly embrace the opportunity of circulating the good news.

SELF-FREEZING ICE-CREAM. ✠

- 1 quart rich milk.

- 8 eggs—whites and yolks beaten separately and very light.

- 4 cups sugar.

- 3 pints rich sweet cream.

- 5 teaspoonfuls vanilla or other seasoning, or 1 vanilla bean, broken in two, boiled in the custard, and left in until it is cold.

Heat the *milk* almost to boiling, beat the eggs light, add the sugar, and stir up well. Pour the hot milk to this, little by little, beating all the while, and return to the fire—boiling in a pail or saucepan set within one of hot water. Stir the mixture steadily about fifteen minutes, or until it is thick as boiled custard. Pour into a bowl and set aside to cool. When quite cold, beat in the cream, and the flavoring, unless you have used the bean.

Have ready a quantity of ice, cracked in pieces not larger than a pigeon egg—the smaller the better. You can manage this easily by laying a great lump of ice between two folds of coarse sacking or an old carpet, tucking it in snugly, and battering it, through the cloth, with a sledge-hammer or mallet until fine enough. There is no waste of ice, nor need you take it in your hands at all—only gather up the corners of the carpet or cloth, and slide as much as you want into the outer vessel. Use an ordinary old-fashioned upright freezer, set in a deep pail; pack around it closely, first, a layer of pounded ice, then one of rock salt—*common salt will not do so well.* In this order fill the pail; but before covering the freezer-lid, remove it carefully that none of the salt may get in, and, with a long wooden ladle or flat stick (I had one made on purpose), beat the custard as you would batter, for five minutes, without stay or stint. Replace the lid, pack the ice and salt upon it, patting it down hard on top; cover all with several folds of blanket or carpet, and leave it for one hour. Then remove the cover of the freezer when you have wiped it carefully outside. You will find within a thick coating of frozen custard upon the bottom and sides. Dislodge this with your ladle, which should be thin at the lower end, or with a long carving-knife, working every particle of it clear. Beat again hard and long until the custard is a smooth, half-congealed paste. The smoothness of the ice-cream depends upon your action at this juncture. Put on the cover, pack in more ice and salt, and turn off the brine. Spread the double carpet over all once more, having buried the freezer out of sight in ice, and leave it for three or four hours. Then, if the water has accumulated in such quantity as to buoy up the freezer, pour it off, fill up with ice and salt, but do not open the freezer. In two hours more you may take it from the ice, open it, wrap a towel, wrung out in boiling water, about the lower part, and turn out a solid column of cream, firm, close-grained, and smooth as velvet to the tongue.

Should the ice melt very fast, you may have to turn off the water more than twice; but this will seldom happen except in very hot weather. You need not devote fifteen minutes in all to the business after the custard is made. You may go into the cellar before breakfast, having made the custard overnight, stir in the cold cream and flavoring, get it into the freezer and comfortably packed down before John has finished shaving, and by choosing the times for your stolen visits to the lower regions, surprise him and the children at a one-o'clock dinner by the most delicious dessert in the world. I have often laughed in my sleeve at seeing *my* John walk through the cellar in search of some mislaid basket or box, whistling carelessly, without a suspicion that his favorite delicacy was coolly working out its own solidification under the inverted barrel on which I chanced to be leaning at his entrance.

Any of the following receipts for *custard* ice-cream may be frozen in like manner. Do not spare salt, and be sure your ice is finely cracked, and after the second beating do not let the air again into the freezer. If you cannot get dry rock salt, that which settles at the bottom of fish-barrels will do just as well. Keep the freezer hidden, from first to last, by the ice heaped over it, except when you have to lift the lid on the occasions I have specified.

CHOCOLATE ICE-CREAM. ✠

- 1 quart of cream.
- 1 pint new milk.
- 2 cups sugar.
- 2 eggs beaten very light.
- 5 tablespoonfuls chocolate rubbed smooth in a little milk.

Heat the milk almost to boiling, and pour, by degrees, in with the beaten egg and sugar. Stir in the chocolate, beat well three minutes, and return to the inner kettle. Heat until it thickens well, stirring constantly; take from the fire and set aside to cool. Many think a little vanilla an improvement. When the custard is cold, beat in the cream. Freeze.

ALMOND ICE-CREAM.

- 3 oz. sweet almonds and 1 oz. of bitter, blanched, and, when cold, pounded to a paste, a few at a time, in a Wedgewood mortar, adding
- 2 tablespoonfuls of rose-water to prevent oiling.
- 3 pints cream—fresh and sweet.
- Nearly 2 cups of sugar.
- 1 tablespoonful of arrowroot, wet up with cold water.

Heat one pint cream almost to boiling, add the sugar, and when this is melted, the almonds. Simmer ten minutes, stirring often, remove from the fire, and let it stand together ten minutes longer in a covered vessel. Strain the cream, pressing the bag hard to get the full flavor of the almonds, return to the inner saucepan and stir in the arrowroot until the cream thickens—say five minutes. When cold, beat very light with an egg-whip, adding gradually the rest of the cream. It should be light in half an hour. Then freeze.

If you wish to mould your cream in fancy shapes, open your freezer two hours after the second stirring and transfer the cream to a tight mould, having given it a third vigorous beating. Pack this down in ice and salt, and let it stand two hours longer than you would have done had it remained in the freezer.

COFFEE ICE-CREAM.

- 3 pints of cream.
- 1 cup of black coffee—very strong and clear.
- 2 cups sugar.
- 2 tablespoonfuls arrowroot, wet up with cold water.

Heat half the cream nearly to boiling, stir in the sugar, and, when this is melted, the coffee; then the arrowroot. Boil all together five minutes, stirring constantly. When cold, beat up very light, whipping in the rest of the cream by degrees. Then freeze.

I cannot say certainly that this can be frozen without turning, although I see no reason why it should not, since the arrowroot gives it the consistency of custard.

ITALIAN CREAM. ✠

- 2 pints of cream.
- 2 cups of sugar.
- 2 lemons—juice and grated peel.
- 2 tablespoonfuls of brandy.

Sweeten the cream and beat in the lemons gradually, not to curdle it; add the brandy and freeze in a patent freezer, or by turning quickly. In turning the freezer, open twice during the operation, to stir and beat the contents smooth.

LEMON ICE-CREAM. ✠

- 1 quart cream.
- 2 lemons—the juice of one and the grated peel of one and a half.
- 2 cups of sugar.

Sweeten the cream, beat the lemon gradually into it, and put at once into the freezer. Freeze rapidly in a patent freezer, or the acid is apt to turn the milk.

You may make orange ice-cream in the same way.

PINE-APPLE ICE-CREAM. ✠

- 1 quart of cream.
- 1 large ripe pine-apple.
- 1 lb. powdered sugar.

Slice the pine-apple thin, and scatter the sugar between the slices. Cover it, and let the fruit steep three hours. Then cut, or chop it up in the syrup, and strain it through a hair sieve or bag of double coarse lace. Beat gradually into the cream, and freeze as rapidly as possible.

You may, if you like, reserve a few pieces of pine-apple, unsugared, cut into square bits, and stir them through the cream when half frozen.

PEACH ICE-CREAM ✠

Is very nice made after the preceding receipt, with two or three handfuls of freshly cut bits of the fruit stirred in when the cream is half frozen.

RASPBERRY OR STRAWBERRY ICE-CREAM. ✠

- 1 quart ripe sweet berries.
- 1 lb. sugar.
- 1 quart fresh cream.

Scatter half the sugar over the berries and let them stand three hours. Press and mash them, and strain them through a thin muslin bag. Add the rest of the sugar, and when dissolved beat in the cream little by little. Freeze rapidly, opening the freezer (if it is not a patent one) several times to beat and stir.

Or,

You may have a pint of whole berries, unsugared, ready to stir in when the cream is frozen to the consistency of stiff mush. In this case add a cup more sugar to the quart of crushed berries.

FROZEN CUSTARD WITH THE FRUIT FROZEN IN. ✠

- 1 quart milk.
- 1 quart cream.
- 6 eggs, and three cups of sugar beaten up with the yolks.
- 1 pint fresh peaches, cut up small, or fresh ripe berries.

Heat the quart of milk almost to boiling, and add gradually to the beaten yolks and sugar. Whip in the frothed whites, return to the custard-kettle, and stir until it is a thick, soft custard. Let it get perfectly cold, beat in the cream and freeze. If you let it freeze itself, stir in the fruit after the second beating; if you turn the freezer, when the custard is like congealed mush.

TUTTI FRUTTI ICE-CREAM. ✠

- 1 pint of milk.
- 1 quart of cream.
- Yolks of 5 eggs—beaten light with the sugar.
- 3 cups of sugar.
- 1 lemon—juice and grated peel.
- 1 glass of pale Sherry, and ½ lb. crystallized fruits, chopped.

Heat the milk almost to boiling; pour by degrees over the eggs and sugar, beating all together well. Return to the fire, and *boil* ten minutes, or until set into a good custard. When cold, beat in the cream, and half freeze before you stir in half a pound of crystallized fruit—peaches, apricots, cherries, limes, etc., chopped very fine. Beat in with these the lemon and wine; cover again, and freeze hard.

In all fruit ice-creams the beating of the custard should be very hard and thorough, if you would have them smooth.

LEMON ICE. ✠

- 6 lemons—juice of all, and grated peel of three.
- 1 large sweet orange—juice and rind.
- 1 pint of water.
- 1 pint of sugar.

Squeeze out every drop of juice, and steep in it the rind of orange and lemons one hour. Strain, squeezing the bag dry; mix in the sugar, and then the water. Stir until dissolved, and freeze by turning in a freezer—opening three times to beat all up together.

ORANGE ICE. ✠

- 6 oranges—juice of all, and grated peel of three.

- 2 lemons—the juice only.

- 1 pint of sugar dissolved in 1 pint of water.

Prepare and freeze as you would lemon ice.

PINEAPPLE ICE.

- 1 juicy ripe pineapple—peeled and cut small.

- Juice and grated peel of 1 lemon.

- 1 pint of sugar.

- 1 pint water, or a little less.

Strew the sugar over the pineapple and let it stand an hour. Mash all up together, and strain out the syrup through a hair-sieve. Add the water and freeze.

CHERRY ICE.

- 1 quart cherries, with half the stones pounded in a Wedgewood mortar.

- 2 lemons—the juice only.

- 1 pint of water, in which dissolve 1 pint of sugar.

- 1 glass of fine brandy.

Squeeze out the bruised cherries and stones, in a bag over the sugar; add the water, then the brandy, and freeze.

It will require a longer time to freeze than other ices, on account of the brandy.

CURRANT AND RASPBERRY ICE (*Fine.*)

- 1 quart red currants.
- 1 pint raspberries—red or white.
- 1 pint of water.
- 1½ pint of sugar.

Squeeze out the juice; mix in the sugar and water, and freeze.

STRAWBERRY OR RASPBERRY ICE.

- 1 quart berries. Extract the juice and strain.
- 1 pint sugar—dissolved in the juice.
- 1 lemon—juice only.
- ½ pint of water.

RIPE FRUIT FOR DESSERT

ORANGES

May be put on whole in fruit-baskets, or the skin be cut in eighths half way down, separated from the fruit and curled inward, showing half the orange white, the other yellow. Or, pass a sharp knife lightly around the fruit, midway between the stem and blossom end, cutting through the rind only. Slip the smooth curved handle of a teaspoon carefully between the peel and body of the orange, and gently work it all around until both upper and lower halves are free, except at stem and blossom. Turn the rind, without tearing it, inside out, making a white cup at each end—the round white fruit between them.

SALADE D'ORANGE.

Pare and slice large sweet oranges; sprinkle powdered sugar thickly over each slice, and pour a couple of glasses of wine on the top. Sprinkle powdered sugar over all, and serve at once, or the fruit will lose its freshness.

You may omit the wine if you like.

Do not let any fruit intended to be eaten fresh for dessert lie in the sugar longer than is absolutely necessary. It extracts the flavor and withers the pulp.

AMBROSIA.

- 8 fine sweet oranges, peeled and sliced.
- ½ grated cocoanut.
- ½ cup powdered sugar.

Arrange the orange in a glass dish, scatter the grated cocoanut thickly over it, sprinkle this lightly with sugar, and cover with another layer of orange. Fill up the dish in this order, having cocoanut and sugar for the top layer. Serve at once.

APPLES.

Wash and polish with a clean towel, and pile in a china fruit-basket, with an eye to agreeable variety of color.

PEACHES AND PEARS.

Pick out the finest, handling as little as may be, and pile upon a salver or flat dish, with bits of ice between them, and ornament with peach leaves or fennel sprigs.

One of the prettiest dishes of fruit I ever saw upon a dessert-table was an open silver basket, wide at the top, heaped with rich red peaches and yellow Bartlett pears, interspersed with feathery bunches of green, which few of those who admired it knew for *carrot-tops*. Wild white clematis wreathed the handle and showed here and there among the fruit, while scarlet and white verbenas nestled amid the green.

Send around powdered sugar with the fruit, as many like to dip peaches and pears in it after paring and quartering them.

STRAWBERRIES, RASPBERRIES, AND BLACKBERRIES.

Never wash strawberries or raspberries that are intended to be eaten as *fresh* fruit. If they are so gritty as to require this process, keep them off the table. You will certainly ruin the flavor beyond repair if you wash them, and as certainly induce instant fermentation and endanger the coats of the eaters' stomachs, if, after profaning the exquisite delicacy of the fruit to this extent, you complete the evil work by covering them with sugar, and leaving them to leak their lives sourly away for one or two hours.

Put them on the table in glass dishes, piling them high and lightly, send around powdered sugar with them and cream, that the guests may help themselves. It is not economical perhaps, but it is a healthful and pleasant style of serving them—I had almost said the only decent one.

"But I don't know who picked them!" cries Mrs. Fussy.

No, my dear madam! nor do you know who makes the baker's bread, or confectioner's cakes, creams, jellies, salads, etc. Nor, for that matter, how the flour is manufactured out of which you conjure your dainty biscuit and pies. I was so foolish as to go into a flour-mill once, and having seen a burly negro, naked to the waist, with his trousers rolled up to his knees, stand in a bank of "fine family flour," a foot deep in the lowest part, on a July day, shovelling it into barrels for the market, I rushed into the outer air a sicker and a wiser woman.

I *know* GOD made strawberries. "Doubtless," says Bishop Butler, "HE could have made a better berry, but HE never did!" The picker's light touch cannot mar flavor or beauty, nor, were her fingers filthy as a chimney-sweep's, could the delicate fruit suffer from them as from your barbarous baptism. You would like to know who picked them. I should inquire instead, "Who washed them, and in what?" I recollect seeing a housekeeper, who was afflicted with your inquiring turn of mind, wash strawberries in a wash-hand basin!

CURRANTS AND RASPBERRIES.

Pick the currants from the stems, and mix with an equal quantity of raspberries. Put into a glass bowl, and eat with powdered sugar.

FROSTED CURRANTS.

Pick fine even bunches, and dip them, one at a time, into a mixture of frothed white of egg, and a very little cold water. Drain them until nearly dry, and roll in pulverized sugar. Repeat the dip in the sugar once or twice, and lay them upon white paper to dry. They make a beautiful garnish for jellies or charlottes, and look well heaped in a dish by themselves or with other fruit.

Plums and grapes are very nice frosted in the same way.

PRESERVES AND FRUIT JELLIES

Use none but porcelain, or *good* bell-metal kettles for preserves and jellies. If the latter, clean thoroughly just before you put in the syrup or fruit. Scour with sand, then set it over the fire, with a cupful of vinegar and a large handful of salt in it. Let this come to a boil, and scour the whole of the inside of the kettle with it. Do not let your preserves or anything else stand one moment in it after it is withdrawn from the fire; fill the emptied kettle instantly with water and wash it perfectly clean, although you may mean to return the syrup to it again in five minutes. By observing these precautions, preserves and pickles made in bell-metal may be rendered as good and wholesome as if the frailer porcelain be used.

Use only fine sugar for nice preserves. Moist or dark sugar cannot be made to produce the same effect as dry white.

Do not hurry any needful step in the process of preserving. Prepare your fruit with care, weigh accurately, and allow time enough to do your work well. Put up the preserves in small jars in preference to large, and, when once made, keep them in a cool, dark closet that is perfectly dry. Keep jellies in small stone china jars, or glass tumblers closely covered. You can procure at most china and glass stores, or house-furnishing establishments, metal covers with elastic rims for these, which can be used from year to year.

Cover jellies and jams with tissue paper, double and wet with brandy, pressed closely to the conserve before you put on the lid, or paste on the thick paper. Examine your shelves frequently and narrowly for a few weeks to see if your preserves are keeping well. If there is the least sign of fermentation, boil them over, adding more sugar.

If jellies are not so firm after six or eight hours as you would have them, set them in the sun, with bits of window glass over them to keep out the dust and insects. Remove these at night and wipe off the moisture collected on the under sides. Repeat this every day until the jelly shrinks into firmness, filling up one cup from another as need requires. This method is far preferable to boiling down, which both injures the flavor and darkens the jelly.

PRESERVED PEACHES. ✠

Weigh the fruit after it is pared and the stones extracted, and allow a pound of sugar to every one of peaches. Crack one-quarter of the stones, extract the kernels, break them to pieces and boil in just enough water to cover them, until soft, when set aside to steep in a covered vessel. Put a layer of sugar at the bottom of the kettle, then one of fruit, and so on until you have used up all of both; set it where it will warm slowly until the sugar is melted and the fruit hot through. Then strain the kernel-water and add it. Boil steadily until the peaches are tender and clear. Take them out with a perforated skimmer and lay upon large flat dishes, crowding as little as possible. Boil the syrup almost to a jelly—that is, until clear and thick, skimming off all the scum. Fill your jars two-thirds full of the peaches, pour on the boiling syrup, and, when cold, cover with brandy tissue-paper, then with cloth, lastly with thick paper tied tightly over them.

The peaches should be ready to take off after half an hour's boiling; the syrup be boiled fifteen minutes longer, *fast*, and often stirred, to throw up the scum. A few slices of pineapple cut up with the peaches flavor them finely.

PRESERVED PEARS

Are put up precisely as are peaches, but are only pared, not divided. Leave the stems on.

PEACH MARMALADE. ✠

Pare, stone, and weigh the fruit; heat slowly to draw out the juice, stirring up often from the bottom with a wooden spoon. After it is hot, boil quickly, still stirring, three-quarters of an hour. Add, then, the sugar, allowing three-quarters of a pound to each pound of the fruit. Boil up well for five minutes, taking off every particle of scum. Add the juice of a lemon for every three pounds of fruit, and a very little water in which one-fourth of the kernels have been boiled and steeped. Stew all together ten minutes, stirring to a smooth paste, and take from the fire. Put up hot in air-tight cans, or, when cold, in small stone or glass jars, with brandied tissue-paper fitted neatly to the surface of the marmalade.

A large, ripe pineapple, pared and cut up fine, and stirred with the peaches, is a fine addition to the flavor.

PRESERVED QUINCES. ✠

Choose fine yellow quinces. Pare, quarter, and core them, saving both skins and cores. Put the quinces over the fire with just enough water to cover them, and simmer until they are soft, but not until they begin to break. Take them out carefully, and spread them upon broad dishes to cool. Add the parings, seeds, and cores, to the water in which the quinces were boiled, and stew, closely covered, for an hour. Strain through a jelly-bag, and to every pint of this liquor allow a pound of sugar. Boil up and skim it, put in the fruit and boil fifteen minutes. Take all from the fire and pour into a large deep pan. Cover closely and let it stand twenty-four hours. Drain off the syrup and let it come to a boil; put in the quinces carefully and boil another quarter of an hour. Take them up as dry as possible, and again spread out upon dishes, setting these in the hottest sunshine you can find. Boil the syrup until it begins to jelly; fill the jars two-thirds full and cover with the syrup. The preserves should be of a fine red. Cover with brandied tissue-paper.

PRESERVED APPLES.

Firm, well-flavored pippins or bell-flower apples make an excellent preserve, prepared in the same manner as quinces. A few quinces cut up among them, or the juice of two lemons to every three pounds of fruit improves them.

QUINCE MARMALADE. ✠

Pare, core, and slice the quinces, stewing the skins, cores, and seed in a vessel by themselves, with just enough water to cover them. When this has simmered long enough to extract all the flavor, and the parings are broken to pieces, strain off the water through a thick cloth. Put the quinces into the preserve-kettle when this water is almost cold, pour it over them and boil, stirring and mashing the fruit with a wooden spoon as it becomes soft. The juice of two oranges to every three pounds of the fruit imparts an agreeable flavor. When you have reduced all to a smooth paste, stir in a scant three-quarters of a pound of sugar for every pound of fruit; boil ten minutes more, stirring constantly. Take off, and when cool put into small jars, with brandied papers over them.

QUINCE CHEESE

Is marmalade boiled down *very* thick, packed into small pots. It will turn out as firm as cheese, and can be cut in slices for luncheon or tea.

APPLE BUTTER.

This is generally made by the large quantity.

Boil down a kettleful of cider to two-thirds the original quantity. Pare, core, and slice juicy apples, and put as many into the cider as it will cover. Boil slowly, stirring often with a flat stick, and when the apples are tender to breaking, take them out with a perforated skimmer, draining well against the sides of the kettle. Put in a second supply of apples and stew them soft, as many as the cider will hold. Take from the fire, pour all together into a tub or large crock; cover and let it stand twelve hours. Then return to the kettle and boil down, stirring all the while until it is the consistency of soft soap, and brown in color. You may spice to taste if you please.

Keep in stone jars in a dry, cool place. It should keep all winter.

PRESERVED CRAB-APPLES. ✠

The red Siberian crab is best for this purpose. Pick out those that are nearly perfect, *leaving the stems on*, and put into a preserve-kettle, with enough warm water to cover them. Heat this to boiling, slowly, and simmer until the skins break. Drain, cool, and skin them; then, with a penknife, extract the cores through the blossom ends. Weigh them; allow a pound and a quarter of sugar and a teacupful of water to every pound of fruit. Boil the water and sugar together until the scum ceases to rise; put in the fruit, cover the kettle, and simmer until the apples are a clear red, and tender. Take out with a skimmer; spread upon dishes to cool and harden; add to the syrup the juice of one lemon to three pounds of fruit, and boil until clear and rich. Fill your jars three-quarters full of the apples, pour the syrup in, and, when cool, tie up.

PRESERVED GREEN-GAGES AND LARGE PURPLE PLUMS. ✠

Weigh the fruit and scald in boiling water to make the skins come off easily. Let them stand in a large bowl an hour after they are peeled, that the juice may exude. Drain this off; lay the plums in the kettle, alternately with layers of sugar, allowing pound for pound; pour the juice over the top and heat slowly to a boil. Take out the plums at this point, very carefully, with a perforated skimmer, draining them well through it, and spread upon broad dishes in the sun. Boil the syrup until thick and clear, skimming it faithfully. Return the plums to this, and boil ten minutes. Spread out again until cool and firm; keeping the syrup hot on the fire, fill your jars three-quarters full of the fruit; pour on the scalding syrup, cover to keep in the heat, and, when cold, tie up.

Or,

If you do not care to take the trouble of peeling the fruit, prick it in several places with a needle, and proceed as directed.

UNIQUE PRESERVES. ✠

Gather young cucumbers, a little longer than your middle finger, and lay in strong brine one week. Wash them and soak a day and a night in fair water, changing this four times. Line a bell-metal kettle with vine-leaves, lay in the cucumbers, with a little alum scattered among them; fill up with clear water; cover with vine-leaves, then with a close lid, and green as for pickles. Do not let them boil. When well greened, drop in ice-water. When perfectly cold, wipe, and with a small knife slit down one side; dig out the seeds; stuff with a mixture of chopped raisins and citron; sew up the incision with fine thread. Weigh them, and make a syrup, allowing a pound of sugar for every one of cucumbers, with a pint of water. Heat to a lively boil, skim, and drop in the *fruit*. Simmer half an hour, take out and spread upon a dish in the sun while you boil down the syrup, with a few slices of ginger-root added. When thick, put in the cucumbers again; simmer five minutes and put up in glass jars; tying them up when cold.

DAMSONS

Are put up in the same manner as plums, but pricked instead of skinned.

PRESERVED ORANGE PEEL. (*Very nice.*) ✠

Weigh the oranges whole, and allow pound for pound. Peel the oranges neatly and cut the rind into narrow shreds. Boil until tender, changing the water twice, and replenishing with hot from the kettle. Squeeze the *strained* juice of the oranges over the sugar; let this heat to a boil; put in the shreds and boil twenty minutes.

Lemon peel can be preserved in the same way, allowing more sugar.

ORANGE MARMALADE. ✠

Allow pound for pound. Pare half the oranges and cut the rind into shreds. Boil in three waters until tender, and set aside. Grate the rind of the remaining oranges; take off and throw away every bit of the thick white inner skin; quarter all the oranges and take out the seeds. Chop, or cut them into small pieces; drain all the juice that will come away, without pressing them, over the sugar; heat this, stirring until the sugar is dissolved, adding a *very* little water, unless the oranges are very juicy. Boil and skim five or six minutes; put in the boiled shreds, and cook ten minutes; then the chopped fruit and grated peel, and boil twenty minutes longer. When cold, put into small jars, tied up with bladder or with paper next the fruit, cloths dipped in wax over all. A nicer way still is to put away in tumblers with self-adjusting metal tops. Press brandied tissue-paper down closely to the fruit.

LEMON MARMALADE

Is made as you would prepare orange—allowing a pound and a quarter of sugar to a pound of the fruit, and using but half the grated peel.

PRESERVED PINEAPPLE. ✠

Pare, cut into slices, take out the core of each one, and weigh, allowing pound for pound of sugar and fruit. Put in alternate layers in the kettle and pour in water, allowing a teacupful to each pound of sugar. Heat to a boil; take out the pineapple and spread upon dishes in the sun. Boil and skim the syrup half an hour. Return the pineapple to the kettle and boil fifteen minutes. Take it out, pack in wide-mouthed jars, pour on the scalding syrup; cover to keep in the heat, and, when cold, tie up, first putting brandied tissue-paper upon the top.

PINEAPPLE MARMALADE.

Pare, slice, core, and weigh the pineapple; then cut into small bits. Make a syrup of a teacup of water to two pounds of sugar; melt, and heat to a boil. Heat the chopped pineapple in a vessel set within one of boiling water, covering it closely to keep in the flavor. When it is smoking hot all through, and begins to look clear, add to the syrup. Boil together half an hour, stirring all the while, or until it is a clear, bright paste.

PRESERVED CITRON OR WATER-MELON RIND.

Pare off the green skin, and the soft, white, inner rind. Cut into strips or into fanciful shapes. Allow a pound and a quarter of sugar to each pound of rind. Line your kettle with vine leaves and fill with the rind, scattering a little pulverized alum over each layer. Cover with vine-leaves, three thick; pour on water enough to reach and wet these, and lay a close lid on the top of the kettle. Let all steam together for three hours; but the water must not actually boil. Take out your rind, which should be well greened by this process, and throw at once into very cold water. It should lie in soak, changing the water every hour, for four hours.

For the syrup, allow two cups of water to a pound and a quarter of sugar. Boil, and skim it until no more scum comes up; put in the rind, and simmer gently nearly an hour. Take it out, and spread upon dishes in the sun until firm and almost cool. Simmer in the syrup for half an hour; spread out again, and, when firm, put into a large bowl, and pour over it the scalding syrup.

Twelve hours later put the syrup again over the fire, adding the juice of a lemon and a tiny strip of ginger-root for every pound of rind. Boil down until thick; pack the rind in jars and pour over it the syrup. Tie up when cool.

A very handsome sweetmeat, although rather insipid in flavor. The reader can judge whether, as the charity boy said of the alphabet, and the senior Weller of matrimony, it is worth while to go through so much and get so little.

PRESERVED GINGER. ✠

Pare the roots of fresh green ginger and lay in cold water fifteen minutes. Boil in three waters, changing the hot for cold every time, until very tender; drain, and lay in ice-water. For the syrup, allow a pound and a quarter of sugar for every pound of ginger, and a cupful of water for each pound of sugar. Boil, and skim until the scum ceases to rise. When the syrup is *cold*, wipe the ginger dry and drop it in. Let it stand twenty-four hours. Drain off and reheat the syrup. This time put the ginger in when blood warm. Do not look at it again for two days. Then reboil the syrup, and pour over the ginger scalding hot. In a week drain off once more, boil, and add again while hot to the ginger; cover closely. It will be fit for use in a fortnight.

PRESERVED CHERRIES. ✠

Stone the cherries, preserving every drop of juice. Weigh the fruit, allowing pound for pound of sugar. Put a layer of fruit for one of sugar until all is used up; pour over the juice and boil gently until the syrup begins to thicken.

The short-stem red cherries, or the Morellas are best for preserves. Sweet cherries will not do.

PRESERVED STRAWBERRIES. ✠

Pound for pound. Put them in a preserving kettle over a slow fire until the sugar melts. Boil twenty-five minutes, fast. Take out the fruit in a perforated skimmer and fill a number of small cans three-quarters full. Boil and skim the syrup five minutes longer, fill up the jars, and seal while hot.

Keep in a cool, dry place.

STRAWBERRY JAM. ✠

- For every pound of fruit three-quarters of a pound of sugar.

- 1 pint red currant juice to every 4 pounds strawberries.

Boil the juice of the currants with the strawberries half an hour, stirring all the time. Add the sugar when you have dipped out nearly all the juice, leaving the fruit quite dry, and boil up rapidly for about twenty minutes, skimming carefully. Put in small jars, with brandied tissue-paper over the top.

You can omit the currant juice, but the flavor will not be so fine.

RASPBERRY JAM. ✠

- ¾ lb. of sugar to every lb. fruit.

Put the fruit on alone, or with the addition of a pint of currant juice to every four pounds of fruit. Boil half an hour, mashing and stirring well. Dip out most of the boiling juice before adding sugar, and cook twenty minutes more. Blackberry jam is very nice made as above, leaving out the currant juice.

GOOSEBERRY JAM

Is made in the same manner as raspberry, only the currant juice is omitted, and the gooseberries boiled one hour without the fruit, and another after it is put in. The fruit must be ripe.

RIPE TOMATO PRESERVES. ✠

- 7 lbs. round yellow, or egg tomatoes—*peeled.*
- 7 lbs. sugar, and juice of three lemons.

Let them stand together over night. Drain off the syrup and boil it, skimming well. Put in the tomatoes and boil gently twenty minutes. Take out the fruit with a perforated skimmer, and spread upon dishes. Boil the syrup down until it thickens, adding, just before you take it up, the juice of three lemons. Put the fruit into the jars and fill up with hot syrup. When cold, seal or tie up.

GREEN TOMATO PRESERVES. (*Good.*)

- 8 lbs. small green tomatoes. Pierce each with a fork.
- 7 lbs. sugar.
- 4 lemons—the juice only.

- 1 oz. ginger and mace mixed.

Heat all together slowly, and boil until the fruit is clear. Take it from the kettle in a perforated skimmer, and spread upon dishes to cool. Boil the syrup thick. Put the fruit into jars and cover with hot syrup.

PRESERVED FIGS. ✠

- The weight of ripe figs in sugar.

- Peel of one lemon and juice of two.

- A little ginger.

Cover the figs with cold water for twelve hours. Then simmer in water enough to cover them until tender, and spread out upon a sieve to cool and harden. Make a syrup of the sugar, and a cup of cold water for every pound. Boil until clear of scum; put in the figs and simmer ten minutes. Take them out and spread upon dishes in the sun. Add the lemons and ginger; boil the syrup thick; give the figs another boil of fifteen minutes, and fill the jars three-quarters of the way to the top. Fill up with boiling syrup, cover, and, when cold, seal up.

BAKED APPLES. ✠

Cut out the blossom end of sweet apples—Campfields or Pound Sweets—with a sharp penknife; wash, but do not pare them; pack them in a large pudding-dish; pour a cupful of water in the bottom, cover closely with another dish or pan; set in a moderate oven, and steam until tender all through. Pour the liquor over them while hot, and repeat this as they cool. Set on the ice several hours before tea, and, when you are ready, transfer them to a glass dish, pouring the juice over them again. Eat with powdered sugar and cream. Apples baked in this way are more tender and digestible, and better flavored, than those baked in an open vessel. Campfields are particularly good.

APPLES STEWED WHOLE. ✠

Pare, and with a small knife extract the cores of fine juicy apples that are not too tart; put into a deep dish with just enough water to cover them; cover and bake, or stew, in a moderate oven, until they are tender and clear; take out the apples, put in a bowl, and cover to keep hot; put the juice into a saucepan, with a cupful of sugar for twelve apples, and boil half an hour. Season with mace, ginger, or whole cloves, adding the spice ten minutes before you remove the syrup from the fire. Pour scalding over the apples, and cover until cold.

Eat with cream.

BAKED PEARS.

Sweet pears may be baked just as sweet apples are—*i. e.*, steamed without being pared or cored.

Or,

If large, cut in half, put into a deep dish, with a very little water; sprinkle them with sugar, and put a few cloves, or bits of cinnamon, or a pinch of ginger among them. Cover closely, and bake until tender.

STEWED PEARS. ✠

If small and ripe, cut out the blossom-end, without paring or coring; put into a saucepan, with enough water to cover them, and stew until tender; add a half cupful of sugar for every quart of pears, and stew all together ten minutes; take out the pears, lay in a covered bowl to keep warm; add to the syrup a little ginger or a few cloves, boil fifteen minutes longer, and pour over the fruit hot.

Or,

If the pears are not quite ripe, but hard and disposed to be tough, peel them, cut out the blossom-end, leaving on the stems, and stew until tender in enough water to cover them. Take them out, set by in a covered dish to keep warm; add to the liquor in the saucepan an equal quantity of the best molasses and a little ginger; boil half an hour, skim, and return the pears to the saucepan. Stew all together twenty minutes, and pour out.

These are very good, and will keep a week or more, even in warm weather. I have canned them while boiling hot, and kept them sweet a whole year.

BAKED QUINCES.

Pare and quarter; extract the seeds and stew the fruit in clear water until a straw will pierce them; put into a baking-dish with a half cupful of sugar to every eight quinces; pour over them the liquor in which they were boiled; cover closely, and steam in the oven one hour; take out the quinces, lay them in a covered bowl to keep warm; return the syrup to the saucepan, and boil twenty minutes; pour over the quinces, and set away covered, to cool. Eat cold.

FRUIT JELLIES.

CURRANT, BLACKBERRY, STRAWBERRY, ETC. ✠

Put the fruit into a stone jar; set this in a kettle of tepid water, and put it upon the fire. Let it boil, closely covered, until the fruit is broken to pieces; strain, pressing the bag (a stout coarse one) hard, putting in but a few handfuls at a time, and between each squeezing turning it inside out to scald off the pulp and skins. To each pint of juice allow a pound of sugar. Set the juice on alone to boil, and while it is warming divide the sugar into several different portions, and put into shallow pie-dishes or pans that will fit in your ovens; heat in these, opening the ovens now and then to stir it and prevent burning. Boil the juice just *twenty minutes* from the moment it begins fairly to boil. By this time the sugar should be so hot you cannot bear your hand in it. Should it melt around the edges, do not be alarmed. The burned parts will only form into lumps in the syrup, and can easily be taken out. Throw the sugar into the boiling juice, stirring rapidly all the while. It will "hiss" as it falls in, and melt very quickly. Withdraw your spoon when you are sure it is dissolved. Let the jelly just come to a boil, to make all certain, and take the kettle instantly from the fire. Roll your glasses or cups in hot water, and fill with the scalding liquid. If these directions be strictly followed, and the fruit is at the proper state of ripeness, there need be no dread of failure. I have often had the jelly "form" before I filled the last glass.

I wish it were in my power, by making known the advantages of the process I have described, to put an end to the doubts and anxieties attendant upon the old-fashioned method of boiling jelly into a preserve. This plan is so simple and safe, the jelly made so superior in flavor and color to that produced by boiling down juice and fruit, that no one who has ever tried both ways can hesitate to give it the preference. I have put up jelly in no other way for eighteen years, and have never failed once.

Strawberry jelly should have a little lemon-juice added to that of the fruit. Both it and blackberry, and very ripe raspberry jelly, are apt to be less firm than that made from more tart fruits; still, do not boil it. Set it in the sun, as I have directed at the beginning of the section upon preserves and fruit jellies, filling one cup from another as the contents shrink. The sun will boil it down with less waste, and less injury to color and taste, than the fire will. Cooking jelly always darkens it.

Put brandied tissue-paper over the top of each glass when cold and firm, paste a thick paper over it, and keep in a dry place.

RASPBERRY AND CURRANT JELLY. ✠

To two parts red raspberries or "Blackcaps," put one of red currants, and proceed as with other berry jelly.

The flavor is exquisite. This jelly is especially nice for cake.

WILD CHERRY AND CURRANT JELLY. ✠

Two-thirds wild cherries (stones and all) and one of red currants. A pound of sugar to a pint of juice, and make as you do plain currant jelly.

This, besides being very palatable and an excellent table jelly, is highly medicinal, good for coughs and any weakness of the digestive organs. I put it up first as an experiment, and because I chanced to have the cherries. Now I would not pass the winter without it, unless obliged to do so by a failure of the fruit crop.

PEACH JELLY. ✠

Crack one-third of the kernels and put them in the jar with the peaches, which should be pared, stoned, and sliced. Heat in a pot of boiling water, stirring from time to time until the fruit is well broken. Strain, and to every pint of peach juice add the juice of a lemon. Measure again, allowing a pound of sugar to a pint of liquid. Heat the sugar very hot, and add when the juice has boiled twenty minutes. Let it come to a boil, and take instantly from the fire.

This is very fine for jelly-cake.

GREEN FOX GRAPE JELLY ✠

Is made after the receipt for currant jelly, only allowing a pound and a half of sugar to a pint of juice.

Ripe grapes require but pound for pint.

QUINCE JELLY. ✠

Pare and slice the quinces, and add for every five pounds of fruit a cup of water. Put peelings, cores, and all into a stone jar; set this in a pot of boiling water, and, when the fruit is soft and broken, proceed as with other jellies.

CRAB-APPLE JELLY. ✠

Cut Siberian crab-apples to pieces, but do not pare or remove the seeds. The latter impart a peculiarly pleasant flavor to the fruit. Put into a stone jar, set in a pot of hot water, and let it boil eight or nine hours. Leave in the jar all night, covered closely. Next morning, squeeze out the juice, allow pound for pint, and manage as you do currant jelly.

Should the apples be very dry, add a cup of water for every six pounds of fruit.

There is no finer jelly than this in appearance and in taste.

CANNED FRUITS AND VEGETABLES

Within a few years canned fruits have, in a great measure, superseded preserves. They are cheaper, more wholesome, and far less difficult to prepare. Attention to a few general rules will insure success to every housekeeper who sensibly prefers to put up her own season's supply of these to purchasing those for double the cost, which are not nearly so good.

First, examine cans and elastics narrowly before you begin operations. See that the screw is in order, the can without crack or nick, the elastic firm and closely fitting.

Secondly, have the fruit boiling hot when sealed. Have upon the range or stove a pan in which each empty can is set to be filled after it is rolled in hot water. Lay elastic and top close to your hand, fill the can to overflowing, remembering that the fruit will shrink as it cools, and that a vacuum invites the air to enter; clap on the top without the loss of a second, screw as tightly as you can, and as the contents and the can cool, screw again and again to fit the contraction of metal and glass.

Thirdly, if you use glass cans (and they are cheapest in the end, for you can use them year after year, getting new elastics when you need them) keep them in a cool, dark place, and dry as well as cool. The light will cause them to ferment, and also change the color.

CANNED BERRIES. ✠

Heat slowly to boiling, in a large kettle. When they begin to boil, add sugar in the proportion of one tablespoonful to each quart of fruit. Before doing this, however, if there is much juice in the kettle, dip out the surplus with a dipper or cup. It will only increase the number of cans to be filled, without real advantage to you. Leave the berries almost dry before putting in the sugar. This will make syrup enough. Boil all together fifteen minutes, and can.

Huckleberries, grapes, blackberries, currants, raspberries, cherries, and strawberries put up in this way are very good, eaten as you would preserves, and make pies which are scarcely inferior to those filled with fresh fruit.

CANNED PEACHES. ✠

Pare, cut in half and stone, taking care not to break the fruit; drop each piece in cold water so soon as it is pared. The large, white freestone peaches are nicest for this purpose. Firmness of texture is a desideratum. The fruit should be ripe, but not soft. Allow a heaping tablespoonful of sugar to each quart of fruit, scattering it between the layers. Fill your kettle and heat slowly to a boil. Boil three minutes, just to assure yourself that every piece of fruit is heated through. Can and seal. It is safe to put a cupful of water in the bottom of the kettle before packing it with fruit, lest the lower layer should burn.

CANNED PEARS. ✠

For the finer varieties, such as the Bartlett and Seckel, prepare a syrup, allowing a pint of pure water and a quarter of a pound of sugar to a quart of fruit. While this is heating, peel the pears, dropping each, as it is pared, into a pan of clear water, lest the color should change by exposure to the air. When the syrup has come to a fast boil, put in the pears carefully, not to bruise them, and boil until they look clear and can be easily pierced by a fork. Have the cans ready, rolled in hot water, pack with the pears and fill to overflowing with the scalding syrup, which must be kept on the fire all the while, and seal.

The tougher and more common pears must be boiled in water until tender; thrown while warm into the hot syrup, then allowed to boil ten minutes before they are canned.

Apples may be treated in either of the above ways as their texture may seem to demand.

CANNED PLUMS. ✠

Prick with a needle to prevent bursting; prepare a syrup allowing a gill of pure water and a quarter of a pound of sugar to every three quarts of fruit. When the sugar is dissolved and the water blood-warm, put in the plums. Heat slowly to a boil. Let them boil five minutes—not fast or they will break badly, fill up the jars with plums, pour in the scalding syrup until it runs down the sides, and seal.

Greengages are very fine put up in this way; also damsons for pies.

CANNED TOMATOES. ✠

"I don't hold with any of these new-fangled notions," said an old lady to me, when I mentioned that my canning was over for the summer. "I was beguiled, two years ago, into putting up some *tomaytesses* in cans, and if I'm forgiven for that folly I'll never tempt Providence in the same manner again."

"They didn't keep, then?"

"Keep! they sp'iled in a week! 'Twas no more'n I expected and deserved for meddling with such a humbug."

"Perhaps you did not follow the directions closely?"

"Indeed I did! I cooked the tormented things, and seasoned 'em with butter and salt, all ready for the table, and screwed the tops down tight. But, in course, they sp'iled!"

"Were you careful to put them into the cans boiling hot?"

"'Twould have cracked the glass! I let 'em get *nice and cold* first. I didn't suppose it made any difference about such a trifle as that!"

Poor old lady! I think of her and her mighty temptation of Providence whenever I can tomatoes, for heat *does* make a difference—all the difference in the world in this sort of work.

Pour boiling water over the tomatoes to loosen the skins. Remove these; drain off all the juice that will come away without pressing hard; put them into a kettle and heat slowly to a boil. Your tomatoes will look much nicer if you remove all the hard parts before putting them on the fire, and rub the pulp soft with your hands. Boil ten minutes, dip out the surplus liquid, pour the tomatoes, boiling hot, into the cans, and seal. Keep in a cool, dark place.

CANNED TOMATOES AND CORN. ✠

Boil the corn on the cob, when it is in nice order for roasting, twenty minutes over a good fire, and cut off while hot. Have your tomatoes skinned and rubbed to a smooth pulp. Put in two measures of them for every one of the cut corn; salt as for the table, stirring it well in, and bring to a hard boil. Then, can quickly, and as soon as they are cold set away in a cool, dark place.

PRESERVED GREEN CORN. ✠

Boil on the cob until the milk ceases to flow when the grain is pricked. Cut off the corn and pack in stone jars in the following order:—A layer of salt at the bottom, half an inch deep. Then one of corn two inches in depth, another half-inch of salt, and so on until the jar is nearly filled. Let the topmost layer of salt be double the depth of the others, and pour over all melted—not hot—lard. Press upon this, when nearly hard, thick white paper, cut to fit the mouth of the jar. Keep in a cool place. Soak over night before using it.

Green corn is difficult to can, but *I know* it will keep well if put up in this way. And, strange to tell, be so fresh after the night's soaking as to require salt when you boil it for the table. Should the top layer be musty, dig lower still, and you will probably be rewarded for the search.

BRANDIED FRUITS

BRANDIED PEACHES OR PEARS. ✠

- 4 lbs. fruit.
- 4 lbs. sugar.
- 1 pint best white brandy.

Make a syrup of the sugar and enough water to dissolve it. Let this come to a boil; put the fruit in and boil five minutes. Having removed the fruit carefully, let the syrup boil fifteen minutes longer, or until it thickens well; add the brandy, and take the kettle at once from the fire; pour the hot syrup over the fruit, and seal.

If, after the fruit is taken from the fire, a reddish liquor oozes from it, drain this off before adding the clear syrup. Put up in glass jars.

Peaches and pears should be peeled for brandying. Plums should be pricked and watched carefully for fear of bursting.

BRANDIED CHERRIES OR BERRIES. ✠

Make a syrup of a pound of sugar and a half gill of water for every two lbs. of fruit. Heat to boiling, stirring to prevent burning, and pour over the berries while warm—*not* hot. Let them stand together an hour; put all into a preserving-kettle, and heat slowly; boil five minutes, take out the fruit with a perforated skimmer, and boil the syrup twenty minutes. Add a pint of brandy for every five pounds of fruit; pour over the berries hot, and seal.

CANDIES

MOLASSES CANDY. ✠

- 1 quart good molasses.
- ½ cup vinegar.
- 1 cup sugar.
- Butter the size of an egg.
- 1 teaspoonful saleratus.

Dissolve the sugar in the vinegar, mix with the molasses, and boil, stirring frequently, until it hardens when dropped from the spoon into cold water; then stir in the butter and soda, the latter dissolved in hot water. Flavor to your taste, give one hard final stir, and pour into buttered dishes. As it cools, cut into squares for "taffy," or, while soft enough to handle, pull white into sticks, using only the buttered tips of your fingers for that purpose.

SUGAR-CANDY. ✠

- 6 cups of sugar.
- 1 cup of vinegar.
- 1 cup of water.
- Tablespoonful of butter, put in at the last, with
- 1 teaspoonful saleratus dissolved in hot water.

Boil fast *without stirring*, an hour, or until it crisps in cold water. Pull white with the tips of your fingers.

Since children must eat candy, this is the best you can give them. It is very nice. Flavor to taste.

PICKLES

Use none but the best cider vinegar; especially avoid the sharp colorless liquid sold under that name. It is weak sulphuric acid, warranted to riddle the coat of any stomach, even that of an ostrich, if that bird were so bereft of the instinct of self-preservation as to make a lunch of bright-green cucumber-pickle seven times a week.

If you boil pickles in bell-metal, do not let them stand in it one moment when it is off the fire; and see for yourself that it is perfectly clean and newly scoured before the vinegar is put in.

Keep pickles in glass or hard stoneware; look them over every month; remove the soft ones, and if there are several of these, drain off and scald the vinegar, adding a cup of sugar for each gallon, and pour hot over the pickles. If they are keeping well, throw in a liberal handful of sugar for every gallon, and tie them up again. This tends to preserve them, and mellows the sharpness of the vinegar. This does not apply to *sweet* pickle.

Pickle, well made, is better when a year old than at the end of six months. I have eaten walnut pickle ten years old that was very fine.

Keep your pickles well covered with vinegar.

If you use ground spices, tie them up in thin muslin bags.

CUCUMBER OR GHERKIN PICKLE. ✠

Choose small cucumbers, or gherkins, for this purpose. They are more tender, and look better on the table. Reject all over a finger in length, and every one that is misshapen or specked, however slightly. Pack in a stone jar or wooden bucket, in layers, strewing salt thickly between these. Cover the top layer out of sight with salt, and pour on cold water enough to cover all. Lay a small plate or round board upon them, with a clean stone to keep it down. You may leave them in the brine for a week or a month, stirring up from the bottom every other day. If the longer time, be sure your salt and water is strong enough to bear up an egg. If you raise your own cucumbers, pick them every day, and drop in the pickle. When you are ready to put them up, throw away the brine, with any cucumbers that may have softened under the process, and lay the rest in cold fresh water for twenty-four hours. Change the water then for fresh, and leave it for another day. Have a kettle ready, lined with green vine-leaves, and lay the pickles evenly within it, scattering powdered alum over the layers. A bit of alum as large as a pigeon-egg will be enough for a two-gallon kettleful. Fill with cold water, cover with vine-leaves, three deep; put a close lid or inverted pan over all, and steam over a slow fire five or six hours, not allowing the water to boil. When the pickles are a fine green, remove the leaves and throw the cucumbers into very cold water. Let them stand in it while you prepare the vinegar. To one gallon allow a cup of sugar, three dozen whole black peppers, the same of cloves, half as much allspice, one dozen blades of mace. Boil five minutes; put the cucumbers into a stone jar, and pour the vinegar over them scalding hot. Cover closely. Two days afterward scald the vinegar again and return to the pickles. Repeat this process three times more, at intervals of two, four, and six days. Cover with a stoneware or wooden top; tie stout cloth over this, and keep in a cool, dry place. They will be ready for eating in two months. Examine every few weeks.

PICKLED MANGOES. ✠

- Young musk or nutmeg melons.

- English mustard-seed two handfuls, mixed with

- Scraped horseradish, one handful.

- Mace and nutmeg pounded, 1 teaspoonful.

- Chopped garlic, 2 teaspoonfuls.

- A little ginger.

- Whole pepper-corns, 1 dozen.

- ½ tablespoonful of ground mustard to a pint of the mixture.

- 1 teaspoonful sugar to the same quantity.

- 1 teaspoonful best salad oil to the same.

- 1 teaspoonful celery-seed.

Cut a slit in the side of the melon; insert your finger and extract all the seeds. If you cannot get them out in this way, cut a slender piece out, saving it to replace,—but the slit is better. Lay the mangoes in strong brine for three days. Drain off the brine, and freshen in pure water twenty-four hours. Green as you would cucumbers, and lay in cold water until cold and firm. Fill with the stuffing; sew up the slit, or tie up with pack thread; pack in a deep stone jar, and pour scalding vinegar over them. Repeat this process three times more at intervals of two days, then tie up and set away in a cool, dry place.

They will not be "ripe" under four months, but are very fine when they are. They will keep several years.

PEPPER MANGOES. ✠

Are put up in the same way, using green peppers that are full grown, but not tinged with red.

They are very good, but your fingers will smart after thrusting them into the peppers to pull out the seeds. For this purpose I have used, first, a small penknife, to cut the core from its attachment to the stem-end of the pepper, then a smooth bit of stick, to pry open the slit in the side and work out the loose core or bunch of seed. By the exercise of a little ingenuity you may spare yourself all suffering from this cause. Should your fingers burn badly, anoint them with sweet-oil and wear gloves that night. Cream will also allay the smart.

PICKLED CABBAGE (*Yellow.*)

- 2 gallons vinegar.

- 1 pint white mustard seed. }

- 4 oz. ginger. }

- 3 oz. pepper-corns. }

- 1 oz. allspice. } pounded fine.

- 2 oz. cloves. }

- 1 oz. mace. }

- 1 oz. nutmeg. }

- 2 oz. turmeric. }

- 1 large handful of garlic, chopped.

- 1 handful scraped horseradish.

- 4 lbs. sugar.

- 2 oz. celery seed.

- 3 lemons, sliced thin.

Mix all and set in the sun for three days.

To prepare the cabbage, cut in quarters—leaving off the outer and green leaves—and put in a kettle of boiling brine. Cook three minutes. Take out, drain, and cover thickly with salt. Spread out in the sun to dry; then shake off the salt, and cover with cold vinegar in which has been steeped enough turmeric to color it well. Leave it in this two weeks, to draw out the salt and to plump the cabbage. They are then ready to pack down in the seasoned vinegar. Do not use under six weeks or two months.

PICKLED CABBAGE (*Purple.*)

Quarter the cabbage. Lay in a wooden tray, sprinkle thickly with salt, and set in the cellar until next day. Drain off the brine, wipe dry, lay in the sun two hours, and cover with cold vinegar for twelve hours. Prepare the pickle by seasoning enough vinegar to cover the cabbage with equal quantities of mace, cloves, whole white peppers; a cup of sugar to every gallon of vinegar, and a teaspoonful of celery seed for every pint. Pack the cabbage in a stone jar; boil the vinegar and spices five minutes and pour on hot. Cover and set away in a cool, dry place.

This will be ripe in six weeks.

PICKLED ONIONS.

Peel the onions, which should be fine white ones—not *too* large. Let them stand in strong brine for four days, changing it twice. Heat more brine to a boil, throw in the onions, and boil three minutes. Throw them at once into cold water, and leave them there four hours. Pack in jars, interspersing with whole mace, white pepper-corns, and cloves. Fill up with scalding vinegar in which you have put a cupful of sugar for every gallon. Cork while hot.

They will be ready for use in a month, but will be better at the end of three months.

GREEN BEANS AND RADISH PODS.

Take young French or "string" beans, and radish pods just before they change color; green and pickle as you do cucumbers and gherkins.

NASTURTIUM-SEED. ✠

Take the green seed after the flower has dried off. Lay in salt and water two days, in cold water one day; pack in bottles and cover with scalding vinegar, seasoned with mace and white pepper-corns, and sweetened slightly with white sugar. Cork, and set away four weeks before you use them.

They are an excellent substitute for capers.

PICKLED BUTTERNUTS AND WALNUTS. ✠

Gather them when soft enough to be pierced by a pin. Lay them in strong brine five days, changing this twice in the meantime. Drain, and wipe them with a coarse cloth; pierce each by running a large needle through it, and lay in cold water for six hours.

To each gallon of vinegar allow a cup of sugar, three dozen each of whole cloves and black pepper-corns, half as much allspice, and a dozen blades of mace. Boil five minutes; pack the nuts in small jars and pour over them scalding hot. Repeat this twice within a week; tie up and set away.

They will be good to eat in a month—and very good too.

PICKLED CAULIFLOWER. ✠

Pick the whitest and closest bunches. Cut into small sprays or clusters. Plunge into a kettle of scalding brine and boil three minutes. Take them out, lay upon a sieve or a cloth, sprinkle thickly with salt, and, when dry, brush this off. Cover with cold vinegar for two days, setting the jar in the sun. Then pack carefully in glass or stoneware jars, and pour over them scalding vinegar seasoned thus:

To one gallon allow a cup of white sugar, a dozen blades of mace, a tablespoonful of celery-seed, two dozen white peppercorns and some bits of red pepper pods, a tablespoonful of coriander-seed, and the same of whole mustard. Boil five minutes. Repeat the scalding once a week for three weeks; tie up and set away. Keep the cauliflowers under the vinegar by putting a small plate on top.

SLICED CUCUMBER PICKLE. (*Very nice.*)

- 2 dozen large cucumbers, sliced, and boiled in vinegar enough to cover them, one hour. Set aside in the hot vinegar.
- To each gallon of cold vinegar allow—
- 1 lb. sugar.
- 1 tablespoonful of cinnamon.
- 1 teaspoonful ginger.
- 1 teaspoonful black pepper.
- 1 teaspoonful celery-seed.
- 1 teaspoonful of mace.
- 1 teaspoonful allspice.
- 1 teaspoonful cloves.
- 1 tablespoonful turmeric.
- 1 tablespoonful horseradish, scraped.
- 1 tablespoonful garlic, sliced.
- ½ teaspoonful cayenne pepper.

Put in the cucumbers and stew two hours.

The pickle will be ready for use so soon as it is cold.

PICKLED WATER-MELON RIND. (*Extremely nice.*)

- Equal weight of rind and white sugar.
- ½ ounce white ginger to a gallon of pickle.
- 1 pint vinegar to every pound of sugar.
- 1 tablespoonful turmeric to a gallon of pickle.
- Mace, cloves, and cinnamon to taste.

Take the thickest rind you can get, pare off the hard green rind, also the soft inner pulp. Lay the pieces—narrow strips or fanciful cuttings—in brine strong enough to float an egg, and let them remain in it ten days. Then soak in fair water, changing it every day for ten days. Cover them with clear water in a preserving-kettle, heat slowly and boil five minutes. Take them out and plunge instantly into ice-water. Leave them in this until next day. Give them another gentle boil of five minutes in strong alum-water. Simmer carefully, as a hard boil will injure them. Change *directly* from the alum to the ice-water again, and do not disturb them for four hours. After a third boil of five minutes, let them remain all night in the last water to make them tender. Next day add to enough water to cover the rinds sufficient sugar to make it quite sweet, but not a syrup. Simmer the rinds in this ten minutes, throw the water away, and spread them upon dishes to cool. Meanwhile prepare a second syrup, allowing sugar equal in weight to the rind, and half an ounce of sliced white ginger to a gallon of the pickle, with a cup of water for every two pounds of sugar. When the sugar is melted and the syrup quite hot, but not boiling, put in the rinds and simmer until they look quite clear. Take it out, spread upon the dishes again, while you add to the syrup a pint of vinegar for every pound of the sugar you have put in, one tablespoonful of turmeric to a gallon of pickle; mace, cloves and cinnamon to taste. Boil this up, return the rind to it, and simmer fifteen minutes. Put up in glass jars. It will be fit for use in two weeks.

This is a very handsome and delicious pickle, although it may seem to be made upon the principle of the Frenchman's pebble-soup.

GREEN TOMATO SOY. ✠

- 2 gallons tomatoes, green, and sliced without peeling.
- 12 good-sized onions, also sliced.
- 2 quarts vinegar.
- 1 quart sugar.
- 2 tablespoonfuls salt.
- 2 tablespoonfuls ground mustard.
- 2 tablespoonfuls black pepper, ground.
- 1 tablespoonful allspice.
- 1 tablespoonful cloves.

Mix all together, and stew until tender, stirring often lest they should scorch. Put up in small glass jars.

This is a most useful and pleasant sauce for almost every kind of meat and fish.

SWEET TOMATO PICKLE. (*Very good.*) ✠

- 7 lbs. ripe tomatoes, peeled and sliced.
- 3½ lbs. sugar.
- 1 oz. cinnamon and mace mixed.
- 1 oz. cloves.
- 1 quart of vinegar.

Mix all together and stew an hour.

RIPE TOMATO PICKLE. (*No. 2.*)

- 2 gallons tomatoes, peeled, but not sliced.
- 1 pint vinegar.

- 2 lbs. sugar.
- Mace, nutmeg, and cinnamon to taste.

Put all on together, heat slowly to a boil, and simmer one hour. Put up in glass jars.

SWEET PICKLE—PLUMS, PEARS, PEACHES, OR OTHER FRUITS. ✠

- 7 lbs. fruit, pared.
- 4 lbs. white sugar.
- 1 pint strong vinegar.
- Mace, cinnamon, and cloves.

Pare peaches and pears; prick plums and damsons, tomatoes, "globes" or husk-tomatoes (otherwise known as ground-plums). Put into the kettle with alternate layers of sugar. Heat slowly to a boil; add the vinegar and spice; boil five minutes; take out the fruit with a perforated skimmer and spread upon dishes to cool. Boil the syrup thick; pack the fruit in glass jars, and pour the syrup on boiling hot.

Examine every few days for the first month, and should it show signs of fermenting set the jars (uncovered) in a kettle of water, and heat until the contents are scalding.

Husk-tomatoes—a fruit which looks like a hybrid between the tomato and plum—are particularly nice put up in this way.

PICKLED PEACHES.

- 10 lbs. fruit—pared.
- 4½ lbs. sugar.
- 1 quart vinegar.
- Mace, cinnamon, and cloves to taste.

Lay the peaches in the sugar for an hour; drain off every drop of syrup, and put over the fire with about a cup of water. Boil until the scum ceases to rise. Skim; put in the fruit and boil five minutes.

Take out the peaches with a perforated skimmer, and spread upon dishes to cool. Add the vinegar and spices to the syrup. Boil fifteen minutes longer, and pour over the fruit in glass jars.

PICKLED PEACHES (*unpeeled.*)

Rub the fur off with a coarse cloth, and prick each peach with a fork. Heat in *just* enough water to cover them until they almost boil; take them out, and add to the water sugar in the following proportions:—

- For every 7 lbs. of fruit

- 3 lbs. of sugar.

- Boil fifteen minutes; skim, and add—

- 3 pints of vinegar.

- 1 tablespoonful (each) of allspice, mace, and cinnamon.

- 1 teaspoonful celery-seed.

- 1 teaspoonful cloves.

Put the spices in thin muslin bags. Boil all together ten minutes, then put in the fruit, and boil until they can be pierced with a straw. Take out the fruit with a skimmer, and spread upon dishes to cool. Boil the syrup until thick, pack the peaches in glass jars, and pour this over them scalding hot.

You may pickle pears in the same way without peeling.

PICKLED CHERRIES. ✠

Morella, or large red tart cherries, as fresh as you can get them. To every quart allow a large cup of vinegar and two tablespoonfuls of sugar, with a dozen whole cloves and half a dozen blades of mace.

Put the vinegar and sugar on to heat with the spices. Boil five minutes; turn out into a covered stoneware vessel, cover, and let it get perfectly cold. Strain out the spices, fill small jars three-quarters of the way to the top with fruit, and pour the cold vinegar over them. Cork or cover tightly. Leave the stems on the cherries.

PICKLETTE. ✠

- 4 large crisp cabbages, chopped fine.

- 1 quart onions, chopped fine.

- 2 quarts of vinegar, or enough to cover the cabbage.

- 2 lbs. brown sugar.

- 2 tablespoonfuls ground mustard.

- 2 tablespoonfuls black pepper.

- 2 tablespoonfuls cinnamon.

- 2 tablespoonfuls turmeric.

- 2 tablespoonfuls celery-seed.

- 1 tablespoonful allspice.

- 1 tablespoonful mace.

- 1 tablespoonful alum, pulverized.

Pack the cabbage and onions in alternate layers, with a little salt between them. Let them stand until next day. Then scald the vinegar, sugar, and spices together, and pour over the cabbage and onion. Do this three mornings in succession. On the fourth, put all together over the fire and heat to a boil. Let them boil five minutes. When cold, pack in small jars.

It is fit for use as soon as cool, but keeps well.

DRINKS

COFFEE.

Never buy the ground coffee put up in packages, if you can get any other. The mere fact that after they have gone to the expense of the machinery and labor requisite for grinding it, the manufacturers can sell it cheaper per pound than grocers can the whole grains, roasted or raw, should convince every sensible person that it is adulterated with other and less expensive substances. Be that as it may, coffee loses its aroma so rapidly after it is ground that it is worth your while to buy it whole, either in small quantities freshly roasted, or raw, and roast it yourself; or stand by and see your respectable grocer grind what you have just bought. You can roast in a pan in the oven, stirring every few minutes, or in the same upon the top of the range. Stir often and roast quickly to a bright brown—not a dull black. While still hot, beat up the white of an egg with a tablespoonful of melted butter and stir up well with it. This will tend to preserve the flavor. Grind just enough at a time for a single making.

TO MAKE COFFEE (*boiled.*)

- 1 full coffee-cup (½ pint) of ground coffee.

- 1 quart of boiling water.

- White of an egg, and crushed shell of same.

- ½ cup of cold water to settle it.

Stir up the eggshell and the white (beaten) with the coffee, and a very little cold water, and mix gradually with the boiling water in the coffee-boiler. Stir from the sides and top as it boils up. Boil pretty fast twelve minutes; pour in the cold water and take from the fire, setting gently upon the hearth to settle. In five minutes, pour it off carefully into your silver, china, or Britannia coffee-pot, which should be previously well scalded.

Send to table *hot.*

To make Coffee without Boiling.

There are so many patent coffee-pots for this purpose, and the directions sold with these are so minute, that I need give only a few general rules here. Allow rather more coffee to a given quantity of water than if it were to be boiled, and have it ground *very* fine. Put the coffee in the uppermost compartment, pour on the water very slowly until the fine coffee is saturated, then more rapidly. The water should be boiling. Shut down the top, and the coffee ought to be ready when it has gone through the double or treble set of strainers. Should it not be strong enough, run it through again.

Café au Lait.

- 1 pint very strong *made* coffee—fresh and hot.

- 1 pint boiling milk.

The coffee should be poured off the grounds through a fine strainer (thin muslin is the best material) into the table coffee-pot. Add the milk, and set the pot where it will keep hot for five minutes before pouring it out.

Tea.

- 2 teaspoonfuls of tea to one *large* cupful of boiling water.

Scald the teapot well, put in the tea, and, covering close, set it on the stove or range one minute to warm; pour on enough boiling water to cover it well, and let it stand ten minutes to "draw." Keep the lid of the pot shut, and set in a warm place, but do not let it boil. Fill up with as much boiling water as you will need, and send hot to the table, after pouring into a heated china or silver pot.

The bane of tea in many households is unboiled water. It can never extract the flavor as it should, although it steep for hours. The kettle should not only steam, but bubble and puff in a hard boil before you add water from it to the tea-leaves.

Boiling after the tea is made, injures the flavor either by deadening or making it rank and "herby."

The English custom of making tea upon the breakfast or tea-table is fast gaining ground in America. It is at once the best and prettiest way of preparing the beverage.

CHOCOLATE. ✠

- 6 tablespoonfuls grated chocolate to each pint of water.
- As much milk as you have water.
- Sweeten to taste.

Put on the water boiling hot. Rub the chocolate smooth in a little cold water, and stir into the boiling water. Boil twenty minutes; add the milk and boil ten minutes more, stirring frequently. You can sweeten upon the fire or in the cups.

COCOA NIBS, OR SHELLS. ✠

- 1 quart of boiling water.
- 2 ozs. of cocoa nibs.
- 1 quart fresh milk.

Wet the shells or nibs up with a little cold water; add to the boiling, and cook one hour and a half; strain, put in the milk, let it heat almost to boiling, and take from the fire.

This is excellent for invalids.

PREPARED COCOA. ✠

- 1 quart of water, boiling.
- 2 ozs. prepared cocoa—Baker's is best.
- 1 quart of milk.

Make as you do chocolate—only boil nearly an hour before you add the milk, afterward heating *almost* to boiling. Sweeten to taste.

MILK TEA (FOR CHILDREN.)

1 pint fresh milk and the same of *boiling* water. Sweeten to taste.

RASPBERRY ROYAL. ✠

- 4 quarts ripe berries.

- 1 quart best cider vinegar.

- 1 lb. white sugar.

- 1 pint fine brandy.

Put the berries in a stone jar, pour the vinegar over them, add the sugar, and pound the berries to a paste with a wooden pestle, or mash with a spoon. Let them stand in the sun four hours; strain and squeeze out all the juice, and put in the brandy. Seal up in bottles; lay them on their sides in the cellar, and cover with sawdust.

Stir two tablespoonfuls into a tumbler of ice-water when you wish to use it.

RASPBERRY VINEGAR. ✠

Put the raspberries into a stone vessel and mash them to a pulp. Add cider-vinegar—no specious imitation, but the genuine article—enough to cover it well. Stand in the sun twelve hours, and all night in the cellar. Stir up well occasionally during this time. Strain, and put as many fresh berries in the jar as you took out; pour the strained vinegar over them; mash and set in the sun all day. Strain a second time next day. To each quart of this juice allow

- 1 pint of water.

- 5 lbs. of sugar (best white) for every 3 pints of this liquid, juice and water mingled.

Place over a gentle fire and stir until the sugar is dissolved. Heat slowly to boiling, skimming off the scum, and as soon as it fairly boils take off and strain. Bottle while warm, and seal the corks with sealing wax, or bees'-wax and rosin.

A most refreshing and pleasant drink.

BLACKBERRY VINEGAR

Is made in the same manner as raspberry, allowing 5½ lbs. sugar to 3 pints of juice and water.

BLACKBERRY CORDIAL.

- 1 quart of blackberry juice.
- 1 lb. white sugar.
- ½ oz. grated nutmeg.
- ½ oz. powdered cinnamon.
- ¼ oz. allspice.
- ¼ oz. cloves.
- 1 pint best brandy.

Tie the spices in thin muslin bags; boil juice, sugar, and spices together fifteen minutes, skimming well; add the brandy; set aside in a closely covered vessel to cool. When perfectly cold, strain out the spices, and bottle, sealing the corks.

ELDERBERRY WINE.

- 8 quarts of berries.
- 4 quarts of boiling water poured over the berries.

Let it stand twelve hours, stirring now and then. Strain well, pressing out all the juice. Add

- 3 lbs. of sugar to 4 quarts of juice.
- 1 oz. powdered cinnamon.
- ½ oz. powdered cloves.

Boil five minutes, and set away to ferment in a stone jar, with a cloth thrown lightly over it. When it has done fermenting, rack it off carefully, not to disturb the lees. Bottle and cork down well.

CRANBERRY WINE.

- Mash ripe berries to a pulp; put into a stone jar.

- Add 1 quart of water to 2 quarts of berries.

Stir well and let it stand two days. Strain through a double flannel bag; mash a second supply of berries, equal in quantity to the first, and cover with this liquid. Steep two days more; strain; add

- 1 lb. sugar for 3 quarts of liquor,

and boil five minutes. Let it ferment in lightly covered jars; rack off and bottle.

This is said to be very good for scrofula.

STRAWBERRY WINE.

3 quarts of strawberries, mashed and strained. To the juice (there should be about a quart, if the berries are ripe and fresh) add

- 1 quart of water.

- 1 lb. of sugar.

Stir up well and ferment in a clean, sweet cask, leaving the bung out. When the working subsides close tightly, or rack off into bottles.

This is said by those who have tasted it to be very good.

CURRANT WINE.

Pick, stem, mash, and strain the currants, which should be very ripe.

- To 1 quart of juice add

- ¾ lb. white sugar.

- ½ pint of water.

Stir all together long and well; put into a clean cask, leaving out the bung, and covering the whole with a bit of lace or mosquito net. Let it ferment about four weeks—rack off when it is quite still, and bottle.

JAMAICA GINGER-BEER.

- 1 bottle Jamaica Ginger Extract.
- 1 oz. cream-tartar.
- 6 quarts water.
- 1 lb. sugar.

Stir until the sugar is melted, then put in the grated peel of a lemon, and heat until blood-warm. Add a tablespoonful of brewers' yeast; stir well and bottle, wiring down the corks. It will be fit for use in four days.

This is a refreshing and healthful beverage mixed with pounded ice in hot weather.

RAISIN WINE.

- 1 lb. white sugar.
- 2 lbs. raisins, seeded and chopped.
- 1 lemon—all the juice and half the grated peel.
- 2 gallons boiling water.

Put all into a stone jar, and stir every day for a week. Strain, then, and bottle it. It will be fit for use in ten days.

LEMONADE OR SHERBET.

- 3 lemons to a quart of water.
- 6 tablespoonfuls of sugar.

Pare the yellow peel from the lemons, and, unless you mean to use the Sherbet immediately, leave it out. It gives a bitter taste to the sugar if left long in it. Slice and squeeze the lemons upon the sugar, add a very little water, and let them stand fifteen minutes. Then fill up with water; ice well, stir, and pour out.

ORANGEADE

Is made in the same manner, substituting oranges for lemons.

STRAWBERRY SHERBET. (*Delicious.*) ✠

- 1 quart of strawberries.

- 3 pints of water.

- 1 lemon—the juice only.

- 1 tablespoonful orange-flower water.

- ¾ lb. white sugar.

The strawberries should be fresh and ripe. Crush to a smooth paste; add the rest of the ingredients (except the sugar), and let it stand three hours. Strain over the sugar, squeezing the cloth hard; stir until the sugar is dissolved; strain again and set in ice for two hours or more before you use it.

REGENT'S PUNCH. (*Fine.*)

- 1 lb. loaf-sugar or rock candy.

- 1 large cup strong black tea—(made).

- 3 wineglasses of brandy.

- 3 wineglasses of rum.

- 1 bottle champagne.

- 2 oranges—juice only.

- 3 lemons—juice only.

- 1 large lump of ice.

This receipt was given me by a gentleman of the old school, a connoisseur in the matter of beverages as of cookery. "Tell your readers," he writes, "that better punch was never brewed." I give receipt and message together.

ROMAN PUNCH.

- 3 coffee cups of lemonade—(strong and sweet.)

- 1 glass champagne.

- 1 glass rum.

- 2 oranges—juice only.

- 2 eggs—whites only—well whipped.

- ½ lb. powdered sugar, beaten into the stiffened whites.

You must ice abundantly—or, if you prefer, freeze.

SHERRY COBBLER.

- Several slices of pineapple, cut in quarters.

- A lemon, sliced thin.

- An orange, sliced thin.

- ½ cup of powdered sugar.

- 1 tumbler of Sherry wine.

- Ice-water.

- Pounded ice.

Take a wide-mouthed quart pitcher and lay the sliced fruit in order at the bottom, sprinkling sugar and pounded ice between the layers. Cover with sugar and ice, and let all stand together five minutes. Add then two tumblers of water and all the sugar, and stir well to dissolve this. Fill the pitcher nearly full of pounded ice, pour in the wine, and stir up from the bottom until the ingredients are thoroughly mixed. In pouring it out put a slice of each kind of fruit in each goblet before adding the liquid.

It is best sucked through a straw or glass tube.

NECTAR. ✠

Make as above, substituting a little rose-water for the pineapple, and squeezing out the juice of the orange and lemon, instead of putting in the slices. Sprinkle nutmeg on the top.

This forms a delicious and refreshing drink for invalids.

CLARET PUNCH. ✠

- 1 bottle of claret.
- ¼ the quantity of ice-water.
- 2 lemons, sliced.
- ½ cup powdered sugar.

Cover the sliced lemon with sugar and let it stand ten minutes. Add the water; stir hard for a whole minute, and pour in the wine. Put pounded ice in each glass before filling with the mixture.

EGG NOGG. ✠

- 6 eggs—whites and yolks beaten separately and very stiff.
- 1 quart rich milk.
- ½ cup of sugar.
- ½ pint best brandy.
- Flavor with nutmeg.

Stir the yolks into the milk with the sugar, which should first be beaten with the yolks. Next comes the brandy. Lastly whip in the whites of three eggs.

CHERRY BOUNCE.

- 4 lbs. of sour and the same quantity of sweet cherries.
- 2½ lbs. white sugar.
- 1 gallon best whiskey.

Crush the cherries to pieces by pounding in a deep wooden vessel with a smooth billet of wood. Beat hard enough to crack all the stones. Put into a deep stone jar, mix in the sugar well, and cover with the whiskey. Shake around briskly and turn into a demijohn. Cork tightly and let it stand a month, shaking it every day, and another month without touching it. Then strain off and bottle.

It is better a year than six months old.

If the Maltese cross appears but seldom in the section devoted to drinks, it is because most of my information respecting their manufacture is second-hand. In my own family they are so little used, except in sickness, that I should not dare to teach others, upon my own authority, how to prepare them. Indeed, the temptation I felt to omit many of them reminded me of a remark made, introductory of preserves, by one of the "Complete Housewives," who, all five together, drove me to the verge of an attack of congestion of the brain, before I had been a housekeeper for a week. Said this judicious lady:—"Preserves of all kinds are expensive and indigestible, and therefore poisonous. *Therefore*"— again—"I shall not give directions for their manufacture, except to remark that barberries stewed in molasses are economical, and a degree less hurtful than most others of that class of compounds."

Then I reflected that I might, upon the same principle, exclude all receipts in which cocoanut is used, because it is rank poison to me; while a dear friend of mine would as soon touch arsenic as an egg. A large majority of the beverages I have named are highly medicinal, and deserve a place in the housekeeper's calendar on that account. Many, so far from being hurtful, are beneficial to a weak stomach or a system suffering under general debility. *None which contain alcohol in any shape should be used daily, much less semi- or tri-daily by a well person.*

This principle reduced to practice would prove the preventive ounce which would cure, all over the land, the need for Temperance Societies and Inebriate Asylums.

THE SICK-ROOM

The sick-chamber should be the most quiet and cheerful in the house—a sacred isle past which the waves of domestic toil and solicitude glide silently. This is not an easy rule to obey. Whoever the invalid may be, whether the mother, father, or the sweet youngling of the flock, the foundations of the household seem thrown out of course while the sickness lasts. You may have good servants and kind friends to aid you, but the hitch in the machinery is not to be smoothed out by their efforts. The irregularity does not annoy you: you do not notice it if the attack be severe or dangerous. All other thoughts are swallowed up in the all-absorbing, ever-present alarm. You count nothing an inconvenience that can bring present relief, or possible healing to the beloved one; disdain for yourself rest or ease while the shadow hangs above the pillow crushed by the helpless head. But when it passes, when the first transport of thankfulness has subsided into an abiding sense of safety, the mind swings back to the accustomed pivot, and your eyes seem to be suddenly unbound. You find, with dismay, that the children have run wild, and the comfort of the whole family been neglected during your confinement to the post of most urgent duty; with displeasure, that the servants have, as you consider, taken advantage of your situation to omit this task, and to slur over that;—in fine, that nothing has been done well, and so many things left altogether undone, that you are "worried out of your senses"—a phrase that too often signifies, out of your temper.

And it is just at this juncture—when you are called to fifty points of attention and labor at once, and are on the verge of despair at the conglomeration worse conglomerated arising before you; fidgetting to pick up dropped stitches in the web you were wont to keep so even—that the invalid becomes most exacting. "Unreasonable," you name it to yourself, even though it be John himself who calls upon you every third minute for some little office of loving-kindness; who wants to be amused and fed and petted, and made generally comfortable as if he were a six-months-old baby; who never remembers that you must be wearied out with watching and anxiety, and that everything below-stairs is going to destruction for the want of a balance-wheel. The better he loves you the more apt is he to fancy that nobody but you can do anything for him; the more certain to crave something which no one else knows how to prepare. And when you have strained muscle and patience a *little* further to get it ready, and with prudent foresight made enough to last for several meals, it is more than probable that his fickle taste will suggest something entirely different for "next time." "Just for a change, you know, dear. One gets so tired of eating the same thing so often!"

He might be more considerate—less childish—you think, turning away that he may not see your change of countenance. When you have taken so much pains to suit him exactly! It is harder yet when he refuses to do more than taste the delicacy you hoped would tempt him.

"It is very nice, I suppose, my love," says the poor fellow, with the air of a martyr. "But it does not taste right, somehow. Maybe the children can dispose of it. If I had a lemon ice, or some wine jelly such as my mother used to make, I am sure I could relish it. I always did detest sick peoples' diet!"

If he is very much shaken as to nerves, he will be likely to say, "*messes.*"

"I am fairly wild!" said a loving wife and mother, and thrifty housekeeper, to me one day, when I called to see her.

She had just nursed her husband and three children through the influenza. All had been down with it at once. That form of demoniacal possession is generally conducted upon the wholesale principle. One of her servants had left in disgust at the increased pressure of work; the weather was rainy, blowy, raw; the streets were muddy, and there was no such thing as keeping steps and halls clean, while the four invalids were cross as only toothache or influenza can make human beings.

"I am fairly wild!" said the worthy creature, with tears in her eyes. "I cannot snatch a minute, from morning until night, to put things straight, and yet I am almost tired to death! I was saying to myself as you came in, that I wouldn't try any longer. I would just sit still until the dirt was piled up to my chin, and *then I would get upon the table!'*

How often I have thought of her odd speech since! sometimes with a smile—more frequently with a sigh. But with all my pity for the nurse and housekeeper, I cannot conceal from myself—I would not forget, or let you forget for a moment—the truth that the sick one is the greater sufferer. It is never pleasant to be laid upon the shelf. The resting-place—falsely so-called—is hard and narrow and uneven enough, even when the tramp of the outer world does not jar the sore and jaded frame; when there is no apparent need for the sick person to be upon his feet, and for aught that others can see, or he can say, he might just as well stay where he is for a month or two. But when, the rack of pain having been removed, the dulled perceptions of the mind re-awaken to sensitiveness, and there comes to his ear the bugle-call of duty—sharp, imperative;—when every idle moment speaks to him of a slain opportunity, and the no longer strong man shakes his fetters with piteous cries against fate, do not despise, or be impatient with him. He is feverish and inconsiderate and capricious because he is not himself. You see only the poor wreck left by the demon as he tore his way out of him at the Divine command. Gather it up lovingly in your arms, and nurse it back to strength and comeliness. The sick should always be the chief object of thought and care with all in the household.' If need be, let the dirt lie chin-deep everywhere else, so long as it is kept out of that one room. There be jealous in your care that nothing offends sight and smell.

There should be *no* smell in a sick-chamber. To avoid this, let in the air freely and often. Cologne-water will not dispel a foul odor, while disinfectants are noisome in themselves. Bathe the patient as frequently and thoroughly as prudence will allow, and change his clothing, with the bed-linen, every day. Do not keep the medicines where he can see them, nor ever let him witness the mixing of that which he is to swallow. So soon as his meals are over, remove every vestige of them from the room. Even a soiled spoon, lying on table or bureau, may offend his fastidious appetite. Cover the stand or waiter from which he eats with a spotless napkin, and serve his food in your daintiest ware.

My heart softens almost to tearfulness when I recall the hours, days, weeks, I have myself spent in the chamber of languishing, and the ingenuity of tenderness that, from my babyhood, has striven to cheat the imprisonment of weariness, and make me forget pain and uselessness. The pretty surprises daily invented for my entertainment; the exceeding nicety with which they were set out before me; the loving words that nourished my spirit when the body was faint unto death,—these are events, not slight incidents, in the book of memory. When I cease to be grateful for them, or to learn from them how to minister unto others of the like consolation, may my heart forget to beat, my right hand lose her cunning!

Do not ask your charge what he would like to eat to-day. He will, of a surety, sicken with the effort at selection, and say, "Nothing!" But watch attentively for the slightest intimation of a desire for any particular delicacy, and if you are assured that it cannot hurt him, procure it, if you can, without letting him guess at your intention. Feed him lightly and often, never bringing more into his sight than he may safely eat. A big bowl of broth or jelly will either tempt him to imprudence, or discourage him. "Am I to be burdened with all that?" cries the affrighted stomach, and will have none of it. While he is very weak, feed him with your own hand, playfully, as you would a child, talking cheerily of something besides his food, and coaxing him into taking the needed nutriment as only a wife and mother can, or as nobody but John could beguile you to effort in the same direction.

Study all pleasant and soothing arts to while away the time, and keep worry of every kind away from him. A trifle at which you can laugh will be a burden to the enfeebled mind and body, and he has nothing to do but lie still and roll it over until it swells into a mountain. When he can be removed without danger, let him have his meals in another room, changing the air of each when he is not in it. Every one who has suffered from long sickness knows the peculiar loathing attendant upon the idea that all food is tainted with the atmosphere of the chamber in which it is served, and if eaten in bed, tastes of the mattress and pillows. The room and all in it may be clean, fresh, and sweet, but the fancy cannot be dismissed. And it is wiser to humor than to reason with most sick fancies.

A hired nurse is a useful, often a necessary thing, but while you are upon your feet, and mistress of your own house, delegate to no one the precious task of catering for the dear sufferer. It is an art in itself. I hope a practical knowledge of it will be taught in Women's Medical Colleges, when they are an established "institution" with us.

I wish it were proper to record here the name of one of the kindest and best family physicians I ever knew, who had charge of my not very firm health during my girlhood. He owed much—I suppose no one ever knew really how much—of his success in his practice to his tact and skill in devising palatable and suitable nourishment for his patients. I well remember the childish pleasure with which I would hear him say when the violence of the attack had passed—"Now, my dear child, we must begin with kitchen physic!" and the glow of amused expectation with which I used to watch him, as, with an arch show of mystery, he would beckon my mother from the room to receive his "prescription;" the impatience with which I awaited the result of the conference, and the zest with which I ate whatever he ordered.

If I could have persuaded him to manage this department of my work, it would win for me the degree of M.D. with a new meaning—Mistress of Dietetics.

THE SICK-ROOM

BEEF TEA. ✠

- 1 lb. *lean* beef, cut into small pieces.

Put into a jar without a drop of water; cover tightly, and set in a pot of cold water. Heat gradually to a boil, and continue this steadily for three or four hours, until the meat is like white rags, and the juice all drawn out. Season with salt to taste, and when cold, skim. The patient will often prefer this ice-cold to hot. Serve with Albert biscuit or thin "wafers," unleavened, made by a receipt given under the head of BREAD.

MUTTON BROTH. ✠

- 1 lb. lean mutton or lamb, cut small.

- 1 quart water—cold.

- 1 tablespoonful rice, or barley, soaked in a very little warm water.

- 4 tablespoonfuls milk.

- Salt and pepper, with a little chopped parsley.

Boil the meat, unsalted, in the water, keeping it closely covered, until it falls to pieces. Strain it out, skim, add the soaked barley or rice; simmer half an hour, stirring often; stir in the seasoning and the milk, and simmer five minutes after it heats up well, taking care it does not burn.

Serve hot with cream crackers.

CHICKEN BROTH. ✠

Is excellent made in the same manner as mutton, cracking the bones well before you put in the fowl.

VEAL AND SAGO BROTH.

- 2 lbs. knuckle of veal, cracked all to pieces.
- 2 quarts of cold water.
- 3 tablespoonfuls best pearl sago, soaked in a cup of cold water.
- 1 cup cream, heated to boiling.
- Yolks of two eggs, beaten light.

Boil the veal and water in a covered saucepan very slowly until reduced to one quart of liquid; strain, skim, season with salt, and stir in the soaked sago (having previously warmed it by setting for half an hour in a saucepan of boiling water, and stirring from time to time.) Simmer half an hour, taking care it does not burn; beat in the cream and eggs; give one good boil up, and turn out.

This is excellent for consumptives.

BEEF AND SAGO BROTH.

- 2 lbs. of beef—cut up small.
- 2 quarts of water.
- 1 cup of sago, soaked soft in a little lukewarm water.
- Yolks of three eggs.
- Salt to taste.

Stew the beef until it falls to pieces; strain it out, salt the liquid and stir in the sago. Simmer gently one hour, stirring often. Add the beaten yolks: boil up once and serve.

This is a strengthening and nice soup. Eat with dry toast.

ARROWROOT JELLY (*Plain.*) ✠

- 1 cup *boiling* water.
- 2 heaping teaspoonfuls of best Bermuda arrowroot.

- 1 teaspoonful lemon juice.
- 2 teaspoonfuls of white sugar.

Wet the arrowroot in a little cold water, and rub smooth. Then stir into the hot, which should be on the fire and actually boiling at the time, with the sugar already melted in it. Stir until clear, boiling steadily all the while, and add the lemon. Wet a cup in cold water, and pour in the jelly to form. Eat cold with sugar and cream flavored with rose-water.

An invaluable preparation in cases where wine is forbidden.

ARROWROOT WINE JELLY. ✠

- 1 cup boiling water.
- 2 heaping teaspoonfuls arrowroot.
- 2 heaping white sugar.
- 1 tablespoonful brandy *or* 3 tablespoonfuls of wine.

An excellent corrective to weak bowels.

ARROWROOT BLANC MANGE. ✠

- 1 cupful *boiling* milk.
- 2 dessertspoonfuls best arrowroot, rubbed smooth in cold water.
- 2 teaspoonfuls white sugar.
- Vanilla or other essence.

Boil until it thickens well, stirring all the while. Eat cold with cream, flavored with rose-water, and sweetened to taste.

SAGO

May be substituted for arrowroot in any of the foregoing receipts, when you have soaked it an hour in water poured over it cold, and gradually warmed by setting the cup containing it in hot water. Boil rather longer than you do the arrowroot.

SAGO GRUEL. ✠

- 2 cups water.
- 2 tablespoonfuls sago.
- 3 teaspoonfuls white sugar.
- 1 glass of wine.
- 1 tablespoonful lemon juice.
- Nutmeg to taste, and a pinch of salt.

Put the sago in the water while cold, and warm by setting in a saucepan of boiling water. Stir often, and let it soften and heat for one hour. Then *boil* ten minutes, stirring all the while; add the sugar, wine, and lemon, and pour into a bowl or mould to cool. Eat warm, if preferred. The wine and nutmeg should be omitted if the patient be feverish.

INDIAN MEAL GRUEL. ✠

- 2 quarts of boiling water.
- 1 cup of Indian meal, and
- 1 tablespoonful flour, wet up with cold water.
- Salt to taste—and, if you like, sugar and nutmeg.

Wet the meal and flour to a smooth paste, and stir into the water while it is actually boiling. Boil slowly one hour, stirring up well from the bottom. Season with salt to taste. Some sweeten it, but I like it better with a little pepper added to the salt.

If a cathartic is desired, omit the wheat flour altogether.

OATMEAL GRUEL

Is made in the same way.

MILK AND RICE GRUEL.

- 1 quart boiling milk.

- 2 tablespoonfuls (heaping) of ground rice, wet with cold milk.

- 1 saltspoonful of salt.

Stir in the rice-paste and boil ten minutes, stirring all the while. Season with sugar and nutmeg, and eat warm with cream.

You may use Indian meal instead of rice-flour, which is an astringent. In this case, boil an hour.

DRIED FLOUR FOR TEETHING CHILDREN.

- 1 cup of flour, tied in a stout muslin bag and dropped into cold water, then set over the fire.

Boil three hours steadily. Turn out the flour ball and dry in the hot sun all day; or, if you need it at once, dry in a moderate oven without shutting the door.

To use it—

Grate a tablespoonful for a cupful of boiling milk and water (half and half). Wet up the flour with a very little cold water, stir in and boil five minutes. Put in a little salt.

TAPIOCA JELLY. ✠ (*Very good.*)

- 1 cup of tapioca.

- 3 cups of cold water.

- Juice of a lemon, and a pinch of the grated peel.

- Sweeten to taste.

Soak the tapioca in the water four hours. Set within a saucepan of boiling water; pour more lukewarm water over the tapioca if it has absorbed too much of the liquid, and heat, stirring frequently. If too thick after it begins to clear, put in a very little boiling water. When quite clear, put in the sugar and lemon. Pour into moulds. Eat cold, with cream flavored with rose-water and sweetened.

TAPIOCA BLANC-MANGE. ✠

- 1 cup of tapioca soaked in two cups cold water.

- 3 cups boiling milk.

- 3 tablespoonfuls white sugar.

- Rose-water or vanilla.

Soak the tapioca four hours, and stir, with the water in which it was soaked, into the boiling milk. Sweeten and boil slowly, stirring all the while, fifteen minutes. Take off, flavor and pour into moulds.

Eat cold with cream. Wash tapioca well before soaking.

ARROWROOT CUSTARD. (*Nice.*)

- 2 cups of *boiling* milk.

- 3 heaping teaspoonfuls arrowroot, wet up with a little cold milk.

- 2 tablespoonfuls white sugar, beaten with the egg.

- 1 egg very well beaten.

Mix the arrowroot paste with the boiling milk; stir three minutes; take from the fire and whip in the egg and sugar. Boil two minutes longer, flavor with vanilla or rose-water, and pour into moulds.

RICE-FLOUR MILK.

- 2 cups of milk, *boiling.*

- 2 tablespoonfuls rice-flour, wet up with cold milk.

- 2 tablespoonfuls white sugar.

Boil ten minutes, stirring all the while, and flavor to taste. Eat warm with cream.

SAGO MILK. ✠

- 3 tablespoonfuls sago, soaked in a large cup cold water one hour.

- 3 cups boiling milk.

- Sweeten and flavor to taste.

Simmer slowly half an hour. Eat warm.

TAPIOCA MILK

Is made in the same way.

BOILED RICE. ✠

- ½ cup whole rice, boiled in just enough water to cover it.

- 1 cup of milk.

- A little salt.

- 1 egg, beaten light.

When the rice is nearly done, turn off the water, add the milk and simmer—taking care it does not scorch—until the milk boils up well. Salt, and beat in the egg.

Eat warm with cream, sugar, and nutmeg.

PANADA. ✠

- 6 Boston crackers, split.

- 2 tablespoonfuls white sugar.

- A good pinch of salt, and a little nutmeg.

- Enough *boiling* water to cover them well.

Split the crackers, and pile in a bowl in layers, salt and sugar scattered among them. Cover with boiling water and set on the hearth, with a close top over the bowl, for at least one hour. The crackers should be almost clear and soft as jelly, but not broken.

Eat from the bowl, with more sugar sprinkled in if you wish it. If properly made, this panada is very nice.

BREAD PANADA, OR JELLY. ✠

Pare some slices of stale baker's bread and toast nicely, without burning. Pile in a bowl, sprinkling sugar and a very little salt between; cover well with *boiling* water, and set, with a tight lid upon the top, in a pan of boiling water. Simmer gently, until the contents of the bowl are like jelly. Eat warm with powdered sugar and nutmeg.

CHICKEN JELLY. (*Very nourishing.*) ✠

- Half a raw chicken, pounded with a mallet, bones and meat together.

- Plenty of cold water to cover it well— *about* a quart.

Heat slowly in a covered vessel, and let it simmer until the meat is in white rags and the liquid reduced one half. Strain and press, first through a cullender, then through a coarse cloth. Salt to taste, and pepper, if you think best; return to the fire, and simmer five minutes longer. Skim when cool. Give to the patient cold—just from the ice—with unleavened wafers. Keep on the ice. You can make into sandwiches by putting the jelly between thin slices of bread spread lightly with butter.

CALVES' FEET BROTH.

- 2 calves' feet.

- 2 quarts cold water.

- 1 egg, beaten up with two tablespoonfuls milk for each cupful of broth.

- Pepper and salt.

Boil the feet to shreds; strain the liquor through a double muslin bag; season to taste, and set by for use, as you need it. Warm by the small quantity, allowing to each cupful a beaten egg and two tablespoonfuls of milk. Give a good boil up to cook these, and serve "with thin, crisp toast. If the patient can take it, a dash of lemon-juice improves the broth.

TOAST WATER. ✠

- Slices of toast, nicely browned, without a symptom of burning.
- Enough boiling water to cover them.

Cover closely, and let them steep until cold. Strain the water, sweeten to taste, and put a piece of ice in each glassful. If the physician thinks it safe, add a little lemon-juice.

APPLE WATER. ✠

- 1 large juicy pippin, the most finely-flavored you can get.
- 3 cups of cold water—1 quart if the apple is very large.

Pare and quarter the apple, but do not core it. Put it on the fire in a tin or porcelain saucepan with the water, and boil, closely covered, until the apple stews to pieces. Strain the liquor *at once*, pressing the apple hard in the cloth. Strain this again through a finer bag, and set away to cool. Sweeten with white sugar, and ice for drinking.

It is a refreshing and palatable drink.

JELLY WATER. ✠

- 1 large teaspoonful currant or cranberry jelly.
- 1 goblet ice-water.

Beat up well for a fever-patient.

Wild cherry or blackberry jelly is excellent, prepared in like manner for those suffering with summer complaint.

FLAX-SEED LEMONADE. ✠

- 4 tablespoonfuls flax-seed (whole.)
- 1 quart boiling water poured upon the flax-seed.
- Juice of two lemons, leaving out the peel.
- Sweeten to taste.

Steep three hours in a covered pitcher. If too thick, put in cold water with the lemon-juice and sugar. Ice for drinking.

It is admirable for colds.

SLIPPERY-ELM BARK TEA.

Break the bark into bits, pour boiling water over it, cover and let it infuse until cold. Sweeten, ice, and take for summer disorders, or add lemon-juice and drink for a bad cold.

APPLE TODDY. ✠

Boil a large juicy pippin in a quart of water, and when it has broken to pieces strain off the water. While it is still boiling-hot, add a glass of fine old whiskey, a little lemon-juice, and sweeten to taste.

Take hot at bed-time for influenza.

MILK PUNCH. ✠

- 1 tumbler of milk, well sweetened.
- 2 tablespoonfuls best brandy, well stirred in.

I have known very sick patients to be kept alive for days at a time by this mixture, and nothing else, until Nature could rally her forces. Give very cold with ice.

EGG AND MILK PUNCH ✠

Is made by the preceding receipt, with an egg beaten very light with the sugar, and stirred in before the brandy is added.

ICELAND OR IRISH MOSS LEMONADE. ✠

- 1 handful Irish or Iceland moss, washed in five waters.

- 2 quarts boiling water, poured upon the moss, and left until cold.

- 2 lemons, peeled and sliced, leaving out the peel.

- Sweeten very well and ice.

Do not strain, and if it thicken too much, add cold water.

Excellent for feverish colds and all pulmonary troubles.

ICELAND OR IRISH MOSS JELLY. ✠

- 1 handful moss, washed in five waters, and soaked an hour.

- 1 quart *boiling* water.

- 2 lemons—the juice only.

- 1 glass of wine.

- ¼ teaspoonful cinnamon. (Measure scantily.)

Soak the washed moss in a very little cold water; stir into the boiling, and simmer until it is dissolved. Sweeten, flavor, and strain into moulds. You may use two glasses of cider instead of one of wine for a fever-patient, putting in a little less water.

Good for colds, and very nourishing.

SEA-MOSS BLANC-MANGE

Is made in the same way, using boiling milk instead of water, and leaving out the lemons and wine. Flavor with vanilla or rose-water.

DRY TOAST.

Pare off the crust from stale light bread; slice half an inch thick and toast *quickly*. Graham bread is very nice toasted.

Butter lightly if the patient can eat butter.

MILK TOAST. ✠

Toast as just directed; dip each slice, as it comes from the toaster, in boiling water; butter, salt slightly, and lay in a deep covered dish. Have ready in a saucepan enough boiling milk to cover all well. When your slices are packed, salt this very slightly; melt in it a bit of butter and pour over them. Cover closely and let it stand five minutes before using it. It is excellent when made of Graham bread.

This is a good dish for a family tea as well as for invalids.

UNLEAVENED BISCUIT, OR WAFERS. ✠

Mix good, dry flour to a stiff dough with milk; salt, and roll out thin. Cut into round cakes and roll these again almost as thin as letter-paper. Bake very quickly.

They may also be mixed with water. These are very simple and palatable, and go well with all kinds of broth, especially oyster-soup.

DRIED RUSK. (See *Bread.*)

BEEF STEAK AND MUTTON CHOPS.

Choose the tenderest cuts and broil over a clear hot fire with your wisest skill. Let the steak be rare—the chops well-done. Salt and pepper, lay between two *hot* plates three minutes, and serve to your patient. If he is very weak, do not let him swallow anything except the juice, when he has chewed the meat well.

The essence of rare beef—roast or broiled—thus expressed, is considered by some physicians to be more strengthening than beef-tea, prepared in the usual manner.

SANGAREE OR PORTEREE.

One-third wine or porter mixed with two-thirds cold water. Sweeten, grate nutmeg on the top, and ice.

Serve dry toast with it. Taken hot, it is good for a sudden cold.

WINE WHEY.

- 1 pint boiling milk.

1 large glass pale wine, poured in when the milk is scalding hot. Boil up once, remove from the fire and let it cool. Do not stir it after the wine is put in. When the curd forms, draw off the whey and sweeten.

HERB TEAS

Are made by infusing the dried or green leaves and stalks in boiling water, and letting them stand until cold. Sweeten to taste.

Sage tea, sweetened with honey, is good for a sore throat, used as a gargle, with a small bit of alum dissolved in it.

Catnip tea is the best panacea for infant ills, in the way of cold and colic, known to nurses.

Pennyroyal tea will often avert the unpleasant consequences of a sudden check of perspiration, or the evils induced by ladies' thin shoes.

Chamomile and gentian teas are excellent tonics taken either cold or hot.

The tea made from blackberry-root is said to be good for summer disorders. That from green strawberry leaves is an admirable and soothing wash for a cankered mouth.

Tea of parsley-root scraped and steeped in boiling water, taken warm, will often cure strangury and kindred affections, as will that made from dried pumpkin-seed.

Tansy and rue teas are useful in cases of colic, as are fennel seeds steeped in brandy.

A tea of damask-rose leaves, dry or fresh, will usually subdue any simple case of summer complaint in infants.

Mint tea, made from the green leaves, crushed in cold or hot water and sweetened, is palatable and healing to the stomach and bowels.

MINT JULEP. ✠

Some sprigs of green mint, slightly bruised in a tumbler with a teaspoon. Put in a generous teaspoonful of white sugar; add gradually, stirring and rubbing lightly, enough water to fill the glass three-quarters of the way to the top. Fill up with pounded ice; stir hard; pour into a larger glass that you may shake up well, and put in two tablespoonfuls fine brandy.

This is called a "hail-storm julep."

EAU SUCRÉ. ✠

Dissolve three or four lumps of loaf sugar in a glass of ice-water, and take a teaspoonful every few minutes for a "tickling in the throat," or a hacking cough. Keep it ice-cold.

A simple, but often an efficacious remedy.

THE NURSERY

All food intended for infants should be very thoroughly cooked. The numerous varieties of farinaceous substances—biscotine, farina, rice-flour, arrowroot, etc., however nourishing may be their properties when rightly prepared, are harsh and drastic when underdone. Unless you have a nurse whom you know for yourself to be faithful and experienced, always superintend the cooking of baby's food. It can do no harm—it may prevent much—if you examine it every day to see that it is right as to quality and quantity. Do not aim at variety in this branch of your profession. Confine a child under three years of age to a very limited bill of fare. His stomach is too delicate an organ to be tampered with. Let milk—scalded or boiled, as a rule—be the staple, mixed with farina, barley, or something of the sort. Let him munch Graham bread and light crackers freely. Remove far from him hot bread and griddle-cakes. When he has cut his carnivorous teeth, Nature says—"This creature wants meat." And Nature's supply is seldom in advance of the demand. If he did not need what the teeth are designed to chew, you may be sure they would not be given him. Grant him the novel food sparingly and with discretion as to kind. Rare beef and well-boiled mutton, tender roast or boiled chicken and turkey are safe. Withhold fried meats of every description. Do not let him touch veal or pork in any shape. Mince the meat very finely to save his digestive apparatus all unnecessary work. Mealy old potatoes—*never* new or waxy—young onions, boiled in two waters; fresh asparagus, green peas, and dry sweet potatoes should suffice for vegetables, with, of course, rice and hominy. For dessert, once in a while, a simple custard, a taste of home-made ice-cream, rice and farina puddings, Graham hasty pudding; the inner part of a well-roasted apple, and, in their season, ripe peaches and apples, will not harm him, taken in moderation, if he be well and strong.

Pare the fruit always. The skin of an apple is as bad for him as a bit of your kid gloves would be; that of a grape more indigestible than sole-leather. Raisins—"skins and all"—are unfit for anybody to eat. Pulp and pits, they are poisonous for baby. Ditto, pickles, pastry, and preserves. Ditto, most kinds of cake and all sorts of fruit puddings.

Give him light suppers, and put him to bed early in a dark room. He will not grow better in a glare of artificial light than will your camellias and azalias.

Always see for yourself that his last waking thoughts are pleasant; that he shuts his eyes at peace with the world and in love with you; that his feet are warm, his stomach easy, and his body not overloaded with blankets and quilts; also, that the nursery is clean and freshly aired. These are better prescriptions for sound slumber than all the old wives' fables of the excellent properties of that pernicious drug—Soothing Syrup.

FARINA. ✠

- 1 cup *boiling* water.
- 1 cup fresh milk.
- 1 large tablespoonful Hecker's Farina, wet up with cold water.
- 2 teaspoonfuls white sugar.
- A pinch of salt.

Stir the farina into the boiling water (*slightly* salted) in the farina kettle (*i. e.*, one boiler set within another, the latter filled with hot water). Boil fifteen minutes, stirring constantly until it is well-thickened. Then add the milk, stirring it in gradually, and boil fifteen minutes longer. Sweeten, and give to the child so soon as it is cool enough.

You may make enough in the morning to last all day; warming it up with a little hot milk as you want it. Keep in a cold place. Some of the finest children I have ever seen were reared upon this diet. Do not get it too sweet, and cook it well. Be sure the farina is sweet and dry.

BARLEY.

It sometimes happens that milk disagrees with a delicate infant so seriously that it is necessary to substitute some other article of diet for a few days. I have known barley water to be used, in such cases, with great success.

- 2 cups *boiling* water.

- 2 tablespoonfuls pearl barley—picked over and washed.

- A pinch of salt.

- 2 teaspoonfuls white sugar—*not* heaping.

Soak the barley half an hour in a very little lukewarm water, and stir, without draining, into the boiling water, salted very slightly. Simmer one hour, stirring often, and strain before sweetening.

ARROWROOT. ✠

- 1 cup of boiling water.

- 1 cup fresh milk.

- 2 teaspoonfuls best Bermuda arrowroot, wet with cold water.

- 1 *small* pinch of salt.

- 2 even teaspoonfuls white sugar, dissolved in the milk.

Stir the arrowroot paste into the salted boiling water; stir and boil five minutes or until it is clear; add the sweetened milk, and boil ten minutes, slowly, still stirring.

If the child has fever, or cannot digest milk, substitute hot water for it. It is, however, a dangerous experiment to forbid milk altogether for an infant. I should rather diminish the quantity, putting in, say, one-third or one-fourth as much as the receipt names, and filling up with boiling water.

RICE JELLY. ✠

- ½ cup whole rice, well-washed and soaked two hours in a little warm water; then added, with the water, to that in the kettle.

- 3 pints cold water.

- 1 small pinch of salt, put into the water.

- Sweeten to taste with loaf sugar.

Simmer the rice half an hour; then boil it until it is a smooth paste, and the water is reduced one-half. Strain through double tarlatan, sweeten, and give to the child.

This is an admirable preparation for an infant suffering with weakness of the bowels. If there is no fever, you may put one-third part milk, boiled with the rice. Give a few spoonfuls every hour or half hour.

MILK AND BREAD. ✠

- 1 cup boiled milk.

- 2 tablespoonfuls stale Graham bread.

- A very little sugar.

Crumble the bread into the boiled milk, sweeten, and when cool enough, feed to the child with a spoon.

WHEATEN GRITS. ✠

- 4 tablespoonfuls grits (cracked wheat) soaked in a little cold water one hour, and then put into the kettle.

- 1 quart boiling water.

- 1 cup milk.

- A pinch of salt.

Boil the soaked grits in the quart of water one hour, stirring up often; add the milk and boil half an hour longer. Sweeten to taste, and if the child is well, pour cream over it. This is designed for children over a year old. It is slightly cathartic; especially if the milk be omitted, and is most useful in regulating the bowels. When this can be done without drugs, it is far better.

HOMINY AND MILK. ✠

- ½ cup *small* hominy.

- 1 scant quart of cold water.

- Pinch of salt.

Boil one hour, stirring often. While hot, mix some soft with new milk, sweeten to taste and feed to baby with a spoon.

This is also relaxing to the bowels, and should not be given if the child is disposed to summer complaint.

GRAHAM HASTY PUDDING. ✠

- 1 cup Graham flour, wet up with cold water.

- 1 large cup *boiling* water and same quantity of milk.

- 1 saltspoonful of salt.

Stir the wet flour into the boiling water, slightly salted. Boil fifteen minutes, stirring almost constantly. Add the milk and cook, after it has come again to a boil, ten minutes longer. Give with sugar and milk for breakfast.

Eaten with cream, nutmeg, and powdered sugar, this is a good plain dessert for grown people as well as children.

RICE FLOUR HASTY PUDDING

Is made as above, substituting two heaping tablespoonfuls rice flour for the Graham.

MILK PORRIDGE.

- 1 tablespoonful Indian meal } wet to a paste with cold

- 1 tablespoonful white flour } water.

- 2 cups boiling water.

- 2 cups milk.

- A *good* pinch of salt.

Boil the paste in the hot water twenty minutes; add the milk and cook ten minutes more, stirring often.

Eat with sugar and milk, stirred in while hot.

MUSH AND MILK.

- 1 cup Indian meal, wet up with cold water.

- 2 quarts cold water.

- Salt to taste.

Boil two hours; stirring often with a wooden spoon or a stick.

To be eaten hot with milk and sugar.

CONDENSED MILK.

This is perhaps the safest substitute for the "good milk from one cow," which few mothers in town can procure. Keep the can in a cool place and mix according to directions.

SUNDRIES

Cleaning Pots, Kettles, and Tins

Boil a double handful of hay or grass in a new iron pot, before attempting to cook with it; scrub out with soap and sand; then set on full of fair water, and let it boil half an hour. After this, you may use it without fear. As soon as you empty a pot or frying-pan of that which has been cooked in it, fill with hot or cold water (hot is best) and set back upon the fire to scald thoroughly.

New tins should stand near the fire with boiling water in them, in which has been dissolved a spoonful of soda, for an hour; then be scoured inside with soft soap; afterward rinsed with hot water. Keep them clean by rubbing with sifted *wood*-ashes, or whitening.

Copper utensils should be cleaned with brickdust and flannel.

Never set a vessel in the pot-closet without cleaning and wiping it thoroughly. If grease be left in it, it will grow rancid. If set aside wet, it is apt to rust.

Knives.

Clean with a soft flannel and Bath brick. If rusty, use wood-ashes, rubbed on with a newly cut bit of Irish potato. This will remove spots when nothing else will. Keep your best set wrapped in *soft* white paper; then in linen, in a drawer out of damp and dust.

Never dip the ivory handles of knives in hot water.

Silver.

Wash, after each meal, all that is soiled, in *very* hot soft water, with hard soap. Wipe hard and quickly on a clean towel; then polish with dry flannel. If discolored with egg, mustard, spinach, or beans, by any other means, rub out the stain with a stiff toothbrush (used only for this purpose), and silver soap.

For years I have used no other preparation for cleaning silver than the Indexical silver soap, applied as I have described. After rubbing with a stiff lather made with this, wash off with hot water, wipe and polish while hot. There is no need for the weekly silver cleaning to be an event or a bugbear, if a little care and watchfulness be observed after each meal. Silver should never be allowed to grow dingy. If Bridget or Chloe will *not* attend properly to this matter, take it in hand yourself. Have your own soap-cups—two of them—one with common soap, the other with a cake of silver soap in the bottom. Have for one a mop, for the other a stiff brush—a toothbrush is best. Use your softest towels for silver.

Besides being clean and easy of application, the silver soap will not wear away the metal as will whiting or chalk, or plate-powder, however finely pulverized.

CHINA AND GLASS.

There are few of the minor crooks in the lot of the careful housewife that cause her more anxiety and more discouragement than the attempt to teach domestics how to wash up dishes.

"I've heard that Mrs. —— is very *exact* about some things, such as washing up dishes and the likes of that!" said a woman to me, with an affected laugh, having called to apply for the then vacant position of cook in my kitchen. She had high recommendations, a whine engrafted upon her native brogue, and spoke of me in the third person—a trick of cheap (and bogus) gentility that tries my nerves and temper to the very marrow of my spine. "I was a-saying to myself, as I came along, that Mrs. —— must have been *very* onlucky in her girls if she had to tache them how to wash up dishes. I always thought that was one of the things that came *kinder nat'ral* to every cook."

"Mrs. ——'s" experience goes to prove that the wrong way of doing this must "come natural" to the class mentioned, and that Nature is mighty in woman. The fact that the right way is *not* to pile unrinsed dishes and plates in a big pan with a loose bit of soap on top, and pour lukewarm water over all; then with a bit of rag to splash said water over each separately, and make another pile of them upon the kitchen-table, until the last is drawn, reeking with liquid grease, sticky and streaming, from the now filthy puddle of diluted swill; then to rub them lightly and leisurely with one towel—be they many or few—is as difficult of comprehension to the scullionly mind as would be a familiar lecture upon the *pons asinorum*.

Yet the right and only neat method is so simple and easy! Rinse the greasy plates, and whatever is sticky with sugar or other sweet, in hot water and transfer to a larger pan of *very* hot. Wash glass first; next silver; then china—one article at a time, although you may put several in the pan. Have a mop with a handle; rub upon the soap (over which the water should have been poured) until you have strong suds. There is a little implement made by the "Dover Stamping Co.," a cup of tinned wire, called a "soap-shaker," that greatly facilitates this process of suds-making, without waste of soap. Wash both sides of plate and saucer, and wipe *before putting it out of your hand.* Draining leaves streaks which can be felt by sensitive finger-tips, if not seen. If china is rough to the touch, it is dirty. Hot, clean suds, a dry, clean towel, and quick wiping leave it bright and shining. Roll your glasses around in the water, filling them as soon as they touch it, and you need never crack one. A lady did once explain the dinginess of her goblets to me by saying that she was "afraid to put them in hot water. It *rots* glass and makes it so tender! I prefer to have them a little cloudy." This is literally true—that she said it, I mean. Certainly not that a year's soak in hot water could make glass tender.

WASHING WINDOWS.

Dissolve a little washing-soda in the water if the glass is very dim with smoke or dirt. Do not let it run on the sash, but wash each pane with old flannel; dry quickly with a soft, clean towel, wiping the corners with especial care. Polish with chamois skin, or newspapers rubbed soft between the hands.

TO CLEAN CARPETS.

Sprinkle the carpet with tea-leaves; sweep well; then use soap and soft, warm water for the grease and dirt spots. This freshens up old carpets marvellously. Rub the wet spots dry with a clean cloth.

TO CLEAN PAINT.

Scour with a flat brush, less harsh than that used for floors, using warm soft suds; before it dries wash off with old flannel dipped in clean cold water, and wipe dry with a linen towel or cloth. Go through the whole process quickly, that the water may not dry upon and streak the paint.

TO KEEP WOOLENS.

Beat out all the dust, and sun for a day; shake very hard; fold neatly and pin—or, what is better, sew up—closely in muslin or linen cloths, putting a small lump of gum-camphor in the centre of each bundle. Wrap newspapers about all, pinning so as to exclude dust and insects.

These are really all the precautions necessary for the safety even of furs, if they are strictly obeyed. But you may set moths at defiance if you can, in addition to these, secure, as a packing-case, a whiskey or alcohol barrel, but lately emptied, and still strongly scented by the liquor. Have a close head, and fit it in neatly. Set away in the garret, and think no more of your treasures until next winter.

TO WASH DOUBTFUL CALICOES.

Put a teaspoonful of sugar of lead into a pailful of water, and soak fifteen minutes before washing.

TO CLEAN A CLOTH COAT.

Rub soap upon the wristbands and collar; dip them in boiling-hot suds—and scrub with a stiff clean brush. Treat the grease and dirt spots in the same way. Change the suds for clean and hot as it gets dirty. Wet and brush the whole coat, the right way of the cloth, with fresh suds, when you have scoured out the spots, adding three or four tablespoonfuls of alcohol to the water. Stretch the sleeves, pocket-holes, wristbands, and collar into shape, folding the sleeves as if they had been ironed, also the collar. Lay upon a clean cloth, spread upon the table or floor, and let it get perfectly dry in the shade, turning over three or four times without disturbing the folds.

TO CLEAN SILK.

To Remove Grease Spots.—Scrape Venetian or French chalk fine; moisten to a stiff paste with soap-suds; make it into flat cakes by pressing between two boards, and dry in the sun or oven. Keep these for use. When you need them, scrape one to powder and cover the spot with it, laying the silk upon a fine clean linen or cotton cloth. Lay two or three folds of tissue-paper upon the chalk, and press it with a hot iron for a minute or more, taking care it does not touch the silk. Raise the paper and scrape off the grease with the chalk. Split a visiting-card, and rub the place where the spot *was*, with the inside, to restore the lustre. The silk should be pressed on the wrong side.

If the spot be discovered at once, simply rub the wrong side hard with powdered French chalk, and leave it to wear off.

To Wash Silk.—Mix together

- 2 cups cold water.
- 1 tablespoonful honey.
- 1 tablespoonful soft soap.
- 1 wineglass alcohol.

Shake up well; lay the silk, a breadth at a time, on a table, and sponge both sides with this, rubbing it well in; shake it about well and up and down in a tub of cold water; flap it as dry as you can, but do not wring it. Hang it by the edges, not the middle, until fit to iron. Iron on the wrong side while it is very damp.

Black and dark or sober-colored silks may be successfully treated in this way.

To Smooth Wrinkled Silk.—Sponge on the right side with very weak gum-arabic water, and iron on the wrong side.

TO RENEW WRINKLED CRAPE.

Stretch over a basin of boiling water, holding it smooth, but not tight, over the top, and shifting as the steam fairly penetrates it. Fold, while damp, in the original creases, and lay under a heavy book or board to dry. It will look almost as well as new.

TO RESTORE THE PILE OF VELVET.

If but slightly pressed, treat as you would crape. Steam on the right side until heated through. If very badly crushed, wet on the wrong side; let an assistant hold a hot iron, bottom upward, and pass the wet side of the velvet slowly over the flat surface—a sort of upside-down ironing. When the steam rises thickly through to the right side, it will raise the pile with it. Dry without handling.

To Curl Tumbled Feathers.

Hold over the heated top of the range or stove, not near enough to burn; withdraw, shake them out, and hold them over it again until curled.

To Clean Straw Matting.

Wash with a cloth dipped in clean salt and water; then wipe dry at once. This prevents it from turning yellow.

To Wash Lawn or Thin Muslin.

Boil two quarts of wheat-bran in six quarts, or more, of water, half an hour. Strain through a coarse towel and mix in the water in which the muslin is to be washed. Use no soap, if you can help it, and no starch. Rinse lightly in fair water. This preparation both cleanses and stiffens the lawn. If you can conveniently, take out all the gathers. The skirt should always be ripped from the waist.

To Wash Woolens.

Wash in clean, hot soap suds; rinse out in clear, hot water, and shake out the wet without passing through the wringer. Worsted dress-goods should never be wrung when washed.

To Wash White Lace Edging.

Have a quart bottle covered with linen, stitched smoothly to fit the shape. Begin at the bottom and wind the lace about it, basting fast at both edges, even the minutest point, to the linen. Wash on the bottle, soaping it well, rinse by plunging in a pail of fair water, and boil as you would a white handkerchief, bottle and all. Set in the hot sun to dry. When quite dry, clip the basting-threads, and use the lace without ironing. If neatly basted on, it will look nearly as well as new—if not quite.

Black Lace.

- ½ cup rain water, or very soft spring water.

- 1 teaspoonful borax.

- 1 tablespoonful spirits of wine.

Squeeze the tumbled rusty lace through this four times, then rinse in a cup of hot water in which a black kid glove has been boiled. Pull out the edges of the lace until almost dry; then press for two days between the leaves of a heavy book.

TO SPONGE BLACK WORSTED DRESSES.

Sponge on the right side with a strong tea made of *fig leaves*, and iron on the wrong.

This process restores lustre and crispness to alpaca, bombazine, etc.

TO CLEAN VERY DIRTY BLACK DRESSES.

2 parts soft water to 1 part alcohol, or if there be paint spots upon the stuff, spirits turpentine. Soap a sponge well, dip in the mixture and rub, a breadth at a time, on both sides, stretching it upon a table. Iron on the wrong side, or that which is to be inside when the stuff is made up. Sponge off with fair water, hot but not scalding, *before you iron*. Iron while damp.

TO REMOVE STAINS FROM MARBLE.

Make a mortar of unslacked lime and very strong lye. Cover the spot thickly with it and leave it on for six weeks. Wash it off perfectly clean, and rub *hard* with a brush dipped in a lather of soap and water. Polish with a smooth, hard brush.

IRON MOULD

Is as nearly ineradicable as it is possible for stain to be. *Try* moistening the part injured with ink, and while this is wet, rub in muriatic acid diluted with five times its weight of water. I have heard that the old and new stain can sometimes be removed together by this operation.

MILDEW

Is likewise obstinate. If anything will extract it, it is lemon-juice mixed with an equal weight of salt, powdered starch, and soft soap. Rub on thickly and lay upon the grass in the hot sun; renewing the application two or three times a day until the spot fades or comes out.

I have also used salt wet with tomato-juice, often renewed, laying the article stained upon the grass. Sometimes the stain was taken out, sometimes not.

INK.

While the stains are yet wet upon the carpet, sponge them with skim-milk *thoroughly*. Then wash out the milk with a clean sponge dipped again and again in fair water, cold. Exchange this presently for warm; then rub dry with a cloth. If the stain is upon any article of clothing, or table, or bed linen, wash in the milk well, afterward in the water.

Dry ink stains can be removed from white cloth by oxalic acid, or lemon-juice and salt.

STAINS OF ACIDS AND ALKALIES.

Treat acid stains with hartshorn; alkaline with acids. For instance, if the color be taken out of cloth by whitewash, wash with strong vinegar.

GREASE SPOTS.

- 1 quart boiling water.

- 1 oz. pulverized borax.

- ½ oz. of gum camphor.

Shake up well and bottle. It is excellent for removing grease spots from woolens.

CURE FOR BURNS.

- One-third part linseed oil.

- Two-thirds lime water.

Shake up well; apply and wrap in soft linen.

Until you can procure this keep the part covered with *wood-soot* mixed to a soft paste with lard, *or*, if you have not these, with common molasses.

TO STOP THE FLOW OF BLOOD.

Bind the cut with cobwebs and brown sugar, pressed on like lint. *Or*, if you cannot procure these, with the fine dust of tea. When the blood ceases to flow, apply laudanum.

TO RELIEVE ASTHMA.

Soak blotting or tissue paper in *strong* saltpetre water. Dry, and burn at night in your bed-room.

I *know* this to be an excellent prescription.

ANTIDOTES TO POISON.

For *any* poison swallow instantly a glass of cold water with a heaping teaspoonful of common salt and one of ground mustard stirred in. This is a speedy emetic. When it has acted, swallow the whites of two raw eggs.

If you have taken corrosive sublimate take half a dozen raw eggs besides the emetic. If laudanum, a cup of *very* strong coffee. If arsenic, first the emetic, then half a cup of sweet oil or melted lard.

COLOGNE WATER. (*Fine.*) (*No. 1.*)

- 1 drachm oil lavender.
- 1 drachm oil bergamot.
- 2 drachm oil lemon.
- 2 drachm oil rosemary.
- 50 drops tincture of musk.
- 8 drops oil of cinnamon.
- 8 drops oil of cloves.
- 1 pint of alcohol.

COLOGNE WATER. (*No. 2.*)

- 60 drops oil of lavender.
- 60 drops oil of bergamot.
- 60 drops oil of lemon.
- 60 drops orange-flower water.
- 1 pint of alcohol.

    Cork and shake well.

HARD SOAP.

- 6 lbs. washing soda.
- 3 lbs. unslaked lime.

Pour on 4 gallons boiling water.

Let it stand until perfectly clear, then drain off. Put in 6 lbs. clean fat.

Boil until it begins to harden—about two hours—stirring most of the time.

While boiling, thin with two gallons of cold water, which you have poured on the alkaline mixture after draining off the four gallons. This must also settle clear before it is drawn off. Add it when there is danger of boiling over.

Try the thickness by cooling a little on a plate. Put in a handful of salt just before taking from the fire. Wet a tub to prevent sticking; turn in the soap and let it stand until solid. Cut into bars; put on a board and let it dry.

This will make about forty pounds of nice soap; much better for washing (when it has dried out for two or three months) than yellow turpentine soap.

BAR SOAP.

Buy a box at a time; cut into small squares and lay upon the garret-floor to dry for several weeks before it is used.

SOFT SOAP.

- 10 lbs. grease.
- 6 lbs. soda (washing).
- 8 gallons hot water.

Let it stand for several days until the grease is eaten up. If too thick, add more water. Stir every day. If wood-ashes are used instead of soda, boil the mixture.

CPSIA information can be obtained
at www.ICGtesting.com
Printed in the USA
LVHW011122160820
663324LV00003B/1011